British Political Biography

Edited by
Chris Cook

BRITISH POLITICAL BIOGRAPHY

E. J. FEUCHTWANGER

GLADSTONE

ST. MARTIN'S PRESS   NEW YORK

British Political Biography
Edited by Chris Cook

Copyright © E. J. Feuchtwanger, 1975

For information, write:
St. Martin's Press, Inc., 175 Fifth Avenue,
New York, N.Y. 10010

Printed in Great Britain

Library of Congress Catalog Card Number: 75-7712

First published in the United States of America in 1975

Designed by Gerald Cinamon

FOR P.M.F.

CONTENTS

PREFACE

Of the making of books there is no end – nowhere more so than in British history of the nineteenth century. Paradoxically, this is some justification for writing another life of Gladstone. Some twenty years ago the last major biography, by Sir Philip Magnus, appeared. Since then historians have done a great deal of work on Victorian England and have altered our view of it in many respects. One of the guiding considerations in the writing of the present book has, therefore, been to take into account the results of this recent scholarship. To do full justice to Gladstone, whose energy was many times that of ordinary mortals, within a biography of limited proportions is, however, virtually impossible;

the emphasis here is fairly and squarely on Gladstone's political life; his private life and his manifold activities as scholar, theologian and in other fields have been comparatively neglected.

Author and publisher have felt disinclined to burden this book with an excessive apparatus of footnotes; for instance, references to Morley's *Life of Gladstone*, which would have to appear on almost every page, have been avoided. Morley's *Life* remains a remarkable achievement, particularly as it appeared so soon after the G.O.M.'s death, and it contains much of the more important documentation, even if it is not always quite correctly quoted.

My thanks are due to Professor M. R. D. Foot who gave me valuable advice and encouraged me to go ahead with an intrusion into a field which is very much his own. My friend and colleague, Mr F. C. Mather, gave me the benefit of his great learning on many points of detail. The editor of this series, Mr Chris Cook, assisted at the birth as well as in subsequent development of the book. Last, but not least, my wife made many improvements of style to the manuscript. In the preparation of the typescript Miss Susie Kirkby, Mrs Marie Clark and Miss Judy Collingwood gave willing and expert help.

1

LIVERPOOL
UNDERNEATH
1809–32

Mr Gladstone in his prime had a personality of titanic proportions, capable of moulding the pattern and context of the world within which he had his being. It is natural to search his origins and upbringing for clues to his almost superhuman strength and energy as well as to the the complexities of his private and political character. Gladstone's family background is far more fully documented than is the case with many men who have become famous, but the influence of this background on his personal development and political attitudes remains in the last resort a matter of interpretation.

The figure of Sir John Gladstone, William's father, towers like a colossus in the annals of the Gladstone family. The career of the statesman is difficult to imagine without the moral and material foundations laid by the father. John Gladstones was born in Leith in 1764, the eldest son of Thomas Gladstones, a corn merchant with a variety of other business interests of modest importance. The family home was pervaded by the Bible-based religious faith of the Scottish Lowlands. John was deeply moulded by this background and the strong sense of personal accountability to God engendered by his parental religion never left him for the rest of his life. His restless energy, however, drove him to seek new opportunities elsewhere and he took the decisive step in 1781 when he moved to Liverpool. There he entered into a partnership with Edgar Corrie, another Lowland Scot, who was about to venture on a major scale into the Liverpool corn trade. John Gladstones brought to this partnership the experience acquired in his father's business, his personal judgement and acumen, and capital of £1500 partly supplied by his father and partly borrowed on his own account. It was now that he dropped the final 's' in his name for convenience's sake, a change not formalized until 1835. It was the beginning of a career that was to make John Gladstone into one of the great merchant magnates of Liverpool and lead to the accumulation of a family fortune of some three-quarters of a million pounds by the end of his life. The religious scruples, the conflict between personal piety and worldly ambition that had restricted his father Thomas to trading modestly at Leith did not inhibit John. Later on even the stark discrepancy between the precepts of evangelicalism and the owner-ship of hundreds of West Indian slaves did not sap the imperious energy of the merchant prince of Liverpool.

The size of John Gladstone's business operations and of his fortune grew rapidly once he was established at Liverpool. By 1795, at the age of thirty, he was already worth £16,000, enough to retire on. His acquisitive instinct drove him on relentlessly; from the corn trade his interests spread into real property, shipping, insur-ance, sugar, cotton and West Indian plantations. In 1803 he placed his first mortgage on a Demerara estate, a connection which was to involve him in so much controversy. By 1799, he was worth £40,000; the growth of his fortune accelerated to bring it to over £200,000 by the end of the Napoleonic Wars.[1] He was an uneasy business partner, determined to get his way even when others had the day-to-day responsibilities, and inclined to pursue quarrels with fierce animosity.

Along with the rise in John Gladstone's commercial stature went his growing involvement in the political life of Liverpool. His father Thomas had inclined to the Whigs and when John came to Liverpool he associated with a group of radicals who drew their main strength from Unitarians, Quakers and Scots Presbyterians like himself. These men resented the hold which the established Tory and Anglican families, working through the Corporation and the closed franchise, had on the politics of the city. Nationally, these Liverpool 'Jacobins' applauded the enlightened policies of Pitt in the 1780s, condemned the slave trade and wanted a wider parliamentary franchise. They had their brief moment of glory when their candidate, William Roscoe, was elected in 1806 as one of Liverpool's two Members of Parliament. John Gladstone was among his supporters, but in the next few years his political outlook began to change. He had for some time been estranged from the Scots Presbyterian Church in Liverpool and by 1804 was a member of the Church of England. As his judgement and confidence as a man of affairs grew he fell out of sympathy with the intellectual approach to political issues of his former friends. He saw no future in the ineffectual Whigs of Liverpool, in their criticism of the war and of King and Country and he was by instinct not an opposition man. More specifically, he now supported a vigorous pursuit of the French War and of the Continental Blockade. This fitted in well with the development of his commercial interests in the West Indies, which could only gain from the exclusion of foreign colonial produce from Europe brought about by the blockade. He opposed those Liverpool merchants whose interests lay in the American trade and who were reluctant to see the blockade enforced against American ships. He lost all his earlier sympathy for the Americans and their policy of neutrality. He became alarmed at the dependence of the growing textile industry on American cotton and wanted to see alternative sources developed in India. This again fitted in with his long-standing opposition to the trading monopoly of the East India Company. Even though he disliked the privileges lavished on John Company, John Gladstone was in fact a mercantilist. He wanted to see the power of the state used for the assertion of commercial advantage. Here as in other matters he was drawing closer to Toryism, but he was too liberal in background and conviction to go the whole way. It was thus that he hitched his political fortunes to Canning, the most liberal among leading Tories. In 1812 John Gladstone, now an important figure in the public life of Liverpool, was more than any other man responsible for persuading George Canning to contest the representation of the city. There were in that year four candidates fighting for the two seats: General Gascoygne, for so many years the candidate of the Corporation Tories; Canning, the candidate of some Whigs and progressive Tories; and Henry Brougham and Thomas Creevey, sponsored by John Gladstone's former Whig–Radical friends. In a fiercely fought election, in which John Gladstone came in for much abuse as a renegade, Canning and Gascoyne emerged victorious. Liverpool had been given a new political configuration which lasted virtually until the first Reform Bill. For John Gladstone the association with Canning opened up vistas of wider political ambitions. One of William's earliest recollections was being taken to the dining-room of the Gladstone house in Rodney Street where a great dinner for Mr Canning was being held to celebrate the election victory of October 1812. Scarcely three years old, he was made to stand on a chair and directed to say to the company: 'Ladies and Gentlemen.'[2]

John Gladstone married twice. His first wife, Jane Hall, the daughter of a Liverpool merchant, was an almost permanent invalid and died childless after six years of marriage in 1798. Two years later the widower married Anne Mackenzie Robertson, the twenty-eight-year-old daughter of the provost of Dingwall, Andrew Robertson, who had himself died in 1796. Anne was of pure Highland stock and on her mother's side could count Robert the Bruce and even the Royal Stewarts among her ancestors. The Robertsons of Dingwall were of higher social standing than the Gladstones of Leith, but the wealth and even more the prospects of John Gladstone of Liverpool were greatly superior to those of the minor Highland lairds from whom his bride was descended. Anne was a frail beauty, destined, like John's first wife, to lead the life of a semi-invalid. There was surely significance in the fact that this strong, powerful man should for the second time have tied himself to a weak, frequently suffering woman and to have borne willingly the regime imposed by her rarely interrupted ill-health. Anne and John had their evangelical religion and background in common, but for her, lacking his overwhelming worldly preoccupations, this intense evangelical faith was and became increasingly the central reference point of her life. Through her, it enveloped her family.

Anne came to the house in 62 Rodney Street which John had built for his first wife. Frail as she was, she yet managed to bear her husband six children. Four arrived in fairly rapid succession between December 1802 and January 1807: Anne, Tom, Robertson and John Neilson. Then there was a gap of nearly three years until the birth of the youngest son on 29 December 1809: William Ewart, so named after one of his father's closest associates, known to his family as Willy. The youngest daughter, Helen, was born after another interval of four and a half years in 1814. In the meantime, John Gladstone, as part of his property investments, had been acquiring the Litherland estate at Seaforth outside Liverpool. Here he decided to build himself a new house on a grander scale, Seaforth House, the construction of which began in 1811 and which had become the permanent family home by 1815. It was right on the water's edge and from its windows one could see the ships passing up the Mersey, many of them carrying John Gladstone's cargoes. The house could be lonely and was exposed to the gales, but its outhouses, trees and orchards provided the setting for many childhood adventures of the Gladstone boys. Here Willy grew up. His father had built St Thomas's Church at Seaforth which, like the other churches built by him, appeared in his balance-sheet as part of his capital. The pew rents brought him a 5 per cent return on these investments. The Rector, the Reverend William Rawson, carefully chosen for his evangelicalism and personally vouched for by Dr Simeon, was also in charge of a school at which the sons of gentlemen, including the Gladstone boys, could be educated and here Willy received his first schooling.

The contrast in character between Willy's father and mother was profound. John Gladstone was overpowering, strongly motivated to struggle with and dominate his environment. For all his deep religious faith he was utterly engrossed in the affairs of this world. Anne Gladstone's life was entirely filled with her religion and her family. Sin, inadequacy in the sight of God, submission to His will, acceptance of suffering and death, the high cliffs, abysses and ravines as well as the consolation of calvinistic evangelicalism were ever present to her. She implanted this, her own mental world, deeply into her children. Unlike her husband, she shrank from contact with the larger world outside her home and took refuge behind her chronic state of ill-health, yet from her couch she dominated the family, and even her husband did willing obeisance at the shrine. From his mother's example, William received an ideal of pure womanhood that inspired his view of the opposite sex throughout his life. He venerated his father and even as a fully grown man of rising distinction preserved towards him an attitude of filial piety and submission. In later life he spoke of the 'torrents of tenderness' that flowed from his father. Yet subconsciously the overbearing figure of his father may well have sparked a resentment which, severely repressed as it was, added to his many inner tensions as an adult. For a child of his time and circumstances little Willy was not isolated from his parents, certainly less so than many of the aristocrats who were later to be his political colleagues. For one thing he lived with his family and attended Mr Rawson's establishment until at the age of nearly twelve he went to Eton. On the other hand, both his parents were relatively old when Willy was born and there was an age gap between him and his older sister and brothers. No doubt servants, nurses, governesses, like Nurse Brown, the subject of his earliest recollection, also loomed large in his childhood. Another pillar of the Gladstone household was Anne, the eldest child, who took many burdens off her mother's shoulders. The younger children, Willy and Helen, owed much to her influence. She had the deep evangelical faith of her mother, but while her health lasted a more youthful zest and gaiety. For the last six years before her death in 1829 she was an invalid, probably suffering from tuberculosis and, even more than her mother, took on, in the minds of her family, the character of a saint.

Religion enveloped the Gladstone home and a constant sense that all of life is a reckoning with God was the deepest mark it left upon William. However much his theological position might change in course of time, this cardinal element of his evangelical upbringing never left him. In his own autobiographical sketch of his childhood, written late in life, he is still examining his record of eighty years earlier for devoutness, love of God, innocence and sin. This sense of accountability extended not only to things spiritual: one of the most marked characteristics of Gladstone the man was the immense care with which he sought to avoid any waste of God's most precious gift, time, and he displayed the same hatred of waste when material resources were at stake, particularly the public funds so often entrusted to him. These traits had already been firmly implanted in him as a child. The Gladstone home, permeated as it was with calvinistic religion, was nevertheless not puritanical. There was no disposition to eschew comfort, there was some gaiety of a restrained intimate kind; some interest in painting and music. John Gladstone lacked culture and polish and William envied the cultivated background of Arthur Hallam when their friendship began at Eton. John Gladstone was, however, glad to see his family acquiring tastes which he had never had the opportunity to develop.

The sense of sin and man's wickedness inculcated by Gladstone's upbringing was profound, yet it was largely abstract. The family lived a very sheltered life, secure under the wing of a powerful father; real evil and viciousness never came their way. All those who knew Gladstone as a man have noted his remarkable and genuine innocence. When combined with the relentlessly earnest self-accusation, revealed particularly in his diary, this innocence gives the impression of a priggishness which to the modern mind must seem unattractive, but on its own terms had all the qualities of sincerity. There was an undercurrent of strong emotion in the Gladstone family, verging often on the neurotic. The fierce quarrels of John, the father, the fears, anxieties and withdrawal of Anne, the mother, the depressions of Tom, the eccentricities of Helen, the preoccupation of all the family with illness, frequently psycho-somatic, and death, all these indicated a highly charged atmosphere. William also had this deeply emotional nature and when he was a man it was one of the secrets of his power as a political leader. In his case, however, it was perfectly controlled and canalized, and the control mechanism was his intellect.

Willy's intellectual gifts became evident early on. He was highly articulate, almost precocious as a child. His family delighted in his ability to tell stories and he experienced the thrill of being able to spellbind his audience. 'Darling Willy has been delighting me with his clever stories and sayings, his beautiful black eyes looked so brilliant,' wrote his sister Anne when he was barely nine. Perhaps it was a foretaste of the oratorical gifts of the mature Gladstone. Facility and verbal skill of a high order always remained one of the hallmarks of his intellect. In the meantime, John Gladstone's ambitions and plans for his sons were developing. He himself had increasingly felt the urge to play a political role on a stage wider than the local one. In spite of his intimate association with Canning he found this difficult. The nomination for Liverpool, which he coveted, eluded him. In 1818 he at last got into Parliament as member for Lancaster; two years later, in the election caused by the death of George III, he transferred to Woodstock. He was one of the most knowledgeable among back-benchers on commercial and currency questions and did much useful work on committees. He also contributed to the evolution of Canning's views on trade questions, though the two were by no means always in agreement. Nevertheless there was a certain discrepancy between his eminence in business and his relatively modest place in politics. He was acutely aware of the social and educational limitations that hampered his political progress. Thus his ambitions were transferred to his sons. Eton and Oxford were the obvious avenues through which they could achieve the national political career which was no longer open to him. It must have been a strong impulse indeed that made him choose Eton as a school for his boys. He could not fail to have been aware that the religious atmosphere there was in total contrast to the evangelical upbringing he had given his children. However great his confidence in his sons and their adherence to the values instilled in them, he and even more his wife must have been fearful of the temptations they might be exposed to at Eton and the mental anguish they might suffer. As it turned out, Tom, the eldest son, went to Eton; Robertson, the second son, did not, because the business career for which he seemed destined could be better prepared for elsewhere. John Neilson, the third son, determined early on to go into the navy and was not to be dissuaded by his family. By the time Willy arrived at Eton in September 1821 the school had proved much less than a success for Tom, who had on numerous occasions asked to be taken away. It had also become obvious that neither Tom nor the other two Gladstone boys were of the calibre to live up to their father's high expectations. John's hopes were, therefore, increasingly centred on William and they were reciprocated by no less intense a motivation to do well.

Without such a firm purpose a boy of William's disposition and background would have found it hard indeed to adjust to the new world of Eton, even with the help of his brother Tom to guide him in his early steps. When he wrote in his autobiographical sketch that 'at this time there was not in me any desire to know or excel' he did himself less than justice, though he admits that even by Easter 1822 when his 'remove' was under the famous Hawtrey, later Headmaster and Provost, there was 'a change' and he was 'inspired with a desire to learn and do'. Henceforth he made rapid academic progress; the classics provided the ideal substance on which he could show his intellectual paces free from any emotional pressure. He also rose remarkably well to the general challenge of his new environment. Under the formidable Dr Keate, who boasted of having flogged more than eighty boys in a day, Eton was far removed from Arnold's ideal of a school for Christian gentlemen. It was one thing for boys with the confidence derived from an assured social background to thrive in such a world, but it was far more difficult for a boy like William Gladstone, who was well aware of his social and cultural inferiority compared with many of his aristocratic contemporaries. Yet he was not unduly shocked by the rough and boisterous side of school life and was not above watching with curiosity and even mild enjoyment the fights which were so much a feature of it. Only the religious tone of Eton really shook him, but his conscience, finely tuned by his evangelical upbringing, was proof against it. As the entries in his diary, which he began in July 1825, show, he examined his own conduct severely all the time and never lost the sense of having to account for it in the sight of God.

It was a milestone in William's Eton career when in October 1825 he was elected to the Literary Society, a debating club later well known as 'Pop'. Here he came together with a great many of the friends among whom he had established himself: Charles Canning, the son of his political patron saint, Gerald Wellesley, later Dean of Windsor, James Milnes Gaskell of Unitarian parentage, Lord Lincoln, later his close political colleague and, above all, Arthur Hallam, son of the Whig historian. Hallam, destined to die at the age of twenty-two, made a deep impression upon William, as he did upon Tennyson and so many others. An emotional friendship with many ups and downs bound the two together, as was often the case among public schoolboys living in an all-male society. William made his debut as an orator in the Literary Society with a speech on the education of the poor. His success as a debater added to his growing prestige in the school. He began to taste the power which his great verbal facility was putting into his hands.

The other extra-curricular activity which drew attention to William Gladstone was his editorship of the *Eton Miscellany*, a school magazine, which he launched with George Selwyn, later Bishop of New Zealand and of Lichfield. William produced a lot of the material himself, particularly in the second volume which appeared during his last six months in the school. He learnt to express himself fluently on paper and to work under pressure, and he displayed the remarkable powers of concentration and application which in later life contributed to the superhuman impression he so often gave.

There was no touch of modernity about the education at Eton. All his life Gladstone was to believe that a sound training in the classics was the basis of a well-tuned mind. Science always remained a closed book to him. But his natural intellectual ability was so great that his capacity to learn and to assess critically developed apace. For the first time he was away from the highly positive yet limited atmosphere of his home. His little band of friends was a remarkable and distinguished group. He read widely, he developed a burning interest in public affairs, encouraged by his father. Only in his religious conscience did he cling steadfastly to precepts instilled in his childhood. It was a formidable combination.

It has often been said that the public schools as they developed in the nineteenth century performed the function of amalgamating the upper sections of the middle class with the aristocracy and landed gentry. Eton performed this work of assimilation for Gladstone perhaps even more perfectly than Harrow had earlier done for Peel. Highly motivated, conscious of growing success, his schooldays, like his childhood, left Gladstone with no trace of rebelliousness against the system, no kicking against the pricks. For all his critical faculties and the liberal elements in the Canningite political outlook, his mind was cast in a conservative mould and always remained so. His youth was not a struggle against adversity, but the ascent of an eagle. As he looked back on his Eton days, he called them 'a time of very great and numerous delights'.

William had been entered as a simple commoner at Christ Church, not as a gentleman commoner, like many men of large fortune and aristocratic birth. John Gladstone, much as he hoped his son would make the right connections, did not want him to waste his time. Most of the brief interlude between Eton and Oxford William spent with a private tutor near Manchester. It was during this time that he paid a visit to a silk-manufactory at Macclesfield, where, as he wrote later, the shortcomings of a policy of protecting the home market first dawned on him. When William went up to Oxford in October 1828 he was determined to fulfil the bright academic promise of his schooldays. Many of the habits formed and friends made at Eton went with him. Lincoln, Canning, Milnes Gaskell and Doyle were still his companions; Hallam, now at Cambridge, was the notable absentee. Among new friends, Sidney Herbert and Manning were two who were to bulk large in Gladstone's life. There were also the two brothers Acland, Joseph Anstice, later Professor of Classics at King's College, London, until his early death at the age of thirty, F.D.Maurice and others. There were again long discussions on religion and politics and wide reading to which the diary bears remarkable witness. Neither the evangelical movement nor the enlightenment had made much impression at Oxford; high churchmanship was vigorous enough, though the Tractarian movement still lay in the future. There was something of an intellectual renaissance, of which the presence of Gladstone and the many brilliant young men around him was itself an indication. Oriel, which elected its fellows on merit, was the centre: here Whately, later to play an important role in the affairs of Ireland as Archbishop of Dublin, tried to bring some of the rationalist values of the enlightenment to bear on the teaching of the classics, while

Newman was beginning to turn his mind to a revival of the Church.[3] Gladstone stuck firmly to his evangelical roots and his diary shows his constant wrestling with himself and his sense of sin and weakness. If anything his need for self-abasement was heightened now by his efforts to control his sexual emotions, of which he had become painfully aware at Eton. In one respect his evangelical dogmas were beginning to loosen. Even before he went up to Oxford he had long debates with his sister Anne, then slowly dying of consumption, on predestination and baptismal regeneration which made him abandon the oppressive rigours of the calvinistic position. A conversation with Mrs Gaskell, the unitarian mother of his friend, also made a deep impression on him. 'Surely we cannot entertain a doubt as to the future of any person truly united to Christ by faith and love, whatever may be the faults of his opinion,' she said to him. Whatever the change in his evangelical assumptions, they were not caused by Oxford. The state of religion there, so unsatisfactory to the young Gladstone, must have made him cling the more tightly to his faith. At the end of his life, when he was perhaps too much concerned to explain his early lack of liberalism, he wrote:

> I was not in sympathy with the high and dry Toryism of contemporary Oxford which I never loved. But what estranged me from it was not I think the true love of liberty, which I had not yet learned: it was its hostility to Evangelicalism which my early training had taught me to regard as another name for Christianity.[4]

If his religious views did not change greatly at Oxford, his political opinions were influenced both by the prevailing atmosphere at the university and by events. In politics Oxford was profoundly Tory, to the right of the position which William, following his father and Canning, held when he went up. On the major question of the day, Catholic Emancipation, William was at odds with the predominating strongly hostile opinion at Oxford, although he shared the deep horror of popery fashionable at the university. The next great question of the day, reform, found him, however, firmly in the most orthodox Tory camp. Later in life he claimed that 'It was a great accident which threw me into the anti-liberal attitude which having taken it up I held with energy. It was the accident of the Reform Bill of 1831.' He saw in it 'an element of anti-Christ' and felt that he had been misled by Canning's hostility to reform. But would Canning, if he had still been alive in 1830, have adopted the outright opposition to electoral reform of Wellington and Peel? It is more likely that Gladstone's ability to foresee, like so many Tories, utter ruin in the prospect of reform arose naturally out of his general political opinions as they had developed. His conservative cast of mind, the remote and rarefied world in which he lived, his inexperience of practical politics and habit of defining his political views by pure logic, his veneration of aristocracy and noble blood, perhaps even the fear that a reformed Parliament would open the door to a triumphal return of the Papacy to Britain, all this made him identify more completely than before with a policy of outright resistance. He disagreed with his father, who with his more empirical approach saw the need for some concessions to appease the reformers. The process of self-education which was later to lead William to liberalism was at this stage deepening his Toryism and making him adopt some rather extreme positions. As he was to put it later, Oxford failed to teach him to set the due value on the imperishable and inestimable principle of English liberty.

William's academic career at Oxford was crowned with a double first, 'the best that had been gained for many years'. He continued the study of the classics with care and relish; familiarity with the great Greek and Roman authors became second nature to him and throughout his life he walked in their company. Yet his perception of the classical world was almost entirely confined to what was noble and monumental; in later life he was to devote much ingenuity to discerning the roots of Christianity in the pagan era. The cruelty and sensuality of the Greeks and Romans lay entirely outside his vision. He found the study of mathematics, which in the Oxford of his time was divorced from any connection with the natural sciences, irksome, but decided to carry on for the sake of maintaining his chance of a double first. His intellectual development owed as much to his voracious reading as to any formal educational process. He founded an essay club, known from his initials as the Weg to which many of his friends belonged. Some discussions held there might sound jejeune to our ears, but some first-class minds were sharpening themselves against each other. The forum where glory really came to Willy was the Debating Society, later the Union, which had been founded only a few years previously. He made his first speech there in February 1830 during his second year, but it was in his final session that he really made his mark. In November 1830 during the meeting which elected him President he moved a motion of no confidence in the Duke of Wellington's government. His attitude was perhaps determined more by the fact that most of the Canningites had left the Duke's administration than by any profound difference of political principle. The Duke was about to resign, as a result of his outright condemnation of parliamentary

reform. It was the same Canningite distrust that made William dis-
approve of the proposal that Peel should take Huskisson's place as
one of the members for Liverpool. His most famous speech in the
Debating Society was made on 17 May 1831 in the course of a three-
day debate on the Reform Bill. Gladstone presented the bill as a
threat to the very foundations of society. Proud as he was of his
son's widely acknowledged brilliance, John Gladstone, now a
moderate reformer, could not wholly agree with his sentiments. It
was soon after this speech that Lord Lincoln, William's friend,
decided to bring him to the attention of his father, the ultra-Tory
Duke of Newcastle. William's last speech in the Debating Society
was against the immediate emancipation of the slaves. It was the
first time that he had in public to defend the institution with which
his father, through his West Indian plantations, had become so
deeply involved.

The same filial piety that made William defend slavery, no matter
how painful the dilemma of conscience, dictated prolonged discussions
with his father concerning his choice of career. His growing awareness of the world's sinful state ripened in him the conviction that
he must enter the Church. In April 1830 he wrote a long letter to
his father, its circuitous sentences propelled by his intense emotion,
giving the reasons for his wish to take orders.[5] Wisely his father
told him to defer a final decision. On his twenty-first birthday he
wrote in his diary: 'Politics are fascinating to me; perhaps too
fascinating.' In November 1831 William achieved the final triumph
of a double first at the end of a year of high political drama which
had strongly involved him. Shortly afterwards he was able to tell
his father that he was now willing to take up a political career. He
saw a great crisis approaching in the history of mankind: enlightened
self-interest is made the substitute for the old bonds of unreasoned
attachment and the stability of society might be threatened.
The Church would be under attack and would need defenders in
politics. Thus he resolved his inner doubts, but again and again in
his long political career he would feel that he had missed his true
vocation. His life in politics was a constant quest for God and for
the great causes in which the will of God could be discerned.

Gladstone's education was rounded off by a long continental tour,
mainly in Italy. It was an important stage in his religious development. He was in a susceptible state, for doubts about his decision
to forsake the Church for a secular career still assailed him. The
great monuments of the Church in Italy, especially St Peter's,
impressed him deeply. Under the impact of this emotional experience

he moved farther beyond his evangelical roots and came to the High Anglican position which he held for the rest of his life. He also began to study the English Book of Common Prayer with much greater zeal, where previously the teachings of the Bible had been pre-eminent with him. At Naples on 13 May 1832 he wrote in his diary:

Of late and today in particular, I have been employed in examining some of the details of the system of the English Church, as set forth in the Prayer Book, with which I was before less acquainted. To coming into Catholic countries, and to some few books, I owe glimpses which now seem to be afforded me of the nature of a Church, and of our duties as members of it, which involve an idea very much higher and more important that I had previously had any conception of.

His new appreciation of the Church, henceforth an intense pre-occupation for him, did not extend to Roman Catholicism and the Papacy. If anything the fears and prejudices he had imbibed with his mother's milk were deepened by his Italian tour. After seeing the Pope in the Sistine Chapel on Palm Sunday, 15 April 1832, he wrote:

As a *sight* it came up not to my expectations of solemn splendour, but rather *down* to the idea one naturally forms of the present condition of popery as a system of faded gauds whose vices and whose virtues are rapidly passing away, and which already is little more than a record of its own past existence.[6]

While at Milan with his brother John Neilson in July 1832, on his return from the Italian tour, William received the letter from his friend Lord Lincoln offering him the parliamentary seat at Newark of which his father, the Duke of Newcastle, was the patron.

On the threshold of his political career, William Ewart Gladstone had become a man of great potentialities and infinite complexities. He had great physical strength, perfect health, fine looks; a formidable intellect, enormous powers of concentration, the highest personal efficiency in the use of time and effort. At Oxford the process of growing away from his family background had gone much beyond Eton. The close family bonds outwardly continued, but there was much that now separated him from his brothers and his surviving sister. The deference to his father was undiminished, but John Gladstone could not follow him into the regions of intellectual and cultural refinement which he now inhabited. The growing expectations placed in him by his father had been amply fulfilled by his academic record and by the notice he was beginning to attract.

For all his sense of sin and unceasing self-examination, there was strong ambition pulsating within him. His triumphs as an orator confirmed his awareness of the power he could exercise over men. In such a man growing confidence produced a self-righteousness which clearly irked some of his contemporaries. Such must have been the feelings of the young Oxford bloods who beat him up in his rooms at Christ Church during his second year. Another potent dimension was added to Gladstone's character by his ardent emotionalism. He was himself frightened not merely by the sexual manifestations of his emotional nature but by the onrush of feelings that would sweep him impulsively hither and thither on any matter that fully involved him. He felt the need not only to render account to his God but to engage in an unceasing struggle for self-mastery. From these struggles he emerged victorious, perfectly in control of himself, exemplary in patience and courtesy, yet with his inner fires merely banked, ready to blaze up when stirred by the righteous cause.

Gladstone was always in need of causes to which he could fully commit himself. When he had found one he would display energies awesome to ordinary mortals; and it was through the pursuit of causes that he could impose order on the volcanic forces that raged within him. A man so preoccupied with his conscience and his own mysterious self had little psychological energy to enter into the feeling of others. A degree of insensitivity in dealing with human beings was one of the principal weaknesses of Gladstone as a man of affairs. Politically, he was now increasingly identified with the main stream of a Tory party from which most of the leading liberal Tories had departed. It was a position strongly reinforced by his religious development towards Anglicanism: the role of the Church within the fabric of society now preoccupied him intensely. His was not an instinctive Toryism such as it might have been had he come from an established landed family. He had arrived at his strongly Tory views by a logical process, remote from practical experience. His powerful critical faculty which had carried him to this point from the Canningite Toryism of his youth might well in due course carry him elsewhere even though his view of man and society would at bottom always remain conservative and reverential. For the moment his opinions were effective in securing him an entry into the parliamentary arena.

2

THE
RISING HOPE
1832–41

The Duke of Newcastle's offer of a parliamentary seat at Newark came to Gladstone as an event of 'extraordinary import'. His conscience was deeply agitated: the old doubts about the choice of a secular career rose up again; the Duke's well-known hostility to Canning, 'the most profligate Minister the country had ever had', disturbed Gladstone and he also feared that his independence as a Member would be limited by the Duke. These qualms were eased when he realized that his father was entirely in favour of accepting the offer.

Newark was an old scot-and-lot borough the boundaries of which remained unaffected by the reform legislation of 1832 and which continued to return two members.[1] It was one of the limited number of boroughs still regarded as proprietary after the Reform Bill. The Duke of Newcastle's influence had, however, been challenged well before 1832. In 1829 Serjeant Wilde, a Whig, had made it a hard fight for the Duke's candidate, Sadler, of Factory Act fame. The Duke reacted by serving eviction notices on forty disobedient tenants. This in turn provoked a protest meeting to petition Parliament and the Duke, when informed of this, sent the curt note by which he has become known to history: 'that he had a right to do as he liked with his own'. It did not save him from losing control of the borough in the 1831 election, when Wilde was swept to the head of the poll. In the contest which Gladstone was now about to enter, the first for a reformed Parliament, there were two other candidates: Wilde again, and Handley, a Tory, who had won the second seat in 1831. There were now some 1600 registered electors, each with two votes, a medium-sized constituency by the standards of the reformed electoral system. The Duke was thought to control some 700 votes, and had therefore to exert himself to influence the other hundred or so required to win.

Gladstone's election addresses contained all the claims to be expected from a 'thorough Conservative candidate' as a local Tory journal called him: 'a warm and conscientious attachment to our Government as a limited Monarchy, and to Union of our Church and State'; 'strict adherence to our national engagements – the defence, in particular, of our Irish Establishments'; 'the observance of a dignified and impartial foreign policy'; 'we must watch and resist that unenquiring and undiscriminating desire for change among us which threatens to produce, along with partial good, a melancholy preponderance of mischief'. One passage startled his ultra-Tory patron: 'it is a duty to endeavour by every means that labour may receive adequate remuneration; which, unhappily, among several classes of our fellow-countrymen, is not now the case'. In this connection Gladstone advocated 'the allotment of cottage grounds' and this was one plank at any rate which he could still recall with pride nearly sixty years later in the run-up to the last general election of his public life. Slavery, however, was the issue which caused him most distress in his first contest. His father had attained national notoriety as a slave- and plantation-owner. The family's Demerara estate had been the centre of a slave rising in 1823 which was brutally suppressed. A national outcry had been caused by the death in prison of the missionary John Smith who was being treated by the frightened and infuriated planters as a scapegoat for the rising. John Gladstone, with his combative temperament, leapt into this bitter controversy with letters to the press and pamphlets, defending slavery and the planters and attacking the abolitionists. He called Wilberforce 'a well-meaning, but mistaken man', and spoke of 'the more intemperate, credulous, designing, or interested individuals who have placed themselves in his train'. As recently as 1830 he had published a considered defence of slavery, couched in the form of a letter to Sir Robert Peel, outlined the insurmountable difficulties in the way of emancipation and compared the Negro's lot favourably with that of the lower classes at home.

It is hardly surprising, therefore, that William came under heavy attack on the slavery question. Quotations from his father's pamphlets were flung at him. Nationally the Anti-Slavery Committee listed him among nineteen parliamentary candidates who were strong supporters of slavery. William had to defend himself and his family with elaborate sophistries. Privately he told his sister Helen that he was 'unable to see the difficulties of emancipation . . . in so strong a light as my father does'.[2] While there is no reason to suppose that he was not in fundamental agreement with his father on slavery at this stage, filial duty must in this case have subjected him to severe, if largely subconscious, tensions.

William took his full share of the rumbustious side of electioneering at Newark. He wrote a characteristic account of some of the problems involved:

. . . to kiss the daughters. This latter was for me rather a novel occupation . . . it was far from my desire to do anything that would either encourage a forward or embarrass and distress a retiring person . . . therefore I availed myself of the privilege whose exercise was not only conceded but expected . . . not apparently either to the displeasure or the detriment of the parties concerned. I fancy however that my performances were considered to be rather sparing: for a report was circulated, that I was a married man. On this and other subjects I am sure it is a sacred and solemn duty to be cautious, and to manifest a marked coolness of manner when there is anything like forwardness exhibited in a female: yet it is perhaps an easier matter than would be conceived, to observe delicacy without fastidiousness . . .[3]

For the rest Gladstone was struck by the fact that feeling between the classes was determined by ignorance rather than malice and that the poor were on the whole reasonable and moderate. He also felt that the Dissenters, numerically strong at Newark, were not all voting for the same party. He noted that among questions put to him the largest number concerned slavery. Thus his electoral analysis, at the very start of his political career, was quite sophisticated by modern standards. When the poll was completed on 13 December 1832 Gladstone emerged in the lead, with 887 votes, followed by Handley with 798. Wilde, with 726 votes, lost his seat. A more detailed breakdown of the poll shows that 582 electors split their votes between Gladstone and Handley, 175 plumped for Gladstone, 33 for Handley, 413 for Wilde. The remainder of the 1516 electors who cast valid votes were split between Gladstone and Wilde (130) and Handley and Wilde (183) respectively.[4] The high tide of radicalism evoked by the battle for reform had receded, but the youthful Gladstone appears to have had some personal attraction as a candidate. The cries of 'he's a lad' which occasionally greeted him and the coffin labelled 'Young Gladstone's Ambition' paraded by his opponents around the streets had not damaged him. In his first speech as an elected member he was anxious to assure the people of Newark that he was the Duke of Newcastle's man on grounds of principle alone and that therefore he genuinely represented the views of those who had voted for him: 'You return me to parliament, not merely because I am the Duke of Newcastle's man: but because both the man whom the Duke has sent, and the duke himself, are *your men.*'

Gladstone had no qualms about entering the House of Commons as the member for a proprietary borough. It was not until his views began to diverge seriously from those of the Duke in the middle 1840s that his position caused him any discomfort. During his first long stay at Newark he had met the Duke at Clumber and had been impressed by the grandeur of his aristocratic position as well as by his personal kindness; the Duke for his part seemed to be well satisfied with the views on religion and politics expressed by his protégé. Gladstone remained blissfully ignorant of the methods by which the Duke's agents exerted electoral pressure and influence at Newark. The one aspect that did cause him serious concern was the amount spent on 'treating'. His father and the Duke had agreed to share his election expenses: when the bills came in they were more than twice what had been expected. William now started a battle with his committee of supporters at Newark about open public houses and the prevalence of drunkenness during elections. This battle continued intermittently throughout the thirteen years of his connection with the borough.

At Westminster Gladstone joined the decimated band of Tories. Some 160 of these were confronted by over 500 Whigs, Radicals and Irish Repealers according to Gladstone's own calculations. There were certainly fewer Tories than Radicals and Repealers. It was a formative period in the development of the modern constitution, of the political system and of the parties. In the crucible of the reform crises the party labels Whig and Tory had taken on more positive meaning, and the terms Liberal and Conservative were coming into use. Under the impact of Catholic Emancipation the Tory position had crumbled and the Duke of Wellington's outright opposition to a change in the franchise had brought the Whigs into office. They in turn were carried along the path of reform by a tide of popular feeling. The battle against reform had given the resisters renewed cohesion and organization. Nevertheless, the party situation was still confused in the first reformed Parliament. The view was commonly held that the disappearance of some of the instruments through which governments had in the past disciplined their back benches, for example nomination boroughs, would weaken party cohesion. What remained of the Tories after the election of 1832 was led in the House of Commons by Sir Robert Peel, but it was a leadership given, initially at any rate, with characteristic reluctance and only half-heartedly accepted by many who called themselves Tories. Gladstone had many things in common with the man who was to become his hero and mentor. Peel was also the son of a man who had amassed great wealth and had satisfied his political ambitions vicariously by raising up his son through Harrow and Oxford, to graduate into the ruling aristocracy. As in Gladstone's case the assimilation was not perfect: a barrier remained between Peel and the landed gentlemen whom he led which contributed to his fall in 1846. Like Gladstone, Peel retained some of the outward marks of his middle-class origin, in particular a slight but noticeable accent. Both men concealed much passion beneath a controlled exterior and both were imbued with a high seriousness. In other ways Gladstone could hardly have been in complete political harmony with his leader. Peel had been Canning's most prominent rival and had resigned in 1827 when Canning became Prime Minister because he could not serve under a pro-Catholic. Peel's conversion to Catholic Emancipation might have commended him to Gladstone but it earned him a deep-seated suspicion from all true Tories that was not allayed by his conduct during the reform crisis. Certainly an ultra-Tory like the Duke of Newcastle never forgave Peel. The cleavage between irreconciled ultras and Peel was in fact the most serious and persistent division among Tories. Gladstone, however, was politically still malleable. His votes in the House for Irish coercion, against the admission of Jews to Parliament and dissenters to the universities, for the Corn Laws and Ashley's Factory Act, marked him out as the most orthodox of Tories; the articles which he wrote at this time for the *Liverpool Standard* tell the same story. His real preoccupation was still with the position of the Church and his political views were derived from this central anxiety.

Gladstone's first words in the House of Commons were spoken on election petitions and were of little consequence. The reporters had difficulty in distinguishing between him and his brother Tom, who sat for Portarlington. He himself regarded as his maiden speech his intervention in reply to Lord Howick during the debates on abolition of slavery. Son of Lord Grey the Prime Minister and until April 1833 Under-Secretary for the Colonies, Howick had specifically attacked the overseer of the Gladstone estates in Demerara, John Maclean, and cited the Vreedenhoop plantation as a leading example of the pressure put upon the slaves to obtain higher output. Tom Gladstone was able to make the first speech in defence three nights after Howick, arguing that better methods of management had been introduced in a humane manner. William had to wait nearly three weeks before he was able to speak, a period of sore trial. On 3 June 1833, after attending a meeting of the West Indian planter interests at the house of Lord Sandon, one of Liverpool's M.P.s, he at last caught the Speaker's eye. It was a moderate speech, outwardly calm, but it showed signs of the agonizing dilemma under which William and his family had lived for at least ten years and which John Gladstone had imperiously forced upon them. William rebutted Howick's charges in detail, with a wealth of statistics. But to his own admission that slavery was inherently abhorrent he could only return the conventional arguments that the Negro was not ready for immediate emancipation and in a free state would be his own worst enemy. He emphasized the dangers to property everywhere of any attack on property-owners. 'My leading desire was, to benefit the cause of those, who are now so sorely beset,' William wrote in his diary. Loyalty to his father, his family and their friends thus remained uppermost with him, and it was taken for granted that he and his brother would be at the disposal of the planter interests. Painful as the predicament must have appeared even to him, there was no kicking against the pricks. The speech was well received; Stanley, the Colonial Secretary who was leading the fight for abolition, congratulated him and so did Fowell Buxton, Wilberforce's successor as leader of the abolitionists. Two days later Sir Robert Peel came up to him 'most kindly and praised the affair of Monday night'. The fact of the matter was that the Gladstone family had improved the economic efficiency of their plantations and were in many respects pioneers of new methods. They tried to ensure humane treatment of their slaves, but were largely in the hands of their local agents. John Gladstone was one of the foremost opponents of slave emancipation and played a prominent part in the fight against emancipation. At a much later period of his life William Gladstone felt he had little to be proud of in this episode, but asked that allowance should be made for the generally more backward state of opinion on this issue and claimed that even then he had little confidence left in those acting for his family in the West Indies. Had emancipation come a year or two later, William, by then an established parliamentary hand, might have taken a position more independent of his father and family.

He made a speech more characteristic of his true position and beliefs a few weeks later on what was the most controversial measure of the session, the Church Reform (Ireland) Bill, which among other things abolished ten redundant bishoprics in Ireland. The major point of principle raised by the proposed reforms of the Church of Ireland was whether Church revenues which were or might become superfluous could be appropriated to lay purposes. On this issue all Conservatives were, however, united in opposition, considering it a spoliation of property and part of a broader attack on the Established Church in England as well as Ireland. Peel was personally in favour of some reforms of the Irish Church but he was entirely opposed to appropriation. Gladstone in his speech opposed the bill on much wider grounds: the state, by opting for religious liberty, was failing to distinguish between truth and falsehood; it needed an established Church as its guide to divine truth and it was entitled to tax to maintain a national Church. This argument was becoming the central obsession of his public life. He also saw in this particular bill a threat to the union of England and Ireland and naturally he opposed what he saw as the misappropriation of Church revenues for lay purposes. The position of the member of Newark was an extreme one; Stanley called it 'singular'. Nevertheless it was not greatly out of line with Tory views in general at a time when the reform of the Church in England as well as Ireland was the most controversial issue in politics and provided the clearest dividing-line between the parties. The fact that the Church of Ireland was an alien Church which with all its rich endowments served only a tenth of Ireland's inhabitants was of no consequence at this stage of his career.

During his first parliamentary session Gladstone became a member of the recently founded Carlton Club and was admitted to Lincoln's

B

Inn. He moved into the Albany and led an active social life, limited only by his concern to avoid frivolity. His fine singing voice, trained by regular lessons, was a considerable social asset. In August 1833, after the end of the session, he paid his first visit to Fasque, the estate in Kincardineshire purchased by his father in 1830 and now the permanent family seat. It was there that the news reached him in October of Hallam's death – 'this intelligence was deeply oppressive even to my selfish disposition' he notes in his diary. He met and held much discourse with Dr Chalmers, the Scottish divine, whom he greatly admired and who influenced him considerably.

Gladstone's second session of Parliament in 1834 saw the break-up of Grey's ministry. His own major contribution in debate was on a bill, abortive as it turned out, allowing the admission of Dissenters to Oxford and Cambridge without a religious test. This and other grievances of the Nonconformists, yet another aspect of the whole problem of the established Church, were pressing for relief with increasing urgency. Gladstone again took the High Anglican line of defending the *status quo* at the two ancient universities, which he called the preparatory seminaries to the Church Establishment, and of attacking the principle of religious liberty. It was a line more extreme than that taken by his leader, Peel, who was always anxious to show that the Tories were not averse to 'the correction of proved abuses and the redress of real grievances' as he was to to put it later in the Tamworth Manifesto. In this instance Peel, while opposing the bill and in general arguing in a similar vein to his young follower, carefully avoided impugning the principles of toleration.

The Church and Ireland were again the two most contentious issues of the session and together they brought down Grey's government. First there was the loss of Stanley, who by a strange irony was later as 14th Earl of Derby to face Gladstone as a Conservative and Protectionist, when the member for Newark had become first a free-trader and then a Liberal. The vexed question of the appropriation of Irish Church revenues drove Stanley out of the Cabinet; with him resigned Graham, later to be a close associate of Gladstone in Peel's great ministry and as Peelite after 1846. Lord John Russell had 'upset the coach', and the 'Derby Dilly' moved away from the Whigs. Shortly afterwards the government got into deep water on Irish coercion with O'Connell and his followers and Grey resigned in disgust. Efforts by the King to promote a coalition between moderate Whigs and Peel proved illusory and Melbourne took Grey's place in the Whig Cabinet. In November 1834, after the end of the session, William IV dismissed the Melbourne Cabinet, the last time that a

British monarch took such action. The occasion was Althorp's elevation to the peerage as Lord Spencer on the death of his father. The removal of Stanley and Althorp had put Lord John Russell in a strong position and Melbourne proposed to the King that he should succeed Althorp as Leader of the House. The King could not stomach the promotion of the most radical of the principal members of the Whig Cabinet and this was the ground for the dismissal. Melbourne was the last man to cling to office, having called the premiership 'a damned bore' when he assumed it.

The way was thus open for a return of the Tories and, as it happened, Gladstone's first brief taste of office. Unfortunately Peel was travelling in Italy when the Whigs fell and for some three weeks Wellington acted as caretaker, while a young gentleman usher scoured the Continent to find Peel and deliver the King's summons. Relations had been strained between Wellington and Peel ever since the dramatic events of 1831 and 1832 and they had improved again only recently as the Whig government's prospects waned. It is not impossible that Wellington's period as caretaker doomed Peel's government to failure from the start. It could only hope to succeed by attracting moderate support as much as possible, for example Stanley and his followers, and Wellington's hard-line image, so prominently displayed at the outset of the Tory return, made this more difficult.

Nevertheless, Peel returned post-haste, arriving on 8 December, accepted the King's commission and thus implicitly sanctioned the dismissal of the Whigs. For the next few days he faced great pressures, political as well as from place-seekers, in forming his government. Disraeli described it thus in *Coningsby*:

People sprang up like mushrooms; town suddenly became full. Everybody who had been in office, and everybody who wished to be in office; everybody who had ever had anything, and everybody who ever expected to have anything, were alike visible. All of course by mere accident, one might meet the same men regularly every day for a month, who were only 'passing through town'.[5]

The young member for Newark was not 'passing through town', but staying at the family's home in Edinburgh when on 17 December the call reached him from Sir Robert. He left immediately for London, with his father's advice 'to take anything with work and responsibility'. Peel offered him a seat at the Admiralty or Treasury boards but preferred him to take the latter as he would be in more immediate communication with himself. It was a tribute to the parliamentary reputation Gladstone had made for himself, but also a consequence of Peel's urgent need to bring forward new men to fill the gaps which political vicissitudes and the passage of time had left in the Tory ranks. Among other young men who were given their first experience of office at this time were Sidney Herbert and Lord Lincoln, Gladstone's Oxford friends and for long to remain his political companions. At his interview Peel told Gladstone in confidence that a dissolution was imminent and one of the first acts of the new Junior Lord of the Treasury was to issue another address to the electors of Newark. It showed that he had travelled some way politically: while accusing the Whig government, in its final stages, of dangerous radicalism, he declared the reform of abuses 'a sacred duty... not inimical to true and determined Conservative principles'. He was unopposed at Newark.

As soon as the election was over Peel invited him to become Under-Secretary for War and the Colonies, John Stuart-Wortley, his original choice, having failed to win a seat. It was an office for which Gladstone was well fitted through his connection with the West Indies and it was particularly important with the Secretary of State, Lord Aberdeen, in the Lords. It was the start of another long political association with a man who personified some of the best qualities of aristocratic statesmanship. The two months which Gladstone held this office were too short to enable him to make any public or parliamentary mark, but he earned praise from the permanent officials of the department, including the two redoubtable officials who carried the emancipation, James Stephen and Henry Taylor. The latter was much impressed with a paper Gladstone wrote on Negro education in the West Indies, a subject dear to his heart, which was left for action to his successor. His performance on a bill dealing with conditions on emigrant ships, left by his predecessors, seems to have been less impressive.[6]

The elections nearly doubled the number of Tories in the House, to somewhere near 300, but it was not a majority. Survival still depended on the ability of Peel to draw to his side enough of the followers of Stanley and other moderate Whigs. It had been a major blow that neither Stanley nor Graham was prepared to join the Tory government and had confined themselves to promising support. In the event Stanley's support was grudgingly and conditionally given and the number of moderate Whigs prepared to follow him in keeping the Tories in office was smaller than had been expected. On the other side of the House the Lichfield House compact pointed to a consolidation of Whigs, Radicals and O'Connellites. The Tories lost the first division in the new Parliament on the appointment of the

Speaker, and their control of the House was thenceforth always in doubt. Soon it was only a matter of time and tactics when Peel should resign. When Lord John Russell moved a motion renewing the conflict over the appropriation of Irish Church revenues the end was in sight. Gladstone was one of the government speakers in the debate which ended in a Tory defeat by thirty-three votes. Concerning this speech, Gladstone noted in his diary that 'this matter of speaking is really my strongest religious exercise'. Although some members of the government, including Wellington, still had a hankering to continue the fight, possibly by again seeking a junction with Stanley, Peel was generally supported when he decided to resign.

What had been achieved by his hundred days (his precise period in office was four months)? For the King it was an unequivocal defeat, showing that the royal prerogative could no longer be used, in conjunction with the House of Lords, to defeat the House of Commons. For Peel it provided a first opportunity to prove his remarkable powers as head of a government. He began to show that grasp of all business in all departments that made a comparison with the legendary Younger Pitt seem for the first time not unreasonable. He firmly established his own leadership of a Conservative party capable of carrying out moderate, realistic and necessary reforms. In setting up the Royal Commission on the Church, the government had created an instrument through which the Church could put its own house in order and thus meet one of the major lines of attack on the established order. The Conservative party in its parliamentary and electoral strength was consolidated and there is little substance in the contention, often made at the time, that but for the action of the King, a stronger reaction towards the Tories would in due course have taken place. An altogether more clear-cut party situation had now been established on both sides of the House.[7] As for Gladstone, he had laid the foundation for a long career in high office, he had made his mark as one of the up-and-coming men in the party and had begun to acquire a reputation as a sound man of business. There was added to his high-minded but innocent addiction to principle a new dimension of practical grasp, or at any rate the beginnings of it. He was no longer a young High Tory unsullied by realism but a working member of a Conservative government that had gone to the country under Peel and behind the Tamworth Manifesto.

Out of office Gladstone was for a spell preoccupied with private affairs and his parliamentary attendances were not as assiduous for the remainder of the 1835 session and in 1836 as they had been. He fell deeply in love with Caroline Farquhar, daughter of Sir Thomas Farquhar of Polesden Lacey. His unsuccessful courtship of this light-hearted girl vexed him deeply and makes him appear a hopeless bundle of inhibitions, innocence, priggishness and pedantry. Much of the courtship was conducted by letters to the object of his affection and to her parents and brother, seeking earnestly for clarification almost in the manner of diplomacy. Differing attitudes to religion and amusements were slowly listed and a common denominator sought. The image of pure womanhood, which Gladstone had acquired from his sister Anne and his mother, prevented him from striking a chord in an ordinary girl of flesh and blood.[8] In July 1836 Caroline Farquhar married a younger son of Lord Grey of the Reform Bill; as General Grey and Queen Victoria's tactful Private Secretary he helped a generation later to ease the difficult relationship between the monarch and her Liberal Prime Minister. The anguish of his affair punctuates his diary: 'A large family party, made very scanty use of my opportunity: learned my blindness and stupidity by afterthought, ruminated long at night by my open window.' And when it was all over and he was given a report of her wedding: 'I had not known of it before: it is as it was to me in respect of pain: but in respect of good I see distinct reasons for glorifying God: I therefore hope that even the pain will in His good time turn to good'[9] followed by much devout sentiment in French; and indeed most of the references to the Farquhar affair in the diary are in Italian, perhaps a defensive mechanism when writing about a matter so deeply emotional.

While William's affections were thus engaged his mother died in September 1835. He nursed her during the last two weeks of her life and described the symptoms of her final illness and the circumstances of her death with the morbid fascination characteristic of the age. No sooner was this crisis passed than his brother Robertson's choice of a Unitarian for his bride caused serious dissension. William attempted, quite gratuitously, to draft articles of a religious agreement between his brother and his intended. It earned him a rebuke from his father. On the day of the wedding in January 1836 which he attended with reluctance, he wrote in his diary, in Italian: 'Would to God that I had been able to lift up my hands to bless them . . . but my blessing, such as it was, at least got out of my mouth.' Eighteen months later, by which time he had moved out of the Albany into a house in Carlton Gardens owned by his father, William himself embarked upon another wooing. This time his choice had fallen upon Lady Frances Douglas, eldest daughter of the Earl and Countess of Morton, described again as a girl of 'child-like buoyancy of heart and spirit'. Gladstone had made little progress as a suitor since Caroline Farquhar and his courtship was as gauche as ever, though the anguish at his rejection was not quite so bitter. He could even write in his diary, after receiving a crushing reply through Dean Ramsay, who acted as intermediary: 'A day of abject prostration. Probably more gloomy from severe seasickness – let the truth be told.' Again it took him an embarrassingly long time to accept his rejection as final and the affair contributed to the low state he was in early in 1838. He escaped through feverish work on his first major literary effort, *The State in its Relations with the Church*. In these private misfortunes and aberrations the modern mind perceives the comic element before almost anything else; but in their contemporary context they shed much light upon the character of the young Gladstone: the great force of his emotions powerfully repressed by a procrustean moral and religious frame-work, the compelling need to proceed from first principles undiluted by any reference to practicality, the other-worldly innocence paired with a high intellect.

Such tribulations did not, however, seriously interrupt Gladstone's public career nor the process of wide reading and self-education of which his diary gives such remarkable evidence. He became person-ally acquainted with many of the great men of the age, from the Duke of Wellington to O'Connell and from Wordsworth to Pusey, and was brought into contact with them in the conduct of his public business. He cultivated his Newark constituency through occasional visits and speeches and was re-elected without a contest in 1837, when the accession of Queen Victoria brought about a general election. It was a tribute to his growing reputation as a young Tory politican that the Manchester Conservatives insisted on nomi-nating him in spite of his initial refusal. In their appeal to the Manchester electors they called him 'by universal admission, one of the most useful members in the House of Commons, and perhaps the most promising young statesman of the day'. The Whigs in reply said that his parliamentary record showed him to be the highest of Tories obstructing every useful reform, and 'a true Cumberlander'.[10] The Duke of Cumberland was to all progressive men the symbol of the blackest reaction. Manchester was a forlorn hope for Toryism, but Gladstone, by fighting the contest *in absentia*, made the Tory humiliation even worse. Overall the general election produced a further slight improvement in the Tory position, in spite of the fact that ministers could now boast the favour of the new monarch. Some losses in Ireland and Scotland were more than made up for by advances in the English counties. Melbourne and his ministers were in office only through the support of O'Connell and confronted a powerful opposition led by Peel, the outstanding statesman of the day. The major problem which had faced Peel in the previous Parliament, the cleavage between his own cautious path combining reform with resistance and the policy of outright blockage frequently adopted by the Tory peers, was considerably lessened in the new Parliament, for the Whigs were not now strong enough for any major legislative initiative. Stanley now formally joined the Tories.

Colonial questions bulked large in Gladstone's parliamentary work, because he had been at the Colonial office and because of his continued connection with the planter interest. In 1836 he was appointed to a select committee to inquire into the working of the apprenticeship system, the intermediate stage between slavery and full emancipation. The committee had been set up on a motion of Fowell Buxton, the abolitionist leader, and reflected the public anxiety aroused by reports of cruel treatment and the desire to see the system ended before the statutory date fixed for 1840. Gladstone frankly represented the planter interest on the committee and in his examination of witnesses the thrust of his questioning revealed more often than not his concern to rebut the accusations made against the planters.[11] He made his last major intervention on the floor of the House in defence of the planters in March 1838 with a speech that was widely admired, on a motion to bring the apprenticeship system to a premature end that year. His intervention was important in securing the rejection of the motion and his own analysis of the division shows that, while a clear majority of Tories as well as the government were with him, ministers had a small majority of their own followers against them. It was indeed 'a moment of delight', but none the less a barren victory, for further public pressure did in fact end the apprenticeship system in August 1838. A parliamentary triumph could no longer assuage Gladstone's inner doubts and his efforts were increasingly turned towards improving the position of the Negro. He had heard much about it on another select committee of which he was a member, concerned with the treatment of aborigines in the Empire. His work on it shows his faith in Britain's mission and obligation towards her subject peoples, which in later life counterbalanced his anti-imperialism.

A colonial matter of a different type with which Gladstone concerned himself was Canada. In his various speeches on this subject one can detect the note of anti-imperialism which at this stage of his life was merely an aspect of the fashionable pessimism about the permanence of the tie between colonies and mother country, but which in later life became an integral part of his liberalism. On the immediate problem of the Canadian rebellions, however, Gladstone, like most Conservatives, advocated a firm line. In the House of Commons a crucial debate took place in March 1838, when Sir William Molesworth, the prominent Radical, moved a motion of censure on Lord Glenelg, the Colonial Secretary. The Tories were caught between their general support for the government's suppression of the Canadian uprisings, their reluctance to combine with the Radicals and the impatience of many of them to throw the Whigs out. Peel had no desire to take office again before the time was ripe. Gladstone took his full share in the consultations held between the leading Conservatives at this time, and in the debate on the Molesworth motion he made a speech which earned him praise from Peel and even Disraeli, recently returned for Maidstone.

The Church and religion, however, continued to be nearest Gladstone's heart and occupied much of his parliamentary efforts. Looking back at this phase in his career in one of the autobiographical memoranda he wrote towards the end of his life he felt that he was 'in concurrence with the general views of the Tory party. But I went beyond them in State Churchism.' This was certainly the nub of his position that the Church was the nation as a spiritual entity and the state was its secular counterpart. The state had a duty to sustain the Church in every respect and full citizenship was impossible without membership of the Church. This outlook coloured Gladstone's attitude on most issues of the time, the Irish Church, the various disabilities of the Dissenters and other non-Anglicans, church rates, education at home and in the colonies. Many of his early votes were cast, sometimes in small minorities, against measures to remedy entirely legitimate grievances of non-Anglicans, for example against the bill to facilitate the registration of Dissenters' marriages. In one of his more important speeches, on an ingenious Whig scheme in the session of 1837 to deal with church rates, another dissenting grievance, he claimed that the Established Church existed to carry home to the door of every man in the country who was willing to receive them the blessings of religion and the ordinances which its ministers were appointed to dispense. In June 1839 he made another widely noticed speech on Lord John Russell's Education Bill. The bill provided for the increase of the annual school grant from £20,000 to £30,000, an educational committee of the Privy Council and a non-confessional school for teacher-training. It would have increased the degree of state control imposed on the two school societies, the Anglican National Society and the Nonconformist British and Foreign. It was welcomed by the Nonconformists, but Anglicans had for some time prepared to resist any attack on the considerable advantage they enjoyed in the education field through the National Society. Gladstone in his speech proclaimed once more the duty of the state to uphold a particular form of religion rather than adopt an even-handed neutrality between different denominations. When he asked rhetorically what the government was bringing the country to, Lord John Russell interjected, 'At least not to bigotry and intolerance,' to which Gladstone riposted, 'The noble lord would be more accurate if he said to latitudinarianism and atheism.' More positively Gladstone had since 1837 worked actively to further the Anglican effort in education by strengthening the National Society, particularly in teacher-training, and by setting up diocesan boards of education. He worked together with a group of young Anglican Tories which included his old Oxford friend Acland, Ashley, Lord Sandon, the member for Liverpool, and Praed, the other up-and-coming young Tory whose premature death in 1839 cut short a promising career. This campaign was part of the Anglican revival of confidence after the low point reached as a result of the attacks on the Church during the reform era. In this revival the Oxford Movement was a major source of intellectual energy.

Gladstone had left Oxford before Keble's Assize Sermon and the publication of the first of the *Tracts for the Times* in 1833 had given the Movement something like an official existence. At the end of his life he wrote: 'The Oxford Movement properly so called . . . had no direct effect upon me. I did not see the Tracts and to this hour I have read but few of them.' Nevertheless he shared the principal preoccupation of the Movement, the position of the Church, and its mysticism appealed to him; in the late 1830s and early 1840s he was regarded as a Tractarian and identified himself with the attitudes of the Tractarians on important public issues. He had many links with the principal figures of the Oxford Movement and when he wrote his first book, *The State in its Relations with the Church*, in 1838 his two closest friends, James Hope, later Hope-Scott, and Manning were also under the influence of the Movement. There were many impulses that finally drove Gladstone to authorship, not only his own obsession with the Church but the central place the Church occupied in politics and in the Tory party. It was under intellectual attack from the philosophical Radicals, under practical attack from reformers of all kinds. The Establishment suffered from a variety of defenders, some taking a narrowly Erastian position; this again generated a predilection for disestablishment among some of the Tractarians. Indeed Gladstone claimed that the immediate impulse to write came from a series of lectures on the principles of Church establishment delivered by his friend Dr Chalmers in London in 1838 which seemed to him to give a thoroughly unsatisfactory explanation for the supremacy of Parliament over the Church. For his own peace of mind he had to cut through this maze of confusions and set up a firm base of principles for his conviction that the Church should have a pre-eminent place reserved for it in the national life and that religious liberalism was wrong. As ever, Gladstone needed a cause to release his energies and with the formation of a Conservative government possible at any time he felt the requirement of 'a definite principle on religious matters'. The actual writing of the manuscript was concentrated into two months and damaged his eyesight; it was a kind of catharsis at a time of inner doubt brought on by private and public tribulations. James Hope, who filled in Gladstone's life something of the place Arthur Hallam had once held in it, was left to put the finishing touches to the manuscript.

The key to Gladstone's arguments is that there is more than a marriage of convenience between Church and state. Both of them have moral functions in pursuit of which the state has the duty to distinguish between truth and error and therefore to support the true religion of the Established Church.[12] Enough of the English people were still members of the Church to make it the conscience and teacher of the nation. This was still the guiding concept behind the Church reforms of the 1830s, but circumstances were rapidly rendering it unrealistic (certainly Gladstone's rigorous application of the concept was, to say the least, untimely). It was not long before he himself was to see that this scheme no longer fitted the realities of his time and the publication of the book brought him much embarrassment. In spite of this he never looked back on the writing of it as an error, perhaps not only because of the contribution it made to what he considered a necessary public debate, but because it helped, as it were by a process of elimination, in his own development. Among the reactions to the book the most famous are those of Peel and Macaulay. Peel remarked, after a cursory examination of the book, 'that young man will ruin a fine career if he writes such books as these' and for a while there was a coolness in their relations. Peel, that eminently pragmatic statesman who had steered a careful course between Church reform and defence of the Establishment, could hardly appreciate so unrealistic an excursion into abstruse dogma. It was a widely shared view and James Mozley, another Tractarian, reported people as saying 'poor fellow'. Macaulay met Gladstone in Rome in December 1838, just as the book was appearing in England and decided to review it in the *Edinburgh Review*. With his mordant wit he produced an article which has remained better known than the book, not least for the phrase 'the rising hope of those stern and unbending Tories, who follow, reluctantly and mutinously, a leader whose experience and eloquence are indispensable to them, but whose cautious temper and moderate opinions they abhor'. There was perhaps more than a grain of truth in this but the truncated version quoted in myriads of places ever since did Gladstone a serious injustice. The book pleased hardly anybody entirely. *The Times* spoke of 'new-fangled Oxford bigotries', many Tractarians could not accept his high view of the state and all Radicals and Dissenters were naturally in outright opposition.

As soon as the manuscript was finished in the summer of 1838, Gladstone left for the Continent. Hope dealt with Murray, the publisher, and sent Gladstone the proofs. It was on this trip that his courtship of Catherine Glynne, his future wife, began.[13] It still suffered from the inhibitions and handicaps that had rendered his previous wooings abortive. An attempt at a proposal in the moonlit Colosseum in January 1839 was a dismal failure; instead there were convoluted letters which kept the attachment barely alive. After Gladstone's return to England there were many more months of inconclusive approaches, in spite of frequent meetings and shared social occasions. Fortunately Miss Glynne was more mature than William's earlier loves and had herself been made wiser by previous disappointments. She discerned the deeper qualities beneath the somewhat frightening and gauche front presented by Gia – the Glynnes' nickname for William. The engagement was finally announced in June 1839; a week later Catherine's sister Mary got engaged to Lord Lyttelton and the double wedding took place a month later. For William it was a splendid match: as the fourth son of a Liverpool merchant he was socially well below what Catherine might have expected and even financially his expectations were not grand by the standards of the aristocracy; only his political expectations were regarded as outstanding. The Glynnes were connected through Catherine's mother with the great political clans of the Wyndhams and the Grenvilles and thus related to the Elder and the Younger Pitt. Through the Lytteltons there was a connection with all the great Whig families, the Spencers, Lambs, Leveson-Gowers and the Cavendishes. The Glynnes were a closely knit family with their own private language, 'Glynnese'. Their seat was Hawarden Castle and Catherine's older brother Sir Stephen, whom Gladstone had known at Eton, was M.P. for Flintshire. Catherine proved a perfect foil for William and she could share his essential innocence and simplicity and their domesticity had an intimate gaiety about it. Sometimes in later life, at moments of special happiness, William and Catherine would link arms and sing:

> A ragamuffin husband and a rantipoling wife,
> We'll fiddle it and scrape it through the ups and downs of life.

Yet Catherine also understood the great complexities of his character and shared his deep religious sense.

Courtship, marriage, depression about the reception of his book, renewed doubts about his choice of career, all this made little difference to the steady flow of his public life or to his gargantuan appetite for work. He sat on countless public and parliamentary committees, he carried on his ordinary parliamentary work, he published a further book in 1840, *Church Principles Considered in their Results*, which evoked almost no response. On colonial questions a decidedly more liberal trend became evident in his parliamentary speeches. In April 1839 he spoke on the suspension of the Jamaican Constitution. The Assembly in the island had refused to carry out any further duties because of the pressure upon it from London for better treatment of the natives, and the Melbourne government in reply suspended the Jamaican Constitution. The whole Conservative opposition, among them Gladstone, attacked the suspension, but Gladstone was no longer so much defending the planters as attacking ministers for their dictatorial practice. When the government's majority dropped to five in this debate they resigned and the famous Bedchamber crisis was precipitated. Gladstone's intervention in the debates on the Chinese Opium War in 1840 were almost in his later anti-imperial, *ruat coelum fiat justitia* vein. He called it an 'unjust and iniquitous war' and accused Palmerston of using the British flag 'to protect an infamous contraband traffic'. In an unfortunate slip of the tongue he appeared to suggest that the

Chinese had poisoned wells as their only means of defending themselves against the English residents engaged in the opium trade. This remark he was not allowed to forget, and he was accused of justifying the poisoning of wells in order to deprive English women and children of water. On this occasion his highly moral stand regardless of national self-interest isolated him somewhat from many on his own side. Perhaps the opium-addiction of his sister Helen made this a matter which touched him personally rather closely. In almost his last speech of Parliament, in May 1841, Gladstone attacked the government's proposals to reduce the duty on foreign-produced sugar. Now his arguments were almost entirely based on the danger that the slave trade would be encouraged, 'that monster which while war, pestilence, and famine were slaying their thousands, slew from year to year with unceasing operation its tens of thousands'. Needless to say he was reminded by many of those who spoke against him of his 'West Indian' past. It was the government's defeat on the sugar duties that set in train the long-delayed departure of the Whigs from office.

On the eve of his first prolonged spell in office Gladstone, aged thirty-one, spoke like one whose political future was assured. He could afford at times to take an unpopular line. Can his first eight years in the House of Commons really be summed up in Macaulay's phrase about the rising hope of stern, unbending Tories? Ever since he had held office in Peel's government in 1835 he was thoroughly a ministerialist. The Tory party was traditionally an alliance between large numbers of country gentlemen, some of them with extreme or at any rate politically unrealistic views, most of them unsuited or unwilling to hold office, and a smaller group of 'official men', some of them aristocratic, others nearer the type of the professional politician, who were capable of holding office. Gladstone clearly belonged to the second group and was increasingly regarded as a member with great prospects ahead of him. He kept close to Sir Robert Peel and followed him with a devotion not untinged with ambition. He appeared in his wake when Peel was projecting himself to a wider public, for example at his installation as Lord Rector of Glasgow University in January 1837, as a moderate and efficient statesman worthy of support by respectable men outside the landed classes. From 1838 onwards he was more and more in the inner councils of his leader and the publication of the state and Church book was only a momentary irritation, though it troubled Gladstone a good deal. In one of his late autobiographical fragments he wrote:

For Robert Peel had given me a forward position in the party though he was repelled and dismayed when my book on Church and State appeared. (I remember that when I came back from the Continent in January 1839 he (not rudely) shirked me in the street and I went after him and spoke to him.)

Gladstone was clearly to the right of Peel's balanced and empirical position in two fields only: the West Indian problems and the Church. On the former it was filial duty that held him in check; yet it was on colonial questions, particularly Canada, that, as he himself saw it, he 'made a first break in my Toryism'. On the Church his attitude went to the roots of his being and his religious development; in practice he did not ever make a break with Peel's policy of cautious reform, of which the appointment of the Ecclesiastical Commission was the most striking outcome. Thus Gladstone did not belong to the ultras, nor, obviously, to the group known as 'fanatick Agriculturalists'. The appearance of ultra-Toryism arose above all from Gladstone's need to make for his great energies a clear path of principle through the perplexities of the world.

3

GOVERNING
PACKAGES
1841–6

The election of 1841 was the first to conform approximately to the model of general elections familiar today. The government dissolved Parliament, in effect at a moment of their own choice. Admittedly the Melbourne ministry was defeated by a majority of one on a vote of no confidence on 4 June 1841; but they had already taken the decision some weeks previously to seek an early dissolution. In the elections the Conservative opposition which had up to then been in a minority was returned with a clear majority. This had never happened before in British history and it was not to happen again until after the second Reform Act of 1867. The fall of the Whigs had been a long time a-coming. First there was the false start of the Bedchamber crisis. Then at the opening of the session of 1840, the impatience of his followers for office and the mistaken prognostications of his whips had led Sir Robert Peel towards another false dawn – the government won in a no-confidence debate with a majority of twenty-one. All this was not modern, for in the twentieth century an opposition hardly ever expects to beat a government in a parliamentary vote on an issue of confidence. But it was again a modern feature of the election of 1841 that for the first time, in a reformed Parliament with a more representative electorate, the voters inclined to the right. It was demonstrated that contrary to expectation democratic electorates tire of reform after a dose of it and that their basic instincts are conservative. As *The Times* put it after the results had become clear: 'No other nation has ever witnessed the spectacle, now exhibited by Great Britain to the admiration of the world, of a triumphant reaction of sound public opinion against the progress of a partially successful democratical movement.'

For Gladstone there was a contest at Newark in 1841, but it was not a very serious one, as the challenger had put in an appearance very late in the day. Gladstone now shared the Tory representation of the borough with Lord John Manners, soon to be a member of the Young England group. Their personal relations were good, but Gladstone never acquired any sympathy for this group of romantic political dilettantes. In his election address Gladstone made a point of explaining his attitude on the Poor Law and the Corn Laws. The unpopularity of the New Poor Law was a major liability for the Whigs in this election, but Gladstone had himself come in for criticism at Newark because earlier that year he had voted for the second reading of the bill renewing the Poor Law Commission. In this he had followed Peel, who was enough of a Benthamite to approve of the 1834 Poor Law in principle though he criticized its harshness in detail. Gladstone took much the same line in the House and in his election address, showing again how much he was by this time an 'official man' in the party. On the Corn Laws he similarly adopted the cautiously balanced support that was Peel's own position at that time.

The general election as a whole gave the Tories a majority of near eighty. There were gains everywhere, most markedly again in the English counties, but least of all in Scotland because of the controversy over lay patronage. The Tories were still predominantly an English party. Following old-fashioned rather than modern procedure, the Whigs remained in office to meet the new Parliament and only resigned when they were defeated on an amendment to the loyal address at the end of August. Discussions with the Prince Consort and his secretary Anson had already ensured that this time the question of appointments in the Royal Household would not prevent the Tories from taking office. Peel himself had preferred to postpone this moment for as long as possible. Since 1837, if not earlier, the Conservative opposition had been so powerful that it could block any action of the Whigs it chose to. This state of affairs suited Peel; he was only too well aware of the size of the task facing any government, particularly in connection with the 'condition of England' question in the heyday of Chartism and the Anti-Corn-Law League. The Tory party had been difficult enough to lead when a battle in defence of state and Church was uniting it; Peel may well have perceived that it would become even more difficult to maintain Conservative cohesion when defence was no longer so necessary. On the other hand Peel was above all a constructive statesman and he now had unprecedented power to take action. This prospect was also to prove a happy release for his acolyte Gladstone from his perplexities about his true cause and vocation.

It was Gladstone's ambition to become Chief Secretary for Ireland, though he would have been content to remain outside the Cabinet. The incipient liberalism which he had shown on Canada and other colonial subjects had begun to trouble his conscience on the state of Ireland. It was only on the maintenance of the Established Church of Ireland that he still maintained his inflexible position. Peel shrewdly perceived that Ireland was not the place for the author of *The State in its Relations with the Church*. Instead Peel offered him the Vice-Presidency of the Board of Trade under Ripon. At first this seemed a disappointment, for Gladstone, the most clearly established younger man in the inner counsels of the party, had a right to expect more. In his late autobiographical fragments he wrote: 'In a spirit of ignorant mortification I said to myself at the moment: the science of politics deals with the government of men, but I am set to govern packages.' He did not see that he was in fact being offered a pivotal position. The interview, in which Peel patiently and, as it turned out, entirely truthfully pointed this out, was full of the professions of inadequacy and ignorance without which Gladstone could rarely move. In fact his long association with his father had given William a good deal of knowledge and experience of commerce and trade, even if it was at second hand. His ineffectual chief was in the Lords and he would therefore have ample scope to make his mark. With the excessive degree of scruple typical of him, Gladstone brought up one point of substance which he considered might bar him from joining Peel's government: his more liberal attitude to the terms to be exacted from China at the conclusion of the Opium War. Peel set his mind at rest on this score by pointing out that being at the Department of Trade he could 'leave the question suspended'. Shortly after his appointment Gladstone was disturbed by newspaper articles that he had been shunted to the Board of Trade because of differences with the Prime Minister on Church questions. He wrote Peel a long letter in which he disclaimed any intention of giving hope to the ultra-Tories against the moderate policies of his leader. It was fortunate that Peel was in no way put off by the tortuous and overscrupulous ways of his young recruit.

With the country in a severe depression of trade, alarmed by the Chartist disorders, assailed by the Anti-Corn-Law League and faced with a budget deficit accumulated by the Whigs over several years, Peel's government was immediately confronted with major decisions on economic policy. Even the Whig government had recognized this in its dying days, and besides proposing a reduction of the sugar and timber duties had come out in favour of substituting for the sliding scale of the 1828 Corn Law a fixed duty of 8 shillings a quarter. This programme had all the appearance of a belated attempt to court the free trade vote. Earlier Joseph Hume's Select Committee on Import Duties had given the official imprimatur to the view that a reduction of duties would lead to an increase in trade and therefore no loss of revenue. The condition of the country as well as the terms of the political debate therefore demanded action from Peel. His answer turned out to be a three-pronged plan of action: the imposition of an income tax, the introduction of a reduced sliding-scale duty on corn and the reduction of duty on a broad range of imports. In the planning of all three steps Gladstone played an important role and on the third of them all the detailed work was his. The income tax had been introduced by the Younger Pitt in the dire emergency of the Revolutionary Wars and had been abandoned in 1816. The psychological barrier to its revival was formidable indeed. In the discussions that went on among ministers Gladstone was consulted at an early stage and produced, in November 1841, a powerful memorandum in which he advocated, as the only alternative to a revival of the income tax, a revival of the house tax. It was clear to most of his colleagues that this would be even more unpopular and inequitable than an income tax and Gladstone's memorandum therefore served to weaken the opposition to the income tax inside the government. In the form the tax finally took in the 1842 budget it was levied at 7*d*. in the pound and there was an exemption limit of £150.

On the Corn Laws Gladstone had hitherto accepted that they were essential to the prosperity of the landed interest though he did not support the more extreme positions of the agriculturalists. Early in 1841 he had campaigned on behalf of his brother John at a by-election in Walsall. It was the first election in which the Anti-Corn-Law League fielded a candidate of their own and in doing so brought about the withdrawal of the official Whig candidate who was not a free-trader. As the League was so active in the contest Gladstone armed himself with pamphlets in favour of the Corn Laws and drew from them most of the material for his speeches. He refused a challenge by Cobden to meet him in public discussion. Once he was installed at the Board of Trade, Gladstone's views evolved very rapidly. Whereas initially he was mainly interested in the difficulties caused through speculation under the existing sliding scale and was concerned with better protection for the farmers, by the beginning of 1842 he was proposing to Peel a short, steep sliding scale which would have offered virtually no protection to the domestic producer once the price of wheat had risen above 61*s*. a quarter.[1] This was a more extreme proposal than the various solutions put forward by his chief, Ripon. The sliding scale which Peel eventually adopted dropped from 20*s*. when wheat was at 51*s*. a quarter to a nominal 1*s*. when it was at 73*s*. Gladstone saw this as a virtual prohibition of imports when wheat was below 70*s*. a quarter and was outraged that Peel and his colleagues were prepared, for political reasons, to stick to a higher degree of protection than they themselves regarded objectively as necessary. It induced in him the first symptoms of the tendency to threaten resignation at the slightest affront to his conscience which was to assail him many times in later years.[2] He reported Peel as 'thunderstruck' at this suggestion of resigning and hinting at a dissolution of the government; in retrospect Gladstone also blamed Peel for lack of 'management' in not talking him round by more reasoned argument. In any case Peel seems to have been by no means inept in handling Gladstone and his young lieutenant soon submitted, confessing his lack of wider political perception. Peel's adroit manoeuvring meant that on the Corn Law changes there was only one casualty from the Cabinet, the Duke of Buckingham, who had been appointed Lord Privy Seal to reassure the agriculturalists.

On the third of Peel's three major taxation changes, the reduction
of tariffs, the detailed work was entirely done by Gladstone. In
terms of sheer administrative and parliamentary effort it was the
most laborious part of the programme. Many of the more important
officials of the Board of Trade, men like John McGregor and G.R.
Porter, were convinced free-traders and had produced most of the
evidence before the Select Committee on Import Duties.[3] They were
therefore suspect to the Conservatives and Gladstone had to use
them with caution, relying much on his own investigations and
information. In particular Peel and his colleagues were not prepared
to swallow wholesale the argument of free-trade officials that
reductions of duty would in nearly all cases lead to increases in
revenue and they in fact made considerable allowances for loss of
revenue. The income tax was therefore the essential counterpart
to tariff reductions, not only because of the existing deficit, but also
to make up for these expected further losses of revenue. Out of
1200 dutiable articles, 750 had their duty reduced, with an expected
loss to the exchequer of £270,000. In addition, reductions of two
major revenue-producing duties, on timber and coffee, would lead
to losses of £600,000 and £170,000 respectively. Altogether the
government budgeted for a revenue loss of over £1·1 million. The
sugar duties were left intact on this occasion and it is worth noting
that while the free-trade implications of this major reform of the
tariff received most attention from contemporaries and ever since,
the new tariff also enshrined the principle of increased imperial
preferences. For Gladstone the biggest burden of the reform consisted in the large number of parliamentary interventions he had
to make, well over a hundred in the spring and summer of 1842,
and the endless deputations from trading interests that he, sometimes together with Peel and Ripon, had to receive. In the House
of Commons it was not the official opposition who posed the greatest
problem. Lord John Russell again put forward his fixed duty of
8 shillings a quarter on corn and Gladstone refuted him with great
ability and complete sincerity. The agriculturalists on the Tory
benches were more dangerous to the government: already suspicious
over the Corn Law, they were outraged by the admission of live
imported cattle at a low rate of duty. Gladstone chided them gently
by saying that as ornaments of the science of agriculture 'they
did not always cherish a sense of the benefits derived from the skill
and enterprise applied to it but were rather inclined to rely over-
much on the so-termed Protection of legislative enactments'. At
the end of this debate, on 23 May 1842, on the technical question of

taxing foreign livestock by weight, some eighty-five Tories voted against the government, who were supported by 172 of their usual opponents. It was an ominous signal of future divisions in the Tory party.The deputations which Gladstone had to receive at the Board of Trade helped him greatly in his parliamentary defence of the new tariff and also forwarded his general education.

> I learnt the nature and conditions of their trades, and armed with this admission to their interior, made careful notes and became able to defend in debate the propositions of the tariff and to show that the respective businesses could be carried on and not ruined as they all said.[4]

It was during one of these deputations that he first saw Bright, 'rather fierce, but very strong and very earnest'.

Gladstone considered this first revision of the tariff he was associated with far more troublesome than any of the others he was subsequently concerned with. Peel's economic package was also a decisive step in the economic development of Britain and indeed of the world, in which the British economy held a central place. The drift was now inexorably towards free trade and this and subsequent steps opened the way for a great expansion of international trade. Customs receipts over a period did not drop, but declined steeply as a percentage of public revenue and of import values. In buying more from abroad Britain helped to develop these countries as markets for her goods. In domestic politics bold measures had been taken to combat the severest depression hitherto experienced. Some of the wind was taken out of the sails of the Anti-Corn-Law League, but what remained of the Corn Laws was dangerously exposed. O'Connor and the Chartists applauded the income tax. The agriculturalists on the Tory benches had received the measures with 'sulky acquiescence'. Neither Peel nor Gladstone had suddenly become doctrinaire free-traders; indeed, as Disraeli, of all men, reminded the House during the budget debates, there was a Tory free-trade tradition going back to Pitt, and Gladstone's chief, Ripon, was a survivor from the Liverpool–Huskisson excursion into free trade. Gladstone changed his views on the substance of the matter with characteristic impulsiveness; but on the principle he still spoke with caution and late in life he wrote that he held 'by Protection during the Peel government as an accommodation to temporary circumstances'. He spoke in fact far from cautiously in the debate on a free-trade motion by Lord Howick in February 1843: he lost the thread of his argument; his free-trade convictions, basically shared by his colleagues, remained only thinly veiled and

Peel vainly tried by gestures to stop him from doing too much damage. Understandably his reputation with his party 'on this question oozed away with rapidity' and he began to be regarded as a renegade. Cobden, on the other hand, now wrote of him as a Puseyite who had been quite absorbed by Peel, but was nothing without him. He had moved a long way from the position of his father who remained a staunch supporter of the Corn Laws and something of a mercantilist in his general views on trade and on the responsibilities of the state towards commerce. These differences did not interfere with John Gladstone's pride in his son's success; it was a crowning moment when Peel, under his reserved exterior a warm-hearted man, found time to write him a letter praising his son: 'At no time in the annals of Parliament has there been exhibited a more admirable combination of ability, extensive knowledge, temper and discretion.' The way was now open for William's promotion to the Cabinet; it came in May 1843 when Ripon moved to the Board of Control and Gladstone succeeded him. There was nearly a hitch, due again to his overscrupulous conscience. Parliament, acting on the advice of the Ecclesiastical Commission, had provided for the union of the two Welsh bishoprics of St Asaph and Bangor when a vacancy should occur. In this way a new see could be created for Manchester. This proposal aroused much opposition, partly local, partly inspired by the Oxford Movement, and from this point of view Gladstone opposed it. Peel was firm in his intention to stick to what Parliament had decreed and determined to resist anything like Puseyite pressure. Gladstone was in an agony of mind and consulted Manning and Hope-Scott. They advised him not to stand on so narrow an issue and he later admitted that they had been his good angels. How often at crucial moments in his career Gladstone was saved from the consequences of his oversensitive conscience! It was a matter which his detractors always held against him.

Two major achievements mark Gladstone's tenure of the Presidency of the Board of Trade, a further round of tariff reductions and the regulation of the railways. The tariff reductions were brought forward in two stages; the politically dangerous sugar duties were tackled in 1844, the other reductions with the budget of 1845. Sugar still earned a far higher proportion of the customs than any other item. With a duty of 63*s.* a hundredweight on foreign-grown sugar, the West Indian planters had a virtual monopoly, yet could not increase their production to keep pace with demand. The question was further complicated by the fact that foreign slave-grown sugar had to remain barred from the British market. The essence of the government's proposals was to reduce the margin of imperial preference to a mere 10*s*. a hundredweight.[5] This was opposed by the West Indian interest; the government was defeated, on a cleverly worded amendment to increase the colonial preference margin again, by a combination of the opposition with Conservative malcontents of all kinds, including those with West Indian connections. It was part of the atmosphere of mistrust and misunderstanding between Sir Robert Peel and a growing number of Tory back-benchers. The government managed to get this vote reversed, but Peel made a speech which only deepened the mutual sense of grievance. Gladstone's comment at the time was that 'a great man had committed a great error' and when he reflected on the incident more than fifty years later he had not changed his mind. Gladstone was at this time beginning to have doubts which led him to resign over the Maynooth grant; he had also not been happy with Peel's and Graham's refusal to enter into any compromise with Ashley over the ten-hour clause in his Factory Bill earlier that session. By the time the second stage of the tariff reductions was announced by Goulburn in the 1845 budget, Gladstone had in fact resigned over Maynooth. He was therefore not able to pilot them through the House, although he had done all the preparatory work on them. In scale these reductions were even bigger than those of 1842, but as the favourable effects of the earlier reforms were by now generally acknowledged the political battle was far less fierce. Import duties on 430 out of over 800 articles still in the Book of Tariffs were completely abolished; the duty on raw cotton and the excise duty on glass were abolished, these two items alone causing a loss of revenue of over £1·3 million. The import duty on coal was also removed; in return the income tax was extended for another three years.

The period of Gladstone's sojourn at the Board of Trade was crucial in the development of the railways. By 1840 some 1500 miles of railways had been opened, a figure which had risen to 2500 by 1845. The following five years, the years of the railway mania in which Gladstone's Act of 1844 was an important factor, saw an increase in the mileage open to traffic to 6500.[6] In 1840 the Whigs had passed a Railway Regulation Act as a result of which a small railway department was set up at the Board of Trade. One of Gladstone's first tasks in connection with railways was to pilot through the House in 1842 a bill designed to strengthen the 1840 Act. It was based on the experience of the department and had been first introduced in similar form in 1841, but had fallen victim to the pressure of business in that session. The 1844 Act was, however, very much Gladstone's own brain-child. It was based on the findings of a select committee; the principal witness before this committee, Samuel Laing, the Law Clerk of the Railway Department, put forward views which were mostly prompted by Gladstone. He was determined to get legislation on to the statute book ahead of the great pressure for new railway promotions which was building up, and he defended his proposals against considerable hostility in the Cabinet. The main provisions were powers to regulate profits at a maximum of 10 per cent for a new railway; if profits exceeded 10 per cent in three consecutive years, rates could be forced down or the line purchased by the state. These powers were to come into effect after twenty-one years. Gladstone was forced by the powerful railway interests to accept amendments by which an act of Parliament was required in each specific case either for rate reduction or purchase. In order to provide immediately cheaper travel for the less well-off, the act laid it down that companies were to run one cheap train each weekday, to stop at every station, run at a speed of at least twelve miles per hour at a fare not exceeding one penny a mile and to have covered carriages. These became known as 'parliamentary' trains. In addition, Gladstone recommended that the Board of Trade in its negotiations with railway companies should pursue a policy of 'equivalents', mainly that advantages coveted by the companies such as protection against competition should be offset by rate revisions. If this policy had been consistently carried out, it would have been beneficial and it was an original idea contributed by Gladstone. As a whole the act was potentially a strong weapon in the hands of the state for controlling the railways and could have led to early nationalization, had the relevant clauses been implemented. It shows Gladstone at this stage as a believer in beneficent government and remote from any doctrinaire *laissez-faire* approach.

After the passage of this act Gladstone seems to have been concerned to minimize his personal involvement in railway affairs. To Peel he wrote: 'My own connection with railway interests, in part personally, but much more through very immediate relatives, is such as in point of public decency to offer serious impediment . . .' He tried to persuade Peel to set up a separate railway department; instead a Railway Board was established within the Board of Trade, the old railway section in strengthened form. In his remaining few months at the Board of Trade Gladstone left the business of the new Railway Board mainly to Dalhousie, his Vice-President. The

Gladstone family had had a stake in railways ever since the famous Liverpool and Manchester Railway was projected in the 1820s and by the 1840s something like a quarter of the great family fortune was in railways; therefore William was right to reduce his official dealings with this industry.

Gladstone's energy was such that this intense preoccupation with politics, administration, finance and commerce in no way diminished his concern for what always remained his first love: religion and the Church. 'I contemplate the former chiefly as a means of being useful in the latter,' he wrote to his father in 1843. At bottom he continued to sympathize with the Oxford Movement. In a long article entitled 'Present Aspect of the Church', which he published in October 1843, he described it as a necessary reaction against some of the narrowness of Evangelicalism, for example on the doctrine of grace, from which he had himself escaped. To be still regarded as a Puseyite in the early 1840s was not politically useful and it says much for Peel's magnanimity that he took Gladstone into his Cabinet in spite of it. By 1843 even Tories looked upon the Tractarians as a romanizing coterie of esoteric clerics. Gladstone, however, was all the while finding his own path through the maze of theological and ecclesiastical complexities, just as he was in the field of secular policy. He steered by the light of his powerful intellect and his absolute intellectual honesty. Hope-Scott and Manning were the two men with whom he was most intimate at the time and whom he consulted most on religious matters. The publications of Froude's *Remains* in 1838 and of Tract X C in 1841 had made Gladstone uneasy about the romanizing tendencies in the Oxford Movement. In the former an immature mind gave vent to strong emotions against the Reformation. In the latter Newman tried to argue that it was possible to put a Catholic interpretation upon the Thirty-nine Articles. Nevertheless Gladstone remained committed to the Movement, and was not prepared to lend himself to any persecution of Tractarians at Oxford. When anti-Puseyite forces tried to block the election of Isaac Williams, a minor Tractarian, to the professorship of poetry early in 1842, Gladstone moved for compromise. Gone was the rigidity that had made him adopt such illiberal religious positions in the 1830s and the attempt to blackball a man for doctrinal differences outraged him. On the other hand he supported the Anglo-Prussian scheme for a Bishopric of Jerusalem, a matter which pushed Newman, who hated Continental Protestantism, to the brink of his break with the Anglican Church. Gladstone, too, had his reservations about facile attempts to establish communion with other Churches, but he had by this time become sufficiently tolerant and ecumenical 'to brave misconstruction for the sake of union with any Christian men, provided the terms of union were not contrary to sound principles'. No doubt his friendship, based on mutual admiration, with Bunsen, the remarkable Prussian envoy and amateur scientist, also inclined him to favour this project. In October 1843 again, when Manning revealed to him the truth about Newman's position, Gladstone was thunderstruck, 'so bewildered and overthrown that I am otherwise wholly unfit'. His disapproval was great and so it was when W.G.Ward's book *The Ideal of a Christian Church* was published in 1844. It castigated the flaws and the extreme Protestantism of the Church of England and held up against it as an ideal the treasures preserved by the Church of Rome. Gladstone reviewed this book in the *Quarterly* with great emotion; he felt it ill became a man to speak as Ward had done of what still was, but soon was to be no longer, his own communion. Yet he refused to support the manner in which the Heads of Houses at Oxford proceeded against Ward, as he had earlier opposed their proceedings against Pusey. Thus Gladstone in this turbulent period of English religious history remained a High Anglican with a basic sympathy for the Oxford Movement before it was broken up by secession. He belonged to the Movement only indirectly, although in the popular view he was still a Puseyite. As he grew in practical experience he abandoned the narrow views of his Church–state days and fully accepted the implications of religious liberty. One can only marvel at the way in which, amid his preoccupations with tariffs, railways and telegraphs, he found time to wrestle with the subtleties of theology and ecclesiastical doctrine. It was, however, his deep convictions and commitments on these matters that drove him to the breach with Peel over the Maynooth grant.

Ireland, the bane of British governments in the nineteenth century, had been relatively quiet in the first two years of Peel's government. Then O'Connell's repeal movement became active again, but the Liberator, as opposed to the rising 'Young Ireland' party, was too old to risk real revolution. Nevertheless, Peel and his colleagues took the threat seriously; what they were really afraid of was a combination of Irish and English malcontents, both in and out of Parliament. On this occasion, Peel's firmness was effective in calling O'Connell's bluff. His monster meeting at Clontarf in October 1843 was broken up, he was subsequently arrested and for the time being the repeal movement was checked. It was not in

Peel's nature to rest on purely negative measures and he wanted to use the breathing-space gained for a more constructive approach. In particular it seemed important to conciliate Irish Catholics and the Irish hierarchy. The priesthood had been a prime factor in the agitation; Irish middle-class Catholics could be a prime factor for stability. The trouble was that any concession for Catholicism touched a raw nerve in England, and nowhere more so than in the Tory party. Anti-popery sentiment was never far away and the impending break-up of the Oxford Movement had aroused renewed fears. Among Conservatives Peel's apostasy on Catholic Emancipation was not forgotten. Concessions to Irish Catholics could be seen as the prelude to disestablishment of the Irish Anglican Church, establishment of Roman Catholicism, repeal of the Union, major subversions of Church and Constitution in England, the maintenance of which was the main function of the Conservative party. Gladstone was therefore not as over-sensitive as he has sometimes been depicted when he felt that his support for concessions to Irish Catholics would make him look a time-server in the eyes of many who remembered his writings on Church and state. No doubt the position of Newman and the conversion of his sister Helen to Catholicism, which had occurred two years earlier, also weighed on his mind.

The possibility of pleasing Irish Catholics by improving the position of Maynooth College, the long-established priests' seminary, was in the air throughout the summer of 1844. Gladstone was unhappy from the beginning, not because he failed to see the need to remedy Irish grievances, but because of his past pledges. In one of his early memoranda on the problem, in February 1844, he wrote that Peel's mind was set on an increase of the grant, but that this would raise large expectations which could not be fulfilled. For a time Gladstone was persuaded to let matters take their course. It was at this stage, in July 1844, that he made the staggering proposal to Peel that he should be appointed envoy to the Vatican. The opening of relations with the Vatican was being considered by Peel, but nevertheless the proposal was, to put it mildly, an unusual one to make for a Cabinet minister and would probably have spelt the end of Gladstone's political career had it been accepted. To the end of his life he included this step among his 'recorded errors' and attributed it to the strong element of fanaticism in his mind. It was certainly an indication of his strong feelings on the Anglican Church, Catholicism and their relations; a measure also of his impulsiveness and his continued need for a righteous cause to steer him through the shoals of public and private dilemmas.

Another four months elapsed before it became finally clear that an increase of the parliamentary grant to Maynooth College as well as certain other changes and improvements in the statutes of the college would be one of the 'messages of peace' to Ireland. When the matter came before the Cabinet at the end of November 1844 Gladstone had to tell his colleagues that he would have to go, though he hinted somewhat obscurely that he did not disagree with the policy nor would he necessarily oppose it as a private member. During the next two months while the Maynooth bill was in preparation Peel made valiant efforts to persuade Gladstone to stay; in the course of one interview the Prime Minister remarked somewhat fatalistically that Maynooth coupled with Gladstone's retirement would probably wreck the government. Gladstone himself passed through a time of heart-searching, confiding in his wife and Manning. He found it hard to leave the scene of his fruitful labours and his little son Willy, aged four, was taken to have a last look at his father's room at the Board of Trade. His resignation speech on 4 February 1845 was over-elaborate; it is chiefly remembered for Cobden's remark that after listening for an hour with pleasure 'I know no more why he left the government than before he began'. The general feeling was summed up in the comparison with the lady's footman who jumped off the Great Western train at forty miles an hour to pick up his hat – a disproportion between cause and effect. Many, including Disraeli, thought Gladstone's career at an end. He himself in later life wrote that he was 'inevitably regarded as fastidious and fanciful, fitter for a dreamer or possibly a schoolman, than for the active purposes of public life in a busy and moving age,' but he expressly excluded this resignation from his list of recorded errors and always regarded his course of action as correct. After Gladstone had resigned, Sir Robert Inglis, member for Oxford and leader of the Church party, asked him to lead the opposition to the Maynooth bill. He reminded Gladstone of the mistake made in 1829 of not accepting his advice to send the Duke of Cumberland into Ireland with 30,000 troops. 'As that good and very kind man spoke the words my blood ran cold, and he too helped me onwards in the path before me,' Gladstone wrote of this incident nearly fifty years later. When the Maynooth bill came to its second reading in April he supported it, but half the Tory party voted against. It was the worst split yet and the wound was deep. The bill passed because the Whigs, though not the Dissenters, supported it and the disaffected Tories were leaderless. The country gentlemen were not yet prepared to follow Disraeli, and Gladstone had refused himself. More than ever he was a ministerialist, in spite of his resignation. Even on a matter which touched his religious views so closely, he now gave priority to justice and stable government for Ireland. As for the Established Church of Ireland, 'I separated myself in mind from all attempts to rearrange or curtail it or compound for a fresh lease of existence on its behalf.' He told Manning that he 'looked upon the Maynooth measure as what is called buying time – a process that presupposes the approach of the period of surrender'.

Gladstone's departure from the government did not affect his friendly personal relations with ministers and he continued to give them political help from the back benches. He helped particularly with the tariff reforms which he had prepared while still in office and published a pamphlet in which he explained and justified the movement of the last few years towards freer trade. In fact his resignation from a trade department made some Tories in those sensitive days suspect that it must be due to differences on trade policy. Gladstone was beginning to be accused of pushing Peel towards free trade. In fact the last speech he made in that Parliament, in July 1845, was again on the vexed question of sugar duties. In a four-hour speech he helped the government against a motion by Palmerston alleging that preferences for colonial sugar amounted to a breach of old treaties with Spain. Peel, usually so sparing of praise, said to him, 'That was a wonderful speech, Gladstone.'

In the summer of 1845 Gladstone had plans to visit Ireland with Hope-Scott. The conviction that Ireland was a place of destiny for Britain was already with him. The illness of his sister Helen at Baden-Baden forced him to go to the Continent instead and he was in Germany for two months in the autumn of 1845. In Munich he met the Liberal Catholic theologian Döllinger, friend of Acton and later leader of the German Old Catholics who resisted the doctrine of papal infallibility, and with him had many hours of theological discussion. Then he had to deal with the distressing situation of his sister, an opium addict who swallowed an overdose of laudanum just as he arrived. In his relations with Helen, William was often seen at his worst. In her the tensions which he managed to control and turn to good account so marvellously led to eccentricity, breakdown and hysteria. When she had been converted to Catholicism a few years previously and again on this occasion he tried to dictate the course of action in censorious and unctuous memoranda to his

family. Perhaps he realized subconsciously that his own psychological make-up was not so far removed from hers. He was torn
between his strong family sense and shame at Helen's conduct.
The days in Baden-Baden were gloomy for him; the news of
Newman's reception into the Church of Rome reached him there
and he was without the steadying presence of Catherine. He must
have reflected a great deal on how his former views on Church and
state had been shattered by realities. Only six months earlier, when
Newman had written him an understanding letter on his Maynooth
resignation, he had replied: 'The state cannot be said now to have a
conscience, at least not by me, in as much as I think it acts, and
acts wilfully, and intends to go on acting, in such a way as no
conscience can endure.' Could his political vocation, about which
he had always had his doubts, continue or was it providentially
shattered?

When Gladstone returned to England at the end of November
1845 he found the country in the throes of crisis over the Corn
Laws and the threatened famine in Ireland. Peel's hand had just
been forced by the publication of Lord John Russell's *Letter to the
Electors of the City of London* in which he announced his own
conversion to the repeal of the Corn Laws. Peel found his Cabinet
hopelessly divided in the face of his own conviction that the Corn
Laws had to be immediately suspended and in short order repealed.
When faced with the imminent loss of Stanley and Buccleuch he
decided on 5 December to resign. Gladstone had known for a long
time that Peel and Graham held the view that the Corn Laws,
which for political reasons were adjusted only in 1842 rather than
repealed, could not survive another crisis. In September 1843 he
reported Graham as saying that it would be all over with the Corn
Law if in a bad harvest foreign corn would not come in until the
duty got down to the shilling and Gladstone agreed with this. The
Queen now called on Lord John Russell to form a government, but
difficulties about the allocation of offices frustrated him. 'One
intemperate and headstrong man [Grey] objected to another
gentleman [Palmerston] having one particular office.' Peel thereupon resumed office, with a grim determination born of pent-up
resentment against his recalcitrant and purblind back-benchers.
He had a reasonable hope of being able to carry the repeal of the
Corn Laws, but his expectations of maintaining the unity of his
party in the process must have been much lower. Perhaps he no
longer cared too much about his party, but he certainly felt that
he was serving the true course of conservatism. It was Peel's

conviction that without repeal England would now be threatened
by grave disorder and even revolution.

Upon resuming office on a free-trade programme Peel lost only
one colleague of importance, Stanley. This was itself remarkable in
view of the divisions in the Cabinet only a few weeks earlier. The
desire to keep the Whigs out and carry on the Queen's government
was still strong; had the feeling inside the government accurately
foreshadowed the sentiments of the Tory back benches in the
House of Commons the unity of the party would have been preserved. The place at the Colonial Office vacated by Stanley was
offered by Peel to Gladstone. His decision to rejoin the government
was an important factor in enabling Peel to carry on. The decision
was not arrived at without some searchings of conscience. Although
Gladstone had been dissatisfied with the degree of agricultural
protection retained in 1842 and had shared Peel's and Graham's
views on the precariousness of the Corn Law ever since, he wished
to be certain that repeal was now really necessary before going
back on his own publicly stated position. 'Nothing could have been
more base than to propose the law in 1842 for the chance of a run
of good harvests and with the intention of withdrawing it upon the
first notion, not even the experience, of a bad one.' Only when he
was convinced did he accept Peel's offer and he did so finally aware
of the possible impermanence of the reconstituted ministry.

Gladstone's appointment as Colonial Secretary made it necessary
for him to vacate his seat at Newark. Although some of his constituents were ready to support his re-election, he thought it
improper to stand again contrary to the wishes of the Duke of
Newcastle. The Duke, naturally, was not prepared to forgive one
who had betrayed the landed interest. His attitude reflects the
bitterness among country gentlemen which enabled Lord George
Bentinck and Disraeli to build up a protectionist party in the session
of 1846. Not even the ingenuity of Bonham, the redoubtable Conservative party manager, enabled Gladstone to find a seat in the
remainder of this Parliament, again a reflection of the way in which
the landed interest was closing up against Peel and his supporters.
Gladstone was therefore a minister without a seat in the House for
six months, unthinkable in modern times. During the dramatic
repeal debates he was an absentee.

Gladstone's short second innings at the Colonial Office was not of
major significance. At a time when dispatches still took weeks and
months to travel between Whitehall and the colonies little impact
could be made in so short a time. Gladstone had to appoint a new

c

Governor-General of Canada; Lord Cathcart had been virtually selected when he took over. In his instructions to Cathcart Gladstone gave expression to the liberal sentiments on colonial self-government that he had already expressed in his speeches on Canada before 1841. On James Stephen's advice, however, he kept his instructions very general and laid down no real guidance on what was then the crucial question in Canada, the transition to responsible government. Gladstone aroused opposition in Australia by advocating the resumption of transportation, though his motives were humanitarian.[7] In New South Wales the opposition was led by Robert Lowe, his adversary on reform twenty years later. Gladstone also became involved in a bitter personal quarrel with Lord George Bentinck over the retirement of an Indian judge. It was the only personal feud he ever got involved in during his long public life and even Stanley was unable to compose it before Bentinck died. On the whole, however, Gladstone's tenure at the Colonial Office was compared favourably with the high-handed impulsiveness frequently exhibited by his predecessor.

In the meantime in his absence the drama in the House of Commons was running its course. Mutual resentment, pressure from the agricultural interest in the constituencies, Peel's refusal to offer any 'compensations' to the Protectionists, were driving the Tory party apart. As soon as the third reading of the Corn Law Repeal Bill had been passed on 25 June 1846 a 'blackguard combination' of Whigs, Radicals, Irish and Protectionists defeated the government on the Irish Coercion Bill and Peel resigned. Just as the ultra-Tories in the Reform Bill crisis had been prepared to go to almost any length against those whom they considered guilty of a betrayal, so the country gentlemen now turned against Peel and they found leaders in Lord George Bentinck and Disraeli. In the first major division on the tariff proposals in February 1846 the government had had a majority of 97; but only 112 Conservatives voted for Peel and 231 against him. This remained then and afterwards a measure of the split in the Tory party and of the extent of Peelite support. In the main it was the 'ministerialists' who were for Peel; the rest, country gentlemen and others, were against him. In so far as there was a tactical reasoning behind the decision of those Protectionists who trooped through the lobby with some of their most inveterate enemies to defeat the government on Irish Coercion, it was the desire to get rid of Peel personally. This would open the way to a rapid dissolution not called by Peel but by someone else, if necessary Russell, so that the Conservative party could then

reunite under a new leader. It turned out that Peel was too formidable a figure, inspiring fierce loyalty in men of great stature,
among them Gladstone, to make such a solution feasible. It was,
however, worthy of note that only 69 of the Protectionist party of
250 or so could actually bring themselves to follow Bentinck and
Disraeli into the lobby to destroy Peel's government; of the remainder, 74 abstained and 105 supported the government. This left
at least some hope of reconciliation for the future.

When, a few days earlier, Gladstone in his room at the Colonial
Office received Peel's memorandum advising immediate resignation
after the defeat in the House that was clearly in prospect, he was
dismayed. He would have preferred the Duke of Wellington's
solution of a defiant appeal to the country. When after the defeat
the Cabinet met for the shortest session Gladstone could ever
remember, no one dissented when Peel advised the resignation of
the entire government. 'It amounted therefore to this – no one
proposed to go on without him.' Thus in the summer of 1846
Gladstone found himself without office, without a seat in the House
of Commons and without a party.

For all the doubts about his political vocation that from time to
time assailed him, politics was too much in his blood now to be
lightly relinquished. He pondered much on the future and in the
days following the fall of the government he talked to many of the
principal figures, including Peel himself. Would it be possible to
put the party together again? Who could do it? Aberdeen and
Goulburn told him that he himself was spoken of as a possible new
leader if he returned to the House of Commons. As for Peel, even
Gladstone found the famous tribute he paid to Cobden in his resignation speech distasteful. Was it deliberately designed to make the
breach irreparable? When Gladstone saw the fallen Prime Minister
himself, he found him determined never to resume the position
he had given up and to keep himself free from all party ties. Peel
spoke much about the tremendous and ever-growing pressure of
business. 'He could not tell what it was to end in, and he did not
venture to speculate even for a few years upon the mode of adminis-
tering public affairs.' Gladstone told him that 'he had been prime
minster in a sense in which no other man had been it since Mr Pitt.
Your government has not been carried on by a cabinet, but by the
heads of departments each in communication with you.' Gladstone
came away feeling the renewed strength of the ties that bound him
to this man. It was to take him many years to resolve his own
political future.

4

A PARTY

OF

OBSERVATION

1846–53

For a man of Gladstone's ardent temperament
these uncertain years after the crisis of the summer of 1846 were
difficult. He had now lost his political as well as his ecclesiastical
moorings and there were no all-absorbing tasks to which he could
devote the great talents which he had revealed as a member of
Peel's administration. Much as he had learnt and greatly as he had
grown he was still in his personal convictions a High Anglican, the
structure of whose personality had been formed by the evangelicalism of his family and whose views on the nature of society remained
conservative.

Even in his private affairs there was much to disturb his peace of mind. The agonies of his sister Helen continued after William had arranged her return to London. Catholic friends of hers reported to the Commissioners in Lunacy that she was being held under restraint by her family, but Tom and William were able to convince Lord Ashley, one of the commissioners, that the case required no further action. There is no doubt that William terrified her and that his presence worsened her symptoms, while he in his turn could not come to terms with her Catholicism. His father's attitude to Helen was in comparison more relaxed and balanced. It was not till the end of 1848 that she was cured of her opium addiction and the more severe symptoms of hysteria. William was deeply grieved by the circumstances of her cure, the laying on of relics by Dr Wiseman who had six years earlier received her into the Catholic Church.

The financial plight of the Glynne family and the Hawarden estate made even greater calls on William's energies. Sir Stephen Glynne had invested heavily in Oak Farm, a small property in Staffordshire with promising deposits of coal and iron. An enthusiastic agent developed furnaces, forges and rolling mills on the credit of the Hawarden estates. In this manner many landed families had made their fortunes in the industrial revolution and the prospects seemed good. Sir Stephen's two brothers-in-law, William and Lord Lyttelton, had taken shares in the company upon their marriage. In the financial panic of the autumn of 1847 the enterprise crashed and had to be put into liquidation. One solution advocated by William's father was to sell the Hawarden estate. The Glynnes could not bring themselves to do this and William agreed with them. He had desperately tried to stave off the crash and on him fell the heavy burden, stretching over years, of nursing the estate back to health. He also incurred a considerable financial commitment and in course of time came to sink some quarter of a million pounds into it. This labour was to him an ordinance of God and he always regarded it as invaluable preparation for his work in public finance, supplementing from a different angle his experience at the Board of Trade. It taught him 'to sail close to the wind'. When it became possible to reopen the house at Hawarden in 1852 William and Catherine occupied it jointly with Sir Stephen, and it became their home for the rest of their lives. William loved it deeply and it forms the permanent backcloth to his life.

In Gladstone's public life the most urgent need of the moment was to return to the House of Commons. It was not easy for a Peelite to find a constituency. The resources of the government had failed to find one for Gladstone when he was Colonial Secretary and the chances were even slimmer now. He turned down a suggestion to stand against one of Russell's newly appointed ministers in the summer of 1846 because he felt the new government needed a fair trial. The opening which occurred for him early in 1847 through the retirement of Estcourt, one of the two members for Oxford University, was therefore doubly welcome. It released him from political limbo and it was an honour which he and his family deeply coveted. It was perhaps a strange moment in his career to enter into an association with the university when his own views on the position of the Church and on religious toleration were undergoing so much change. It has generally been held that his connection with Oxford, which lasted for eighteen years and which he was very reluctant to give up, complicated his political development, but for a long time he was not prepared to admit this to himself. The university was itself changing and Gladstone was well aware of the need for it. He had often disagreed with the policy pursued by the university authorities, for example in their treatment of Pusey and Ward; neither on the academic nor on the theological side was he satisfied with the *status quo* at Oxford. The Tractarian movement was now shattered, but its influence was not at an end and some of its members were still respected. A new liberal renaissance was, however, creating a counter-movement. Men like Jowett, later Master of Balliol, A.P.Stanley, A.C.Tait, both to rise high in the Church, Arthur Hugh Clough the poet, J.A.Froude the historian and H.G.Liddell, Dean of Christ Church, were all beginning to hold positions of influence. They owed much to Germany, the new biblical criticism of David Friedrich Strauss, the philosophy of Hegel and the historical school of Ranke. As time went on, some of these ideas began to produce the frightening spectre of religious doubt and much of Gladstone's later work on religion was to be devoted to this battle between faith and doubt.

The Oxford contest was highly complicated and fiercely fought. Edward Cardwell was in the field before Gladstone. He had been Peel's Secretary of the Treasury, was politically closely identified with Peel and in his religious views much nearer to his chief than Gladstone – some called him Peel-and-water. High and Low Churchmen, Tories and liberals combined to back him. In days when reform of the university appeared as a threat to some, desirable to others, Cardwell seemed a candidate who would promote reform but do so safely. Then Gladstone, more famous and distinguished, appeared, backed initially mainly by High Churchmen and Tractarians and only a few isolated liberals; yet Gladstone's increasing religious liberalism was already causing alarm in the High Anglican camp. Finally another candidate appeared, Charles Gray Round, who had once taken a first at Balliol and was member for North Essex. High Churchmen of the old Protestant orthodoxy and evangelicals supported him, as did six Heads of Houses, while not a single one supported Gladstone. Significantly Round was also a Protectionist. Cardwell withdrew after a while, for he could offer nothing that Gladstone could not offer better. Most of the liberals now switched their support to Gladstone, but in terms of ecclesiastical faction the contest remained highly confused, illustrating that the old party labels had little meaning. Round and Gladstone were fiercely attacked for their own past ecclesiastical professions and votes. Gladstone had to explain away his support for Maynooth. On the other hand it stood him in good stead that he had spent years of effort in launching the episcopalian training college at Glenalmond; yet his old tutor and present warden of the college, Charles Wordsworth, refused him his vote because of his turn towards religious toleration. Even his elder brother Tom, who remained an evangelical and was not a little jealous of his successful younger brother, only supported him under parental duress. Gladstone's voting for the Dissenters' Chapels Bill, which protected the legal titles of Nonconformist congregations to their chapels, was much held against him; this bill of 1844 did not really raise any issue of principle between Church and Chapel, but was one of his earliest departures from rigid Church–state views and was actuated by nothing more than an elementary sense of justice. The most difficult accusations he had to rebut were those levelled against him on account of his refusal to vote for the degradation of Ward two years earlier and because of his sister's conversion to Catholicism. It was again shown that religious controversy lent itself as well as any other to the throwing of mud. Gladstone won the second Oxford seat with a vote of 997 against Round's 824, while Sir Robert Inglis retained the seat he had wrested from Peel in 1829 with 1700 votes. Analysis showed that Gladstone had polled the votes of 157 electors with first-class degrees, while Round only got 46.[1]

The contest at Oxford was part of the general election of 1847, one of the most confused of the century. After a period during which party lines had become increasingly clear-cut, the appearance of the Peelites created once more a fluid situation. As events were to show, the party situation did not simply return to the conditions prevailing before 1832. With a wider electorate parties had to exist as organizations; the question now was which new combination of parties was eventually going to emerge. Peel and his colleagues had given the country effective executive government, but in doing so had strained the party system beyond what it could bear at that stage. The pressure from 'Fremantle and his clique', Peel's whips, was an aspect of the resentment on the Tory back benches. Peel now went to the opposite extreme and determined to stay aloof from all party connections. This created a difficult situation for his former colleagues, particularly for those younger men, Gladstone foremost amongst them, who were looking forward to a future of constructive work. Personal loyalty and policy debarred them for the moment, and as it turned out for a long time to come, from either rejoining the Protectionists or linking up with the Whigs. Yet the Peelites included nearly all the 'official men' of the Conservative party. This was their strength, it was the weakness of the Protectionists and it proved to be the opportunity of Disraeli. But how was this strength to be realized if their leader Peel was refusing to organize his followers in any way? Gladstone, the man with the greatest potentialities for the future among Peel's supporters, found this situation increasingly frustrating as the years passed by. Looking back in 1855 on this period he had this to say of Peel:

It might have been in his power to make some provision for the holding together, or for the reconstruction of that great Party which he has reared . . . But although that party was the great work of so many years of his matured life, his thought seemed simply to be, 'It has fallen, there let it be.'

Yet Gladstone was himself in the grip of many inhibitions. To go back to the Protectionists 'penitent' was impossible, for him and all of Peel's colleagues; but there might well be a drift back among the lesser fry who had supported Peel, especially if there was no organization to keep them in line. To join the Whigs was impossible and Gladstone completely agreed with his three friends and colleagues, Lord Lincoln, Sidney Herbert and Dalhousie, who were invited by Lord John Russell to join his government and rejected the offer out of hand. Yet the Whig government could not be allowed to be defeated, otherwise there was a danger of a return to protection. Some of the more fanciful combinations which caught the imagination of contemporaries, for example a union of Peelites and Free-Trade Radicals like Cobden, were not in fact practical politics. Ideologically this situation was very confused: the Peelites could find themselves facing the same way as the Radicals in upholding *laissez-faire*, for instance they opposed Fielden's Ten-Hour Factory

Bill in the session of 1847, while most Whigs and Protectionists supported it. On the other hand Radical Dissenters could combine with ultra-Protestant Protectionists against Peelites tainted with 'Maynooth'. To all this Gladstone added the complexities of his own political profile as it evolved in the later 1840s. In spite of Peel's reluctance, some of his colleagues, especially the younger men, did decide to rally the Peelite forces before the start of the 1847 session and Young, who had been Tory whip before the split, sent out circulars to 240 Conservative members. It was to be a position 'of observation rather than of party opposition to the Government'. Peel was sceptical: 'A party of observation . . . will not succeed. The adherents of a party must be stimulated by something more exciting . . .'[2] Gladstone approved of this effort to organize and when he returned to the House took part in many discussions on how to organize and overcome the apathy of their leader.

The general election of 1847 was not dominated by any one issue. The price of wheat remained so high without the Corn Law that protection could hardly be a rallying-cry. If there was a matter which stirred the electorate it was the old 'No Popery' feeling in which anti-Irish feeling was a potent ingredient. There was an unprecedented number of uncontested seats and the result was difficult to analyse, particularly the relative strengths of Peelites and Protectionists. Gladstone's own estimate of Peelites was as low as sixty, while others gave a figure of over 100, hardly any diminution from the Peelite vote in the Corn Law debates. Overall the Conservatives lost some ground and the Liberals gained, a turnover of about fifty seats. Within the Whig–Liberal camp the Radicals improved their position. Lord John Russell and the Whigs were able to stay in office, secure in the knowledge that the Peelites would prevent a return to Protection. The aloofness of Peel and the contempt of his associates for Whig incompetence made a Whig–Peelite fusion for the moment impossible, while old resentments and the bugbear of protection prevented Conservative reunion. Gladstone chafed increasingly at his chief's policy of keeping the Whigs in office at almost any price; Peel's advice to his colleagues always seemed to be 'get what you can in the right sense from the Government: but do not convulse the country by letting in the Protectionists'. At bottom Gladstone was still predisposed towards a Conservative reunion; as in the case of broken china 'so should the fragments of a political party, shattered by a crisis, be reunited before a new surface has been formed by the constant attrition . . . of public life'. If the Whigs were brought down and the Protectionists, now led by Gladstone's former colleague Stanley, took office, the policy of protection might be exposed for the bluff it increasingly was and therefore might cease to be a barrier to reunion; Disraeli was not yet, before 1850, the obstacle to reunion. It was probably not a realistic argument. As far as the agricultural community was concerned, the collapse of corn prices in the autumn of 1847 and the agricultural depression beginning in 1849 meant that protection was far from being a dead issue, and the attempts of Disraeli to wean his party away from it were for the time being unsuccessful. Nor were the Protectionists in the House of Commons in a mood to have a Peelite leadership grafted back on to them. But Gladstone thought of himself still primarily as a Conservative, even if his views on specific questions were becoming more liberal. In some ways he lagged behind Peel, who, detached as he was, could afford to range ahead freely.

One of the first big issues on which Gladstone had to declare himself was the admission of Jews to Parliament. His vote for Russell's bill to remove Jewish disabilities was courageous. It brought him much opposition from his High Church friends. Pusey attacked him strongly in a letter; when he went to Oxford in July 1848 to receive an honorary degree there were cries of 'Gladstone and the Jew Bill!' Above all it brought into the open his father's smouldering resentment at the new political furrow that William was ploughing. John Gladstone was and remained opposed to the repeal of the Corn Laws; in spite of this he had accepted a baronetcy from Peel; on Jewish disabilities he felt his son had concealed his views from him and from his supporters at Oxford. William's vote lay in the logic of the conviction that had been growing for some years now that the close link between Church and state which he had once envisaged could no longer be realized. His friend Hope-Scott, High Churchman and Tractarian, supported him and wrote to him in terms that might well have expressed his own views:

> On the Jewish question my bigotry makes me Liberal. To symbolize the Christianity of the House of Commons in its present form is to substitute a new Church and Creed for the old Catholic one, and as this is a delusion I would do nothing to countenance it. Better have the legislature declared what it really is – not professedly Christian – and then let the Church claim those rights and that independence which nothing but the pretence of Christianity can entitle the legislature to withhold from it. In this view the emancipation of the Jews must tend to that of the Church.[3]

If Gladstone took a liberal line on the Jewish question, it must be remembered that Disraeli and Lord George Bentinck did the same. Indeed it spelt the end of Lord George's leadership of the Protectionists.

In the session of 1848 the Peelites managed on the whole to pursue a united course on trade questions in support of the Whig government. Two major issues presented themselves, the renewal of the income tax and the repeal of the Navigation Laws, one of the remnants of the old system of protection. On the income tax the Whigs had to withstand, with Peelite support, a combined onslaught of Protectionists and Radicals; the former opposed it as part of a whole financial system they abhorred; the latter wanted reductions of expenditure. The repeal of the Navigation Laws was introduced so late in the session that it could not be carried and the real battle took place the following year. On both these problems Gladstone had no difficulty in supporting his leader and the Russell government. But it was different when the problem of West Indian sugar came up again, a matter that had already strained Peelite unity immediately after the formation of Russell's ministry. The Whigs had then reduced the preference available to West Indian sugar; this had caused difficulties to the West Indian planters which a new bill was designed to remedy. It was a question about which Gladstone knew a lot, because of his West Indian connections, and he was making colonial matters one of his special concerns partly out of interest, partly as an ex-colonial secretary. He considered that Russell's proposals did not offer sufficient relief to the West Indian sugar plantations and he was not prepared to subordinate this view to Peel's overriding preoccupation with keeping the Whigs in office. Together with Goulburn, Herbert, Lincoln and Cardwell he went into the lobby against Peel, Graham and the Whigs.[4] It was the most serious split amongst the Peelites so far and nearly brought down Russell's government, but this was not a prospect that disturbed Gladstone.

When the repeal of the Navigation Laws came before Parliament again in 1849 Gladstone once more took a line somewhat different from Peel and Graham. He wanted to use the opportunity for the negotiation of reciprocal arrangements with other countries, rather than go for outright free trade. He and others had discussions with Peel on this proposal and secured Peel's reluctant consent to sound out ministers. Gladstone could not make any headway, either in or out of the House, and in the end went along with outright repeal. Later in the same session he again differed from Peel and Graham on the Canadian Rebellion Losses Bill. This was to indemnify inhabitants of Lower Canada for losses incurred in the rebellion and it caused great bitterness among the English-speaking minority in Quebec, who saw it as a reward for treason. Lord Elgin, the Governor-General, nevertheless accepted and signed this bill passed by the Canadian Parliament and this step has always been hailed as an important advance in responsible government in Canada. Grey, the Colonial Secretary, upheld Elgin. In the debate in the House of Commons in June 1849 Gladstone said:

> I cannot deny that my sympathies are with the men in Canada who think that those persons who took part in the rebellion ought not to be compensated . . . I am not prepared . . . to be a consenting party to advising the Crown . . . to assent to any Act of a Colonial Legislature which I believe to be essentially dishonourable to Imperial rights.

These were Tory sentiments; Gladstone's budding colonial liberalism had clearly not yet burst into full bloom. Peel in contrast refused to do anything to infringe the principle of representative government in the Colonies. The Peelites were again badly split in the vote on this issue.

In the 1850 session Gladstone and Peel were in opposite camps on a motion brought by Disraeli to relieve agricultural distress by a revision of local taxation, in particular by transferring the cost of the Poor Law to the Consolidated Fund. Gladstone supported this motion on the ground that it would lessen the pressure for a return to protection. Peel tore this argument to shreds, but not without expressing 'the greatest respect and admiration' for his erstwhile lieutenant; 'it is no small consolation to me to hear from him, although in this particular motion we arrive at different conclusions, that his confidence in the justice of those principles for which we in common contended remains entirely unshaken.' On this occasion the Peelites were fairly neatly split down the middle and even Young, the Whip, voted for Disraeli's motion. He wrote to Peel, enclosing a list of the sixty-three Peelites who had voted in this division: 'They will stand by Free Trade but they have no sympathies with and no confidence in the present government.' Gladstone also went into the lobby with the Protectionists and against Peel, Graham, Goulburn, Cardwell and the government on a proposal to widen the franchise in Ireland. At this stage his views on Ireland lagged much behind those of Peel.

This was Peel's last session and he died in July 1850 after a fall from his horse. His detached position in the 1847 Parliament had brought him much personal satisfaction. He stood on a pedestal of public esteem; he was much consulted by the government, particularly by Wood, the Chancellor of the Exchequer, on economic and financial affairs. His advice was of special importance in the financial crisis of 1847, when the functioning of his own Bank Charter Act of 1844 was at stake. Gladstone had remained loyal to Peel in a general sense, but he had found his refusal to lead and organize increasingly irksome and frustrating. He had not turned his back on the desultory efforts made by various politicians to bring about a Conservative reunion, though he realized that Lincoln, or Herbert, or even Goulburn were better placed than he was to take a leading role in the event of reunion. He had no great hopes of such a reunion taking place. On the other hand he was detached from the various efforts to bring Peelites into the Russell government, culminating in the abortive offer of the Admiralty to Graham in January 1849. In contrast to Peel and Graham, Gladstone had no qualms about working for the downfall of the Whigs; he was a free-trader, selectively liberal but basically Conservative.

There is no evidence that during those years Gladstone's interest in politics was not as acute as ever and clearly his ambitions remained high. It is true, however, that his preoccupation with the affairs of Oak Farm and the Hawarden estate as well as the fact that he was out of office and belonged to no organized party may have somewhat reduced the sheer volume of his parliamentary work. In the summer of 1849 he burdened himself with yet another private chore in a manner characteristic of his generosity and utter lack of self-regard. Lady Lincoln, the wife of his friend and political associate, had deserted her husband and gone to the Continent with Lord Walpole, son of the Earl of Orford. Gladstone undertook to find her and persuade her to return, a task which Manning had refused to take on. It was a mission not without its comic-opera aspects. After travelling all round Italy he tracked her down on the shores of Lake Como. She escaped to Verona, where he caught up with her, but she refused to have any truck with him. The evidence of his own eyes showed him that she was pregnant and this was 'the dagger' he had to send back to Lincoln. This venture exposed him to a great deal of ridicule and old Sir John Gladstone was so furious that he threatened to alter his will. Peel on the other hand wrote him a letter recognizing his 'unparalleled kindness and generosity'. Gladstone had to appear as a witness on the Divorce Bill that Lincoln had to bring and as late as 1857 he had to deny in the House of Commons that he had collected evidence in the case for a fee. His transparent innocence carried him through all these trials.[5]

The same quality protected him in what had become for him and

for Catherine their principal charitable work, the rescue of prostitutes. His first attempts to redeem 'fallen women' can be traced
back to his Oxford days. In 1840 he founded a small lay brotherhood
with the older Acland and Hope-Scott, dedicated to works of mercy,
but it did not flourish. By the middle 1840s Gladstone had in its
place embarked upon his rescue missions, 'the discharge of some
humble and humbling office'. It was a strange form of charitable
enterprise to choose and a number of psychological factors may
have brought Gladstone to it and made him cling to it with such
tenacity. The idealized concept of pure womanhood that came to
him from his mother and his sister Anne made the prostitute seem
the ultimate in evil and degradation; the sense of guilt which his
evangelical upbringing had left him had to be assuaged by self-
mortification and the doubts about the validity and sanctity of his
political vocation could be made more tolerable by an enterprise so
close to a priestly calling. For a politician it was risky to be seen
accosting prostitutes and in Gladstone's case it gave rise to a great
deal of rumour; in particular it was said that he gave his attention
mainly to the younger and prettier type of woman to be found in
the West End and there was talk of 'Old Gladeye'. Only on one or
two occasions was there a serious incident, but Gladstone's integrity was so incontrovertible that he came to no harm. During
his second premiership he was warned by Lord Rosebery and by his
private secretary, Sir Edward Hamilton, about the political risks of
his 'nightwalks'. In May 1882 Hamilton wrote in his diary: 'He
gave me three opportunities of putting in my word. . . He quite
admitted the force of my warning word and implied that he would
really give up these night encounters.'[6] He did not give them up,
in spite of further warnings, until old age compelled him to do so.
It may well be that his difficult relations with the Queen in later
years were in part due to slanders that had been retailed to her.

The later 1840s was an uncertain and painful time for Gladstone,
not only in his public and private life, but also in the religious and
ecclesiastical matters which touched him so closely. His coolness
towards Lord John Russell and the Whigs owed much to religious
differences. The aggressive lay protestantism of Lord John was
alien to Gladstone; where Peel had been lukewarm to the Tractarians,
Russell was an active anti-Puseyite. The innocuous Dr Hampden
became the focus of fresh controversy when Russell nominated him as
Bishop of Hereford in November 1847. Not only the High Churchmen were outraged, and Gladstone wrote to his father, 'Never
in my opinion was a fire-brand more wantonly and gratuitously

cast.' When the Dean of Hereford informed Russell that he would be unable to give his vote for Hampden he received the famous but ill-advised reply: 'Sir, I have had the honour to receive your letter of the 22nd inst., in which you intimate to me your intention of violating the law. I have the honour to be your obedient servant, J. Russell.'[7] Hampden was elected and consecrated, all by a hair's-breadth, but he left a trail of secessions to Rome among High Churchmen and Puseyites. Gladstone never felt the tug of Rome himself; it 'never offered itself to me otherwise than as a temptation and a sin'. But he did sense the tug in his friends and it pained him.

Worse was to follow in the Gorham case. Phillpotts, the fiercely High Church Bishop of Exeter, had refused to institute Gorham into a living because of his views on baptismal regeneration. Gorham took his case to the Court of Arches and, when defeated there, appealed to the Judicial Committee of the Privy Council. If Phillpotts had won it would have amounted to a condemnation of the interpretation of the Thirty-nine Articles accepted by most Evangelical Low Churchmen and would probably have produced a major disruption of the Church. As it was, the verdict produced great difficulties for the High Church party, on two grounds. Firstly, the doctrinal point about baptism and the inability of a bishop to insist on the interpretation of the relevant articles; secondly, that a secular tribunal (on the Judicial Committee the only ecclesiastical representatives were the two Archbishops and Bishop Blomfield of London) could determine the teaching of the Church. Gladstone, like many of his friends, was particularly concerned with the second point; the solution which he saw to the problem, in line with his rapidly evolving view of Church–state relations, was 'peaceably to request liberty of conscience for the Church, and cheerfully to pay the price which the state, acting within its own sphere, may think fit to affix to that liberty'. In the long run he remained optimistic about what the Church of England could do if freed in this way. As a leading layman of the High Church party he was well aware of the dangers and dilemmas and launched into a campaign of protest. The outlook was gloomy and there was much disagreement among his friends about what could be done. Some threatened secession to Rome, others disestablishment. Gladstone's own depression was aggravated by the death, only a month after the promulgation of the Gorham judgement, of his second daughter Jessy from meningitis. For a moment his usual self-control seemed to give way and he found release in writing an intensely emotional memoir of the child. The worst consequence of the Gorham case for him was that his two closest friends of recent years, Manning and Hope-Scott, went over to Rome. They were both received on the same day in April 1851. For a year Gladstone had had to watch how Manning in particular was drifting towards the breach with the Church of England; he clutched at straws in the hope that his friend would not go over the brink. When the double conversion finally occurred he was in a state of shock: '. . . I never *can* form I suppose with any other two men the habits of communication, counsel, and dependence in which I have now for from fifteen to eighteen years lived with them both.' With Manning the breach was complete; they returned each other's correspondence and did not meet for many years.[8]

The loss of Manning and Hope-Scott was merely the most personal of the tribulations and controversies that arose for Gladstone out of the Gorham case. Yet 1850 was also the year when foreign affairs for the first time assumed major significance in his political life. The Peelites had been dissatisfied with Palmerston's conduct of foreign affairs for some time. Peel and Aberdeen, who had been his Foreign Secretary, wanted a quieter style of diplomacy and greater regard paid to the traditions and susceptibilities of foreign governments, especially in the wake of the revolutions of 1848. Palmerston was increasingly emerging as the strong man of the government; his chauvinism appealed to the John Bullish middle classes and his support for liberal and national causes abroad attracted a section of the Radicals. When Graham refused to join the Whigs early in 1849 objections to various items in the catalogue of Palmerstonian policies were a factor. Peelite feelings about Palmerston received vigorous expression in the famous Don Pacifico debate in June 1950. Palmerston had espoused the dubious claims of this Gibraltese Jew whose title to British nationality was none too secure. In pursuit of this and other claims he had ordered a naval blockade of Greece. It was part of a policy of keeping up pressure on the autocratic government of King Otto, the Bavarian prince who had been imposed on the Greek people, not least by Palmerston himself. As a result of French pressure there was in the end something of a British climb-down. Stanley moved a motion against Palmerston in the House of Lords which was carried. The Court and the Establishment were solidly against Palmerston and Russell had to retrieve the government's standing. Roebuck, one of the Radical supporters of Palmerston, moved a motion in his favour in the Commons on which the fate of Russell's government depended. Peelites and Protectionists united on this occasion although, according to

Gladstone's testimony, Peel was still annoyed to have to be acting in concert with Disraeli, the man who had plunged the dagger into him so ruthlessly four years earlier. Disraeli in turn acted reluctantly with his colleague in the Lords; it would not have suited his personal book to have turned out the Whigs at this stage, for in a reunited Conservative government he would have been crowded out by the Peelites. Disraeli made a poor speech in the debate, '. . . almost a "cross"' Gladstone called it,[9] but the two men had a good deal of contact in arranging the order of debate. Gladstone made a big three-hour speech invoking the ancient state system of Europe, the conventions of civilized nations, the need for moral conduct in international relations, the right to independence and self-determination of small nations. It was a note he was to sound many times in the future. Russell and other Whigs affected to see him as a new leader of the opposition. It was the first major occasion on which Gladstone had crossed swords with Palmerston, and the repulsion exerted on him by this powerful but to him alien and antagonistic personality greatly affected his future political course. It was soon to be more than counterbalanced by the even greater antagonism to Disraeli. The day after the Don Pacifico debate ended Peel was thrown from his horse and died four days later. Sir George Cornewall Lewis, who later succeeded Gladstone as Chancellor of the Exchequer, commented: 'Upon Gladstone it will have the effect of removing a weight from a spring. . . The general opinion is that Gladstone will renounce his free-trade opinions, and become leader of the Protectionists.'[10]

It turned out to be a false prophecy, not least because of the evolution of Gladstone's views on the nature of the international community. In this evolution his journey to Naples in the autumn and winter of 1850 was crucial. He had long talks with Lacaita, the legal adviser to the British Embassy in Naples, who opened his eyes to the true state of affairs in the Kingdom of the Two Sicilies under the corrupt regime of Ferdinand of Bourbon. He was able to see for himself the travesty of justice perpetrated in Neapolitan courts in the trial of political prisoners. He visited the prisons and saw the degrading conditions under which most of the leaders of the liberal opposition in Naples were kept. He was particularly impressed by the case of Poerio, who had been a minister, was condemned on trumped-up evidence to twenty-four years in irons and was seen by Gladstone in his dungeon chained to a common criminal. All this had a cataclysmic effect on Gladstone; it was 'the negation of God erected into a system of government'. He hurried home in February

1851, leaving his wife in Italy still weak from a miscarriage. He was determined to act. The dictates of justice and morality outweighed every other consideration with him and he was prepared to go against all his preconceived conservative notions on the politics of Europe and the dangers of revolution on the Continent. The ability to let moral conviction prevail in this way was the true greatness of Gladstone, but whereas on previous occasions – the switch to free trade, the widening of his views on religious toleration – the shift had been gradual, on this occasion it came with great suddenness, though its full implications also took years to make themselves felt. Gladstone realized that he could achieve nothing through Palmerston; the jingoistic support for nationalism and self-determination for which Gladstone had attacked him in the Don Pacifico debates had made Palmerston *persona non grata* in the conservative chancelleries of Europe. Gladstone therefore turned to his fellow Peelite Aberdeen, in some ways now the titular leader of the group and an ex-Foreign Secretary. Aberdeen was entirely sympathetic and prepared to do his utmost to alleviate suffering; but he was also a conservative statesman, whose ideas were formed during the Napoleonic wars, who saw the Vienna system as the sheet-anchor of stability and revolution as the great threat to European order. Moreover, he must have been aware of the implications for the Peelites as a group of public action on this issue by the conservative Gladstone. It was just on foreign policy that they were closest to the Protectionists and the views of Aberdeen were indistinguishable from those of Stanley. Aberdeen therefore asked Gladstone to allow him time to work privately on the Austrian government before anything was made public. It was only when after more than four months there had been no reply from the Austrian government that Gladstone decided to make public his *Letters to Lord Aberdeen*. There was insufficient consultation with Aberdeen before publication was finally decided on, but Gladstone's sincerity was so evident that Aberdeen, though irritated, did not hold it against his younger colleague. Shortly after the publication of Gladstone's letters there was in fact a reply from Prince Schwarzenberg, but it promised little action and was full of counter-accusations on the British treatment of Irish and Chartist offenders. The letters caused a sensation; at a stroke Gladstone appeared to have aligned himself with liberals and even revolutionaries right across Europe, from Mazzini to Manin, and to have made enemies of conservatives from Guizot to Princess Lieven. To some extent this was a misunderstanding of Gladstone's complex motives and thought-processes; there was to be frequently in the future a similar discrepancy between his own intentions and actions and the public forces and reactions evoked by them. Even Palmerston now commended him for his new stand and had his *Letters to Aberdeen* distributed to British missions abroad; but Gladstone reassured Aberdeen: 'You need not be afraid I think of Mazzinism from me, still less of Kossuth-ism, which means the other plus imposture, Lord Palmerston and his nationalities.' Great as was the earthquake caused in Gladstone's mind by the suffering he saw in Naples, he was not yet ready to embrace the cause of nationalism in Italy or elsewhere in Europe. It was not because there was any trace of insularity in him; Italy especially he knew and loved deeply and he was at that moment translating Farini's four-volume history of the Papal States from 1815 to 1850. He felt himself a citizen of the Christian civilization of Europe – an attitude entirely in harmony with his basic conservatism.

When Gladstone returned from Naples on 26 February 1851 a letter from Lord Stanley was handed to him at the station asking him to join the government which Stanley was trying to form. 'There *never* was *such* a *complicated* state of affairs,' wrote the Queen to her uncle, the King of the Belgians. It was true of the general political situation and applied *a fortiori* to Gladstone's own position, until the situation was resolved by the formation of the Aberdeen Coalition nearly two years later. In his heart of hearts Gladstone wanted both the general and his personal political uncertainty to be resolved: he saw the need for Parliament to resume 'its natural and usual organisation in the form of two political parties, a Government and an opposition' and his natural ambition drove him to seek office as an outlet for his great constructive talents. Yet with the instinct for self-mortification so deeply implanted in him he was reluctant to grasp prematurely something he really desired. On this occasion Stanley made it easy for him to refuse office, for he proposed putting a small duty back on corn. It was significant, however, that Stanley's bid for Peelite support was made in the first place to Gladstone, showing how great his political stature had become and also that he continued to be regarded as the Peelite most likely to be attracted by Conservative reunion. On Stanley's failure to form a government, Russell resumed office, also without the Peelites. Whigs and Peelites were in fact at this moment being driven increasingly apart by the Ecclesiastical Titles Bill. It had arisen out of the 'No Popery' hysteria that flared up when the Pope appointed Wiseman to be Cardinal of West-

minster and divided England into territorial dioceses. Lord John
Russell in riding the 'No Popery' horse was for the moment
identifying himself with an overwhelmingly popular cause, but in
the long run he was further weakening the already declining position
of his government. So obviously illiberal and demagogic a stance
repelled not only the Peelites but also many leading Radicals, and
it clearly undermined Irish support for the Whigs. All the major
Peelite figures, though not the Peelite back-benchers, were united
in their opposition to the Ecclesiastical Titles Bill, but it took
particular courage for Gladstone and his two closest political
associates Sidney Herbert and Newcastle (as Lincoln now was)
to take this course. They were High Churchmen and the secessions
to Rome of former Tractarians and High Anglicans had given edge
to the anti-Catholic hysteria. Gladstone was particularly suspect:
his two closest friends had just seceded and no doubt Wiseman's
connection with his sister was remembered. Morley considered
Gladstone's speech on the second reading of the Ecclesiastical
Titles Bill in a predominantly hostile House one of his three or
four masterpieces – a paean on religious liberty. This meaningless
piece of legislation was repealed twenty years later during his first
premiership. But Gladstone's conservatism was still at least as alive
as his liberalism. He was opposed to a further reform bill and he
blamed Graham for not speaking out against electoral reform on
behalf of the Peelites. It was known that Lord John Russell had a
great desire to bring in another reform bill and this was yet another
reason why Gladstone would not have been sorry to see him fall.
Oddly enough Palmerston was also opposed to more reform; it
contributed to the growing coolness between him and Russell which
weakened the government.

Nothing was resolved in the session of 1851, the first in which the
Peelites had been without Peel; but neither had the Whigs anything
to show for other than the empty Ecclesiastical Titles Bill. The
Protectionists had revealed their weakness when they failed to take
office. Gladstone still felt frustrated by the leaderless and dis-
organized state of the Peelites and made fresh efforts in the autumn
to galvanize the group into greater cohesion. Effective liaison
scarcely went beyond the triumvirate of himself, Herbert and
Newcastle; Graham was indecisive and Aberdeen lacked all ambition.
The dismissal of Palmerston in December 1851 gave a fresh shake to
the political kaleidoscope. Russell's days were clearly numbered
unless he could enlist the Peelites, but the chances were no better
than before. Mutual suspicion on matters ecclesiastical was still a

virtually insuperable obstacle with the High Anglican triumvirate; an offer to Graham could hardly succeed in isolation and there were doubts if it was seriously meant. Greville considered the Peelite group so divided and scattered 'that it can hardly be called a party'. Soon after the opening of the 1852 session Palmerston had his 'tit-for-tat with Johnny Russell' and brought the government down on a militia bill. Gladstone, who had never been afraid of either Russell's fall or the coming to office of the Protectionists, was one of only ten Peelites, among them Herbert, who voted with Palmerston.

More than ever the Peelites held the key to the situation and among them Gladstone was more than ever before the central figure. Nobody rivalled the energy, tenacity and grasp with which he consulted, organized and evolved policy. Through all the complexities he held to the line which he had for a long time envisaged: he still looked to a Conservative reunion, once protection was finally buried as an issue: 'I thought that a Liberal policy would be worked out with the greatest security to the country through the medium of the Conservative party, and I thought a position like Peel's on the Liberal side of that party preferable . . . to the Conservative side of the Liberal party.' In practice this meant giving the Derby–Disraeli government that was now formed a fair trial on the understanding that they would, after the dispatch of current business, go to the country and let a new Parliament decide the issue of protection and free trade. In the meantime the Peelites would remain entirely independent. As a group the Peelites did in fact take this line, but there were difficulties among them. There was the question, symbolic yet significant, where they were to take their seats in the House. At the beginning of the 1847 session the Peelites had moved to the opposition side of the House, separated from the Protectionists by the gangway. Gladstone and Herbert now wanted to move with the Protectionists over to the government side, remaining below the gangway. Their colleagues prevailed on them to remain on the opposition side below the gangway. Gladstone found that Newcastle, his close associate, was much more suspicious of the Derby government than he was and they had a conversation on a sofa at the Carlton Club which grew 'rather warm'. Most important was the decision of Graham to throw in his lot with Russell, in which Cardwell followed him. He was invited to stand for Carlisle as a free-trader, paired with a Radical. Since he had once been a Whig he spoke of himself as a 'wanderer returned'.[11] Gladstone had to tell him that because he represented Oxford he had to sever his political connection with him, and Graham no longer attended Peelite meetings. It was an amiable and in the event only temporary parting. During this period Russell was trying to put out feelers again towards the Peelites. He discussed Gladstone's position, likely to be the least promising from the point of view of a Whig–Peelite fusion, with Aberdeen. Gladstone recorded this version of the discussion:

> The tenor of his conversation was that my opinions were quite as liberal as his; that in regard to Colonies I went beyond him; that my Naples pamphlets would have been called revolutionary if he had written them, nay that in regard to church matters he saw no reason why there should not be joint action, for he was cordially disposed to maintain the Church of England, and so, he believed, was I.

The general election of 1852 was as confused as its predecessor. There were only 212 contested constituencies out of 374 and a low turn-out. There were no real issues, for the Protectionists, sensing the weakness of their position, talked Corn Laws in the countryside and free trade in the towns. There was still some beating of the Protestant drum, but it helped the Derbyites only in some isolated cases, notably Liverpool, where Cardwell was beaten. In Ireland, where they hoped for gains, the Derbyites approved of Maynooth. Gladstone faced a contest at Oxford, in spite of the tradition that a sitting candidate was not opposed. Dr Marsham, the Warden of Merton, was put up against him by a group of Heads of Houses. Gladstone had contrived to make enemies among almost every section of opinion: the evangelicals disliked him as much as ever, he was suspected of favouring disestablishment by many beyond the High Church party, his opposition to the Ecclesiastical Titles Bill led to 'romanizing' accusations, his support for Jewish emancipation was still held against him. In fact it was difficult for many to understand where Gladstone stood. In spite of all this Gladstone won handsomely; if his supporters had not also had to give votes to Sir Robert Inglis, he would have headed the poll. Analysis showed that more recent graduates were heavily in his favour.

No one could be sure what the result of the election was. There was probably a remaining block of thirty or so Peelites and for the rest the position was so finely balanced that this group could be decisive.[12] Who could foretell what twenty-five or so Free Trade Derbyites would actually do? Undoubtedly the manner in which the election was fought and the result widened the gap between Derbyites and Peelites and brought a Whig–Peelite coalition a step nearer. But Gladstone still stood out to some extent from this general disposition of the Peelites and was not prepared to commit himself against Derby. It is true that he deprecated the bigotry displayed by Derby's followers in the election, but he immediately counter-balanced this by referring to Russell's pandering to 'No Popery' the year before, 'the person to whom I am now invited to transfer my confidence'. This was in reply to Aberdeen who had sent him a letter from Russell making a serious approach to the Peelites. Aberdeen sent Gladstone's letter to Russell with the remark that he was 'hampered by his Oxford constituency'. Russell was a good deal hurt by some of the strictures on past Whig conduct in Glad-stone's letter. Gladstone was therefore determined to 'wait and see' what kind of policy Derby would produce when Parliament re-assembled in November. This was also the policy of the other Peelites and Gladstone met frequently with his colleagues to discuss the situation, generally under the chairmanship of Aberdeen. But more than most of them he was still inclined to throw in his lot with Derby, provided protection was dropped, which it was almost bound to be. The other major difficulty in the path of Conservative reunion lay, to Gladstone's mind, in the personality of Disraeli. In his letter to Aberdeen he referred to the 'unscrupulousness and second motives of Mr D'Israeli, at once the necessity of Lord Derby and his curse'. But personal difficulties could be overcome if political principles did not stand in the way.

This was Gladstone's position on the eve of a decisive movement in his career. He was a liberal Conservative; liberal on the colonies, still his special interest, even something of a colonial reformer, but colonies were of marginal interest; liberal on freedom of religion, a central issue; potentially liberal on foreign policy; a deeply convinced free-trader. But he viewed society as a conservative, felt himself to be a conservative and on specific issues, for example electoral reform, was still wholly conservative.

5

A MOST
RIGID
ECONOMIST
1853–8

When Parliament reassembled in November 1852 Gladstone's position was still genuinely open. He was poised between his hope for Conservative reunion, insistence that protection must be well and truly buried, distrust of Disraeli and fear that no budget on truly sound Peelite lines could be expected from one so 'quackish', unease about Russell and the Whigs and their religious ethos. Through Hardinge, a Peelite who had joined the Derby government, he conveyed to the Conservative leader that there must be explicit adoption of free trade in the Queen's Speech and an immediate budget on sound lines. The Peelite leaders were in session when they received a copy of the relevant paragraph in the Queen's

Speech, which was far from explicit. 'We were all much dissatisfied and disappointed,' wrote Gladstone, but he was still concerned to leave all options open. The next hurdle which faced Derby's government was a free-trade motion moved by Villiers, most inveterate of free-traders, at the end of November. Gladstone knew that the Protectionists must eat dirt, but he was prepared to let them swallow it quietly. He collaborated with Palmerston, then in an independent position after his breach with Russell, in working out a more palatable free-trade resolution, and this was passed by an overwhelming majority from all sections of the House. The government was saved, but not spared the necessity of producing a budget. In the debate Sidney Herbert, politically closest of all to Gladstone, made a slashing personal attack on Disraeli; in doubtful taste he referred to the difficulty Jews had in making converts because of the 'surgical operation' involved in circumcision. The following evening Gladstone went to a party at Lord Derby's and had a long political conversation with his host. Derby sought reassurance about the hostile tone of Herbert's speech and received it; but Gladstone gave nothing away on the future: 'I said that as to relations of parties, circumstances were often stronger than the human will; that we must wait for their guiding, and follow it. . .'

Then, on 3 December 1852, Disraeli opened his first budget. It had been part of the understanding reached with the Peelites when Derby formed his government that there should be an interim budget before the dissolution and a full budget on the reassembly of Parliament. In brief, Disraeli's task was this: he had to offer some 'compensation' to those interests, particularly agriculture, which had considered themselves injured in the past few years of free trade, in return for their acquiescence in the burial of protection. The main compensation which he offered was a halving of the malt tax, for long a bugbear to the landed interest. The main problem he faced was the income tax, which was only renewed for a year in 1851, mainly owing to Radical pressure. Disraeli now made a bold bid for Radical support by distinguishing between 'precarious or industrial' and 'realized or property' income. The stock Radical criticism of the income tax was that it failed to distinguish between earned and unearned incomes, though the distinction which they wanted was not quite the same as is implied by these terms today. Under Disraeli's scheme 'realized' income was to continue to be taxed at 7*d*. in the pound; 'precarious' income only at 5¼*d*. He forfeited any popularity he might have gained through this distinction by lowering the exemption limits to £50 and £100 respectively for the two types of income. Unfortunately for Disraeli the distinction between the two types of income was imperfectly worked out and offended against the canons of financial orthodoxy.

The Peelites were immediately hostile to these proposals which were incompatible with the principles of their late Master. Gladstone was above all offended by the income tax proposals and perhaps even more by the spuriousness of the surplus for which Disraeli was budgeting. He considered it 'the least conservative budget I have ever known' and distrusted both its contents and its author. It soon became clear that the government was facing defeat in spite of Disraeli's desperate efforts to stave it off. Not only the Peelites were hostile, but also the Irish, in whom Disraeli had placed some hope ever since Russell had offended them by the Ecclesiastical Titles Bill. The Irish disliked the extension of the income tax to Ireland as well as Derby's hostility to tenants' rights in Ireland. Gladstone did not speak until the final night of the debate and contrary to usual practice he followed the Chancellor of the Exchequer's winding-up speech. Disraeli ended his speech with the famous remark that he was facing a coalition but 'that England does not love coalitions'. It was a speech of which Gladstone wrote: 'I was on tenterhooks, except when his superlative acting and brilliant oratory from time to time absorbed me and made me quite *forget* that I had to follow him.' He followed him at one o'clock in the morning of 17 December 1852 with a speech that combined great mastery of technicalities 'with a high tone of moral feeling – now rising to indignation, now sinking to remonstrance – which was sustained throughout without flagging and without effort'; so wrote *The Times*. He showed up the shoddiness of Disraeli's work, highlighted the burdens that would be placed on lower incomes and the small relief that would be gained by halving the malt tax. 'My great object was to show the Conservative party how their leader was hoodwinking and bewildering them.' At this crisis in his career he still felt himself to be a Conservative and he said, 'If I vote against the government I vote in support of those Conservative principles which I thank God are common in a great degree to all parties in the British House of Commons, but of which I thought it was the peculiar pride and glory of the Conservative party to be the champions and the leaders.' His speech made the defeat of the government certain. More than ever before he had held the centre of the political stage and had experienced the exhilarating power his oratory gave him over men and events.

The way was now open to the formation of the Whig–Peelite

coalition which had been in the air for such a long time. Lord John Russell's position among the Whigs had been so weakened that he could no longer claim the first place in the new combination; he still took it badly and the problem of placing him in keeping with his dignity almost rendered the coalition abortive before it started. The Peelites, on the other hand, were now able to take the share which they considered befitting to their abilities and importance: the premiership and nearly half the places in the Cabinet. In terms of parliamentary strength the Whigs and their allies were overwhelmingly more important than the Peelites; but on the other hand the still rather exclusive group of Whig office-holders was no larger than the Peelites and considerably less talented. Palmerston was another difficult piece to fit into the jigsaw of the Aberdeen coalition: some thought that when he moved his compromise free-trade resolution he was aiming at joining Derby and perhaps replacing Disraeli as leader of the House. After some hesitation he decided to stick with the Whigs, with whom he had made his political home for the past twenty-five years, and he joined the coalition as Home Secretary. It was a decision of great importance for the future of British politics.[1]

Gladstone's appointment as Chancellor of the Exchequer was even more significant. Many suspected him of personal ambition. Could he really have found an adequate outlet for his talents through Conservative reunion? At the time of the free-trade motion in November Derby was trying to strengthen his government by overtures to Palmerston. Prince Albert was aghast and suggested Gladstone as a more suitable successor to Disraeli as Leader of the House. Derby said he was 'in his opinion, quite unfit for it; he had none of that decision, boldness, readiness, and clearness which was necessary to lead a Party, to inspire it with confidence, and still [more], to take at times a decision on the spur of the moment, which a leader had often to do!'[2] Derby was not ready to drop Disraeli; he would have found a place for Gladstone, but it might not have been adequate. Could Gladstone have served in a position inferior to Disraeli? Whatever may have been suspected, Gladstone's ambition never overcame other motives more important to him. In some ways it was hard for him to sever his old party loyalties, but the atmosphere of the old unregenerate Toryism of the country party was in fact uncongenial to him. His High Tory phase in the 1830s had been an intellectual choice and underneath there was his Canningite heritage from Liverpool. Ideologically there was little to choose between the various combinations that were possible within the central spectrum of British politics. At times Peelite conservatism had more in common with the Manchester radicalism of Cobden and Bright than with Whigs or Tories; though one of the conditions that made the coalition acceptable to Gladstone was the minor part played in it by the Radicals. Only Molesworth, the doyen of radicalism in the House, a follower of Bentham and impeccably aristocratic in background, was a member of Aberdeen's Cabinet. On ecclesiastical matters the election of 1852 had shown the Derbyites to be hardly less objectionable than the Whigs. Acting together with his closest political friends Gladstone could therefore not feel out of place in the new combination.

The move caused Gladstone much difficulty with his friends. They judged him by the results he produced, the fall of Derby, and did not pause to examine the complexity of his motives. The vote on the budget was attributed to deliberate combination against Derby; Northcote, his secretary, said jokingly that Mary Stuart could never get over the presumption which her marriage with Bothwell raised as to the nature of their previous connection. A few nights after the division on the budget a part of Tory revellers at the Carlton Club threatened to throw him out of the window into the Reform. More serious opposition arose at Oxford where he unexpectedly found himself faced with a contest after his appointment as Chancellor. Again there was an unholy alliance of High Churchmen and evangelicals against him. The former denounced the coalition as latitudinarianism in politics that would lead to latitudinarianism in the Church; the latter talked of 'a cabinet more deeply tainted with the leprosy of Tractarianism than any which has yet existed'.[3] Dudley Perceval, son of the Prime Minister who had been assassinated, was put up against Gladstone; it was a bitter contest and the poll was kept open for fifteen days. Gladstone won by 1022 to 898, a narrow majority. The poll was followed by protracted pamphlet warfare. Gladstone was much shaken by this experience; it made him wonder if he should retire from Oxford; it made him more favourable to action on the report of the royal commission of inquiry into the affairs of the university, a commission which he had originally opposed most strenuously, and it moved him closer to the liberals in the university, men like Jowett and Goldwin Smith. More sober-minded High Churchmen, however, continued to regard him as a spokesman for their point of view, the more influential now for being a member of the government, and Sir William Heathcote, who had chaired his committee in 1852, stood by him.

Aberdeen was at first uncertain whether to appoint Graham or

Gladstone to the Exchequer. Russell wanted the former, the Queen the latter. Gladstone reported that there was a feeling that since he had destroyed the budget so he ought to make a new one, and so it was to be. No doubt the prospect appealed to him; loyalty to the Peelite canon of financial policy had been one of the main threads of his political life for over a decade and he now had the opportunity of carrying on this work in a leading role. The budget was also going to be a crucial test for the coalition, whose parliamentary majority was no more secure or predictable than Derby's had been. Gladstone's own analysis was that fifty or so Conservatives who might be favourable to the coalition held the balance. If their support could be secured it would be a justification of the tactics which he more than anybody else had recommended to the Peelites since the election.

Early in February 1853 Gladstone moved into No. 12 Downing Street, the Chancellor's official residence, soon to be renumbered 11. There and at No. 10 next door he was to spend over twenty years. There was an unpleasant correspondence between him and Disraeli about the furniture and the official robes of the Chancellor, in which the ex-Chancellor intimated that his successor was not a man of the world. Then the budget preparations started. Morley prefaced his account of this phase in Gladstone's life with the famous remark that 'there is something repulsive to human nature in the simple reproduction of defunct budgets' and that 'if anything can be more odious than a living tax it is a dead one'. Nevertheless, financial policy held as central a place in the politics of the mid nineteenth century as economic policy does in our day, and it was perhaps even more directly connected with the alignment of parties than it is now. The key to Gladstone's budget, as it had been to Disraeli's, was the income tax. As we have seen, Gladstone had originally been opposed to its revival, but he soon came to accept it as an essential part of Peel's scheme of freeing trade. Most of those on the Radical side of politics had also been prepared to accept it when it was used to weaken the privileged position of the landed interest and to help the consumer. But by the 1850s it had become an almost universally unpopular tax and it was Hume who had moved for its renewal for only a year in 1851 and for the appointment of a select committee of inquiry. Gladstone opposed this committee and refused to serve on it. His view now was that an immediate abolition of the income tax was impossible, but that what he called in his budget speech 'this colossal engine of finance' should not become a permanent feature of the tax system. His bold proposal therefore was to keep the income tax for two more years at 7d., then hold it another two years at 6*d*., then three years at 5*d*., and abolish it altogether by 5 April 1860. Never had a Chancellor planned for the future to this extent. To get the surplus necessary for the further reductions of tariff which he proposed he had to lower the exemption limit to £100. This left him still open to the charge, which Disraeli had tried to meet with his ill-fated scheme, that earned income was carrying an unfair burden compared with property. He firmly stuck to his argument that distinctions in types of income were unsound; but in order to make property pay its due share he instituted a general succession duty in place of the existing legacy duty confined to personal property passing on death. This proved to be the thin end of a very wide wedge and was perhaps in the long run the most effective part of the budget. It required legislation of great complexity. These were the central proposals of the budget, but there were many others: remission of the excise duty on soap; extension of the income tax to Ireland at a reduced rate in return for a cancellation of Irish debts; a conversion scheme to reduce the cost of the national debt.

Gladstone had to work out this complicated scheme almost entirely by personal effort: endless memoranda, many delegations and consultations. The Treasury staff at this time was small, like that of all other departments. He had to put his proposals before the Cabinet, which required a three-hour speech, and before the House, where he spoke for four and three-quarter hours. In the Cabinet all sorts of objections were urged, on mainly political grounds. This was not surprising in view of the precarious parliamentary position of the coalition. Particularly the lowering of the income tax exemption and the extension of the tax to Ireland would, it was feared, lead to adverse reactions from the Radicals and the Irish; similar proposals had destroyed Disraeli's budget. Finally the Cabinet swung into line and defeat on any of the main proposals was made a matter of confidence. The political difficulties which were to be anticipated threw a great weight of responsibility on Gladstone when he introduced the budget in the House on 18 April 1853. The speech was one of the great parliamentary performances of the century. Gladstone noted in his diary: ' . . . my strength held out, thank God. Many kind congratulations afterwards. Herberts and Wortleys came home with us and had soup and negus.'

In the Commons there were four nights of debate on the income tax proposals; on 2 May a hostile amendment was rejected by 323 to 252 votes. Some eighty Conservatives voted in the majority; since there were about forty dependable Peelites, it meant that forty out of the fifty Conservatives who were considered possible supporters of the coalition had been won over from Derby. Even some twenty-five Irish Liberals supported the proposals. There were many more battles in committee on the Income Tax Bill, and the Succession Duty Bill which came later proved even more difficult. On one occasion the government's majority sank to six. But in the end it all went through and Gladstone was established as a great public financier. To modern eyes the contemporary adulation seems somewhat excessive, for so many of the assumptions of the budget did not work out: the debt conversion scheme ran into difficulties, the succession duty brought in a disappointing amount of revenue and above all the ambitious plan to phase out the income tax failed. Partly this was due to the Crimean War, but not entirely. Expenditure had been on a plateau of about £50 million; by 1860 it had risen to £70 million and did not come down again. For the moment, however, Gladstone had emerged as the strong man of the coalition; his budget had demonstrated that Aberdeen's government was more than a nine-days' wonder and more firmly based than Derby's of the year before. The extent of Conservative parliamentary support for the budget had shown the weakness of the Derbyites even as an opposition. Nobody's discomfiture was greater than Disraeli's. He disagreed with Derby about tactics: Dizzy wanted to attack at all costs, Derby to lie low and perhaps draw some of the Peelites back into his camp. Many Tories would have liked to have rid themselves of Disraeli as leader and in the latter weeks of the 1853 session he hardly took part in debates.

Just when the prestige of the coalition was at its height, in the summer of 1853, the storm clouds of the Crimean War began to gather. It was a quirk of fate that this coalition which had its origins entirely in the necessities of British domestic politics should have had to fight the only major war in which Britain was involved between 1815 and 1914. Historians have generally considered it an avoidable war and it certainly did not solve anything. For Gladstone's career the Crimean War was a misfortune, not less because he recovered from it. Yet to the end of his life he always considered the war had been justified, even though twenty years later he took the opposite view of the Eastern Question. To his mind Russia had transgressed the Public Law of Europe in 1853, when she acted on her own in applying pressure on the Turks. Another charge often made is that the divisions in the Cabinet made the war more likely. If either Aberdeen and the peace party or Palmerston and the war party had made policy the war could have been avoided; but

Aberdeen was reluctant to break up the coalition so recently formed. In 1887 Gladstone wrote an article in the *English Historical Review* on the Crimean War in the form of a review of Greville's memoirs. In it he denied that divisions in the Cabinet had produced the drift into war and asserted that he had never served in a Cabinet where there was less dissension. The fact was that Gladstone's role in the conduct of foreign affairs was somewhat marginal and moreover during some of the most crucial weeks, from the latter part of August to October 1853, he was away ill in Scotland. When he took part in Cabinet meetings again the Turks had already declared war on Russia. From that moment on he certainly threw his weight on the side of peace, but it was late in the day and the initiative had largely passed from the hands of the British government. In the middle of October he was away again in Manchester, at the unveiling of a statue erected in memory of Peel. He told Aberdeen that he found the feeling there stronger for peace than for war. He made a speech in which he said 'more on the war question than I intended'. He stressed the need for maintaining the integrity of the Ottoman Empire and the dangers which would arise if an autocratic Russia sought aggrandizement at the expense of the Sultan; but he also admitted the weaknesses of Turkish rule and the anomaly of Turkish dominion over millions of Christians.

Personal difficulties in the coalition did in fact aggravate the crisis. Lord John Russell had hoped to succeed Aberdeen by the end of the summer. Gladstone would probably have left the government if this change had taken place and this was one of the reasons why it could not take place. Then Lord John Russell was still determined to bring in another reform bill. Gladstone had opposed this in the past and was still sufficiently conservative to be unenthusiastic about it now. Palmerston was the strongest opponent of reform in the Cabinet, yet Russell and Palmerston were agreed on a firm policy against Russia. In the middle of December Palmerston resigned, ostensibly on reform, but also because of dissatisfaction with the Cabinet's Eastern policy. The resignation happened to coincide with the so-called massacre of Sinope, the destruction of Turkish ships by the Russians in the Black Sea. Public opinion and Palmerston's friends in the press linked the two events together and Palmerston became the hero of the hour, the man who wanted to stand up to the Tsar, when Aberdeen and the rest of the Cabinet had betrayed British interests. Aberdeen and his colleagues came to realize that the loss of Palmerston might prove fatal to the coalition; the course of diplomacy following Sinope was in any case pushing

D

them towards confrontation with Russia. Newcastle and Gladstone were two of the ministers who now worked for a reconciliation with Palmerston, who was back in office within a few days. At this stage Gladstone no longer harboured the hostility towards Palmerston he had felt in the days when the Whig Foreign Secretary was encouraging revolution and nationalism abroad. He now respected Palmerston's expertise on foreign affairs and may have sympathized a little with him over his opposition to Russell's reform proposals. Just before Palmerston's return to the Cabinet Gladstone wrote to Sidney Herbert, '. . . I had had wishes today that P. was back again on account of the E. Question.'[4] Palmerston and Gladstone were hardly made to be bosom friends, but their political antagonism went in phases. The Cabinet meeting at which Gladstone wished Palmerston to be back again had, on 22 December 1853, decided to agree to French proposals for a joint naval occupation of the Black Sea. Here Gladstone made his one major intervention in the crisis by insisting that Turkey should be required to refer any terms of peace to Britain and France. Commenting on this the historian Kinglake wrote in his history of the Crimea:

> The proposal seemed made to win the Chancellor of the Exchequer; for it fell short of war by a measure of distance which, though it might seem very small to people with common eyesight, was more than broad enough to afford commodious standing-room to a man delighting as he did in refinements and slender distinctions.[5]

As war moved closer, Aberdeen wanted to retire from office. He felt a sense of guilt at having failed to avoid war and he never shook it off for the rest of his life. He consulted Gladstone who dissuaded him from resignation, arguing that it was a just and inevitable war: 'I said we were not fighting for the Turks, but we were warning Russia off the forbidden ground.' Gladstone felt 'a warm and grateful affection for Lord Aberdeen'. A fundamental simplicity and modesty drew the two men together in face of the many complicated *prima donnas* they had to work with. At this time Gladstone also wrote an unsigned article in the *Morning Chronicle*, the organ of the Peelites, defending Prince Albert against the slanderous campaign depicting him as pro-Russian and virtually a traitor. Thus Gladstone faced the war reluctantly and had no sympathy with the chauvinism that swept public opinion. On the other hand he did not in any way share the anti-war feeling of a small group of Radicals such as Bright. He thought it a justified war against a despotism in which England would prove the superiority of her free institutions and of her commercial industrial system which he was himself doing so much to develop. But there were limits beyond which his conscience would not allow him to go. He told Aberdeen: '. . . we were not going to extend the conflagration . . . but to apply more powers for its extinction, and this I hoped in conjunction with all the great Powers of Europe. That I, for one, could not shoulder the musket against the Christian subjects of the Sultan, and must there take my stand.'

It fell to Gladstone to deal with the financial side of the war and this placed him in a situation from which he could hardly emerge with credit.[6] The whole tradition of Peelite finance, summed up in Gladstone's description of Peel as 'a most rigid economist', mixed with war as little as oil does with water. Gladstone was forced to abandon his own principles step by step and when the British public, after a winter of disasters in the Crimea, demanded an all-out effort to win the war, Peelite canons of economy were laughed out of court as petty cheese-paring. Fortunately for Gladstone he was no longer in office by then. It was, however, not only lessons learnt from Peel that governed Gladstone's initial approach to war finance; equally influential were the lessons which everybody thought needed to be learnt from the Younger Pitt and the bad examples of war finance in the Napoleonic period. There was universal agreement that the National Debt was a heavy and damaging burden; war should therefore be financed by taxes and not by loans. In his first provisional budget introduced in March 1854, before the declaration of war, Gladstone doubled the income tax from 7*d.* to 1*s.* 2*d.* Characteristically this was to him not merely a practical but also a moral measure: 'The expenses of war are the moral check which it has pleased the Almighty to impose upon the ambition and the lust of conquest that are inherent in so many nations.' Another argument that Gladstone used against loans as a means of war finance was that with loans 'you go directly to that fountainhead where money is supplied, upon which in a great degree the activity of trade and the cheapness of productions must depend'. Thus loans would restrict production and reduce wages. But Gladstone soon came up against the limits of income tax; one of the chief arguments in his mind against a further increase of it was the fact that it could not be effectively levied on the poorer classes and therefore fell unfairly upon the commercial and professional classes. A strange reversal of much modern argument on taxation! The poorer classes had supported and wanted the war and it was only fair that they should pay their proper share of it. This left only loans and a return to more indirect taxation as sources of revenue.

Gladstone had to resort to both to raise enough revenue; he was afraid that a prolonged war would lead to a return to protection. His policy on loans came in for a good deal of criticism, particularly from the City. The conversion scheme he had proposed in 1853 had already run into trouble and he included it in his list of recorded errors late in life. He now used exchequer bonds and bills to make up for short-term deficiencies in the revenue. He rather disingenuously denied that these were real loans and therefore additions to the National Debt. His critics, in particular Lord Monteagle, who as Thomas Spring-Rice had been a Whig Chancellor of the Exchequer, pounced on his evasions. He also became involved in disagreements with the Bank of England, both on this and the operation of the Bank Charter Act of 1844, with its tight control of the note issue. In fact, 46 per cent of the total expenditure on the Crimean War was met by loans, in spite of the fact that it was a relatively short war.

Another aspect of war finance which was debated a good deal at the time was the question of subsidies to allies. Here again the example of Pitt and his large expenditure on foreign allies was a deterrent. On this matter Gladstone was inclined to adopt a somewhat purist attitude and he insisted on very strict definitions in the grant of money to Sardinia and particularly to Turkey. When the Turkish loan was discussed in the House of Commons in July 1855 Gladstone appeared as a man who put petty financial scruples before winning the war. His popularity at that time was at its nadir. In practice Gladstone was by no means rigid; he was only too well aware that political and diplomatic considerations might have to outweigh financial rectitude as he saw it. His principles were as high as ever, while at the same time his powerful mind could grasp the practicalities of a situation with ruthless logic. When it came to explaining himself he was less happy: over-elaborate qualifications and subtle complexities appeared to the more commonsensical multitude as sheer sophistry. Gladstone's great verbal powers tempted him into out-talking his adversaries and overbearing them by sheer weight of argument. At times it could appear that he was deceiving no one but himself.

In spite of the impending war the Aberdeen government announced an impressive list of measures for the parliamentary session of 1854. It was perhaps an over-ambitious programme, for most of it had to be abandoned; the parliamentary basis of the coalition remained uncertain and there was general agreement only on keeping the government in existence for the time being to prosecute the war. Gladstone was intimately connected with two of the proposed measures; the reform of the Civil Service arising out of the Trevelyan–Northcote Report and the bill to reform the University of Oxford. The structure of various government departments, including the Treasury, had been under review for some time before the coalition took office. Gladstone found that soon after going to the Treasury he needed to examine the conditions of entry into the public service common to all departments under investigation. Sir Charles Trevelyan, the Assistant Secretary of the Treasury, and Sir Stafford Northcote, Gladstone's former secretary at the Board of Trade, were already working on investigations into several of the departments and were given this additional task in April 1853. Northcote had been called back into the public service by Gladstone and he had worked on his committee during his several contests for the Oxford seat. Although he described himself as 'rather a stiff Conservative' and had doubts about serving the coalition government, he was reassured by the presence in it of Gladstone. It was hardly surprising that he made a poor showing in opposing Gladstone in the 1880s, when he was the Tory leader in the Commons. The famous Trevelyan–Northcote Report was presented in November 1854 and recommended that recruitment for a certain number of appointments in government departments should be through open competitive examination; for this purpose appointments would be grouped into categories cutting across departments, according to whether the work was 'mechanical' or 'intellectual'. Promotion would be on merit instead of seniority and could also be from one department to another, so that the fragmentation of the service would be ended.[7]

Gladstone was eager to pass legislation to give effect to the recommendations of Trevelyan and Northcote. The principle of open competition had just been introduced into the Indian Civil Service. Jowett had worked hard towards this end, partly through his connection with Gladstone, and he was now, with Trevelyan and Gladstone, exerting influence towards the adoption of the same principle for the Home Civil Service. Gladstone saw the proposed changes less as an advance towards democracy than as a guarantee of greater efficiency and as a simple act of justice. He ran into considerable opposition from his colleagues and the Queen, mainly on two grounds: Graham emphasized that the patronage available to ministers in filling public appointments was an essential part of the political system and its loss would weaken the executive. Lord John Russell was the chief spokesman for the argument that it was a revolutionary and democratic step: 'Our institutions will be as harshly republican as possible.' Gladstone denied that the kind of

patronage it was proposed to abolish was necessary for the maintenance of party in Parliament, and to Russell he wrote that the change
would not work against the aristocracy but would 'strengthen and
multiply the ties between the higher classes and the possession of
administrative power'. It proved impossible to introduce legislation in the session of 1853: for the moment all that could be
achieved was the setting up of the Civil Service Commission, through
which the principle of competitive examination gradually gained a
foothold in the recruitment of government officials. It was not until
1870, when Gladstone was Prime Minister, that the principle was
generally accepted. The inefficiencies revealed by the Crimean War,
however, kept the cause of administrative reform alive and Gladstone,
more than ever convinced of the need for it, made several speeches
on the subject in the next few years.

Gladstone was a central figure in the highly involved business of
reforming Oxford, but the details of it fit more appropriately into
the story of the university than into his biography. He had been
hotly opposed to the appointment of a royal commission to inquire
into the affairs of the university when Russell proposed it in 1850:
'no worse case was ever more strongly argued' is Morley's comment.
The general development of his views and his experience of affairs
at Oxford had since convinced him that reform could no longer
be resisted. The opposition to the royal commission and the outcry
on the publication of its report in May 1852 had been led by the
same Heads of Houses, gathered together in the Hebdomadal
Board, who had fought Gladstone in three electoral contests.
Gladstone had convinced himself by the end of 1852 that parliamentary intervention, which he had earlier regarded as an evil, had
become necessary and he intimated that he would give it his support.
The power of his influence was by this time well appreciated by
friend and foe alike. When the process of consultation and preparation
for a bill began in December 1853 Gladstone toyed with resigning
his Oxford seat in order to give himself greater freedom of action.
Northcote told him, 'A member elected by the anti-hebdomadal
interest, need not quit his post because he takes part in an anti-
hebdomadal measure.' The burden of correspondence and consultation involved in the Oxford bill would have more than occupied
any normal energetic man, yet Gladstone coped with it while also
preparing the national finances for war. The bill was a compromise
between a draft prepared by Jowett, who all along had been a
driving force for reform at Oxford, and one prepared by Gladstone
himself. Features which owe their origin particularly to Gladstone

were the appointment of parliamentary commissioners to assent to and frame new statutes and the establishment of private halls to provide less expensive education for a larger student body.

During its passage through Parliament the bill suffered a number of amendments in a conservative sense, some from friends of Gladstone's, such as Sir William Heathcote and Roundell Palmer, later Lord Selborne. Heathcote was about to join Gladstone in the representation of the university in place of Sir Robert Inglis and the Gladstonian influence had been used to bring this about. There was a notable intervention by Disraeli in the debates. Speaking about the creation of more professorships, a proposal that owed much to comparisons with German universities, he argued that the talent that in Germany might go into academic life was in England accustomed to going into politics:

> . . . if we have not those profound professors in England, it is because the character of this country is different. . . We are a nation of action . . . however you may increase the rewards of professors – though you may give them £2000 instead of £200 . . . men will look to the House of Commons and not to professors' chairs in the universities.[8]

Small wonder that Gladstone, who had laboured prodigiously on the reform of Oxford, found Disraeli's approach, on this as on other occasions, incurably flippant. Much the most important change made to the bill on the way through Parliament was the provision enabling Dissenters to matriculate and graduate. The Nonconformists were at this time seriously at loggerheads with the coalition. None of their representatives had been included in the government; on a number of minor issues the government had shown that it had no intention of weakening Anglican privileges. Yet the *Census of religious worship* had just shown that about half the churchgoing population were Dissenters. Bright called the Oxford bill 'pusillanimous and tinkering' and a great dissenting agitation was set on foot. The amendments admitting Nonconformists were carried against the government by a combination of Conservatives, Liberals and Radicals. Gladstone opposed these amendments but his position was equivocal. He did not want so profound a change to be imposed on the university from without and for tactical reasons also he thought it necessary to exclude the question of the Dissenters from the bill. On the other hand he was no longer opposed to their admission on principle, provided the teaching and government of the university remained firmly in Anglican hands. In general, the 1854 bill marks a milestone in the modernization of Oxford.

In the autumn of 1854 disappointment over the progress of the campaign in the Crimea cast its shadow over the government. Gladstone was not immediately involved in the problems of military administration that moved into the forefront of public debate. It was, however, relevant to the eventual break-up of the coalition that in the second half of 1854 his relations with Lord John Russell grew very strained. They had collaborated on the Oxford bill which had been introduced in the Commons by Lord John. Then Gladstone, like many of his colleagues, became irritated by Russell's unsatisfied ambition and concern for his *amour-propre* as party leader and ex-prime minister. Lord John had hoped to take Aberdeen's place at a much earlier stage and it still had not happened. It was generally felt that Lady Russell was pushing her husband and Gladstone expressed himself with rare venom on this point:

. . . the depths of a certain woman's restlessness and folly, or the amount of influence it might exercise on the man who for the country's misfortune is her husband, in bringing him both to a pitch of wilfulness and to an abyss of vacillation and infirmity of purpose, which are in themselves a chapter in the history of human nature.[9]

At this time Gladstone and Lord John were also fighting a prolonged battle over an official, T. F. Kennedy, whom the Chancellor of the Exchequer had to dismiss from his post as Commissioner of Woods and Forests and whom Russell defended as a Whig appointment. In the late autumn of 1854 Lord John's resignation over the Kennedy affair seemed likely and Gladstone would have been happy to see him go. Aberdeen took a calmer view and tried to keep Russell in the government, fearing the consequences of his departure. Arthur Gordon, Aberdeen's youngest son, noted in his diary: 'Gladstone, eager and impulsive, is really anxious for a rupture with Lord John . . . there is no *perspective* in his views. All objects, great and small, are on one plane with him, and consequently the tiniest sometimes assume the largest dimensions.'[10] A larger cause of friction soon came along: Russell became, no doubt rightly, very concerned about the state of the army and the military administrative machine; he attacked the Duke of Newcastle in particular and wanted him replaced, oddly enough, in view of past quarrels, by Palmerston. He also wanted to end the division of responsibility between the Secretary of State for War and the Colonies and the Secretary at War. Aberdeen still kept him from resigning; but when Roebuck moved his motion for a committee of inquiry on the conduct of the war in January 1855 Russell suddenly bolted from the government. A few days later Aberdeen's ministry was defeated on Roebuck's motion. It fell to Gladstone to make one of the main speeches in defence of the government and he can have had few less congenial tasks. He had to deal with details of military equipment which were entirely outside his normal fields of interest, but he mastered this alien subject with his accustomed thoroughness. It was to no avail.

A government crisis of unusual complexity now ensued, which would not have been out of place in the French Third or Fourth Republic. The Queen was led to complain that she alone was unable to resign when faced with the apparent reluctance of so many of her ministers to retain or assume the burdens of office. On Aberdeen's advice the Queen first called on Derby to form a government – it was after all the Derbyites who had supplied the bulk of the votes that brought the Aberdeen coalition down. Derby's weakness was that he had no stable parliamentary majority unless he could get the support of the Peelites and other groups; that he had, apart from Disraeli who was still distrusted, hardly any ministerial talent; and that the country was clamouring for Palmerston as the man best fitted to conduct the war. Derby consequently asked Palmerston to join his government and to persuade Gladstone and Sidney Herbert to join also. Palmerston had little incentive to comply with the request, for he knew that if he waited long enough the Queen would have to turn to him. Gladstone still felt some inclination to return to his old political moorings, but he did not want to become separated from other Peelites such as Graham and now had a strong sense of loyalty to Aberdeen. Viewing the situation in retrospect at the end of his life he wrote:

> A strong sentiment of revulsion from Disraeli personally, a sentiment quite distinct from that of dislike, was alone sufficient to deter me absolutely from a merely personal and separate reunion; besides which there would have been no power, unless in company, to give to Conservatism a liberal bias in conformity with the traditions of Peel.

Much about Derby's Conservative party, though perhaps not Derby himself, had no longer been congenial to Gladstone in 1852; after another two years as the protagonist of Peelite financial and administrative policies he had moved even further away from it. For many Tories it was a mutual antagonism: at a party meeting held at a later stage of this ministerial crisis, Lord Derby was greeted by cries of 'No Puseyites; no papists!' and it was estimated that if Gladstone joined Derby up to a hundred Conservatives would have defected. As it was, the decision not to join Derby was largely taken out of his hands by Palmerston. It was an important point in Gladstone's career: Conservative reunion had once more revealed itself as impracticable for him and it was becoming a less and less convincing alternative. Derby was much blamed, not least by Disraeli, for giving up so easily and Gladstone agreed with this judgement in retrospect. It was the occasion when he held out a hand in sympathy to Disraeli whose disappointment had been shattering. Derby would in fact have found it difficult to form a government of which he could have been the effective master.

After Derby's failure the 'andirivieni', as Gladstone called it, went on. The Queen consulted Lord Lansdowne, Whig leader in the Lords. Gladstone always considered it one of his greatest errors, perhaps the greatest error he ever committed, that he did not support Lansdowne and encourage him to accept the Queen's commission. He would have made a Prime Minister more to his liking than Palmerston. Then it was Lord John Russell's turn, but no one except himself thought he had a chance. He came to Gladstone 'his hat shaking in his hand' – but he got a refusal. So it was finally Palmerston's turn. Gladstone was very reluctant to join. To Sidney Herbert, who was somewhat less reluctant, he made the significant remark: '. . . I used to debate with Newcastle, who used to argue that we should grow into the natural leaders of the liberal party. I said, it is now plain this will not be; we get on very well with the independent liberals, but the whigs stand as an opaque body between us and them. . .' The pressure of public opinion to join the patriotic minister for whom all were calling in the middle of a war bore heavily upon the Peelites, and finally they allowed themselves to be persuaded by Aberdeen. For Gladstone, Herbert and Graham, it lasted no more than a fortnight. When Palmerston decided to accept Roebuck's proposed committee of inquiry they resigned from a position that had been uncomfortable for them all along. Gladstone was back in the wilderness and the next four years were to be politically the most perplexing of his life.

In the short term Gladstone and his two Peelite colleagues came in for much abuse. They had deserted the ship in time of danger; their in–out performance made them look ridiculous. Much of the abuse concentrated on Gladstone: he was the ablest Peelite with the greatest potential for the future. The combination of outstanding ability, tender conscience, casuistry and complexity made an irresistible target. The Peelites were more than ever fragmented: Newcastle had fallen victim to the blunders of the Crimea, Argyll and Canning remained in Palmerston's government. The course of the war and foreign policy thereafter created a gulf between Palmer-

ston and Gladstone, though the Italian question was in the end the
key to their reunion. The war, foreign affairs, finance and administrative reform moved Gladstone closer to the Manchester School,
to Cobden and to Bright. In common with them he suffered the
searing experience of being universally unpopular. 'It is hardly
possible to believe one is not the greatest scoundrel on earth, when
one is assured of it from all sides on such excellent authority . . .,'
he wrote to Aberdeen in August 1855. Bright urged Gladstone to
make a new start 'in a Liberal and useful public career'. Religion
still kept Gladstone close to some Tories, for example to his fellow
member for Oxford, Sir William Heathcote, whose seat at Hursley
in Hampshire, where Keble was Vicar, was a meeting-place for
Tractarians and other High Anglicans. Gladstone had much affinity
with Derby and his revulsion from Disraeli was as deep as ever.
In all this confusion of contradictory pulls Gladstone felt the need
for a return to a two-party system. He told the Queen just before
his resignation in 1855 that 'she would have little peace and comfort
in these matters, until parliament should have returned to its old
organization in two political parties'. He also felt the pull of political
ambition and the frustration of seeing his influence on affairs reduced;
his many other interests, literary, ecclesiastical and his growing
family, could not make up for the exhilaration of mastering great
affairs of state. At times there was something feverish about the
way in which he took up an issue and expended himself upon it,
casting prudence to the winds; it was the impulsive, volcanic
side of his nature which to many observers indicated a lack of judgement.

The first such issue was the continuation of the war in the summer
of 1855. He felt the legitimate object of the war, warning Russia
off the Ottoman Empire, had been attained early in 1855 when
Nicholas I accepted the Vienna points, abrogating among other
things the Russian claim to a protectorate over the Christian subjects
of the Sultan. Gladstone, like Cobden and Bright, and eventually
Russell who resigned from the government in July 1855, wanted a
compromise peace. He made two major speeches on the subject, in
May and August 1855, as a result of which much of the press and
public opinion bracketed him with Cobden and Bright as traitors.
After the August speech Bright wrote in his diary: 'Gladstone
made a speech of the highest class, proving his superiority over all
other men in the House.' Even some of his Peelite colleagues,
notably Sidney Herbert, thought he had gone too far and would have
retained more influence with Palmerston if his attack had been more

moderate. If there were three pillars of Gladstonian liberalism, peace, retrenchment and reform, the first two were now firmly in place.

Derby made two approaches to Gladstone in 1856 in the spring and at the end of the year. The second of these, ahead of the 1857 session, was the more important. It produced common action on the budget brought by Cornewall Lewis and much rumour of a junction. The budget kindled all Gladstone's ardour for retrenchment and economy, but his indignation was if anything overdone. Shortly afterwards he was again brought to boiling-point over Palmerston's Chinese policy, a subject which had seen his first major excursion into foreign affairs seventeen years earlier. On this occasion he acted in concert with Cobden and Derby; Disraeli and Lord John Russell joined them in the same lobby. Representatives of the Tory High Church party, for instance Lord Robert Cecil, spoke against Palmerston. It was, however, significant that a considerable number of Tories, mostly back-benchers of the silent kind, preferred Palmerston's rumbustious patriotism to the prescriptions of their own more pacific chiefs. Even so Palmerston was beaten by sixteen votes. He went to the country and he had judged its mood better than the establishment of party leaders in Parliament. The result of this election was curiously ambivalent: it was a triumph for Palmerston, but it was also a victory for liberalism. Palmerston was not only a patriot, he was also still seen as a liberal: in many places the provincial business community supported him strongly. Cobden, Bright and Milner-Gibson lost their seats, because their stand over the Crimean War had made them personally unpopular. But the voting power of the Dissenters, now at the zenith of their strength, made itself felt in many constituencies and through organizations like the Liberation Society. Thus the great Palmerstonian majority was not just the product of a chauvinistic breeze, but of forces that were to make the Gladstonian Liberal party a decade later. Gladstone himself did not realize this yet. At Oxford he had no contest to face that year; the evangelical party, who were happy with Palmerston, were unable to rouse enough enthusiasm for their candidate to make it a contest; the High Church party were more content with Gladstone than they had been for some time. The election as a whole seemed to Gladstone almost an unmitigated disaster: Palmerstonianism triumphant, the Peelites an irrelevant rump, men of the Manchester school, with whom he had discovered some affinities, defeated. Even the Derbyites had on balance suffered by their association with the Peelites immediately before the election and by the talk of reunion. A country Tory M.P. wrote to Colonel Taylor, the Conservative Whip: 'Taking the feelings of the Constituency as to "leaders", I may put them: "Palmerston", "Derby" (not popular), "D'Israeli" (unpopular), "Lord John" (very unpopular), "Gladstone" (extremely unpopular) . . .'[11]

In the new Parliament another of those matters cropped up that drew Gladstone like a moth to a lighted candle – the Matrimonial Causes Bill. Up to this time divorce for most matrimonial offences was possible only through a private act of Parliament and this procedure was available only to the wealthy. This bill, based on the report of a royal commission, withdrew matrimonial jurisdiction from the ecclesiastical courts to a newly established Divorce Court. One of its flaws was that a husband could get a divorce for adultery only, while the wife had also to prove some other offence such as cruelty or desertion. The bill passed the House of Lords where the Archbishop of Canterbury supported it, but when it reached the Commons Gladstone and a number of other High Churchmen fought it tenaciously. It touched all Gladstone's old feelings about the position of the Church and called forth all his great resources of erudition and casuistry. In an article in the *Quarterly* he wrote at this time: 'It seems to be a sign of the general decay of this spirit of traditionary discipline in our own day, that so determined an assault should have been made upon a part of the Levitical Prohibitions, now forming the basis of our ecclesiastical law.'[12] Gladstone used parliamentary delaying tactics on this bill, a foretaste of what he was to experience from the Irish Nationalists a generation later. There were eighteen long sittings in the exceptionally hot summer of 1857. Gladstone, aged forty-seven, was unable to wear down Palmerston, aged seventy-three, who on this, as on some other matters, was thoroughly liberal. Gladstone's Peelite friends were disturbed about this clash with the Prime Minister, which did not fit into the political pattern as they saw it evolving. If they did not join with Palmerston soon, when he seemed set for many years in office, they would be in the wilderness forever. For the public such an exhibition could only evoke old prejudices about the Peelites as a Puseyite coterie. Such considerations meant nothing to Gladstone when he was roused.

During this searing and frustrating period of his life, when his political path was so unclear, Gladstone devoted much time to his Homeric studies, and in 1858 he published three volumes on *Homer and the Homeric Age*. It was an attempt to relate Greek civilization, for which he had a deep reverence, to the story of Christian revelation. To modern scientific scholarship many of Gladstone's ideas and linkages seem sheer fantasy, bordering on the ridiculous, as quixotic as his attempt to keep divorce within the ecclesiastical law in a secular age. On the other hand the work shows the breadth of Gladstone's personality: he is able to overcome frustration in one sphere by creative work in another. It shows his deep sense of the continuity and universality of European civilization; it also shows that the great battle between religion and science, natural or historical, which increasingly threatened Victorian faith was to Gladstone no battle at all.

In February 1858 the government was unexpectedly defeated over the Conspiracy to Murder Bill, arising out of the Orsini case. Palmerston was hoist with his own petard and the chauvinism he had so often appealed to turned against him. He had already strained his credit by appointing the disreputable Lord Clanricarde as Lord Privy Seal. Radicals like Bright and Milner-Gibson now taunted him with having truckled to the French and Disraeli, with characteristic opportunism, joined them in voting Palmerston out. Gladstone also voted against the bill because he felt that the government had not firmly rejected the accusation of complicity in assassination. Once more the ball was in Lord Derby's court and this time, as in 1852, he formed a minority administration. It was in a very weak position, being outnumbered in the House by three to two, and there was little prospect that an election would alter this. Derby made at least two more efforts to get Gladstone, his 'half-regained Eurydice', over to his side: one on the formation of the Conservative government, and a second three months later, in May 1858, when a Cabinet vacancy occurred. Gladstone on both occasions refused, giving as his main reason that he could not alone make such a move without his Peelite colleagues. On the first occasion he received a remarkable letter from Bright, with whom he did not have any close relations at this time, warning him against joining the Derby ministry, 'an inevitable failure', while 'if you remain on our side of the House . . . I know nothing that can prevent your being prime minister . . . I think I am not mistaken in the opinion I have formed of the direction in which your views have for some years been tending.' Bright was thus foreseeing the role that Gladstone would some years hence play in a left-of-centre combination.

Derby's second offer, in May 1858, was remarkable for an exchange of letters between Disraeli and Gladstone. Disraeli had offered to stand down from the leadership of the House in favour of Graham.

When this failed to attract any Peelites, he made a direct appeal to Gladstone:

> Mr Canning was superior to Lord Castlereagh in capacity, in acquirement, in eloquence, but he joined Lord C. when Lord C. was Liverpool's lieutenant . . . it certainly terminated very gloriously for Mr Canning. I may be removed from the scene, or I may wish to be removed from the scene. Every man performs his office and there is a power, greater than ourselves, that disposes of all this . . .

Even this invocation of the Almighty did not draw Mr Gladstone.

Why did Gladstone never return again to the Conservatives once he had been a member of the Aberdeen coalition? The position of Disraeli, more and more firmly entrenched, was certainly one important reason, although Gladstone would never fully admit it. Another reason was that there was in fact much hostility to Gladstone among back-bench Tories, on account of his religious views, his economic liberalism and the whole ethos of his personality. It was a mutual antagonism. After the 1857 election it was, moreover, obvious that the Conservatives had no hope of a stable majority for a long time. Ideologically Gladstone was closer to Derby than to Palmerston, but apart from this the ideological choice was finely balanced. In 1856 Gladstone told Elwin, the editor of the *Quarterly*:

> There is a policy going a-begging; the general policy that Sir Robert Peel in 1841 took office to support – the policy of peace abroad, of economy, of financial equilibrium, of steady resistance to abuses, and promotion of practical improvements at home, with a disinclination to questions of reform gratuitously raised.

This was Gladstone's position throughout the 1850s and beyond. It was therefore important to him, not least because of his strict sense of personal loyalty, to remain in step with the dwindling band of Peelites. Both Herbert and Graham had moved closer to Russell, so that Conservative reunion was no longer a realistic possibility for them; in fact, apart from residual personal loyalties, the Peelites were all at sixes and sevens. What mattered least of all was the position outside Parliament. Gladstone had little contact with the groups and interests, many of them Nonconformist, that were marshalled behind the Whig–Liberal–Radical combination in Parliament – this contact, in many ways his decisive contribution to the formation of the Gladstonian Liberal party, was yet to come. He had no connection with the groups behind the Tory party either, unless one counts his constituents at Oxford and the High Church party or his role as a landowner in Flintshire. It is interesting to reflect that if British politics had not been so firmly focused on

Parliament as they were at least until 1867, Gladstone might not have been so important nor so assiduously courted. Everybody wanted him because of his unequalled gifts as a parliamentarian.

Yet there were voices already writing him off. He was nearly fifty and however powerful as a speaker in the House of Commons he seemed to have lost his way. Nothing is more highly prized in English politicians than judgement. About Gladstone it was said, as it was about Winston Churchill two or three generations later, that he lacked it. He seemed to tilt at windmills, then offer incomprehensible explanations for doing so. He seemed unable to estimate how his actions would strike ordinary men with all their prejudices and foibles. Would he be a magnificent failure?

6

GETTING
UNMUZZLED
1858–65

Gladstone found himself unable to accept office in Derby's government, but he was prepared to undertake one of the most quixotic missions of his career on behalf of that ministry. In November 1858 Sir Edward Bulwer-Lytton, Colonial Secretary and one of two romantic novelists in Derby's government, sent him to the Ionian Islands as Lord High Commissioner Extraordinary. In 1815 these islands had been united into a nominally independent state under a British protectorate; ever since the backwash of the 1848 revolutions hit them they were in a disturbed state and the islanders were demanding union with Greece. Although the British involvement had been mostly a burden, there was reluctance to give it up, because the islands were considered of some strategic importance and their return to Greece might cause international complications. The task was therefore to devise a system of government for these islands that would reconcile their 250,000 inhabitants to continued British control. It was a well-nigh impossible task and it is a measure of Gladstone's eager innocence that he took it on. Bulwer-Lytton and Disraeli were naturally glad to be able to involve him in some official connection with the Conservative government. Gladstone, with his Homeric passion, felt the call of Greece, and the absence of constructive political work had been telling on him. He also had private reasons for going – Catherine's health had suffered from the shock of the death of her sister, Lady Lyttelton. The press greeted the news of Gladstone's appointment and reports of his activities in the islands with ridicule. It all added to his by now widely accepted image of a man of high intellectual ability devoid of practical judgement and side-tracked by quixotic enthusiasms. Sidney Herbert wrote to Graham: 'He really is not safe to go about out of Lord Aberdeen's room. It is heartbreaking to see him throwing so much away.'[1]

For some three months Gladstone and his entourage enjoyed the delights of colonial eminence. There were levees, balls, openings of assemblies, a visit to a feudal Albanian chieftain, delegations from bishops and clergy. Lord Aberdeen's son, later Lord Stanmore, accompanied Gladstone as private secretary and left a vivid account of the proceedings. The details of the political problem facing Gladstone need not detain us and he entirely failed to find a solution. He had a naïve belief that the apparatus of a liberal constitutional state was suitable to these wild and primitive islands; in spite of his passionate concern for the Italian *risorgimento* he as yet failed to understand the force of nationalism. Four years later the islands were in fact united with Greece.

Gladstone returned to England in March 1859. The Conservatives were just in the process of trying to pass their own Reform Bill through the House. It was an attempt to catch the wind of reform and doing it in such a way that the Conservative party would reap an incidental advantage, for example by transferring the 40s. freeholders in boroughs from the county to the borough electorate and by Disraeli's 'fancy franchises'. Gladstone was in principle opposed to electoral reform in the 1850s, though prepared to tolerate a small amount of it. It was said that his absence on the Ionian mission was a convenient excuse for not taking a position on this bill, but in the end he voted for the government and made a speech in which he somewhat irrelevantly praised the proprietary borough system. It was an amendment by Lord John Russell which skilfully brought together the Radicals, who thought the reform insufficient, and the Whigs, who either thought it too much or too little or too much weighted in favour of the Tories. Derby was defeated at the end of March 1859 and managed to get a dissolution from the Queen, in spite of the fact that this Parliament was only two years old.

In the election not only reform but the Italian crisis was an issue. Derby and his colleagues were judged to be pro-Austrian, though in fact they were merely cautious; Palmerston and Russell explicitly supported Italian unification. Gladstone was unopposed at Oxford. The Conservatives somewhat improved their position, but they still had no independent majority. Their survival in office depended on drawing over other support, and Disraeli made a last effort to attract Palmerston as well as Gladstone. It was in vain. The really important development was the growing consolidation on the Whig–Liberal side. The long-standing feud between Russell and Palmerston was healing and just before the first vital vote in the new Parliament there was the famous meeting at Willis's Rooms on 6 June, which can be seen as the foundation of the modern Liberal party. Willis's had once been Almack's, the club where Regency society, including Palmerston, disported themselves. Palmerston helped Lord John Russell on to the platform and John Bright spoke third. The meeting at Willis's was in fact no more than an incident in the emergence of the Liberal party; but English political parties are in the first instance parliamentary phenomena whose ramifications stretch out into the country. The significance of the meeting at Willis's should therefore not be underestimated. A few days later the Derby government was defeated by thirteen votes. Gladstone, curiously enough, was one of the twenty or so independent members who supported the government. He explained the tortuous reasoning behind his vote to his friend Sidney Herbert:

. . . it will not be pleasant to have to give a vote which will appear to mean confidence in the Government. . . Such, however, seems likely to be my fate. For I have not brought myself to think that a man who has been acting as I have wholly out of concert with Opposition, can safely, I would almost say honourably, *enter* Opposition, so to speak, by a vote of such sweeping and strong condemnation as a vote of no confidence must always be, and, of course, intended for the resumption of office.[2]

Yet a few days later Gladstone accepted office as Chancellor of the Exchequer from Palmerston, who had in the meantime emerged as Prime Minister.

Gladstone was emphatic, perhaps a little overemphatic, that he never had 'an easier question to determine than when I was asked to join the government'. More than he cared to admit he was now afraid of being left out in the cold – 'the one remaining Ishmael in the House of Commons'. His acceptance of the Ionian commission showed how desperate he was was to get back into harness. Writing a few years later he said:

> I felt sure that in finance there was still much useful work to be done. I was desirous to co-operate in settling the question of the franchise, and failed to anticipate the disaster it was to undergo. My friends were enlisted, or I knew would enlist: Sir James Graham indeed declining office, but taking his position in the party. And the overwhelming interest . . . of the Italian question . . . joined to my entire mistrust of the former government in relation to it, led me to decide without one moment's hesitation. . .

No doubt the Italian question, so critical in the summer of 1859, was an important factor; and Gladstone could also tell himself that he was not taking a new step: after all, he had held office briefly under Palmerston in 1855. Perhaps he would still have preferred a Derby–Palmerston government, with himself a member and Disraeli suitably relegated. The 1859 combination was more left-ward orientated than Palmerston's 1855 government, which was overshadowed by his personal reputation as a war leader. In 1859 two Radicals of long standing, albeit with aristocratic connections, Milner-Gibson and Villiers, were given office. Cobden was offered the Board of Trade, but he felt that his long opposition to Palmerston on foreign policy made it impossible for him to join. Only Bright was excluded, because to Palmerston's mind his reform agitation had become too much coloured by attacks on 'classes' and established institutions. The composition of the government was an earnest of the intention to tackle the reform question; Gladstone professed that he wanted to see it settled, but it is certain that he did not want to go anything like as far as Bright and many Radicals. The fact was that Gladstone owed the offer of office entirely to his parliamentary standing and if he had turned it down he would have been more isolated than ever. As he told Sir William Heathcote, he had no claims on the Liberal party, having normally voted with Derby; his friends had restrained him from Conservative reunion, therefore he had now to go along with them in Liberal junction.

Gladstone's explanation did not satisfy Oxford. Palmerston was anathema to the High Church party – his liberal and evangelical church appointments, his energetic espousal of the Divorce Bill and his whole personality were offensive to them. On his appointment as Chancellor Gladstone was thus suddenly confronted with yet another contest at Oxford. The opposition found a candidate whose Tory credentials were unexceptionable – Lord Chandos, the son of the now bankrupt Duke of Buckingham, the erstwhile leader of the agriculturalists. Gladstone won by a bigger margin than in 1853, for the Tractarian remnant remained loyal to him; his presence in Palmerston's government swung the evangelicals behind him and his Liberal support was increasing. On the other hand there was some evidence that his following among recent graduates was declining. Already in 1857 Gladstone had declared that he was willing to fight only one more contest at Oxford and there was a growing impression following the 1859 contest that he would seek another constituency.

A chance to carry on the Peelite scheme for the finance of the nation was one of the attractions of office for Gladstone. It was one of his great passions, as his attack on Cornewall Lewis in 1857 had shown. It was bound up with other aspects of Peel's legacy – a restrained foreign policy and limits on defence spending. The experience of the Crimean War and Palmerstonian foreign policy had hardened Gladstone's convictions in this respect, so that his vision of world order was not far removed from that of Cobden and Bright. It was not, certainly not with Cobden, a negative isolationist vision: Bright and Cobden had grasped that in the industrial age the strength of a nation lay in its economic and not in its military potential.[3] Gladstone had in addition the strong sense of European civilization as a unity which arose from his deep studies and understanding of the classical past and of Christianity and the churches. It was almost inevitable therefore that the thrust of Gladstone's political dynamic should bring him into collision with Palmerston and to a lesser extent Russell, and should move him closer to Cobden and Bright and the whole spectrum of politics of which they were the most conspicuous representatives. Only one major issue initially cut across this pattern – Italy, the cause which had enabled Gladstone's conscience to permit the junction with Palmerston. Later the American Civil War separated Gladstone from Cobden and Bright – here he had none of their passionate conviction that justice was on the side of the North. It surprised the world that Gladstone, with his tender conscience, did not resign from the Palmerston government, although he jokingly said that he always took the precaution of carrying a letter of resignation in his wallet. But he did not resign; again his detractors called his displays of conscience a hypocritical cover for his real love of office and power. In fact, Gladstone did not at this time or later share the sometimes facile internationalism of men like Bright; he objected to Palmerston's playing to the gallery by public bluster, but behind the scenes the Prime Minister was a skilful and cautious diplomatist; retrenchment was Gladstone's overriding objective.

In the summer of 1859, immediately after he took office, Gladstone had introduced an interim budget based on the situation left by his predecessor. There was a deficit of nearly £5 million, partly caused by the war in China. In accordance with his principles Gladstone refused to meet this deficit by borrowing or increases in indirect taxation. Instead he raised the income tax from 5*d.* to 9*d.* and thereby created the basis from which he could put his own ideas into operation. It was at this point, in September 1859, that an initiative by Cobden gave him a new opportunity. Cobden had for a long time cherished the idea of a commerical treaty based on free-trade principles between Britain and France, the two leading trading nations of Europe. Bright had brought the idea up again in a Commons speech in July 1859 when, following the peace of Villa-franca, there were the beginnings of another anti-French outburst. In France Michel Chevalier, a follower of Saint-Simon, thought the time was ripe for action and that the proposition could be made palatable to the Emperor. He wrote to Cobden, who realized that Gladstone was the one major figure in the Cabinet who might be sympathetic to the idea. He paid him a visit at Hawarden and during a stroll in the garden put the suggestion of an Anglo-French treaty. It fell on fertile ground. Gladstone was not only anticipating a budget surplus the following year which he was hoping to use for another assault on remaining tariff duties; he was as appalled as Cobden by the rising tide of anti-French hysteria and an opening up of trade would be an admirable way of counteracting it.[4] Gladstone and Cobden between them secured the reluctant consent of Palmerston and Russell to an unofficial approach to the French government. It was to be made by Cobden himself, who was planning to spend part of the winter in Paris. The government depended on Radical votes and Palmerston could therefore not afford to cold-shoulder Cobden. In spite of all obstacles the unofficial negotiations in Paris, beginning with an interview between Cobden and Napoleon, quickly reached the point where they could be given official status, and the treaty was signed in January 1860. The French removed all obsolete prohibitions on the import of British goods and reduced tariffs on a wide range of them. Britain promised to reduce duties on French brandy and wines and the abolition of all remaining tariffs on manufactured goods. The treaty provided only an outline, and Cobden himself engaged in prolonged negotiations in 1860 to make it effective against the many vested interests still clinging to protection, particularly in France. It was an important step in bringing the international movement for free trade to a climax in the 1860s. Unfortunately for those who saw free trade as the key to an era of international concord, national rivalries and war were not to be so easily set aside by trade.

The negotiations for the treaty were conducted to an accompaniment of anti-French feeling and it was Gladstone's view that 'the choice lay between the Cobden treaty and not the certainty, but the high probability of a war'. It was in a way fortunate for Palmerston that the French abandoned the work of Italian unification prematurely at Villafranca, otherwise it would have become extremely difficult to be simultaneously pro-Italian and anti-French. Throughout the closing months of 1859 and into the summer of 1860 Gladstone fought a hard battle in the Cabinet against what he considered excessive defence spending: Cobden, still negotiating in Paris, fed him with information designed to show that the French were not preparing war. Many times Gladstone was on the point of resigning; but he knew that he had insufficient weight to bring the government down and for the sake of being able to carry out his grand financial design he stayed on. He was more realistic than Cobden and Bright; they were disappointed in him and he considered their aims as impractical. In 1862 Gladstone wrote to Palmerston: 'In all good humour, I prefer not being classed with Mr Bright or even Mr Cobden . . .'[5]

The commercial treaty with France became part of the great budget scheme of 1860. Two other budgetary events made it a year of exceptional importance: a reduction in the interest on the National Debt made an additional £2 million available; on the other hand the income tax, bringing in £12 million, was about to lapse unless renewed. Gladstone made three major proposals: in addition to the remission of customs duties arising out of the French treaty, he provided for the abolition of tariffs on nearly 400 articles and thus left only about fifteen articles of any importance subject to duty. The move towards free trade was therefore virtually completed. His second main proposal was to renew the income tax and raise it another penny to 10*d*. He explained in his budget statement why the scheme to abolish the income tax, which he had launched seven years earlier, had failed and laid the blame fairly and squarely on the growth of expenditure, particularly for defence and war. Thirdly, and this proved to be the most controversial of his proposals in 1860, he abolished the excise duty on paper. 'Taxes on knowledge' had for long been an emotive cry and it had been an important aim of radical movements at least since 1815 to abolish them. In addition, this part of Gladstone's budget became entangled in a constitutional conflict between the two Houses of Parliament. Gladstone in his budget statement gave mainly fiscal and practical reasons for the abolition of paper duty – the use of paper in various manufacturing processes, the need to revive small-scale rural paper-making, the difficulty of defining what paper was and how to collect the duty. His hope was that the abolition of the duty would help the cheaper type of book or periodical.

Gladstone put forward his budget proposals in a four-hour speech on 10 February 1860. The sense of drama was heightened by the fact that the statement had to be delayed for four days, because Gladstone fell seriously ill with bronchitis and was still looking pale and drawn when he finally spoke. Lord Robert Cecil wrote in the *Quarterly* of 'the heroic will that mastered even a rebellious uvula in the cause of duty'. The early date of the budget was due to the need to co-ordinate it with the French treaty. The speech was one of Gladstone's great political triumphs; an interesting part of it was his review of the growth of national wealth in recent years, which he attributed largely to freer trade, and his demonstration that national expenditure had increased even faster than wealth. The triumph was short-lived; as controversy began to focus on the paper duty Gladstone became unpopular in parliamentary and political circles, for the proposal was seen as a bare-faced attempt to pander to the Radicals. It was perhaps more than a symbolic gesture when at the end of March 1860 Gladstone resigned from the Carlton Club. On the other hand the French treaty was criticized not only by various vested interests but by some doctrinaire free-traders because it did not go far enough.

The budget did not have an easy passage. For a time it was in competition with the Reform Bill which Lord John Russell had waited for such a long time to enact. Although Gladstone wanted to see reform settled in a moderate way, he begged Lord John 'on my knees', to withdraw his bill, for it is a basic parliamentary rule 'never overlap business'. The Reform Bill died a natural death, for many on both sides of the House did not want it, but it held up the budget. On the paper duty abolition the government's majority dropped to nine and the stage was set for the big battle with the House of Lords. Palmerston wrote to Gladstone: 'You must be aware that your budget is not much liked in the House except by the comparatively small Band of Radicals below the gangway, who are thought to be your Inspirers in financial Matters . . .'[6] Palmerston had never liked the abolition of the paper duties and he told the Queen that the Lords would 'perform a good public service' if they rejected this proposal. When they did so Lady Palmerston, who was in the gallery, applauded.[7]

This was a constitutional crisis. The Radicals demanded that the bill should be sent back to the House of Lords a second time. Gladstone agreed with this, but the Cabinet adopted a compromise proposal that the action of the Lords should be referred to the Commons Committee of Privileges. When Palmerston moved the resolution to this effect 'his language . . . went near to the verge of saying, We mean nothing'. The discrepancy between the Prime Minister and his Chancellor was striking. The abolition of the paper duty could not be carried that year, but the House of Commons reaffirmed that it had the inviolable right to frame bills of supply. The paper duty abolition was proposed again in the 1861 budget and this time Gladstone adopted the device of putting all his financial proposals into a single bill, thus confronting the Lords with the need to accept or reject the budget in its entirety. This has been the practice ever since. Palmerston still opposed the paper duty abolition in 1861 and refused to make the budget a question of confidence. There was not to be another such clash between the two Houses of Parliament on finance till Lloyd George's budget of 1909. The whole train of events had identified Gladstone for a time with the Radicals; it was clearly seen that even the Whigs disliked him, let alone the Tories. His popularity was beginning to grow with the masses who were excluded from the *pays politique*.

While Gladstone and Palmerston were clashing over the paper duty, they were concurrently fighting the battle in the Cabinet over military expenditure. In this fight even Sidney Herbert, Gladstone's close friend, was opposed to him. The problem of the military threat occasioned a great deal of correspondence between Palmerston and Gladstone, in which the former put the case for national defence as a first priority, while the latter stressed the need to avoid panicking into excessive defence expenditure. Similar arguments are heard to this day when defence expenditure is under discussion. Up to 1862

Gladstone lost the battle over defence spending, but thereafter the tide turned. In 1861 total expenditure was £72 million, by 1865 it had dropped to £66 million. After reaching a peak of 10*d.* in the pound in the 1860 budget Gladstone was able to reduce income tax to 4*d.* in 1865. There were also improvements in the exemptions for lower incomes. There were further reductions in indirect taxation, which in most cases, owing to increases in consumption, led to no loss of revenue. Gladstone was particularly proud of having established the Post Office Savings Banks in 1863. It provided a ready means by which the ordinary man could save with full security, while at the same time making available to the national exchequer large sums of money independently of the City.

The passion with which Gladstone pursued his financial aims and the admiration which was lavished on his work both at home and abroad stemmed from a profound belief in the beneficence and inevitability of a free market economy. All shackles and imposts upon it must be removed and it must be allowed to operate on a worldwide scale; the state must provide the limited services which only it could furnish at the lowest possible cost. Gladstone's passion for economy and hatred of waste were not only deeply embedded in his character; it was a genuine fight for an orderly and clean administrative system when much of it was still encumbered by quaint and sometimes corrupt procedures. It was a passion that sometimes invited ridicule: when he went to Corfu in 1858 he had the address on the dispatch bag labels scratched out so that they could be used for the return to the Colonial Office – this was typical of his inordinate attention to small detail when it came to economy. But to the end of his life he was proud of his drive for public economy, reduced and rationalized taxation: thereby he had made life richer and fuller for all classes of the community. In his social philosophy Gladstone was neither an interventionist nor an egalitarian. Society with its multifarious classes and conditions of men could not be altered by a fiat from above or below. A man could raise himself by his own efforts, but there would be no moral benefit to him if he was raised by an outside agency. Gladstone was fully aware of the abject poverty that existed in many places. His work for prostitutes brought him into contact with social degradation; particularly in the 1860s his wife, with his help, developed her charitable work in many directions, orphans, the homeless in London, victims of the Lancashire cotton famine and the East End cholera. Many poor children spent periods of recuperation at Hawarden.[8] But such evils were endemic in the human condition; Gladstone hoped that the progress of industry and commerce, of which he was also fully aware and which roused his imagination, would gradually reduce such evils. But he was also suspicious of the greed and self-interest of industrialists and moneyed men – he had seen so much of it at the Board of Trade and at the Treasury. There must be justice – it was just that the poorer classes should bear their fair share of taxation, but it was unjust that vested interests should be given special protection by the state. In his 1863 budget he proposed to apply income tax to the income of charitable endowments. This aroused a storm of protest and the proposal had in fact to be withdrawn; but in defence of it he made one of his most admired speeches in which he argued that it was unjust to give privileges to endowments which benefited a select number of people at the expense of all. It was general principles of morality and justice that he sought to apply by the use of his powerful logical faculty to specific cases.

Finance and foreign policy moved Gladstone closer to the assorted forces and classes which took up the left in the British political spectrum. As so often in his career what he said and did was taken in a wider and more all-embracing sense than he meant. His attitude on the American Civil War, which now loomed large over British domestic and foreign affairs, showed that he had not moved as far and as fast as his friends and his opponents believed. Gladstone naturally detested slavery, but like many did not see this as the main issue of the Civil War. Lincoln and the federal government themselves did, after all, with great care and deliberation establish the position that the war was about secession and not slavery. After the initial failure of the North to end the secession Gladstone soon came to believe that the attempt to crush the South was vain and that efforts should be made, possibly through British mediation, to end the sickening slaughter. Gladstone did not entirely share the outright emotional sympathy for the South which was common among the upper classes; nor did he really believe in Palmerston's policy of cautiously profiting from the weakness of a powerful state and potential rival. Gladstone never thought that a permanent division of the Union was a British interest and even feared that a truncated North would seek compensation by attacking Canada. On the other hand he did not accept the claim of the North to be fighting for a great moral cause and regarded anti-slavery as the motive of a self-righteous minority. Men on the left as well as on the right saw the Civil War as a struggle for the principles of popular government and a Northern victory as a powerful stimulant to democratic forces everywhere to be either desired or feared. This kind of argument made no appeal to Gladstone; as the war progressed his feelings were rather that the South was genuinely a nation struggling to be free. He was therefore undoubtedly out of step with a good many of the Radicals who had just hailed him over his financial policy; most conspicuously with Bright who became the most prominent propagandist for the Northern cause. But even Cobden was less clear-cut; at least until 1863 he was, for all his sympathy for the North and the Union, not certain that the North could win and thought that British policy would have to be based strictly on non-intervention. The working classes and the press catering for the working-class readership were in fact also divided; some of the older generation of leaders who had grown up in Chartist days were pro-Southern – their anti-capitalism and refusal to follow middle-class radicals like Bright and Cobden led them in that direction.[9] The claim so often made that Bright kept the Lancashire cotton operatives loyal to the Northern cause in spite of the cotton famine seems hard to substantiate; when the North was seen to be winning by 1863 sentiment naturally became more pro-Northern and by that time Indian cotton was easing the famine. Gladstone at the Exchequer was fully aware of the hardship caused by the cotton famine; he gave employment at Hawarden to out-of-work Lancashire operatives.

At the end of 1861 Gladstone played some part in moderating the tone of British protests at the removal of Mason and Sliddell, the two Southern agents, from the *Trent*. His deepest involvement came with the speech he made in Newcastle in October 1862, which contained the phrase that the leaders of the South had made an army and a navy 'and they have made what is more than either, they have made a nation'. At this time the fortunes of the South seemed to be at a peak and Lee was poised to invade the North. Napoleon III, who had much at stake in his Mexican adventure and whose policy was based on a permanent division of the Union, proposed joint Anglo-French mediation. If the North refused the offer, the way would be paved for full recognition of the South. In the Cabinet Russell and Gladstone were the strongest supporters of this proposal; Palmerston was sympathetic but cautious.

At this moment preparations were in hand for Gladstone to visit Newcastle. He was now enjoying an increasing popularity out-of-doors as a successful public financier who had the wellbeing of the people as a whole at heart. The fight over the paper duties had given him something of an image as a tribune of the people; it had in particular helped his credit with the provincial press, itself a pillar of the Radical movement. In April 1862 he had been loudly cheered when he visited the Manchester Exchange. There was a certain convergence of working- and middle-class aspirations at this time; politically conscious working men, largely drawn from the 'labour aristocracy', were prepared to accept the leadership of middle-class manufacturers like Cobden and Bright in causes such as support for the North in the Civil War. Gladstone was a major figure inside the political establishment who seemed worthy of their enthusiasm. Behind the scenes he was, however, leaning over backwards to reassure Palmerston, always deeply suspicious of the support his colleague was getting from the Radicals, that he was not going to Newcastle in the guise of a demagogue and that his visit had the blessing of the respectable men in the party. At the same time he was also telling Palmerston of his support for the mediation proposals: he felt that the South was militarily so successful that it would shortly find it more difficult to make peace on reasonable terms than the North had hitherto found it. He also felt that the suffering in Lancashire might shortly lead to an outbreak which would compromise the position of the British government as a disinterested mediator.

There was irony in the fact that Gladstone's Newcastle visit in 1862, his first major triumph as a popular hero, should become notorious for his pro-Southern *gaffe*. For such it was; in looking back on it thirty-five years later he described it as 'only a mistake but one of incredible grossness'. Adams, the American Minister in London who had devoted himself to the avoidance of a break between Britain and the North, nearly asked for his passport; everybody assumed that the British government was about to recognize the South. Gladstone came under fierce attack by the supporters of the North and was even accused of subscribing to Confederate Loans. Bright wrote to Charles Sumner, the Northern abolitionist leader:

> He has made a vile speech at Newcastle full of insulting pity for the North, and of praise and support for the South. He is as unstable as water in some things, he is for union and freedom in Italy, and for disunion and bondage in America . . . I did not expect that he would step out openly as the defender and eulogist of Jefferson Davis, and his fellow conspirators against God and man.[10]

What Gladstone said may have been indiscreet; but it represented his considered opinion at this time and he continued to put the case for mediation in the Cabinet, based on the assumption that the South had established itself and could not be crushed.

The speech did not diminish his popularity in Newcastle and on Tyneside. It was an area where shipbuilding was a major industry which for years had felt the pressure of American competition, and the workers in the shipyards were not sorry to see the North in trouble. His progress was triumphal: at Gateshead he 'went down the river at the head of a fleet of some twenty-five steamers, amidst the roar of guns and the banks lined or dotted above and below with multitudes of people', and so it was everywhere. When reminded of the occasion twenty years later by a reporter, Mrs Gladstone said: 'Oh, I shall never forget that day! It was the first time, you know, that *he* was received as he deserved to be.'[11] If Newcastle heralded the coming of the People's William, it also showed that the junction of Gladstone and popular Liberalism was not so much a marriage of like minds as a parallel movement of fairly distinct forces.

Gladstone was less often on the point of resigning after 1862 than he had been in the previous two years. He could never be on intimate terms with Palmerston, but whether they wished it or not these two very different horses were yoked to the same political wagon. Palmerston once told a friend, after he had suffered a bout of Gladstone's dialectics: 'You remember the anecdote about Pitt when he was asked what was the first quality of a statesman. He answered, "patience" – and the second? patience; and the third? patience. But Pitt did not know Gladstone.' From time to time there were squalls, as over the service estimates again in 1864, but in all differences there was a lack of acrimony. Ecclesiastical matters were less a cause of friction than they might have been. Palmerston relied almost entirely on Shaftesbury in making his church appointments – 'he does not know, in theology, Moses from Sydney Smith'. In consequence the Palmerston bishops were almost without exception Low Church and evangelical; but he also said to Shaftesbury, 'I should like to be a little cautious in the selection of bishops, so as not unnecessarily to vex my colleagues, some of whom are very high. It is a bore to see angry looks and have to answer questions of affected ignorance.' Gladstone was allowed to make suggestions, which were ignored, but this seemed to make him less inclined to quarrel: he proposed Samuel Wilberforce for the archbishopric of York in 1862, and the following year suggested two Tractarians, J.B.Mozley and R.W.Church, to succeed Stanley as Regius Professor of Ecclesiastical History at Oxford. Gladstone had some respect for Palmerston, his ability and even his liberalism; Palmerston probably disliked Gladstone rather strongly, but usually managed to hide it. He thought the best way to handle him was to bully him a bit; and after lengthy outpourings by Gladstone in Cabinet, Palmerston would say: 'Now my Lords and Gentlemen, let us go to business.'[12] Gladstone was on better terms with Russell than he used to be – his own liberal leanings made him appreciate the great service Lord John had rendered the cause of English political progress for over thirty years. If Russell had had the great abilities of Gladstone and had been less constricted by his background of Grand Whiggery he might have played, at a slightly earlier stage, the part that Gladstone came to play in launching the modern Liberal party.

In some ways Gladstone was more isolated from political friendships than he had been: his Peelite colleagues were dying, one by one, Aberdeen in 1860, Graham and Herbert in 1861 and Newcastle in 1864. Sidney Herbert's premature death hit him hardest, especially as it came after some disagreements over military estimates; for this charming aristocrat, who seemed to be in a special sense a vessel of grace, he had the kind of emotional attachment that in his youth he felt for Arthur Hallam. Another premature death was that of the Prince Consort who had long held Gladstone, with his high seriousness of purpose, in great regard. The Queen was deeply appreciative of a speech Gladstone made in memory of Prince Albert in Manchester in April 1862; he spoke of his 'strong grasp on practical life in all its forms', with which 'he united a habit of thought eminently philosophic; ever referring facts to their causes, and pursuing action to its consequences'. For a time the Queen had the same high opinion of Gladstone that the Prince Consort had had and it was only later that the relationship deteriorated. Gladstone found it hard to flatter and he could never approve of the Queen's Low Church views; at Balmoral the absence of episcopalian services and the Queen's communion with the Scottish kirk were a sore trial to him.

In 1864 the Schleswig-Holstein question dominated foreign affairs and took up much Cabinet time. It was the dawn of Bismarck's age and processes were set in motion that were in due course to render Gladstonian liberalism, as yet hardly born, obsolete. In these events Gladstone played only a secondary role. Palmerston and Russell had created a situation where the Danes could hope for some British support. They did so without any authority from their Cabinet colleagues; when the crisis reached flashpoint at the end of June 1864 it became clear that the Cabinet would not go to war, and that if they did there was a great likelihood that the government would fall. Gladstone was always with the peace party. On the mishandling of the Schleswig-Holstein question, which brought British prestige to as low a point as at any time in the nineteenth century, Derby and Disraeli launched their one real attack on the Palmerston government in years. They had been content to leave a basically conservative ministry in office and had refused any possible combinations with the Radicals to turn them out. But on Denmark they had to let their troops smell battle and it was Gladstone who was put up to follow Disraeli's opening attack. He made the best of a bad case with his usual competence and the government survived with the narrow margin of eighteen votes.

Earlier that year, in April, Garibaldi visited London. He aroused great popular enthusiasm and was the centre of large demonstrations. The campaign for the North and for abolition of slavery, which gathered momentum in 1863, the support and sympathy given to the rebellious Poles in the same year, and the Garibaldi campaign culminating in his visit were all milestones in the revival of the reform agitation. A series of organizations and committees promoted these causes; most of them had an interlocking membership and working- and middle-class radicals came together in these campaigns. There is a direct line of descent from the Working Man's Garibaldian Fund Committee and the middle-class City of London Demonstration Committee, both of which worked together during the Garibaldi visit, to the Reform League, founded in February 1865. Gladstone met Garibaldi several times during his visit; he regarded him as a hero, but found Garibaldi's atheism hard to swallow. Gladstone was present at a great reception for Garibaldi at Stafford House, the home of the Duke of Sutherland and the Italian hero's headquarters during his stay in London. During the reception Gladstone had a long talk with Bright who noted in his diary:

I had a long talk with Mr Gladstone, among other topics upon Ireland and the Irish Church; he thought when the Liberal party is restored to life, that question would come up for settlement, and he should regard it as one of the great purposes of the party, although it would necessarily separate him from the University of Oxford.

After his London visit Garibaldi was to have gone on a prolonged triumphal tour of the provinces. Amongst his friends there were genuine fears for his health and it fell to Gladstone to persuade him to give up the provincial tour. When his sudden departure for Italy was announced there was a storm of Radical protest. The Palmerston government was suspected of wishing to get rid of him before he could further stimulate the democratic movement in the country.

In reply to Radical attacks in the Commons Gladstone had to explain his own part in the general's departure and assure the House that he acted entirely out of concern for Garibaldi's health and wellbeing. If there was a plot by Palmerston to get Garibaldi out of the country as quickly as possible, Gladstone played an unwitting part in it.

It was shortly after the Garibaldi visit, on 11 May 1864, Gladstone made the famous speech in the Commons in which there occurred the phrase: 'I venture to say that every man who is not presumably incapacitated by some consideration of personal unfitness or of political danger, is morally entitled to come within the pale of the constitution.' The House was debating a private member's bill to lower the franchise. Palmerston had warned Gladstone not to commit the government:

If at any future Time our Government should have to bring in a Reform Bill which the present State of public opinion does not appear to favour, it is of great Importance that we should be free to look at the Question without any fresh Pledges – No doubt many working men are as fit to vote as many of the Ten Pounders, but if we open the Door to the Class the Number who may come in may be excessive, and may swamp the Classes above them.

As soon as the words had left Gladstone's mouth and the storm raged, Palmerston's recriminations began:

You lay down broadly the Doctrine of Universal Suffrage . . . I would say, that it was more like the sort of Speech with which Bright would have introduced the Reform Bill which he would like to propose than the Sort of Speech which might have been expected from the Treasury Bench in the present State of Things . . . – The Function of a Government is to calm rather than excite agitation.

Gladstone defended himself by saying that he meant to go no further than the reform proposals which had been put forward by the government in 1860; he denied causing any agitation. Nevertheless his statement caused a sensation: supporters and opponents of reform saw it as a confession that he had been converted to reform and as a deliberate bid for the leadership of a Liberal party committed to reform. How far was it such a bid?

For years now Gladstone had been talked of as a potential leader of the Liberal combination. The 'two terrible old men', Palmerston and Russell, were bound to leave the stage soon and there was no serious rival in sight for Gladstone. His work in public finance, the reduction in taxation and growth in prosperity for which he was given more credit than anybody, made him widely

E

popular across class and interest divisions. He himself had perceived the growth of working-class acceptance of the industrial and capitalist system and the signs of middle- and working-class co-operation in a political cause such as franchise reform. The change in social atmosphere compared with the days of Chartism and the Anti-Corn-Law League was certainly striking. Only the day before he made his speech in the Commons on Baines's bill, he had received a deputation from the Society of Amalgamated Engineers, always regarded as a typical manifestation of the labour aristocracy, who had asked him to modify the rules of the Post Office Savings Bank which he had established so that the union funds could be deposited there. To Gladstone this seemed a remarkable sign of confidence in the established order. He had always felt since he joined the Palmerston government that the reform question, though it was not a cause he regarded with enthusiasm, should be settled. He was now much more aware that it needed to be settled and confident that a moderate settlement would prove both beneficial and acceptable. On this matter he had a good deal of contact with Bright in 1864. Another consideration may not have been far from his mind: the parliamentary position of the government was by no means secure and the poor showing over Schleswig-Holstein might well upset it. In the past Disraeli had shown no compunction about clutching at almost any combination, with the Irish or the Radicals, to obtain or hang on to office. In the last year or two he had been restrained by the broad satisfaction of Derby and the Tory rank and file with the conservative domestic policy of the government. Might not the temptation to bring the government down prove too strong if it could be done through a Tory reform proposal? This was a possibility Gladstone had to counteract and it became a reality only in June 1866 after the failure of the Liberal Reform Bill. Gladstone's professions of surprise at the storm his speech of 11 May 1864 created were therefore genuine enough and he may well have been right when he wrote in his diary: 'It appears to me that it was due less to me, than to the change in the hearers and in the public mind from the professions at least if not the principles of 1859.'

In October 1864 Gladstone went on a provincial speech-making tour, this time in Lancashire, but it was no different from a similar excursion the Prime Minister had made to Bradford only two months earlier. There was, however, a marked difference in his reception. The organizers of Palmerston's visit refused to allow Chartist and Socialist organizations led by George Holyoake to present a petition accusing the Prime Minister of obstructing parliamentary reform; in consequence there was a silent demonstration by a large crowd against Palmerston and at a banquet W. E. Forster, recently elected as member for Bradford, accused him of going back on his promises about parliamentary reform. In contrast Gladstone had a hero's welcome in Lancashire and the crowds listened reverently to his disquisitions on the need for economy, England's moral duty in foreign affairs and the benefits of self-government in the colonies. On economy he was just beginning his last prolonged skirmish with Palmerston and this was therefore the most immediately political of his themes in Lancashire. Communion with large enthusiastic crowds began to strike a deep chord in Gladstone. After the Lancashire visit he wrote in his diary:

So ended in peace an exhausting, flattering, I hope not intoxicating circuit. God knows I have not courted them. I hope I do not rest on them. I pray I may turn them to account for good. It is, however, impossible not to love the people from whom such manifestations come, as meet me in every quarter. . .

The counterpiece to the attraction of the masses was the repulsion of the classes – a distinction which was given wide currency by Gladstone himself at a somewhat later stage. Bright had written to his wife after the reform speech in May: ' . . . he will be more than ever the dread of the aristocratic mob of the West End of London.' And Gladstone himself wrote to his brother-in-law Lord Lyttelton who had told him of the odium towards him in clubland: 'Please to recollect that we have got to govern millions of hard hands; that it must be done by force, fraud, or good will; that the latter has been tried and is answering; that none have profited more by this change of system since the corn law and the Six Acts, than those who complain of it.' Gladstone was increasingly persuading himself that the moral sense of the masses was in many ways sounder than that of their social superiors; that the weight of the working classes was required to counterbalance the power of the higher social orders – this was social justice in the Gladstonian sense. It had nothing to do with equality, but with giving every class its just deserts. Nor did it mean that Gladstone had committed himself to anything like universal suffrage or that he had ceased to believe in aristocratic government.

A few more pieces had to fall into place before Gladstone could be considered fully qualified to lead a rejuvenated Liberal party. Dissenters were a potent force in the Liberal combination – they predominated in the Radical movement. To them Gladstone had

been until recently Oxford and Tractarian and a vigorous defender
of the Establishment and he had therefore a lot to live down. It
was known that he had abandoned most of his earlier inflexible
Church–State positions, but he had still to prove himself in the
eyes of the Dissenters. As his views evolved his votes in the House
of Commons on some of the long-standing grievances of Nonconformists began to change. As early as 1863 he voted for the Burials
Bill which facilitated the holding of Dissenters' funerals in church-
yards; on the more important and embittered problem of church
rates, he did not cast his first vote for abolition until 1866. On the
question of the Irish Church he had long abandoned the ground of
the 1830s when the word 'appropriation' would make him, like
most Anglicans, instantly leap to the defence of the Establishment.
As early as 1847 he wrote, 'We are no longer in a condition to
occupy high and secure ground in arguing for the integrity of the
Irish Church temporalities.' In March 1865 he had to speak on a
Radical motion about the Irish Church; in spite of yet another
warning from Palmerston to tread warily, the burden of his song was:
'I am not loyal to it as an establishment.' As on reform, he accompanied the confession with many reservations and disclaimers, but
many in his audience received the message. Along with this public
evolution of Gladstone's attitudes there went increasing contacts
and correspondence with leading Dissenters.

The most direct tie between Gladstone and his former self was his
Oxford constituency. In 1861 there had been an opportunity for
Gladstone to find a new constituency: there was a petition from
8000 electors asking him to stand for the new constituency of
South Lancashire and there was also an offer to succeed Lord John
Russell in representing the City of London. Gladstone decided to
stand by those of his friends in Oxford who were still loyal to him;
Roundell Palmer whom he wanted as his successor in Oxford
might not have been able to hold the seat, especially as a bill had
just been passed in the teeth of Gladstone's opposition allowing
postal votes in university elections. In the next few years opposition
to Gladstone increased in Oxford; not only his growing identification
with liberalism but also Palmerston's Low Church ecclesiastical
appointments offended many of his former supporters. In 1864 the
Conservatives in Oxford found a new candidate in Gathorne Hardy,
a rising Tory politician who had once been a Unitarian and was now
a High Anglican. Like Disraeli, he was an example of the need the
Tories always had for professional politicians and their willingness
to accept them regardless of social background. Prominent among

Hardy's backers was Lord Robert Cecil; on the eve of the 1865 poll he wrote a strong article in the *Quarterly* on the identification of Church interests with the Conservative party. When the dissolution of Parliament was approaching in 1865, Gladstone's friends prevailed upon him once more to stand, although the view was widely held that his speech on the Irish Church in March had dealt his chances a severe blow. The drawn-out character of nineteenth-century elections, however, made it possible for Gladstone also to accept the renewed offer of the South Lancashire nomination as a reinsurance. Gladstone came 180 votes behind Hardy in the contest that was part of the general election of July 1865. The church parties at Oxford were in deep confusion: High Anglicans were divided between those who still believed in Gladstone's soundness and others who regarded him as a renegade; some evangelicals voted for him because of Palmerston's church appointments; others suspected him of 'Romanizing' in Ireland and being one of 'that extreme party whose religious principles are sufficiently elastic to include in their embrace a Stanley, a Colenso and a Mill, provided they are allowed to chant choral services in their churches, to offer sacerdotal sacrifices at their altars amidst clouds of incense. . .'[13] On the day of Gladstone's defeat, the Bible fell from the hand of the statue of James I in the quadrangle of the Bodleian and this was seen by some as an omen of the coming separation of Church and state.

The defeat at Oxford hurt Gladstone more than he cared to admit. One of his favourite sayings in those days was that for the Church of England it was 'a question between gold and faith: and the gold always carries it against the faith'; namely that by clinging on to every detailed privilege and temporality the Church was failing to read the signs of the times and stood in danger of losing out on the essentials of faith and dogma. From Oxford he hurried to South Lancashire; there, in the Free Trade Hall at Manchester, he spoke the famous sentence, 'I am come among you, and I am come among you unmuzzled.' It was a reference to Palmerston's remark that Oxford had kept his unpredictable colleague conveniently muzzled. In the contest for the three South Lancashire seats Gladstone came third, the only Liberal to be elected alongside two Conservatives. Again more than he cared to admit, Gladstone was affected by the warmth of the welcome that Lancashire, and indeed the English masses, were now prepared to give him. His translation from Oxford was an event of national significance, perhaps the most important outcome of an election otherwise still overshadowed by Palmerston. The Prime Minister had only three more months to live.

Gladstone's transformation was more outward than inward. Only a few days after the election he was writing to one of the Nonconformist leaders with whom he was now in contact, Baldwin Brown, that he still saw grave obstacles to Oxford becoming a national university instead of the Anglican institution it still was; his views on parliamentary reform were still cautious. He was a conservative High Anglican who had, by the light of his powerful intellect and fierce sense of justice, fought his way to a liberal position on religious toleration, on the self-determination of peoples and of individuals. The wider public, who cannot easily distinguish the finer shades of grey, saw it all as a change of front. Gladstone's foes inevitably thought the change fitted in too neatly with his personal advancement to be genuine; his friends forgot about his reservations and welcomed him with open arms as an ally of progress. Some of his finest qualities now made him into a fiercely controversial figure: the elaborate reasoning was seen as casuistry and he was hated as a hypocritical renegade; his huge moral stature and ability to arouse response turned him rapidly into a folk-hero.

7

THE PALE
OF THE
CONSTITUTION
1865–8

The general election of July 1865 appeared on paper to strengthen the Liberal majority. Some 360 followers of Palmerston now confronted 290 supporters of Derby. It was a remarkable triumph for the ageing premier. There was a commitment to reform by many Liberal candidates at the election, by some more than by others, and in the autumn, when Palmerston was preparing for the first session of the new Parliament, Brand, the Chief Whip, told him that a reform bill was expected by his followers. Before the autumn cabinets could meet, Palmerston was dead. There was little doubt that Russell would succeed him; Gladstone was, however, widely talked about as a younger and more plausible

Prime Minister. Even *The Times* featured an article proposing Gladstone as Prime Minister; it was printed while Delane, the editor, was out of town and when he returned the paper's support was promptly switched to Russell. The Queen sent for Russell, who after accepting office asked Gladstone to retain the Treasury and become Leader of the House. He thus became clearly second man in the government, although before finally accepting he offered to let Sir George Grey, who had the purest of Whig credentials, have the lead in the House. Gladstone may well have felt his isolation at this moment, when the removal of Palmerston made him so largely responsible for keeping the diverse Liberal combination together. He was neither a Whig nor did he, for all the reputation he now had outside the House, belong to any of the various Radical factions, and his High Anglicanism still created a barrier between him and most of the men on his side of the House. In the Russell government Gladstone had to shoulder an almost superhuman burden of work: the Prime Minister was an old man and had never been a particularly competent administrator; he, the Foreign Secretary and several other important ministers were in the Lords. During the short-lived ministry there were considerable disagreements between Russell and Gladstone about bringing in new blood; the Chancellor of the Exchequer wanted at an early stage to bring in Robert Lowe in whom he saw a kindred spirit on questions of economy; as it turned out Lowe became the most dangerous enemy of the government's Reform Bill a few months later, whereas inside the Cabinet he might merely have used his influence in favour of a moderate measure. Russell refused to have Lowe because of various past grudges. Gladstone, on the other hand, succeeded in bringing W. E. Forster, destined to be his colleague for many years, into junior office. Forster made it a condition of joining that there should be no question of delaying reform by appointing a commission of inquiry first.

Reform was in the air and even Palmerston might have found it difficult to put it off any longer. Russell, who had for years tried to follow up his handiwork of 1832, was determined to bring a Reform Bill of serious dimensions and to do so quickly, before age and ill-health could prevent him. Gladstone was prepared to use his best endeavours in this cause, but he was more than a little afraid of Russell's rapidity. It was more than ever obvious that the Liberal party was a loosely knit combination: a few on the left of Bright were in favour of the Reform League's programme of manhood suffrage and would oppose anything less; a much larger number on the right did not want the disturbance of any reform and felt that the majority of the country were with them. In this situation the government might easily be heading for a fall before Gladstone could consolidate his position as the future leader of the Liberal amalgam. All kinds of possible political combinations were always being considered and rumoured. Gladstone himself wanted to bring Stanley, Lord Derby's heir, and any other Conservative who might come with him into the government; on the other hand he was opposed to bringing in Bright, for although, as he told Russell, Bright had 'for many years held language of a studious moderation about Reform, in the present critical state of feeling on your own side with respect to the franchise his name would sink the government and their bill together'. The Conservative party, although dispirited, was waiting in the wings. If reform should break up the Liberal combination, the dissident anti-reformers might make common cause with the Tories, or some new centre party might emerge and it could even be that Gladstone with his appeal to some of the young and able High Church Tories might head such a combination. All this was rumour and speculation, but it illustrates how fluid the parliamentary situation was in which Gladstone was now operating. He was thus in favour of tackling reform but would have preferred to proceed more cautiously than Russell, and economy was still of greater interest to him than reform; behind the scenes he hardly conformed to the image of the zealous reformer which some sections of the population had now built around him. He knew that taking the country as a whole the pressure for parliamentary reform was by no means all that strong. On the other hand he thought that Parliament and the Liberal party had been committed to reform since 1859 and that it would be discreditable to the whole parliamentary system to renege on this commitment. He felt that positive benefits would flow from enfranchising more of the independent, sturdy, prosperous working men of the country – their sound moral sense, which he had in recent years come to appreciate, would be a valuable counterpoise to the selfishness of the upper classes which he had come to fear. It was no part of Gladstone's purpose to give the vote to what Bright later called the 'residuum', the bottom stratum of the poor, the ignorant and the feckless, and even Bright himself by opting for 'residential suffrage' wanted to exclude these.

Cabinet committees considered the proposed Reform Bill in the early weeks of 1866. It was finally decided to enfranchise the £7 occupier in the boroughs and the £14 occupier in the counties.

This compared with £6 and £10 in the Palmerston bill of 1860, but the qualifications were now to be based on rental rather than rating, as in 1860, and were therefore thought to be equivalent to or possibly in advance of the £6 and £10 rating proposal. The difference between a rental and a rating qualification became an important issue in the whole reform controversy of 1866 and 1867. Gladstone introduced this bill in a somewhat restrained speech on 12 March 1866. It was the opening of a delicate political manoeuvre. The bill was so moderate that it could well have been passed by a consensus of Liberals, Whigs, Conservatives and Tories, leaving in opposition perhaps only the bulk of the Radicals and a few extreme Tories. But this was not the way things worked out in this Parliament which had been elected only so recently on a Palmerstonian platform. The decisive factor was that a group of Whigs and Liberals, among whom Robert Lowe, the albino, was by far the most able, opposed the government's bill. This meant that the Conservatives in their turn saw an opportunity of defeating the government and therefore also opposed the bill. A contributing factor in bringing about this configuration was Bright's decision to support the bill as a payment on account, even though he was not satisfied with its extent. His verdict was: ' . . . the Bill is an honest Bill; and if it is the least the Government could offer, it may be that it is the greatest which the Government could carry through Parliament . . .' Anything that Bright could support, men of a conservative persuasion must oppose. An additional factor was the publication of statistics which showed that at least a quarter of the existing electorate was already working-class. This gave the opponents of the bill, Liberal or Conservative, the opportunity to argue that the proposed changes would swamp the electorate with working-class voters – and this hardly anybody wanted.

For Gladstone the opposition of Conservatives and Adullamites, as Bright dubbed the Liberal malcontents, meant a far greater commitment to the bill and to the cause of reform than he had initially had. The language in which he now defended the bill made him seem more radical and the bill more far-reaching than either really were. A lot of the Adullamites did not really want to overthrow the government, even less did they want a dissolution and a bruising fight on reform. With careful handling enough of them would have supported the government to enable it to survive. This was a task which Gladstone was unable to perform. He was new to the job of leading the House, he was overworked, he got little help from Russell, who was totally out of touch with back-bench opinion;

some of his Whig colleagues in the Cabinet were suspicious of what he would do 'if thrown . . . into the hands of the radicals' and took little trouble to hide their misgivings about him and his bill. Above all Gladstone was himself – once he believed that principle was involved he took off like a high-spirited horse at the scent of battle. He replied to Lowe's famous question 'if you want venality, ignorance, drunkenness – if you want impulsive, unreflecting violent people – where do you look for them? Do you go to the top or to the bottom?' by saying that the opponents of reform counted the numbers of those to be enfranchised as if they were an invading army. 'But the persons to whom their remarks apply are our fellow Christians, our own flesh and blood . . .' It is hardly surprising that anti-reform Whigs were now full of venom about him: 'not a particle of fact, temper, knowledge of the world . . .', 'neither honest, moderate or gentleman enough . . . to be the Whig minister', 'the impulsiveness of woman without her instinct', 'in a chronic state of conversion', 'that d—d Gladstone, Tory as he was, High Churchman as he is and revolutionist as he will be . . .'[1] Gladstone appealed to public opinion in the country in order to bring pressure to bear on the dissident Liberals. On 6 April 1866 he went to Liverpool and made it clear that the government was staking its life on the bill – he talked about crossing the Rubicon, blowing the bridges and burning the boats, and attacked Lord Grosvenor, titular leader of the Adulla-mites, and Stanley, Derby's heir, both of them Lancashire magnates, as 'selfish aristocrats'. The first major test came on 27 April at the end of the long second reading debate, on an amendment by Grosvenor asking for a redistribution bill to be made public before the Franchise Bill was passed. Gladstone followed Disraeli, who had reminded him of his opposition to the first Reform Bill in the Oxford Union thirty-five years ago. It was one of his great speeches and the core of his stand on reform is perhaps contained in this passage from it:

> I think that the influence [in Parliament] of separate classes is too strong, and that the influence of the public interest properly so called, as distinguished from the interest of sets, groups, and classes of men, is too weak . . . I believe that the composition of the House might be greatly improved and that the increased representation of the working classes would supply us more largely with the description of Members whom we want, who would look not to the interest of classes, but to the 'public interest'.

In the division the government's majority, which after the election had been reckoned to be around seventy, dropped to five. Those in the Cabinet most committed to reform now wanted to dissolve Parliament; the Whigs on the right wing wanted to resign. Both Gladstone and Russell thought the only honourable course was to carry on with the threat of dissolution in the background. The Whigs in the Cabinet were greatly alarmed by this: they thought that Gladstone and Russell would 'dish' them by going to the country on a radical platform. Granville, Halifax (the new title of Charles Wood) and Sir George Grey privately told General Grey, the Queen's Secretary, that they were opposed to a dissolution, implying therefore that the Queen would not have to grant one if Russell, backed by Gladstone, asked for it. The Prime Minister and the Chancellor, however, now tried to be conciliatory and to meet the point of Grosvenor's amendment by bringing in a Redistribution Bill. The reason why they had not brought in redistribution along-side reform was that any such bill was always likely to arouse violent opposition from members whose seats would be disturbed. This now proved to be the case.

The next six weeks were a time of extreme pressure for Gladstone. On top of the reform battle there now came the failure, on 10 May, of the great banking house of Overend & Gurney, which forced him to suspend the Bank Charter Act and to raise bank rate to 10 per cent. The panic in the City ushered in a severe economic depression, which in due course proved to be a powerful stimulant to working-class agitation for reform. Gladstone tried to sleep in the House of Commons, but the members behind him, seeing him nod off, put their feet on the bench and shook it. Disraeli bent every effort to defeating the government. Even though the Conservative party's own statistician, Dudley Baxter, had in a confidential memorandum assured Derby and Disraeli that the party would actually gain from the £14 franchise in the counties, two amendments were put forward, one to raise the qualification to £20, the other to substitute rating for rental value. These amendments were defeated by fourteen and by seven votes respectively, so one more good heave would bring the government down. All was poised on a razor's edge, for earlier an ill-judged procedural amendment by Stanley was lost by twenty-seven votes and the always pessimistic Derby thought the government might win through after all. Unfortunately Gladstone was not the man to make the best of such a situation. His temper became short and his note of high principle and purpose was an irritant in itself. Cranborne (as Lord Robert Cecil now was) wrote of his performance in the *Quarterly*:

The imperiousness which is so irritating to an assembly of English gentlemen has been described by Mr Gladstone's devoted admirers in the press to a virtuous indignation and a consciousness of superior purity, which will not suffer him to treat with forbearance the meannesses and follies of his opponents. Perhaps, if the House fully realized this superiority, it might take his rebukes more meekly and kiss the rod that smites them. But they are a sceptical body of middle-aged men, not believing much in virtuous indignation, and strongly inclined to suspect all claims to special purity of purpose.[2]

The end came on an amendment, indefensible in itself, to substitute rating for rental value in the boroughs. It was moved by Lord Dunkellin, son of Lord Clanricarde and brother of the man who became Ireland's most notorious landlord. On 18 June the government was defeated by eleven votes.

The question facing Russell and his colleagues now was whether to dissolve Parliament, resign or carry on once more, either ignoring the defeat or reversing the verdict on Dunkellin's amendment. Gladstone was initially for dissolving; at this moment, having been by the course of events pushed into an increasingly Radical public posture, he seemed willing to catch the Radical wind and Bright encouraged him in that direction. Brand, the Liberal Chief Whip, warned against dissolution in a divided state in the midst of a financial crisis, but Gladstone thought that the loss of some right-wing elements would be a beneficial purge. The obstacles to a dissolution so soon after the last one were, however, overwhelming. Gladstone regretted to the end of his life that he did not press harder for it, but in retrospect he may well have overestimated his radicalism at that moment. On the other hand he refused to agree to the various expedients proposed to enable the government to remain in office, for he considered them dishonourable. The result was that he had to agree to what was the easiest way out, resignation. Clarendon wrote to Russell at this time: ' . . . it will be fatal to Gladstone whose services and abilities would fit him to guide the destinies of his country if his arrogant ill-temper did not repel the sympathies upon which a leader must rest for support.'[3] The Queen was reluctant to leave Balmoral for Windsor and even more reluctant to accept the government's resignation; she would have liked Russell to remain in office and settle the reform question by consent. But it was not to be and after seven years it was Derby's turn again. Gladstone's longest continuous period in office came to an end.

It was again a decisive moment in the history of British political parties. A Tory–Adullamite coalition might have proved possible. There had been much concerted action between these two groups in opposing the Reform Bill. But the Cave of Adullam, like the Peelites before them, demanded a high price for fusion. Disraeli would have had to go and possibly Derby as well; they might come in under Stanley, but preferably under a Whig such as Clarendon, Russell's Foreign Secretary. Derby, who had so often been lackadaisical about taking office, was not prepared to be pushed aside this time, nor was he at all disposed to drop Disraeli. Thus a minority Conservative government was formed and the dividing-line between the parties remained where it had been.

In the meantime Gladstone had become a popular hero. The masses had been up to now fairly apathetic about reform; it was this that had encouraged the opponents of reform in the Commons to kill the bill. The event itself, however, kindled popular wrath. Shortly after the resignation of the government a crowd of demonstrators moved to the Gladstones' house in Carlton House Terrace and shouted for 'Gladstone and Liberty'. Gladstone was out and at the request of the police Mrs Gladstone and her daughters appeared briefly so that the crowd would disperse quickly. Such was the hostility to Gladstone at this juncture that *The Times* and other papers reported this as a pandering to the lowest type of mob by the ladies of the Gladstone household and compared Gladstone himself to Wilkes and Lord George Gordon.

At this moment, however, Gladstone was already beginning the process of disengagement from the Radical posture into which events had pushed him. He refused to address the demonstration in Hyde Park which was being planned by Beales and the Reform League and which was to become so important in the whole progress of events. In refusing he counselled the London Working Men's Association 'to wait in patience the course of great events' although he covered all this up by warning against 'any illusory or reactionary measures simulating the . . . character of reform' and proclaiming that 'on the hour of defeat I have a presentiment of victory'. No doubt he expected such an 'illusory' Reform Bill to come from the Tories. When the demonstration took place on 23 July and was banned from Hyde Park the result was the famous Hyde Park riots, when, within sight of the most fashionable houses in London, the railings round the park were trampled down. How important these events were in disposing the Tories towards reform is a matter for dispute. On Gladstone they had exactly the opposite effect and impelled him to disengage even more explicitly from any more extreme position he may have been thought to be holding. On 8 August he stated in a published letter: 'I do not agree with the

demand either for manhood or for household suffrage: while I own
with regret that the conduct of the opponents of the Government
measure of this year has done much to encourage that demand,
which, but for such opposition, would scarcely have been heard of.'
Shortly afterwards he thought it wisest to remove himself from the
scene of action and he left with his family for Italy at the end of
September. Before his departure he wrote to Brand:

> So far as I am concerned I now leave the wound of the liberal party
> to the healing powers of nature. . . If we cannot arrive in sufficient
> strength at a definite understanding with respect to the mode of handl-
> ing the question of the franchise, then our line ought to be great patience
> and quietude in opposition.

Gladstone was in Italy for nearly four months and during this
time he met many of the leading men of that country. Ever since
the publication of his letter to Lord Aberdeen in 1851 his name was
revered in Italy and its connotations were unequivocally liberal
and even democratic. This time there was no such cause as there
had been in 1850 to involve him deeply in the political affairs of the
peninsula. The one major problem that remained unresolved at this
time was the future of Rome and the Papal States. Manning had
been the contact between Gladstone and the Vatican and had warned
the Vatican authorities to treat their visitor with care. Gladstone
on his part 'considered himself bound to good conduct in a very
strict sense of the word'. It was his view that whatever the future
of the Pope's temporal power 'an ample provision . . . for the dignity,
safety, independence and becoming sustentation of the Papal
Court is an indispensable condition of any plan . . . it should contemplate the Pope's residence in Rome.'[4] He felt that it would be
against the true interests of the Roman Church and religion if a
government were forced on the Papal States which the inhabitants
did not want and he thought the proper rights of the Church and its
institutions in Italy could be maintained under the normal law of
Italy. Gladstone had two audiences of the Pope, one alone and one
with his family. Pio Nono and his visitor seem to have carefully
skirted the topics which might have caused them to disagree
strongly although the Pope talked freely about the condition of
Italy. It impressed Gladstone that at the beginning of the interview
the Pope asked his visitor to be seated, whereas the Queen kept
her ministers standing. Gladstone was amused by the reported
remark of the Pope about himself and his three political colleagues
who were in Rome at the same time: 'I like but I do not understand
Mr Gladstone; Mr Cardwell I understand, but I do not like; I both

like and understand Lord Clarendon; the Duke of Argyll I neither understand nor like.' Gladstone saw no fewer than ten cardinals and also met the King at Florence. He spent a great deal of time listening to Italian sermons and according to Lord Clarendon lectured his wife and daughters on Dante every morning at eight. But Clarendon had always looked upon him with slightly disdainful amusement. On his way home from Italy Gladstone spent a few days in Paris where he met many leading personalities including the Emperor and made known his opposition to the increasingly military turn of events on the Continent. He arrived back in London on 30 January 1867 and the new session of Parliament was opened on 5 February.

During Gladstone's judicious absence the initiative on how to deal with reform or whether to deal with it at all had passed to Lord Derby and his Cabinet. They finally arrived at the decision to tackle reform in some manner in the session of 1867; considerations of great complexity drove them to this conclusion. There were the Hyde Park riots; there were the great meetings addressed by Bright in the main provincial centres and in London in the autumn of 1866. None of these demonstrations was ultimately decisive with Derby and his colleagues, for they knew what really mattered in the end was the parliamentary situation and not an agitation in the country which they never mistook for the early symptoms of a revolution. It was really a thoroughly respectable agitation, in which working- and middle-class aspirations and organizations came together; Bright himself was not nearly as extreme as he sounded, did not really want manhood suffrage and was prepared to accept a reasonable interim measure. Other calculations weighed more heavily with Derby and Disraeli. On the level of strategy, it was important for them to show that the Conservative party had once again become a governing party, a viable alternative to the Liberals and capable of settling major problems. If the reform question was solved by the Tories the details of the solution could be so arranged that the possible damage to the Conservative party would be minimized, whereas a Liberal scheme would be designed, like that of 1866, to reap maximum advantage for that party. On the tactical level Derby and Disraeli were anxious to hold on to office as long as possible and to exploit the cleavage among their opponents between Radicals and constitutional Liberals. From this point of view the activities of Bright and Beales were an advantage to the Tories and a liability to their opponents. Gladstone saw this clearly. On 30 October 1866 he had written from Rome to Brand, the Liberal

Chief Whip: 'The reform movement is by degrees complicating the question. It is separating Bright from us, and in one sense thus clearing our way. But then it may become too strong for us; or at least too strong to be stayed with our bill of last year.' The personal problem for Gladstone now – and his absence abroad had only postponed it – how to retain his popular following and avoid dissociating himself from Bright publicly while not identifying himself with him too closely for the comfort of the large number of parliamentary Liberals who were still loyal to him. Only in this way could he hope to keep alive the possibility that he might succeed to the leadership of a reunited Liberal party.

Great personal and party issues were therefore at stake in the Reform Bill battle of 1867. There had been many such occasions since 1846, but triumph and disaster never followed each other so hectically as they did in those days of the late winter and spring of 1867. Initially events seemed to conspire to make Gladstone master of the situation. The government hoped to proceed by way of resolutions, thus extracting the maximum benefit from Liberal divisions without having to show their own hand too clearly. Disraeli was, however, soon forced to announce that the government would make public the outlines of their bill before the resolutions were debated. At this stage Disraeli planned to bring in a bill based on giving the vote to every householder who personally paid his rates in the boroughs, 'rated residential suffrage'. The resulting enfranchisement of a large number of working-class electors would be counterbalanced by a variety of plural votes, the old 'fancy franchises' which Disraeli had tried to introduce in 1859. The advantage of these proposals from the Conservative point of view was that they would have established a clear-cut basis of principle for the vote, which it would probably be possible to maintain for a long time to come, and that it was a basis clearly different from that of Gladstone's abortive bill of the previous year. In fact, the enfranchisement would not be all that large, because a lot of householders did not personally pay rates, but 'compounded' for them with their rent, and moreover there would be the counterbalancing factor of the 'fancy franchises'. Unfortunately for Disraeli the Cabinet's unity came to grief over these proposals; first General Peel, whose eye lit up 'with insanity' when he heard the phrase 'household suffrage', threatened to resign. Then, much more formidably, Cranborne refused to be 'bounced' by the statistics which Derby and Disraeli hurriedly gave to the Cabinet. With literally minutes to spare before the crucial party meeting on 25 February, the

Cabinet went back on rated residential suffrage and substituted a £6 rating franchise in the boroughs, £20 in the counties. This ill-fated 'Ten Minutes Bill', so called because of its rapid genesis, was announced to the House by Disraeli that evening.

Gladstone was now in a strong position. He had played his cards wisely since the beginning of the 1867 session, in marked contrast to the irritability and impatience he had shown the previous year. He let it be known, though not publicly, that he disagreed with Bright's agitation in the country. He talked to several members of the Cave of Adullam and left them with the impression that he was a moderate. All this was not a pose but entirely in accordance with his convictions. At the same time he studiously avoided the appearance of being impatient to get back into office. He seemed prepared to let Derby tackle reform if he did it in the right way. All sections of the Liberal party were immediately united against the Ten Minutes Bill; even those who had sheltered in the Cave of Adullam could hardly accept from a Tory government something very similar to what they had refused to accept from their own side. At a party meeting which was held at Gladstone's house on 26 February, the day after Disraeli's announcement, even Grosvenor, the prominent Adullamite, 'mentioned with great praise the judicious way in which Mr Gladstone had led the opposition this session'. Gladstone had no need now to show his own hand; he could adopt a statesmanlike pose, saying that they would await the details of the government's bill and if these proved satisfactory they would give it reasonable support. The danger to the Conservative government and to the whole future of the Tory party was now very great; so great in fact that it contained its own cure. Backed by the feeling of Conservative back-benchers that it would be better to go to some great principle such as household suffrage, suitably hedged around, rather than seek to impose limits which would not be recognized as a final settlement,[5] Derby and Disraeli decided to drop the Ten Minutes Bill and go on without Cranborne, Peel and Carnarvon if necessary. On 2 March they reverted to rated residential suffrage and the three men resigned.

Even now the Conservatives were in a highly precarious position. Cranborne and his resigning colleagues might have organized a 'cave' against the government, the Tory back-benchers might have broken rank. Neither of these things did in fact happen. Cranborne was not by nature a 'caver' who would lead a revolt; the Tory back-benchers were pleased with a proposal that would allow their side to strike before Gladstone could and they were conscious of the restrictions on enfranchisement, through the exclusion of the compound householder, rather than of its possible wide extent. It was, however, the latter potentiality, namely that rated residential suffrage might in fact come to mean effective household suffrage, that had attractions for the left wing of the Liberal party. Yet the proposal also appealed to the Adullamites for much the same reason that it did to the Tory back-benchers, namely that under cover of a principle that would offer some hope of a final settlement there would in fact be a fairly restricted enfranchisement balanced by counterpoises. Some of the Adullamites were so suspicious of Gladstone that as soon as they saw the government reconsidering their position they broke away again from the momentary Liberal unity that prevailed immediately after Disraeli's announcement of a £6 rating bill on 25 February. They preferred to keep Derby in rather than let Gladstone loose again and a good many Whigs who had not voted with the Cave the previous year thought likewise.

All this put Gladstone in a difficult position. Personally he still held the view that enfranchisement should stop short of giving the vote to the 'residuum'. He distrusted Disraeli's bill because of its ambivalent nature. On the one hand the distinction between compounding and personal payment of rates was entirely arbitrary, illogical and unworkable and made the government's bill much less liberal than it ought to have been; on the other hand the various fancy franchises were likely to be swept away in the committee stage, very largely because the Liberal party would have to sweep them away for the sake of its progressive image. This would leave household suffrage pure and simple and this neither Gladstone nor the majority of Liberals were prepared to have. Gladstone was trying at the same time to please the right wing of his party and possibly to draw over some of the supporters of Cranborne, while retaining the support of the Radicals and the progressive forces outside Parliament. In trying to square this circle he also wanted to give the impression of retaining the initiative by forcing his own ideas on the government rather than appearing passively to follow the government's lead. Yet in laying claim to the slogan 'household suffrage', however hedged about, the government had pre-empted the best available base-line. Against this Gladstone put forward the notion of a £5 rating franchise combined with compulsory compounding below £5. This would mean that in boroughs no householder inhabiting a house of under £5 rateable value would have the vote, and all above that level would have it. This was in a way clear-cut, but sounded less bold than the government's rated residential suffrage and Gladstone was not even able to proclaim it fully for tactical reasons.

He was thus having to attack the government's bill as too restrictive and too liberal at the same time. He was having to do this with a following whose dislike of the Conservative bill was due to equally varied reasons and some of whom did not want to bring Derby down. Gladstone was still intent on seizing the initiative and did not correctly gauge the weakness of his position. As a result he invited a series of damaging rebuffs in the three weeks following the introduction of the bill on 18 March. First he found that his party would not follow him into an outright rejection of the second reading of the bill. Since he knew that he could not rely on his following in the committee stage, owing to their diverse views, he had to seek another confrontation before the bill went into committee. This he sought to do by moving an Instruction that the bill should have a fixed-line franchise above which all householders, whether compounders or not, should have the vote and below which nobody would have it. The Instruction did not actually mention the figure of £5 which he had in mind. Gladstone pressed this Instruction on a party meeting held on 5 April. A substantial body of Liberal members stayed away from this meeting; although Bright supported the proposed Instruction there remained a great deal of hostility to it. It was typical of the insensitivity that sometimes blinded Gladstone that he persisted in forcing this move on his reluctant followers. The consequence was the famous Tea-Room revolt only three days later. A group of some fifty Liberal M.P.s, drawn mainly from the left and centre of the party but also including some who simply distrusted Gladstone or feared a dissolution, decided to tell Gladstone that they could not support the Instruction for fear of being ' . . . made to appear in the eyes of their constituents as having been opposed to going into committee upon and fairly considering a bill which gave, ostensibly, that household suffrage which they had always advocated'. Gladstone had therefore to order the Instruction to be withdrawn; he had been thwarted in his attempt to oppose the principle of Disraeli's bill before the committee stage. There can be no doubt that among the Tea-Room Liberals there were a few Radicals, who hoped to get more out of Disraeli than out of Gladstone; notably James Clay, an old friend of Disraeli's, who had been in touch with him since the beginning of the session.[6]

Gladstone still did not fully grasp the weakness of his position. He tried one more move to reassert himself by moving an amendment to take the personal rating provision out of the bill. It was skilfully chosen ground, for Disraeli had erected the personal payment of rates as the cardinal principle in qualifying for the vote. By knocking away this provision the government would be brought down; the Radicals had to vote for it because it removed the main restriction in the bill and opened the way to household suffrage pure and simple; moderate Liberals, Adullamites, even Cranborne Tories might vote for it on the calculation that it would turn the bill into such an extreme one that it could not possibly continue. But on this occasion Disraeli was too skilful for Gladstone. He published a letter in *The Times* to his followers warning them that the amendment was a 'declaration of war', a 'party attack' dictated 'by a candidate for power' who forgot that he 'has had his innings'. Gladstone's position was further weakened by the fact that he had to make it clear, although it was not in the amendment, that his real intention was to go for a £5 limit in the boroughs; thereby the useful ambivalence of the amendment was largely nullified. In the early hours of 13 April 1867 the amendment was defeated by twenty-one votes. It was one of the most decisive encounters between Gladstone and Disraeli. Although Gladstone lost, events were to show that he had not lost the future; but Disraeli by winning had at last established an unequivocal claim to succeed to the leadership of his party. Gladstone wrote in his diary that evening: 'A smash perhaps without example.' Disraeli was fêted at the Carlton and then went home to Mary Anne, who was up waiting for him with champagne and a Fortnum & Mason pie. It was on this occasion that he said to her, 'Why, my dear, you are more like a mistress than a wife.'

An analysis by Brand showed that the forty-five Liberals who voted against their party on 13 April included former Adullamites, a few Radicals, a heterogeneous collection of others, some preferring to see the government settle the question, others hating Gladstone or fearing a dissolution. Only a few of the forty-five had been involved in the Tea-Room revolt; thus there were at least one hundred Liberals who in one way or another had chafed under Gladstone's leadership. He was in a bitter mood and talked of surrendering the leadership. A current joke was 'Why is Mr Gladstone like a telescope? Because Dizzy draws him out, sees through him and shuts him up.'[7] He did in fact give up the day-to-day leadership of the party, but like so many of his moves this one, too, was ambivalent and only had the appearance of withdrawal and resignation. In fact, he was being advised to become more aloof so as to save his reputation from the compromises that were being forced on him as leader. His old friend Acland warned him against the dissident Whigs, 'a narrow clique who want to prevent your being prime minister'. In spite of having apparently lost control of his party Gladstone remained a central figure. His failure on 13 April and the signs that he was not reliably in favour of the greatest possible enfranchisement gave fresh impetus to the extra-parliamentary agitation. It reached another climax in the Hyde Park demonstration of 6 May and these indications of popular feeling undoubtedly helped to create a climate in the House of Commons in which members on all sides wished to see the reform question speedily and finally settled. The effect on Gladstone was to make him sound more radical and democratic again; partly because he was convinced that popular demands must be appeased and partly because it seemed increasingly likely that the Liberal party he might come to lead would have to be more democratic and less Whiggish. In the House Gladstone also remained a central figure; he no longer effectively led the Liberals and he knew he could no longer hope to dictate to the government by moving amendments, yet he could not remain silent. His continued interventions in debate made him the more effective as a kind of butt; the Conservative cohesion owed at least as much to the hatred of Gladstone as to the skill of Disraeli. It was an uncomfortable position for him. On 9 May, three days after the alarming Hyde Park demonstration, he made a long speech on what he considered a restrictive counter-amendment by Disraeli to a Radical amendment to facilitate enfranchisement of some compound householders. As was so often the case, Gladstone had a better grasp of the complex technicalities than anybody, but he bored a House increasingly tired of these complexities. He was heavily beaten and noted in his diary: 'Spoke earnestly and long for compound householder, in vain. Beaten by 322–256. Much fatigued by heat and work.' It was two days later that he spoke to a Reform Union deputation supported by twenty Liberal M.P.s. The Union was the more respectable and middle-class of the two main reform organizations and it was now becoming more active, like the League. If the middle classes could really have been roused it would be more important than any disorder generated by large working-class demonstrations. Gladstone in addressing this deputation finally abandoned his £5 limit and came near to committing himself against the personal rating principle. Thus he had returned to a clearly Radical position; any hope of combining with the Adullamites was deliberately cast aside. The government was thereby relieved from any lingering fear that Gladstone might outflank them on the right. It is likely that Gladstone's move to the left played a part in Disraeli's willingness to accept Hodgkinson's amendment less than a week later. In doing so he removed the most important restrictive feature of his bill and at a stroke enfranchised around 400,000 compound householders. 'Never,' wrote Gladstone in retrospect, 'have I undergone a stranger emotion of surprise than when, as I was entering the House, our Whip met me and stated that Disraeli was about to support Hodgkinson's motion.' When Disraeli after the event dashed off a long letter to Gathorne Hardy, the most likely opponent of his action in the Cabinet, he again used Gladstone as the butt: ' . . . Gladstone got up . . . and made his meditated coup . . . I felt that the critical moment had arrived when . . . we might take a step which would destroy the present agitation and extinguish Gladstone and Co. . . .'

Gladstone's role in the great reform battles of 1866 and 1867 was strange. Throughout his views on the substance of the question were moderate and consistent and the popular hero-worship of him as a zealous reformer was almost a misunderstanding. His leadership in Parliament in the session of 1866 and 1867 was in many ways disastrous; his popular following outside the House earned him fierce hatred inside. But it was not only fear of his potentialities as a demagogue that aroused antagonism; it was the manner in which he flaunted his 'purity of purpose', his High Anglican, Peelite priggishness that tried beyond endurance many men in a worldly, aristocratic assembly. Yet it was his great weight as a man of high principle, allied to his remarkable gifts of intellect and speech, that ultimately gave him the power to dominate, even in failure, the course of events.

The Reform Bill of 1867 and the redistribution measures coupled with it brought about a major change in the political landscape. It was very difficult for politicians to discern what the real implications were. Glyn, who had succeeded Brand as Liberal Chief Whip, wrote to Gladstone: 'All is new and changed and large and I fear I must say in some respects *dark*.' In their mental habits the denizens of the parliamentary world were slow to adjust to the new realities. But one thing was fairly certain: public opinion in the mass was going to count for more. It was in his ability to appeal to that extra-parliamentary opinion that Gladstone was superior to any other major political figure. In the final weeks of the parliamentary battle over reform he had, thwarted as he was in the House, strengthened once more his identification with popular aspirations outside it. In Parliament the far-reaching nature of the Reform Bill as it finally emerged had the effect of mitigating the Liberal divisions. The Left had got what it wanted or more; the Right had nowhere else to go. Gladstone was still held in great suspicion, especially among Whigs; he continued to feel sore at the way the party had treated him and reluctant to assert leadership for fear of finding himself disavowed; he complained when the new session of Parliament opened of his 'crippled means of action'. Disraeli, who succeeded Derby as Prime Minister in February 1868, was still in a minority and sooner or later there would have to be an election. It was, however, in the interests of the Liberal party not to precipitate an election before it could be held on the new register based on the 1867 bill; it was generally thought that the new registers could not be ready before 1869.

At that moment events played a card into Gladstone's hands through which he was able to turn the tables on Disraeli and avenge his defeat on reform. Fenianism had become a force in Ireland and after a period of relative calm Irish national consciousness was reawakening. Two incidents in particular served notice to the British public that Ireland was once more a problem: the rescue of two Fenian prisoners in Manchester in September 1867, when a police officer was killed; more seriously the attempted rescue of two Fenian prisoners in Clerkenwell gaol on 13 December 1867, when twelve people were killed in the explosion of a barrel of gunpowder. A few days later Gladstone spoke at Southport and proclaimed the need for a broadly based attack on Irish problems; the Church, education and the land, the three main Irish grievances, would all have to be tackled. On the Church of Ireland, Gladstone had given up his early rigid Church–state views by the time he resigned over the Maynooth grant. In 1865 he had publicly declared that he could no longer support the establishment of the Irish Anglican Church in principle, although he did not then consider the time ripe for action. At about the same time he was already advocating a scheme to make university education fully available to Irish Catholics. He wrote: '*civil disabilities* are still in 1865 attached to *religious opinions*; and this in the matter of education, which the State professes, and desires, and spends much money to encourage.' A few days after his Southport speech Russell informed him in a letter that he would never again take office. The leadership of the Liberals was open to Gladstone more than ever, but he still needed a way of reasserting himself. The government was beginning to toy with the idea of concurrent endowment in Ireland, essentially the same policy as the Whigs had adopted in the 1830s when 'appropriation' of Irish Church revenues so hotly divided the parties. It was a policy full of pitfalls. In mid-March 1868 Gladstone had an opportunity, on a motion by an Irish member, to make his own position clear – he was in favour of disestablishment and disendowment. Up to this point Manning, now Cardinal of Westminster, had been in touch with Disraeli on the possibilities of concurrent endowment. This contact now ceased abruptly. Within a few days Gladstone tabled his resolutions on the Irish Church. On 4 April he carried the motion to go into committee on the resolutions by sixty-one votes. It was as great a triumph as Disraeli's on personal rating had been almost exactly a year earlier. Gladstone was loudly cheered in the House and a large crowd followed him as he walked home to Carlton House Terrace with his two sons. The Liberal combination had not been so united since the days of Palmerston. With Irish Church disestablishment Gladstone had picked a winner; it united Radicals, Dissenters, Adullamites and all; it divided the Tories because the High Church party was in outright opposition while those of Low or broad church views were prepared to concede that the position of the Irish Church could not remain entirely intact. Any danger that Disraeli might 'dish the Whigs' on Ireland as he had done on reform, was now removed. The first of Gladstone's resolutions was passed at the beginning of May with a majority of sixty-five and the others were allowed to pass without a division. Disraeli clearly could not go on, but he was reluctant to surrender the premiership after barely three months. By-passing his colleagues who might have preferred to resign immediately, he secured the Queen's consent to a dissolution, the appeal to be made preferably to the 'new constituency'. The Queen was already, as Gathorne Hardy put it, 'very anti-Gladstonian'. Disraeli's sharp practice caused a great deal of hard feelings all round, mollified only when he announced that the new registers would be ready in November.

In nailing his colours to the mast of disestablishment in Ireland Gladstone acted from deep conviction. At the same time he had brought off a brilliant parliamentary coup. In retrospect he considered it one of the four occasions in his life – the income tax in 1853, Home Rule in 1886, his desire for a dissolution in 1894 being the other three – when he had shown a special political gift, ' . . . an insight into the facts of particular eras, and their relations one to another, which generates in the mind a conviction that the materials exist for forming a public opinion, and for directing it to a particular end'. The reaction of the voters remained to be seen. Essentially

Gladstone had reasserted his control over a parliamentary combination and his popularity out-of-doors had not necessarily been an asset in this process; on the contrary, suspicion of him among many sections of parliamentary Liberals continued to run high. Out-of-doors the complex cluster of interests and ties, local as well as national, that sustained the parliamentary Liberal connection was now enlarged in a manner that no one could fully assess. Gladstone's personality and reputation, deserved or otherwise, and the policy of disestablishing the Irish Church, which he had now put forward as the central issue of the moment, served as the common denominator for all these intra- and extra-parliamentary groups. It was entirely in accordance with the practice of the age. Organized parties which could have evolved a fully fledged programme did not exist and Gladstone would have considered it entirely improper that he should outline such a programme. As it was, the speeches he made in his constituency of South-West Lancashire[8] in the election campaign were criticized as an excessive playing to the gallery by a party leader, a criticism that had clung to him ever since he had revealed himself as the most effective platform speaker among senior politicians in the early 1860s. In these Lancashire speeches Gladstone again made his Irish policy the central feature; he used it to make a general moral appeal to his audience: 'in the removal of this Establishment I see the discharge of a debt of civil justice, the disappearance of a national, almost a world-wide reproach. . .' He conveyed the image of a man and a party bent on removing injustice wherever it might be found, but the details of how injustices and grievances might be removed in other areas, for example in education, were hardly spelt out.

Disestablishment and disendowment of the Church of Ireland was effective enough as an electioneering gambit in the terms in which an election was perceived in 1868. Disraeli found it difficult to counter Gladstone's initiative effectively. He tried to arouse Protestant and anti-Popery feeling, for example through his ecclesiastical appointments. He appointed Canon McNeile of Liverpool, a famous and controversial evangelical preacher, Dean of Ripon. Any electoral advantages he may have derived from such uses of his ecclesiastical patronage were neutralized by the antagonism aroused among High Churchmen. The High Church party may not have been popular, but it was important among the Anglican clergy who in their turn could influence many among the Tory laity. Disraeli certainly had neither the will nor the capacity to counteract Gladstone's popular appeal and his public oratory. The 'disestablishment' cry proved very effective in rallying the Dissenters behind Gladstone. He had already earlier in the year earned their gratitude by sponsoring a bill abolishing all legal proceedings for the recovery of church rates. Even the Wesleyans, normally Conservative, tended to be drawn to the Liberals and the same was true of the Roman Catholics. The Liberation Society with its substantial Liberal and Radical policy was naturally in wholehearted support and Irish Church disestablishment was a vote-winner along the Celtic fringe. During the campaign Gladstone published a pamphlet entitled 'A Chapter of Autobiography' in which he explained his journey from *The State in its Relations with the Church* to his current position as the champion of disestablishment in Ireland.[9] After his victory he wrote, 'Our three *corps d'armée*, I may almost say, have been Scotch presbyterians, English and Welsh nonconformists, and Irish Roman catholics. . . The English clergy as a body have done their worst against us and have hit us hard. . .'

The Irish Church could not, however, be more than a marginal issue among many groups of voters, such as the politically conscious and organized working men. They could be expected to be an important factor in this election. The Tories had made tentative efforts to draw them over to their side by organizing Conservative working-men's clubs and a central body, the National Union, to link them together. The Liberal whips were throughout the year 1868 negotiating with George Howell, the Secretary of the Reform League, and received a good deal of electoral assistance from the League; James Stansfeld, the Radical M.P., served as intermediary.[10] Such a link owed a great deal to the magic of Gladstone's name and helped to overcome the reservations which politically active working men had about the parliamentary Liberals, let alone the Whigs. Similarly Gladstone's reputation helped to keep intellectuals like Henry Fawcett, Goldwin Smith and G. O. Trevelyan tied to political liberalism. Gladstone took no personal interest in links like that with the Reform League; his preoccupation with the great causes and crusades left no room for what he would have considered the small change of politics.

It had been widely expected that the Liberals would win this election. In the 1865 Parliament they had a paper majority of about seventy and the best the Tories could hope for was to reduce this. In fact the Liberals were surprised by the extent of their victory, increasing their majority to 110. They strengthened their hold in Scotland, Wales and Ireland and in the smaller English boroughs. On the other hand the Tories further improved their position in the

English counties and, what was of great significance for the future, they made some advance in the largest English towns, including London. Lancashire was the only place where Gladstone's Irish policy had clearly misfired. This was perhaps not surprising in view of the strong Orange feeling among the working class which was in the main due to the presence of a large Irish population. The Liberal débâcle in Lancashire cost Gladstone his seat, but he had also been nominated at Greenwich, where he was elected. The election results were so clear-cut that Disraeli took the unprecedented step of resigning immediately instead of waiting for the new Parliament to meet.

Gladstone was engaged in his favourite pastime of felling trees at Hawarden when the telegram reached him announcing the impending arrival of General Grey, the Queen's Private Secretary. He handed it to Evelyn Ashley, Palmerston's former private secretary, who was holding his coat, and said: 'Very significant.' He took up the axe again, but after a while he paused and leaning on the handle of the axe said with deep earnestness: 'My mission is to pacify Ireland.'

Gladstone had little difficulty in constructing his Cabinet.[11] The Queen had reservations about Lord Clarendon, whom Gladstone had marked out as Foreign Secretary. Clarendon had a mischievous tongue and called the Queen 'the Missus' while his nickname for Gladstone was 'Merrypebble'. The Queen's fears were soon set at rest. The accession of John Bright was of great political importance; he was the most prominent of the Radicals, though by no means typical of this heterogeneous section of the party. He had consistently put his trust in Gladstone during the battle over reform and defended him against those Radicals who were suspicious of his underlying conservatism. Gladstone in fact owed a great deal of his popular reputation to Bright. By joining the government Bright would help consolidate the alliance between popular and parliamentary Liberalism and Gladstone worked hard to get his co-operation. At bottom Bright had long been eager for office and allowed himself to be persuaded to become President of the Board of Trade; it was not a happy choice for him, for he had few of the executive and temperamental gifts for running a large government department. Another surprising appointment was that of Lowe as Chancellor of the Exchequer and it was remarkable that he and Bright could sit together in the same Cabinet. Gladstone said that his first Cabinet consisted of three Peelites, himself, Cardwell and Argyll, five Whigs and seven new men. The Whigs were Clarendon, Granville, de Grey, Hartington and Chichester Fortescue. Some other Whigs, among them Russell, Sir George Grey, the Duke of Somerset and Halifax, for one reason or another refused office. The Whigs were important to Gladstone: he still believed in the virtues of aristocratic government and he was much concerned to allay their suspicions of him, even though in sheer numbers they now made up a small section of the party. Many moderate Liberals, country gentlemen and well-established provincial industrialists were still inclined to follow a Whig lead. But there were certainly more 'new' men in the Gladstone government than there had been in the days of Palmerston and Russell: Lowe, Cardwell, Goschen, Childers, Bright, Bruce, Forster – these were all men not to the purple born. Gladstone considered his first Cabinet 'one of the best instruments for government ever constructed' and looked back on it 'with great satisfaction'.

Gladstone was very conscious of the strange destiny that had put him not only at the head of the Liberal party but had enabled him to mould this great amalgam of forces very much in his own image and as an instrument of his crusades. On his fifty-ninth birthday, 29 December 1868, he wrote in his diary: 'I descend the hill of life. It would be truer to say I ascend a steepening path with a burden ever gathering weight. The Almighty seems to sustain and spare me for some purpose of His own, deeply unworthy as I know myself to be.' His sense of mission was great, perhaps dangerously great.

8

ZENITH

1868–73

In terms of legislative achievement the government which Gladstone had now formed was to become one of the greatest of the nineteenth century and by far the most important of the four governments of which he was to be the head. If one wishes to define the substance of Gladstonian liberalism the actions of this government are much the best point of reference. Yet there was no plan in existence which might have charted the course this ministry was to take nor was it certain at the outset that its parliamentary majority would prove stable. The previous Parliament had been one of the least stable of the era since 1832 and it had come at the end of a twenty-year period of fluid party lines. There was no guarantee that Gladstone had been able to impose more than a temporary cohesion upon his followers through the Irish disestablishment policy. Disraeli had not abandoned hope that when this policy came to be put into legislative effect the Irish Church would be as damaging to Liberal unity as reform had been. In retrospect the first Gladstone government looks like the beginning of a new era of coherent political parties with a mass following in the country and of much else that was new and modern about the political system. Certain features of the situation were indeed novel and pointed to the future: Gladstone's role as a link between a parliamentary combination and a popular movement in the country, though Palmerston's role had not been so very different; the immediate resignation of Disraeli once the verdict of the country was clear; the Queen's summons to Gladstone, when perhaps only a few years previously she might in similar circumstances have first turned to Lord Russell or Lord Granville.

But in many other ways the novelty of the situation was not recognized, either by Gladstone or by others. He saw himself as the head of a parliamentary combination and the composition of his Cabinet reflected this. He was aware that many reforms were waiting to be taken up which had been in the air for a long time but had been held up in the days of Palmerston and had been impossible to proceed with in the unstable Parliament of 1865. Even the Conservative government had tried to do something about education; there was a royal commission sitting on the trade unions. His Cabinet colleagues were therefore bound to bring up schemes of various kinds and Gladstone would, once the Cabinet had collectively adopted them, facilitate their passage through Parliament. He personally, however, was above all concerned with his Irish crusade; his control over government policy as a whole was therefore not likely to be as complete as Peel's had been between 1841 and 1846. The 'condition of England' question came to be Peel's main preoccupation during the years of his great government and it supplied a unifying theme over a broad range of subjects to the direction in which Peel steered government policy; Gladstone had no such unifying theme to support his control of policy.

Three major measures were the pillars of Gladstone's Irish policy during this first administration: the Church Bill of 1869, the Land Bill of 1870 and the University Bill of 1873. The first resolved the question with which it dealt; the second reached the statute book but failed to solve the grievances of the Irish peasantry; the third never became law and nearly caused the fall of the government. When Gladstone set out to deal with the Irish Church he had the full backing of a united party behind him, a party which had won a majority in an election fought primarily on this issue. Gladstone was in his element; he was fresh to the premiership, fortified by a sense of mission and operating in a field of peculiar interest to him. There was no longer much opposition to the principle of disestablishment, for the verdict of the electorate had been decisive and it was, moreover, a new and enlarged electorate that few wanted to trifle with. The battle concentrated on disendowment and the attempts by the friends of the Irish Church and the supporters of the Anglican Establishment generally to rescue as much as possible for the dispossessed Church and its clergy and institutions. Gladstone made valiant efforts, some of them perhaps rather naïve, to arrive at an agreed solution with the Irish and English bishops. In these efforts the Queen and Lord Granville played a leading role. The Queen was not in favour of the disestablishment policy in particular and she was by this time clearly opposed to Gladstone's general political line. Nevertheless, relations between her and her Prime Minister still oscillated between friendly courtesy and correct politeness; more marked antagonism was to come later in the life of this ministry and acute hostility did not arise until after the Queen had experienced six years of Disraeli's premiership. The role which the Queen played in the crisis on the Irish Church Bill was entirely helpful. Lord Granville was *persona grata* with the Queen and was often able to smooth relations between her and the Prime Minister. He was at the same time Gladstone's closest political confidant and friend and their correspondence from 1868 until 1886 forms a most valuable source for the history of three of Gladstone's four governments. Granville had the manly charm and openness that always appealed to Gladstone; it was also characteristic that a man of such pure Whig background should in fact have been the person closest to the Liberal leader.

Gladstone introduced the Irish Church Bill in the Commons in a masterly three-hour speech on 1 March 1869. The bill ended the establishment of the Irish Church and the union of the English and Irish Churches from 1 January 1871. Of the £15–16 million of Church revenue, some £10 million according to Gladstone's estimate were to be given back to the disestablished Church to meet its various reasonable necessities and claims, leaving some £5 million to be used for secular purposes, 'mainly for the relief of unavoidable calamity and suffering not touched by the Poor Law'. This meant a decisive rejection of all notions of concurrent endowment; the grants

F

to Maynooth and the Irish Presbyterians, the so-called *Regium Donum*, were in fact to cease. Gladstone was aware that concurrent endowment would logically lead to a kind of free trade in religion; provided a religion could attract a sufficient number of followers it would be impossible to withhold from it some state support. The details of the scheme were of massive complexity and Gladstone showed once more his astonishing gift of not only mastering such details, but of conveying them intelligibly to a large audience. Even Disraeli acknowledged that not a single word had been wasted. The second reading majority was 118, a figure slightly in excess of the nominal Liberal majority. This was regarded as a remarkable triumph after years of thin majorities on major issues that made and unmade governments. Disraeli called it a mechanical majority; what was not generally realized was that it was the harbinger of an age of more strictly defined party lines. The Liberal majority on subsequent major divisions on the Irish Church Bill remained of a similar size. The real battle came in the House of Lords. Efforts by the Queen to prepare a compromise were not effective. Only one English bishop voted for the bill and the two Archbishops abstained. The day was saved for the government by Lord Salisbury who led a group of Tory peers to vote for the second reading, thus causing a split in the opposition ranks. Among High Churchmen the Irish Church, which was generally low, had never been popular and Salisbury was prepared to play the game flexibly, although in principle he was, of course, a strong opponent of Irish Church disestablishment. Cairns, the fiercely Protestant Ulsterman who led the Tories in the Lords, was humiliated and it was a corresponding victory for Granville.

On the committee stage in the Lords, however, the disendowment provisions of the bill were materially altered in favour of the Irish Church; above all the preamble allocating the residual revenues of the Church to non-religious purposes was struck out and thus the notion of concurrent endowment was brought in again. In July the Commons rejected most of the Lords' amendments and for a few days there was a tense situation. The Lords restored their version of the preamble again, but after this show of defiance saner counsels prevailed and Cairns was ready for compromise. The strain of those days, when it looked as if the bill might be lost, was so great that Gladstone became ill and some of the vital negotiations were conducted for him by Granville. His relief when the bill was finally home and dry and a constitutional conflict avoided was great; he told the Queen that it was a beneficent and necessary measure.

The disestablishment bill not only had obvious electoral backing, it united in support the Liberation Society with most of Irish Catholicism and the Irish hierarchy. Even the Vatican steered clear of involvement, in spite of Tory attempts to get it to declare against the bill and despite the fact that the settlement in Ireland was along the lines of '*libera chiesa in libero stato*', a principle that did not commend itself to the Papacy. On this issue Manning gave his full support to Gladstone. Before the Church Bill was out of the way Gladstone turned to the land question in Ireland and on this he could not expect the united support of his own side. The basic problem was that according to English notions of property and contract the Irish peasant was a tenant; in fact and in his own view of himself he was a co-proprietor. The principle that the tenant should have some right to the improvements he had made on the land was recognized, however imperfectly, by previous legislation. The Irish peasant's greatest grievance, however, was eviction and this was often brought about by the imposition of rents which the tenant was unable to pay. The only protection against this evil was to go beyond payment for improvements and to adopt in some form the principle of compensation for disturbance.[1] Gladstone's initial instinct was to give generous recognition to tenant-right and perhaps go the whole way towards fixity of tenure, the principle eventually accepted in his second Land Act of 1881. He soon realized that this was not practical politics given the strength of the landlord interest not only in Ireland but throughout the United Kingdom, not least inside his own Cabinet. He therefore came to base his plan on the extension to the whole of Ireland of the customary understandings which in Ulster gave far-reaching protection to the tenant. Even this idea did not wholly survive when the bill was in its final shape: customary tenant-right was legalized where it existed, in Ulster and elsewhere in Ireland; apart from this the bill attempted to enforce compensation for disturbance. Gladstone relied mainly on his own reading and knowledge in preparing the bill. He was in correspondence with some of the leaders of the now defunct Irish tenant-right movement, but was not much influenced by them. He had the help of Chichester Fortescue, the Chief Secretary for Ireland, and of Sir Edward Sullivan, the Irish Attorney-General, but Fortescue, a timid man, was frequently in disagreement with his chief. Throughout, Gladstone was the driving force in trying to secure justice for the Irish peasantry in face of the offended property sense of his colleagues. Argyll, Cardwell, Clarendon and Lowe were among those in the Cabinet who at various stages resisted the Prime Minister's intentions, and the break-up of the government on the Irish land question was within the bounds of possibility for some weeks in the winter of 1869-70. Bright, on the other hand, had for long been a supporter of land purchase as the cure for the Irish agrarian problem and this solution, at one time also advocated by J.S.Mill, he now pressed on Gladstone. His proposals for 'free trade in land' showed, however, that he also was deeply attached to the sanctity of property. The bill did eventually include the so-called Bright's clauses providing facilities for land purchase; they proved in practice very ineffective, for few Irish peasants could afford the initial deposit.

Gladstone skilfully rode out the divergent views of his colleagues and little of these dissensions leaked out. When he introduced the bill in the House of Commons on 15 February 1870 the public had come to expect legislation on the Irish land problem as inevitable. Thus the Conservatives did not oppose the bill in principle, in spite of its potentially profound implications for all owners of property, and the second reading was carried by 422 votes to 11. But Gladstone had to fight a long and lonely parliamentary battle for the bill during the next three and a half months. His colleagues gave him little assistance, largely because they did not have the knowledge to survive in the morass of the Irish land problem. Even Gladstone's knowledge was acquired in haste, rather than matured over the years as had been the case with the Irish Church.

Two factors in particular made the fight difficult. Irish opinion and the Irish hierarchy were not wholeheartedly behind the bill, for they saw, rightly as it turned out, its practical shortcomings. Moreover, English opinion began to take an unsympathetic turn as the proceedings of the Vatican Council became known. Gladstone wrote to Manning on 16 April 1870:

... I seem to myself to trace the influence of the same bitter aversion to the Roman policy in a matter, to me at least, of the most profound and absorbing interest – I mean the Irish Land Bill . . . the tone and atmosphere of Parliament have changed about the Land Bill; again for the second time within a fortnight I have been obliged to resort to something like menace, the strain thus for me has been extreme, and I regret to say it is not yet over.

The main battle in Parliament was over the clause defining the conditions under which a court could order compensation for eviction. In its final form the clause made such an order possible if the rent was proved to be 'exorbitant'. This greatly weakened the act in practice. On the whole, however, the Irish Land Act aroused less opposition in the Lords as well as in the Commons than could have been expected. It was a monument to the persistence, industry and power of Gladstone. In practice it was only very partially effective, but it prepared the way for Gladstone's own more far-reaching act of 1881. Unfortunately it also showed the Irish that they could never expect satisfactory treatment from the hands of English politicians, however sympathetically inclined. Gladstone found himself trapped in the coils of the Irish question: he could never deliver enough at Westminster to appease the Irish sense of grievance.

Ireland continued to be, in defiance of political expediency, a passionate preoccupation with Gladstone. Concurrently with the Land Bill he was attempting the repeal of the Ecclesiastical Titles Act, which had been passed during the 'No Popery' hysteria of 1851; because of the anti-Catholic feeling provoked by the Vatican Council the repeal failed in the session of 1870, but was finally successful in the session of 1871. Against the opposition of his colleagues and the Queen he secured the release of the Fenian prisoners at the end of 1870. For long he pondered the possibility of establishing a permanent royal residence in Ireland in order to link the Royal Family more closely with John Bull's other island. He also began to see this project as a means of giving employment to the Prince of Wales and counteracting the unpopularity into which the monarchy was drifting as a result of the Queen's constant seclusion. In a long memorandum to Granville of 3 December 1870 he outlined a scheme under which the Prince of Wales would spend half the year in Ireland as the Queen's representative. Lord Bessborough called the idea 'the wildest and most visionary . . . I have ever heard of'.[2] The Queen was not at all anxious for the Prince of Wales to be employed and such ideas played their part in the growing estrangement between the Queen and her Prime Minister.

While the Irish Land Bill was going through Parliament in the session of 1870, the government had also embarked upon another major measure, the Education Bill. Gladstone never had a strong interest in education for its own sake; his concern was above all for the position of the Church and the nature of religious instruction. Throughout the nineteenth century the role of the state in education was bedevilled by the conflict between Anglicans and Nonconformists and whenever that problem cropped up Gladstone consistently emphasized the need for the integrity of religious instruction. He was not prepared to tamper with the way religion was taught for the sake of enabling children of different denominations to attend the same lessons. He preferred a conscience clause, by which, for example, Dissenters could withdraw their children from Anglican religious instruction; he was quite prepared to have teaching provided by public funds restricted to secular instruction. In the late 1860s there was growing pressure for an expansion of the educational system: in 1866 Robert Lowe had talked of 'educating our masters' and the British system was being compared unfavourably with that of foreign nations, particularly Prussia. Two important organizations were founded in 1869 to press for educational reform: the predominantly Nonconformist National Education League campaigned for free, compulsory, non-sectarian schools, and the National Education Union defended the voluntary and denominational schools. Gladstone may well have felt that his government would inevitably have to deal with education sooner or later and that delay would be damaging to the cause of the denominational schools which he had at heart. It would be more difficult to take up the Irish education question if the schools in the rest of Britain had not first been given attention. The two ministers immediately responsible for education were Lord de Grey and Forster; the latter was the real driving force and responsible for drafting the bill, but he did not get a seat in the Cabinet till July 1870. Even though Gladstone did not take the initiative on education, he was prepared to make room for legislation alongside his Irish Land Bill and when the time came he threw himself wholeheartedly into the parliamentary battle.[3]

The main feature of the bill introduced by Forster in February 1870 was that it was designed to supplement voluntary and denominational effort in education and not to supersede it. This had Gladstone's wholehearted approval. The state would intervene only in districts where educational provision was proved to be deficient; after a year's grace to allow voluntary effort to make good the deficiency, school boards with power to levy a rate might establish free schools, make bye-laws for compulsory attendance (so-called 'permissive compulsion'), assist existing schools and pay fees for poor parents. Gladstone would have preferred that state or rate-aided schools should limit themselves to giving secular instruction. When Forster's memorandum on the principles of the bill was being discussed in the autumn of 1869 he commented, '... Why not adopt frankly the principle that the State or local community should provide the secular teaching ...' Had Gladstone's view prevailed the government might have saved itself the damaging conflict with the militant Nonconformists which the bill produced.

After the bill's introduction there was a momentary and deceptive lull, but then it quickly ran into heavy and vocal opposition. The nature of the opposition was, however, complex: on the one hand there were those, led by the Birmingham group of the National Education League round George Dixon and Joseph Chamberlain, who opposed the bill on the broad strategic ground that it did not set up a universal, compulsory, secular system of national education; their opposition on religious grounds to details of the bill was subordinate to this general objection. The general body of Nonconformists were chiefly concerned about the problem of religious instruction and opposed to any use of the rates to support denominational schools. Some prominent dissenters, for example Edward Baines and J.H. Rigg, were firmly attached to the voluntary principle in education; at the other end of the political spectrum Cardinal Manning, preoccupied though he was with the Vatican Council and with special pleading for the Catholic position, was corresponding with Gladstone in a sense broadly sympathetic to the government's policy of supplementing the denominational effort in education. Gladstone and his colleagues could not, on grounds of principle, have satisfied the secularists, though they might have gone further in their direction on issues such as compulsion, where Forster's original draft of the bill had included universal rather than 'permissive' compulsion. It was, however, just on compulsion that Gladstone had reservations and could not bring himself to go all the way. Whatever concessions the government might have made to the secularists, they had to be limited to avoid losing the support of the denominationalists. Without their support the bill could not pass through the Commons and would be rejected by the Lords. The fact that the government frequently relied on Tory support during the passage of the bill further inflamed the anger of militant Nonconformists. Gladstone was, however, anxious to meet Nonconformist grievances as far as possible; it was one of the reasons for the long gap in the parliamentary consideration of the bill between March and June and the main intention behind the substantial amendments which were introduced by Gladstone in June and which included the Cowper–Temple clause. This clause provided that in rate-founded schools no catechism or formulary distinctive of any particular denomination should be taught. Gladstone did not immediately perceive the import of the clause; he accepted Forster's view that 'under the new clause you may teach Transubstantiation in every Board School in England, so long as you don't teach it out of the Penny Catechism'. In his later years Gladstone considered 'Cowper–Temple religion' a moral monster and regretted that his solution of confining publicly provided teaching to secular instruction had not been adopted.

Gladstone was not insensitive to Nonconformist objections to the bill nor unaware of the damage the alienation of organized dissent could do to his party. On the other hand the controversy shows that however much Nonconformists in the country might have come to look up to Gladstone as a leader, he and they differed deeply in their persuasions and attitudes. In March he personally met the great Education League deputation against the bill for which Joseph Chamberlain acted as chief spokesman; in reply the Prime Minister was courteous, Olympian and gave away nothing. It was the first encounter between the two men whose mutual lack of sympathy was eventually to split the party. In July Gladstone spoke sharply against Miall, the Liberationist leader, who had accused him of leading the Nonconformists through the valley of humiliation: 'I hope my hon. friend will not continue his support to the government one moment longer than he deems it consistent with his sense of right and duty. For God's sake, sir, let him withdraw it the moment he thinks it better for the cause he has at heart that he should do so.' In spite of the government's concessions, admittedly limited and to some extent peripheral, the Nonconformists were not reconciled; in their denominational jealousy they did not see that in the long run the threat to all forms of religion came from secularism. For the next few years their opposition focused on Clause 25, under which the fees of poor children in denominational schools could be subsidized from the rates. In spite of all controversy the Education Act of 1870 was perhaps the single most important achievement of Gladstone's first ministry. He himself was not an initiator in this matter as he was on Irish policy; but because so much of the controversy raged round Forster his part has perhaps been underestimated. The Act bore the stamp of much that he believed in: his concern for the work of the Church in education, his preference for voluntary over state action and his distrust of compulsion. In 1888, when reviewing Wemyss Reid's *Life of Forster*, he wrote in the *Nineteenth Century*:

... if we had been dealing with a *tabula rasa*, I should have preferred the provisions of the Scotch Education Act ... which give to the local School Board a free discretion with regard to denominational education ... I am strongly of opinion that arrangements ... should be permitted under which the master who gives the secular teaching should not be disabled from giving religious instruction also ... at other times, and perhaps even within the walls of the school house.[4]

In July 1870, while the House of Commons was discussing the Education Bill, a drama of vastly greater proportions was unfolding on the Continent of Europe, the outbreak of the Franco-Prussian war. It was the first of three major problems of foreign policy which the Gladstone government had to face; the other two were the renunciation by Russia of the Black Sea clauses of the Treaty of Paris and the American claims arising out of the Civil War. The Franco-Prussian War was much the most important of these three issues but it was also the event on which any British government, whatever its political complexion, was least able to exercise any influence. Ever since Palmerston had postured in vain on the Schleswig-Holstein question in 1864 there was a strong current of opinion in Britain against taking up attitudes in the affairs of Continental Europe which could not be sustained by action. The one exception to this rule was Belgium, where British opinion remained sensitive to possible encroachment, particularly by France. This problem had disturbed the Conservative government in 1867 and the Liberal government in 1869. The Conservative government between 1866 and 1868 had been hardly less keen than Gladstone when he held office under Palmerston and Russell to exercise economy in naval and military expenditure. Consciousness of British military weakness in the face of growing Continental tensions was the motive behind a disarmament proposal which Clarendon put forward with the enthusiastic support of Gladstone in January 1870. It was like whispering in the teeth of a gale.

When the crisis over the Hohenzollern candidature for the Spanish throne broke in July 1870 Clarendon had just died and been succeeded by Granville. Bismarck was probably exaggerating when he remarked to Clarendon's daughter in 1871, 'Never in my life was I so glad to hear of anything as of your father's death.' Clarendon undoubtedly had a reputation as a diplomatist on the Continent, but it was probably exaggerated in British eyes and became an article of faith with Gladstone. Nevertheless Clarendon might have been able to act with more effect than Granville and Gladstone in the Franco-Prussian crisis, but it seems unlikely that the final result could have been much different. Gladstone was very pleased to have his friend at the Foreign Office: 'We are happy in being able to fill the office with a man who has the deep calm of Ld. Aberdeen, a strong sense of justice, much foreign knowledge, and singular tact.' When Granville went to the Foreign Office on 5 July, Hammond, the Permanent Under-Secretary, told him that 'he had never during his long experience known so great a lull in foreign affairs'. When the lull was broken with a vengeance in the following few days Gladstone worked together with Granville to restrain the parties to the dispute. Their efforts were somewhat peripheral to the course of the crisis and lagged behind the speed of events. They seem to have been slow to appreciate the gravity of the crisis and Granville had to restrain Gladstone from attending a funeral in Scotland during the critical days. In common with public opinion at that stage they had little sympathy for the position the French had taken up and irritated Paris by supporting the fiction that the candidature was entirely a matter between the Spanish government and the Hohenzollern family.

Once the war had broken out, Belgium became again the chief preoccupation of the British government. Bismarck communicated to the British government the French proposal, made in 1867 and in 1869 and known as the Benedetti draft treaty, to trade South Germany for Belgium. Gladstone and Granville wisely refused to swallow the bait, but their hand was forced when the draft treaty was leaked to *The Times*, where it was published on 25 July 1870. Public opinion was aroused and Gladstone was now concerned that a new Belgian neutrality treaty should be signed with France and Prussia as quickly as possible. It was in fact done within a fortnight, but Gladstone made it clear in the House of Commons that its chief merit in his eyes was that it avoided a situation where Britain might have to act alone in the defence of Belgium. Thus even the concern for Belgian neutrality of successive British governments in the 1860s was more a matter of self-esteem and assertion rather than a realistic commitment.

Up to this point the Gladstone government had conducted a policy which was not specifically Gladstonian and which would not have been materially different under Disraeli. It can be criticized on detail only and its general drift was inevitable. In October 1870 Gladstone reviewed the course of events in an anonymous article in the *Edinburgh Review*.[5] It shows him well in line with public opinion at that moment. He stresses the folly of French policy through which the moral advantage in the war was handed to Prussia. There is a note of complacency when he writes of Britain's enhanced naval security; he deplores the general rise in military establishments, but mentions the work which his colleague Cardwell is doing to improve British military efficiency. Gladstone seems to have had little foreboding at this point that his vision of the international community and of European civilization had been seriously compromised by these momentous events.

Gladstone came out much more in his true colours when it came to the Prussian demand for the annexation of Alsace-Lorraine. In a long memorandum he argued passionately for a British initiative to mobilize the Concert of Europe against this 'violent laceration'. He based his case not on the inviolability of national territory, but on the need to act in accordance with the wishes of the inhabitants of the territories. In a brief note to Granville accompanying this memorandum he wrote: 'I am much oppressed with the idea that this transfer of human beings like chattels should go forward without any voice from collective Europe if it had disposed to speak.' The Cabinet and Granville were not surprisingly unwilling to support the Prime Minister. Gladstone himself was hardly facing up to the dilemma between a moralistic foreign policy and the principle of non-intervention. He allowed himself to be overruled on this occasion; in practice his innocent enthusiasm and Granville's tactful prudence made a useful combination. When one considers how the annexation of Alsace-Lorraine poisoned Franco-German relations for the next half-century, one cannot withhold one's sympathy from Gladstone's views, however impractical they were at that juncture.

Russia's abrogation of the Black Sea clauses of the Treaty of Paris of 1856 arose directly out of the Franco-Prussian War. Russia had regained her freedom of action as a result of her acquiescence in Prussia's actions during the Franco-Prussian clash. Gladstone had never approved of the later phases of the Crimean War and shared the general view that the neutralization clauses could not be maintained. On the other hand his fundamental faith in the Concert of Europe and the sanctity of treaties was outraged by Russia's unilateral opportunist action. To him it was part of the general breakdown of the public law of Europe, of which the Franco-Prussian War and the Italian seizure of Rome were other instances. Yet Gladstone could not be other than disgusted by the war hysteria rapidly unleashed in the country after the receipt of Gortchakoff's circular. 'The tone of the press (though in some respects it may be useful) shows me that we have a highly inflammable and susceptible state of the public mind to deal with', he wrote to Granville, and he was opposed to all actions which might aggravate the risk of war. Of the various options open to it the government chose to work for a conference, so that the Treaty of Paris could be changed in an orderly manner. The risk of war was made to appear real enough to convince even Bismarck that he must put pressure on the Russians to come to the conference table.

The London Conference met and after three months the offending clauses were abrogated by agreement. To this extent Gladstone and Granville had been successful, but it earned them little popularity. The pendulum was beginning to swing against the non-interventionist policy which was itself a reaction against Palmerston's impotent meddlesomeness in his final years. Gladstone was not, of course, an unconditional non-interventionist, but a moralist in international relations. The public felt that Britain had stood by helpless while great decisions were being made and the feeling was widespread that Gladstone was unable to handle foreign affairs. Disraeli was waiting in the wings to come out with more assertive statements about England's imperial mission and her power and these proved to be more in harmony with the mood of the moment.

The third of the three major foreign policy issues which faced the Gladstone government was the settlement by arbitration of the claims and counter-claims of the British and American governments arising out of the Civil War and other matters. It contributed even more than the other foreign policy problems to the unpopularity of the government and the Prime Minister which was making itself increasingly felt after 1870. It was on this matter, however, that the verdict of history has gone most unequivocally in favour of the course taken by Gladstone and his government. Even from the standpoint of *Realpolitik* it was right that every effort should be made to remove the irritants from the Anglo-American relationship. The alarms of 1870 made it relatively easy to set in train the process of dealing with the claims by arbitration. An earlier attempt by Stanley, the Conservative Foreign Secretary, to promote an arbitration treaty had finally come to grief in the American Senate; informed opinion was agreed early in 1871 that another attempt should be made. What could not be anticipated then was that it would take nearly two years of frequently severe bickering before the claims were finally settled; and that during that time the government would often have to take an unpopular stand in order to prevent a breakdown in the face of provocative American demands. The attitude of the United States government was naturally much influenced by its own domestic political exigencies and by the pleasure taken by many American politicians in twisting the Lion's tail. The Americans were particularly unreasonable over the indirect claims: they attempted to make the British liable for a whole chain of ramifying contingencies flowing from the escape of the *Alabama*. The way in which these claims cropped up again and again even after there had been an apparent agreement to drop them caused even Gladstone severe irritation. In the spring of 1871 the Treaty of Washington had after complex negotiations been signed and the British understanding was that the indirect claims had been excluded. When the Americans put their case to the arbitrators early in 1872 the full panoply of indirect claims was back again. Gladstone wrote to the Queen that the conduct of the American Government in this affair was the most disreputable he had ever known in his recollection of diplomacy. From then until June 1872 the progress of the Geneva Arbitration remained a constant preoccupation. Gladstone was determined to go on even though the cohesion of his government was threatened. Some members of the government, notably Halifax, Cardwell and Kimberley, the Colonial Secretary, disliked the way in which the other cheek was being turned to the Americans; Lord Russell, still somewhat prestigious as the former Liberal leader, propounded the same view from outside. Kimberley had written in his journal after the signature of the Washington Treaty in June 1871: 'the more you cringe to the Americans the more they will bluster and bully.'[6] Though Gladstone might have been emotionally inclined to share this view at times he persevered impressively in the face of Cabinet divisions and popular opprobrium. In September 1872 the arbitrators awarded the sum of $15 million to the Americans; although it was much less than had been asked for it stuck in many people's gullets and brought the government further unpopularity. In seeing the Anglo-American arbitration through to its final settlement Gladstone showed most clearly his firm adherence to the principles which governed his view of international relations. For most of the time, however, he had the support of the opposition and there was therefore no striking clash of principle such as occurred a few years later over the Eastern Question.

In the meantime the wide-ranging work of the ministry in domestic reform, unexampled in the nineteenth century, went on. There were few matters in which Gladstone did not have a hand, either in Cabinet discussions or in the House of Commons. His heart was more in it in some cases than in others and in general terms his interest in the legislation of his ministers declined after 1870. In the early days of his government he was keen to advance the principle of open competition in the Civil Service on which he had himself made a start when he was Chancellor of the Exchequer in the Aberdeen government. This required no legislation, but it met with opposition in the Cabinet, especially from Clarendon. Gladstone hit upon a formula by which it was left to the individual minister to decide whether recruitment to his department should be by open competition through the Civil Service Commission set up in 1855. All departments quickly fell into line, except the Foreign Office, which clung to the system of limited competition combined with nomination that was in force before 1870. Lowe as Chancellor of the Exchequer had been the driving force behind these changes and Gladstone had shrewdly helped him to out-manoeuvre opposition in the Cabinet. On the other hand it was also Gladstone who helped Clarendon to plead the special nature of the Foreign Office. He did it with a clear conscience, for in his view the exception of the Foreign Office did not infringe the general principle.

Gladstone moved with great reluctance in abolishing the religious tests for university and college teaching posts at Oxford and Cambridge. It was a matter in which for long he had been deeply involved at Oxford; fundamentally he had not moved from the position that the two ancient universities, though open to non-Anglicans, were essentially Anglican institutions. Even before he became Prime Minister he had realized that this position might not be tenable much longer, but he was reluctant to be himself instrumental in doing something that was so contrary to many of his convictions. It was not till the session of 1871 that he allowed a government bill to go forward abolishing the tests. To some extent he squared it with his conscience by thinking of it as a measure that would forestall even more far-reaching proposals, made by Miall and others, to abolish all clerical fellowships. Once Gladstone had decided that the University Tests Bill should go forward he saw to it that it was vigorously defended against Salisbury's efforts in the Lords to block it.

An example of what Gladstone saw as the limits of reform can perhaps be seen in the trade union legislation of 1871. In some respects this bill which was in the hands of Bruce, the Home Secretary, embodied the pro-labour minority recommendations of the Royal Commission on the Trade Unions. These had been put forward by Frederic Harrison, the Positivist and intellectual friend of the unions. But while Bruce's bill gave the unions a specially protected legal status, it in effect outlawed picketing and thus took away with one hand what it gave with the other. When the Cabinet discussed the bill in January 1871 Gladstone made the significant note: 'principle to punish violence; and in all economical matters the law to take no part.' Trade unionists mounted a vigorous campaign against the picketing clauses of the bill, with the help of friendly Liberal M.P.s such as A.J.Mundella, Thomas Hughes and

Samuel Morley.[7] The most the government would agree to was a separation of the picketing clauses from the rest of the bill; thus two bills became law in 1871, the Trade Union Act and the Criminal Law Amendment Act, and the campaign of the unions was henceforth concentrated against the second. Gladstone was not unaware of the importance of organized labour in society and ever since the early 1860s had put increasing confidence in the more respectable sections of the working class, as his views on parliamentary reform showed, but on grounds of principle he was unwilling to concede a privileged legal position to the unions. *Laissez-faire* feeling in the Liberal party was sufficiently strong to prevent the unions from achieving a change in the law before 1874; the opportunity was thus given to Disraeli's government to meet the demands of organized labour in their trade union legislation of 1875.

Gladstone gave his full backing to Cardwell's army reforms and played a full part in the battle to abolish the purchase of commissions in 1871. Cardwell was one of the few remaining Peelite colleagues of the Prime Minister and was actuated by the same zeal for economy and efficiency; Gladstone refused to accept Cardwell's suggestion that he should stand down in favour of a soldier in order to strengthen the government's position during the difficult parliamentary fight over the abolition of purchase.[8] The obstruction of the Tory 'colonels' in the Commons and the rejection of abolition by the Lords were two of the many incidents which confirmed Gladstone's view of the upper classes as selfish and lacking in moral sense. In his great public speech to his Greenwich constituents in October of that year he said: 'in attacking purchase in the army, we were perfectly well aware that we were assailing class interest in its favourite and most formidable stronghold.' Gladstone was much attacked for the *coup d'état* in which abolition of purchase was carried out by royal warrant; he was called 'the imperious minister'. It was the kind of action that offended purists even on the left like Fawcett. On this occasion Gladstone and Cardwell were backed by a united Cabinet and even the Queen played her part without demur. Shortly afterwards the Lords also rejected the Ballot Bill. This was not a cause that Gladstone had particularly at heart and the support for it among some of his more Whiggish colleagues was lukewarm. But Gladstone knew that the failure of the bill would merely fan popular feeling, just as the failure of reform in 1866 had done. He was angry with the House of Lords and in his public speeches in the autumn he attacked their actions. He was careful at the same time to express his continued support for the House of

Lords as an institution and for the aristocratic contribution to government. The Ballot Bill was eventually passed in the session of 1872.

Gladstone took little interest in Bruce's licensing legislation in the sessions of 1871 and 1872. At the time of the Cobden treaty he had worked in favour of free trade in wine and had tried to open up the wine trade; he had little sympathy with the organized temperance interest. In the House of Commons the bills introduced by Bruce were dealt with to a large extent on a non-party basis; only in the public reaction to the new licensing law did the Liberals become increasingly identified with temperance.[9] Much weight has often been attached to the licensing question as a factor in the decline of Liberal popularity. Modest though the bill of 1872 was, it could help to arouse emotion by being pilloried as an attack on property and liberty and contributed to a public mood that was not helpful to the government.

There could be little doubt that the government and Gladstone himself were becoming unpopular. By-elections told their tale. When on 27 February 1872 the nation's leaders went to St Paul's for a Thanksgiving Service after the Prince of Wales's recovery from his near-fatal illness, Disraeli was cheered to the echo and Gladstone was greeted by silence broken by occasional hoots. The strain of office was telling on the Prime Minister. He was not a man who could ever really relax and further work was his best relaxation. But sometimes now he found it difficult to detach himself from the feverish controversies of which he was so often the centre in the House of Commons; his brain went racing on, rehearsing arguments, and he found it difficult to get to sleep. He spoke much of retirement once he had completed his Irish mission and he would point out that his government had already lasted longer than the previous two Liberal governments with comfortable majorities, Palmerston's in 1857 and Russell's in 1865. Gladstone was suffering from the irritability of temper that afflicted him in 1866 when he led the House for the first time; a sense of proportion had never been his strong point and now the lack of it led him to make mountains out of molehills. Two somewhat unfortunate appointments made by Gladstone in the winter of 1871–2 added to the impression that he was increasingly accident-prone. He appointed Sir Robert Collier, the Attorney-General, to be a paid member of the judicial committee of the Privy Council. Since it was a qualification for this office to have been a puisne judge, Collier was first appointed to the common law bench. In a similar way he appointed the Reverend

W. W. Harvey, a Cambridge graduate, to be rector of Ewelme, where it was a qualification to be a member of the Convocation of Oxford; and in order to qualify Harvey was duly incorporated at Oxford. Both men were entirely suitable for their offices, but the appointments nevertheless raised a storm. Gladstone gave the impression of being a man prepared, for all his conscientiousness, to cut corners and obstinate to boot. He was in fact punctiliousness itself and such cases were for him disproportionately exhausting.

One of the responsibilities which kept Gladstone reluctantly chained to the wheel was what he called the 'Royalty Question' and here his sense of proportion deserted him badly. His great loyalty to the Monarchy as an institution and to the Queen personally made him feel it was his duty to draw her out of the seclusion that was making her unpopular and strengthening the republican movement in the country. In the Queen he met a will as strong as his own and the more he pressed her to undertake public duties the more she fell back on pleading the state of her health and her circumstances as an excuse. On 5 August 1871 Kimberley wrote in his diary:

> Gladstone has worked himself up into a tremendous pitch of excitement about the Queen's going away before the prorogation . . . No doubt petty outbursts of ill-humour because she is asked to forego the breezes of Balmoral for a few days beyond her usual time, are very provoking to a hard worked Minister; but the only wise thing to do in such circumstances is to remember that she must have whims like other women, to shrug one's shoulders and bear philosophically these little annoyances. Unfortunately this is just the last thing that Gladstone can do, and if he does not take care he may get into a serious difficulty about these trifles.

In the summer of 1872 Gladstone was still exchanging lengthy letters and memoranda with the Queen about finding employment for the Prince of Wales by establishing a permanent royal residence in Ireland. It was a plan that had been doomed from the moment Gladstone put it forward in 1870, though it is fair to add that Colonel Ponsonby, who had succeeded General Grey as the Queen's Private Secretary in that year, and others at Court gave it every encouragement. Gladstone returned to the charge again and again, long after it was obvious that it would all be futile. No wonder the Queen felt as she wrote to Ponsonby two years later that in Gladstone's manner there was 'an overbearing obstinacy and imperiousness (without being actually wanting in respect as to form) which she never experienced from *anyone* else, and which she found most disagreeable. It is the same thing which made him so unpopular to his followers, and even to his colleagues.'[10]

As Gladstone's government was declining in vigour and popular esteem in 1872 Disraeli was doing what he could to profit from the breeze. Up to this time he had played his role as Leader of the Opposition in low key, partly from apathy and for various personal reasons, partly because the opportunity did not beckon. There were many in the Tory party who would dearly have liked to find another leader, but once Disraeli had decided to reassert himself such plots and cabals were doomed to futility. By the spring of 1872 Disraeli judged the time had come to sound a clarion call and in a series of programmatic speeches he lightly sketched a Conservative programme and painted a Conservative image. All this showed that deep tides were running against Gladstone's government. It was not only that organized groups like the Nonconformists, labour and the licensed victuallers were aggrieved. The whole ethos of Gladstonian liberalism, self-fulfilment, self-help, individual and social morality, for the moment no longer satisfied the nation as a collectivity as much as it had done. Perhaps Gladstone could have arrested this trend if he had firmly aligned himself with the demands of his more radical followers. Instead he felt increasingly bitter about their ingratitude, whether it was the Nonconformists on education or the temperance interests on licensing or the trade unions on the labour laws. More than ever his inclination was to retire as soon as possible and only his personal causes, above all his desire to complete his Irish mission, made him go on.

The obstacles in the path of Gladstone's Irish mission had grown since the passage of the Land Bill. Anti-Catholic feeling in England and Scotland was roused by the Vatican Council and the proclamation of papal infallibility. Many Nonconformists were anyhow alienated from the Liberal government. In Ireland Butt's Home Rule party was beginning to develop and various specific incidents and events were driving Irish and English opinion as far apart as ever. There were agrarian outrages; the Galway election in 1872 demonstrated to the English the priest-ridden nature of Irish affairs, while the petition arising out of it and the Keogh judgement showed the Irish once more the total lack of understanding with which an English judicial and administrative system was treating them.

If education was to be the area in which Gladstone would make his next attempt to 'pacify Ireland', then there were particular difficulties. The trend in England was towards secular education, but the Irish hierarchy wanted to control their own education;

this no British House of Commons would give them. As early as August 1870 Gladstone had asked Fortescue, then Chief Secretary for Ireland, to prepare the ground for legislation on the Irish University question, but to do so in no 'violent hurry'. The government's legislative programme was full to bursting. At that time Gladstone also told Fortescue: 'It seems to me that in the main we *know* what we ought to give them whether they will take it or not.' Higher education was not the only matter awaiting settlement in Ireland. A royal commission reported on primary education in 1870 and recommended a system that would in practice replace unified with denominational education. Gladstone realized that the obstacles to legislating along these lines were too great and left this question alone, in spite of considerable pressure on him from Ireland to deal with it. Hartington, who succeded Fortescue as Irish Secretary in 1870, wrote to Moriarty, the Bishop of Kerry:

> The speeches which have lately been delivered at public meetings and the requirements of the Roman Catholic bishops (as I understood them), do appear to me to demand an amount of control on their part over the system of State Education which I do not think the Government or Parliament could be justified in conceding.[11]

Hartington himself was keen to legislate on the railways and local government in Ireland, but Gladstone felt that university reform was more urgent.

In the autumn of 1872 he went to work in earnest on the question which had baffled successive governments. He did not consult the Irish bishops for he knew only too well that he could not hope wholly to satisfy them. His solution was to embody a new University of Dublin as a teaching and examining body into which the existing denominational colleges like Trinity College, Dublin, and Maynooth would be combined. It was open to Catholics and Protestants alike, but theology, moral philosophy and history would be excluded from the curriculum. This latter provision did not satisfy the Irish bishops, who were opposed to mixed education. On the other hand it offended radical secularists like Henry Fawcett. In spite of Manning's advice the Irish bishops moved into outright opposition to the bill, breaking the alliance with the Liberal party which had lasted since 1868. On the second reading of the bill thirty-five Irish Liberals voted against the government, and also a few radicals like Fawcett and Horsman. Many Liberals abstained and the government was beaten by three votes. Gladstone made one of his great speeches, but it was to no avail. Manning wrote to him afterwards: 'This is not your fault, nor the bill's fault, but the fault of England

and Scotland and three anti-Catholic centuries.' Perhaps a more prudent and less obstinate man might not have chosen that moment to legislate on the Irish university question; but such a man would probably not have had Gladstone's power to determine the content of the political discourse.

The government decided to resign on their defeat. 'Gladstone seems utterly weary of office and few of us I think will be sorry for rest,' wrote Kimberley in his Journal. There were certainly signs that the great Gladstonian coalition was breaking up and Northcote saw it that way from the other side of the House. On the other hand the government need not have resigned for, as Disraeli pointed out, the vote on the Irish University Bill did not imply any more permanent realignment of parliamentary groups. Gladstone could have dissolved and some of his colleagues thought he should have done so. To quote Kimberley again: 'I regret for my part we did not dissolve . . . Our old programme is completely exhausted: and Gladstone is not the man to govern without "measures", nor is he at all suited to lead a party in difficulties. He must have a strong current of opinion in his favour.'[12] The advice Disraeli received from all quarters was 'that time is required to mature the fast ripening Conservatism of the country' and this was the reason why he refused to take office. It seems only too likely that this view of the situation was correct and that Gladstone therefore missed an opportunity of at least limiting the extent of his impending electoral defeat by not dissolving Parliament in March 1873.

More than four years had elapsed since he became Prime Minister and they were the years of the greatest constructive achievement in the whole period of nearly thirteen years during which he held the premiership. The extent of this achievement would have been impossible without his gargantuan powers of work and his prodigious parliamentary ability. Even where he was not the original initiator, as on the Education Act or the army reforms, it was his concept of his duty as head of the government to put his full weight and prestige into the scales when it was required. At the same time he regarded his role in the Cabinet as *primus inter pares* and he was scrupulous in leaving to departmental ministers their own sphere of action and responsibility. This was one reason among several why he cannot be held to have had the general grasp of government policy that his mentor Peel had had thirty years earlier. He had his own causes, principally Ireland, which he pursued, sometimes beyond the limits of practical politics. If it is the pre-eminent function of statesmen to force the important problems of the time upon the attention of their fellow men, this was a function which Gladstone performed exceedingly well and it is part of his greatness.

Naturally there were shortcomings. Some sprang from his character: he was impetuous, so convinced of his own case that he could be blind to the views of others; he was liable to bear down by sheer weight of argument those who did not agree with him; he could be tactless and obstinate. There was something in him that could attract antagonism as a honey-pot draws bees, the counterpart to the great veneration he inspired. He abhorred even that veneer of cynicism that eases intercourse between the worldly. After 1871 he was no longer at his best; even physically he was often exhausted. Perhaps the greatest shortcoming was that he did not see himself as a party leader in the modern sense, responsible for a permanent combination of interests and groups. He made no attempt to keep in touch with or cultivate his back-benchers and he was not in any sense a parliamentary manager. He dined in the House of Commons only once during his long parliamentary life. His domination was achieved entirely by the force of his personality and not through the skills of management. Denison, the Speaker in the Parliament of 1868, thus described to Granville the appearance of Gladstone at a moment of party disorder during a debate on emigration in 1870: 'In the end the . . . Shepherd appeared on the scene and positively shamed the wolves who drew off one by one pretending that they never meant any harm. The sheep went to the division bleating in full chorus – a capital division as you will see.'[13] He led, as it were, from the outside, as a man *sui generis*, his followers had to take him and his ideas as they found them and if they would not he was quite prepared to depart. Ideologically he was still a Peelite, a liberal–conservative, and there were beginning to be developments for which his outlook had little relevance.

9

BAG

AND

BAGGAGE

1873–80

When Gladstone and his colleagues resumed office after the crisis over the Irish University Bill their position was further weakened. The Parliament of 1868 could, however, run on for another two years or more and there could be time for recovery. Gladstone could still produce great parliamentary performances, for example when he spoke against Miall's motion for the disestablishment of the Churches of England and Scotland; this was, however, a topic where his attitude pained his Nonconformist supporters and which showed up the divisions in the Liberal party. Exhaustion came only in bouts; Gladstone could still fell trees at Hawarden and walk miles at Balmoral. But could he find a cause that would give him and his government renewed vigour, as the Irish Church had done five years earlier, a cause in harmony with the very different mood of 1874?

The summer of 1873 did not pass happily for the government. There had been irregularities, though not amounting to corruption, in the administration of the Post Office. Both Monsell, the Post-master-General, and Lowe, the Chancellor of the Exchequer, had to be moved. Lowe was an unpopular minister, for the remarks he made in 1866 about the working classes clung to him and his pro-posed match tax in the 1871 budget brought forth a demonstration by poverty-stricken match-girls of East London. It made him look more hard-hearted than ever and the suggestion that the Latin pun *ex luce lucellum* should be printed on the match-duty stamps hardly improved his image. Gladstone did him justice when he wrote to him: 'Outstripping others in the race, you reach the goal or con-clusion before them; and being there, you assume that they are there also. This is unpopular.' Lowe went to the Home Office in place of Bruce, another minister who had built up a lot of unpopu-larity over licensing, the labour laws and much else. There were further changes in the senior and junior ranks of the government. Such matters cost Gladstone a great deal of energy and peace of mind and he did not always handle them well. His fundamental concern for justice, fairness and decent dealing cannot be doubted, but his imagination in divining the feeling of others sometimes faltered. On this occasion he needlessly offended Hartington by assuming that he wished to leave Ireland and offering him the Post Office; he did not see that he had erred and wrote to Granville: 'Hartington has many good and fine qualities besides his birth: but I am tempted to say he sells them rather dear.' At this stage Bright was brought back into the Cabinet which he had left three years earlier because of illness. It was hoped that this would go some way towards mending fences with the Nonconformists, but Bright's influence was no longer what it had been and other men like Chamberlain and Dilke were coming to the fore.

Gladstone became Chancellor of the Exchequer when Lowe left the Treasury. This raised the complicated legal question whether he should have to vacate his seat at Greenwich, which was not considered safe, or whether his continuation as First Lord of the Treasury relieved him of the necessity.[1] The balance of the advice given to Gladstone was that he need not seek re-election; but the possibility that this matter might be exploited on the reassembly of Parliament in 1874 was perhaps a minor factor in the precipitate dissolution of Parliament in January of that year. The more serious problem facing Gladstone was how to fill the session of 1874 if this Parliament was to continue. The three major possibilities were to extend household suffrage to the counties, to reform local taxation or to bring in a popular budget based on economy. On the first the party would not be united and the Tories might support it, thus gaining some of the kudos. Gladstone thought they might support Trevelyan who annually brought a private member's motion on the county franchise, but they could not stand or fall by it. Local taxation was not suited to Liberal legislation; there was much agitation against the growing rate burden, particularly in respect of education, and the Tories could always outbid the Liberals in proposing the transfer of burdens to the Exchequer. This left the budget as the most plausible election winner for the Liberals. Gladstone had already set in motion, as soon as he took over from Lowe, an investigation into the financial position and he had hopes of a surplus large enough to enable him to make the abolition of the income tax the central feature of the 1874 budget.

These possibilities were set out in a long letter which Gladstone wrote to Granville on 8 January 1874. In it he toyed with the idea of an immediate dissolution; within the next few days his determination to grasp the nettle hardened. A further factor tilting his decision towards an immediate dissolution was disagreeement with Cardwell and Goschen over the military and naval estimates. This could endanger the surplus on which he proposed to base his budget; it might therefore be better to hold out financial boons to the public in prospect rather than wait and find that they could not be fully realized in practice. On 23 January Gladstone advised his colleagues that he had come to the conclusion that an immediate dissolution of Parliament would be best in the public and the party interest and there was no disagreement. Gladstone's election manifesto burst upon an astonished country the following morning, a Saturday, and even Disraeli, having by chance spent the night in London, was taken by surprise. In the manifesto Gladstone proposed abolition of the income tax, reductions in local taxation and in taxes on articles of popular consumption. He rebutted at length the accusation that the Liberal party had endangered the institutions of the country. In his counter-manifesto Disraeli called it 'a prolix narrative'.

Prime ministers of the nineteenth century had to time their appeals to the country on the basis of very slender evidence. Disraeli fared no better in 1880 than Gladstone did in 1874. No general assessment of the electoral mood could be more than a hazardous guess; the position of particular groups could be estimated, but their real influence in terms of votes was not accurately known. The importance of specific issues and policies was much overestimated and there was a tendency to see the whole process too much in rational terms. Organization was undoubtedly important, for there were still many small constituencies where a handful of votes could be decisive; it depended often on organization whether there would be a contested election at all. In 1874 the Tories had the edge in organization, for Disraeli had given this aspect his personal attention. It was not a field in which Gladstone ever took much interest and which he considered tainted with corruption. In selecting the abolition of the income tax and economy as the core of his appeal Gladstone revealed himself as still a Peelite. What had been the focus of political debate and the basis of his own reputation in 1860 could, however, serve that purpose no longer in 1874. The electors were no longer so interested in details of public money saved; the working class were beginning to look to the public purse as a provider. Gladstone was beginning in some respects to look like a man of the past.

The result of the 1874 election was that over 350 Tories came to face more than 240 Liberals and nearly 60 Irish Home Rulers. The reversal compared with 1868 was drastic. Gladstone had expected the virtual disappearance of Irish Liberalism through the rise of the Home Rule party and it had been foreshadowed by the vote on the Irish University Bill. Leaving aside this special loss, there was a move away from the Liberals in nearly every type of seat in England, Scotland and Wales. On the one hand there was a continued drift of the middle and propertied classes towards Conservatism. It was not only the policies of the Gladstone government which were bringing this about, but extraneous events like the Paris Commune. It can be seen very strikingly in London suburban constituencies like Middlesex where the Liberal poll dropped sharply in 1874. At the same time the Liberals saw their support weakening in large urban, predominantly working-class constituencies. To some extent the prescription of Tory democracy was working, though there is every reason to suppose that a majority of the urban working class still voted Liberal. The disaffection of specific groups, like the National Education League, the United Kingdom Alliance and the Trade Unions, was the third major element in the Liberal weakness in 1874. In 1868 these groups or their equivalents had been the activists in many constituencies and had mobilized the voters

responsive to their particular appeal. Now they had been disappointed by the Gladstone government and were apathetic. Against
such trends Gladstone's cry of economy could make no headway and
was indeed hardly noticed.

Gladstone campaigned vigorously in his own contest at Greenwich. He addressed large open-air meetings in the cold January
weather. Contrary to expectations he retained his seat at Greenwich,
but he was pushed into second place by Boord, a distiller. He took
this very badly, even though he ran well ahead of the other Liberal
candidate. His well-known remark 'we have been borne down in a
torrent of gin and beer', made in a letter to his brother Robertson,
owes probably more to conditions at Greenwich than to a considered
judgement on the whole election. The licensing laws were only one
among many factors in the Liberal defeat.

When the result of the election became clear the choice for the
Cabinet was either to resign immediately or meet Parliament.
Gladstone as an old parliamentary hand much preferred the
second alternative, but was overruled by his colleagues. At the same
Cabinet, on 17 February 1874, he announced to his colleagues his
intention to lay down the Liberal leadership. As there was no one to
succeed him for the moment, Cardwell having for health reasons
accepted a peerage, he did not formally abdicate for the session of
1874. He made it clear that he could not attend the House of
Commons regularly and held himself free to take a line of his own as
an individual. 'I must reserve my entire freedom to divest myself
of all the responsibilities of leadership at no distant time,' he wrote
to Granville in March 1874. His formal withdrawal came in January
1875, ahead of the next parliamentary session.

Gladstone's retirement cannot have come completely as a surprise
for he had spoken of it for a long time. It was entirely in accord
with the view he had taken of his own role in politics. He was in it
to pursue moral causes. In this quest he had come together with the
Liberal party, a complex parliamentary combination, with a large
and varied mass following in the country. They had given him their
support; he had given them his unrivalled gifts as a parliamentarian
and hero of the masses. Together they had accomplished great
things, but now they had run out of causes and he could no longer
discharge his function as link between parliamentarians and masses.
In this coming together there had always been elements of misunderstanding: Gladstone was no democrat, even if the masses thought so;
the Nonconformists responded to his moral appeal, but he remained
a Churchman with a 'Catholic sense'. No doubt there was an element

of hurt pride in his retirement. The electoral verdict, so overwhelming, was a slap in the face. The communion with the masses, even if it was not based on the fullest mutual understanding, had ceased for the moment. Some of the radical intelligentsia in the Liberal party had long forfeited Gladstone's sympathy. The Nonconformists had demonstrated ingratitude, the pride of the Whigs had never completely unbent to him. Gladstone had a genuine desire for repose; he had an urgent inner need to come to grips with new religious problems, the claims of the Vatican, the spread of unbelief. No one could really believe that his break with politics was final and perhaps he did not fully believe it himself. He refused the Queen's offer of a peerage and retained his seat in the House of Commons.

Gladstone's major intervention during the 1874 session was in fact in an entirely individual capacity. Tait, the Archbishop of Canterbury, had prepared a bill to control the spread of ritualism in the Church of England, the Public Worship Regulation Bill. The adoption of Roman Catholic practices, such as the use of incense, by Anglo-Catholic clergy was causing alarm among the great mass of staunchly Protestant Anglicans. Gladstone, although a High Anglican, was not a ritualist, for forms of worship were not a vital matter to him. On the other hand he strongly disapproved of any attempt to persecute the ritualists; in fact, as he wrote to Halifax, 'I have serious doubts whether the whole of the penal proceedings taken in this country with respect to Church matters, from the day of Dr Hampden downwards, have not done considerably more harm than good.' He felt increasingly that disestablishment must lie at the end of that road. Even during the weighty deliberations on the dissolution in January 1874, he addressed a long letter on Archbishop Tait's proposed bill to the Queen; among the matters that divided her from him were her staunchly Protestant-based church views which she shared with the majority of her subjects. In the debates on the Public Worship Regulation Bill Gladstone was in a very isolated position and at one point saw looming ahead of him the painful necessity of announcing his conversion to disestablishment. It did not come to this; but the vast majority on his side of the House, Anglicans and Nonconformists, thoroughly approved of the bill, while Disraeli, seeing its popularity with all but the High Churchmen on his side, jumped in to support it.

During this first year of release from office the chief call on Gladstone's energies came not from political and parliamentary affairs but from his work on Homer and above all on the Vatican Council of 1870. Even when the pressures of politics and public life were greatest upon him the problems of faith, religion and the Church were never far from his mind and his correspondence on these matters was copious. In his decision to retire from active political life there was still an element of that sense of missed vocation that had been with him since he had chosen the political path in his early twenties on the advice of his father. In his work on Homer he was still, as in the 1850s, concerned to show the relationship between Greek civilization and Christian revelation and to present the Greek poet as the precursor of the Bible. The challenge to faith from science and rationalism had become more insistent and religious doubt had become a major threat to the peace of mind of many of Gladstone's contemporaries. To him it was no threat at all, for he held that faith on the one hand and science and reason on the other inhabited different spheres and that there could be no clash between them. His own cast of mind was so remote from that of the sceptic or agnostic that he found it perhaps difficult to understand fully the agonies of doubt to which many were now subjected. He had followed closely the controversies arising out of *The Origin of Species, Essays and Reviews* and Bishop Colenso. His view is best summed up by what he wrote to Professor Jevons in 1874: 'I must say that the doctrine of Evolution, if it be true, enhances in my judgement the proper idea of the greatness of God, for it makes every stage of creation a legible prophecy of all those which are to follow it.' The more extreme liberal and latitudinarian views among some of the clergy he abhorred, since they blurred the distinction between religion and irreligion. In 1869, in one of his most controversial church appointments he made Dr Temple Bishop of Exeter. Temple was a contributor to *Essays and Reviews*; Gladstone, when he was attacked for the appointment, made it clear that in his view Temple had not in his contribution added to the rationalist argument of the book and was not tainted with it.[2]

The Vatican Council of 1870 and the proclamation of papal infallibility was perhaps the greatest defiance of the rationalist tendencies of the age. To Gladstone, who did not in himself feel threatened by these tendencies, it was an appalling over-reaction. He had a great reverence for the Roman Catholic Church; this action, he judged, deprived it of much of its power for good within European civilization. When the Council was in progress he had been frustrated in his intention to intervene, in spite of the obstacles that were being created for his Irish policies. His sympathies were with the liberal Catholics who were his friends, Acton and Döllinger. His relations with Manning, who embraced the decisions of the

Council with the zeal of a convert, declined once more. In 1870 Gladstone was debarred by his official position from mounting a public attack, but the public sensation caused when it came was enhanced by the delay. In September 1874 he went to Munich to see Döllinger, who had in the meantime become the leading Old Catholic in Germany and had been excommunicated. Döllinger kept him abreast of the development of Bismarck's *Kulturkampf*. On this trip Gladstone also saw his sister Helen and tried, again without success, to persuade her to abandon the Roman Catholic religion. Soon after he returned to Hawarden he put pen to paper and in a matter of days wrote his pamphlet on 'The Vatican Decrees in their bearing on Civil Allegiance: a Political Expostulation'. It sold nearly 150,000 copies within weeks. It was a strong attack on ultramontanism and concentrated on the logical incompatibility between the submission to papal infallibility and the civil obligations of Roman Catholics. It was essentially a political pamphlet and only incidentally dealt with the fundamental philosophical problem of authority and freedom. All kinds of political implications were read into the pamphlet. It was seen as Gladstone's bid to reunite his party and ride back to power on a 'No Popery' platform. It certainly helped to repair Gladstone's relations with the Nonconformists; it created difficulties with the Irish and a good many radicals wondered if a man who could thus plunge into abstruse religious controversy could ever lead their party again. Even his old friend Monckton Milnes, Lord Houghton, wrote to Granville about Gladstone's excursion into controversial theology: 'People are calling him Charles the Fifth, and these certainly are not the clocks that he will get to strike harmoniously together.' He was faced with a flood of correspondence; Manning's reply ran to 200 pages. A second pamphlet published by Gladstone in February 1875, in which he replied to his critics, evoked less response although it was even sharper in tone.

In the meantime he had carried out his intention of formally abdicating the Liberal leadership. He sent Granville a list of nine possible causes which the party might take up, ranging from the extension of the suffrage and disestablishment, through retrenchment, to secular education and Irish affairs. He felt that on none of them would it be possible for him to lead a united party and no amount of pressure, not even from his wife, could move him to continue. Forster would have been the best man to succeed him, but his role in the passage of the Education Act made this impossible. The task fell to Hartington, while Granville continued to lead in

the Lords, and thus the Liberal party was once more led by Whigs
of the purest pedigree. Gladstone's position was, however, equivocal.
From time to time he turned up in the House of Commons and sat
on the Opposition Front Bench. Disraeli described one such an
occasion to the Queen: 'Mr Gladstone not only appeared, but
rushed into the debate. The new Members trembled and fluttered
like small birds when a hawk is in the air.' For financial reasons he
sold No. 11 Carlton House Terrace, but bought a cheaper property,
No. 73 Harley Street. Among his family and entourage there was a
feeling that retirement would not be final and this was shared by
the general public. But having deliberately cut himself off from
day-to-day politics it could be no ordinary event or change that
would bring Gladstone back.

The Eastern Question, the Bulgarian atrocities and the country-
wide agitation against the Disraeli government's policies on these
questions drew Gladstone out of his semi-retirement in the summer
of 1876. It was a situation tailor-made for him. There was the moral
cause: the country cynically committed to the support of a corrupt
moribund empire perpetrating evil atrocities. All this for the sake
of alleged national self-interest and as part of a discredited balance-
of-power game. The Concert of Europe had been deliberately enlisted
in the Eastern Question; this, Gladstone liked to think, had been
the one positive result of the Crimean War, which otherwise he
remembered with a guilty conscience. He had himself tried to
maintain this joint European responsibility when Russia renounced
the Black Sea clauses in 1870; now Disraeli had deliberately flouted
it by rejecting the Berlin Memorandum. Sending the fleet to Besika
Bay was precisely the kind of action that Gladstone had fought
against when the Crimean War was in the making. All his deep
suspicions about Disraeli were aroused; he now even suspected him
of being influenced by Judaic sympathy for the Turks and hatred
of Christians. As Gladstone came more fully to grips with the
question of the Balkans he saw the future of the area in terms of
national self-determination, a principle which he had espoused for
Italy and which he was beginning to see as applicable to Ireland.
As a problem of international policy Gladstone could see the Eastern
Question as a perfect demonstration model for his outlook and
attitude, more perfect than any case he had had to deal with during
his premiership.

In beckoning Gladstone out of retirement the domestic repercussions of this foreign imbroglio were at least as important as the
international implications. As the atrocity agitation began to get

under way in August 1876 he could perceive that here was a means by which he might reforge the bond with the masses that had snapped two years earlier. He could not appeal to the material self-interest of the masses, for he was no democrat or egalitarian; for him the bond could only rest on a moral cause and this now lay ready to hand. From the point of view of his relations with the Liberal party the Bulgarian atrocities and the Eastern Question would bring him together again with the Nonconformists and for once his High Church views would no longer be a barrier. It was precisely the High Church party in the Church of England that was to the fore in the atrocity agitation: they were, as it were, the persecuted minority, attacked by the Disraeli government through the Public Worship Regulation Act; they looked towards a communion with the Russian Orthodox Church to which most of the Sultan's Christian subjects belonged.

It is unlikely that Gladstone could have stood out for long from the popular movement that was developing. On 31 July 1876 he at last spoke in the House of Commons on the Eastern Question before the summer recess. While critical of the government, he said little about the Bulgarian atrocities and even spoke of maintaining the integrity of the Turkish Empire. He refused to take part in a debate on 11 August initiated by Evelyn Ashley, his friend and Shaftesbury's son. Looking back on this period twenty years later he wrote: 'I was slow to observe the real leanings of the prime minister, his strong sympathy with the Turk, and his mastery in his own cabinet.' Gladstone was in fact very reluctant to give the impression that his retirement was not genuine; he was truly anxious to get back to his theological studies on punishment and retribution; he had no wish to embarrass Hartington or Granville, for whom his continued presence in Parliament was difficult enough. The Duchess of Manchester, Hartington's mistress, told Disraeli: 'That gentleman is only waiting to come to the fore with all his hypocritical retirement,' but it was far from the truth.

During the second half of August 1876 the pressures built up on Gladstone to speak out on the Bulgarian horrors.[3] W. T. Stead, the well-known journalist, was organizing protest meetings in the North and was writing to him. Liddon and MacColl, noted High Anglican clerics, were due to go to the East to make a personal investigation and MacColl was constantly in touch with Gladstone. Freeman, the historian, was conducting a campaign of his own, chiefly through letters to the newspapers. Even old Lord Russell took a hand. What was most decisive in moving him were the signs that the parliamentary recess had not closed the debate and that it was stirring the masses. On 18 August he read a report in the *Daily News* that a protest rally of working men was going to be held in Hyde Park and he remembered this when he was writing about his role twenty years later. On 28 August he started work on the famous pamphlet 'The Bulgarian Horrors and the Question of the East' and in spite of an attack of lumbago finished most of it in four days. On Sunday, 3 September, he went up to London; 'Papa rushed off to London Sunday night, pamphlet in hand, beyond anything agog over the Bulgarian horrors, which pass description,' wrote his daugher Mary.[4] The British Museum had been alerted and on the Monday 'in six or seven hours, principally at the British Museum, I completed my MS'. The only restraining influences were Granville and Hartington, who were obviously afraid of the consequences of this Gladstonian eruption, but they had no hope of extinguishing the volcano. The next evening they accompanied him to a farce at the Haymarket Theatre to relax after these arduous labours. The following morning the pamphlet burst on the world and sold 40,000 copies within a few days. The breathlessness of these proceedings is an indication of the depth of Gladstone's emotions, once the facts about the situation in the Balkans had been unmistakably established and he had clearly perceived his own role in the matter. These emotions dominated him through the ups and downs of the next three years. 'From that time forward, till the final consummation in 1879–80, I made the eastern question the main business of my life.'

The pamphlet is written in a passionate oratorical style of which its most famous sentence is a fair sample: 'Their Zaptiehs and their Mudirs, their Bimbashis and their Yuzbashis, their Kaimakams and their Pashas, one and all, bag and baggage, shall I hope clear out from the province they have desolated and profaned.' To the modern reader Gladstone's description of Turkish turpitude has faintly racialist overtones. Gladstone's solution to the Balkans problem is only adumbrated rhetorically; the long-term tides of history were no doubt with him when he demanded self-determination for the nationalities of the peninsula, but his opponents and even his colleagues can hardly be blamed for having their doubts about how this could be translated into immediate practical politics. Three days after the publication of the pamphlet Gladstone made the first of his great public speeches on the Eastern Question at Blackheath. It was a memorable occasion. From now on his public oratory became a regular feature of British politics; it had started fifteen years before at Newcastle, but up to now it had consisted of isolated

G

appearances. Now it came to be a campaign, in the tradition of revivalist preaching. The Blackheath speech was more restrained in content than it was in tone. Gladstone was still hoping that the government would modify its pro-Turkish policy; he was reluctant to appear to be coming out of retirement. Granville and Hartington were dragging their feet and he did not wish to make their position too difficult. In the whirlpool of Liberal politics he was so powerful a figure that the mere chance of his return to the leadership was drastically altering the personal and political calculations of all the other leading figures. Forster, still smarting under his failure to become leader in 1875, was active on the Eastern Question and strongly anti-Turk, hoping to use this as a lever to retrieve his position. Hartington was being pushed by his ambitious mistress; he was the brother-in-law of Gladstone's niece and political differences, although kept within bounds and handled with dignity by both men, were felt in the family circle. Lady Frederick Cavendish wrote in her diary a few months later: ' . . . F. [her husband] is nearly wild. How can he leave Cavendish [Hartington] in the lurch, and yet be driven to vote against Uncle W. seems almost inconceivable to him.'[5] Chamberlain, who had entered the House of Commons in 1876, cared little about the Eastern Question, but saw Gladstone's return ('he can't continue in public life for very much longer' he wrote to Dilke) as a means of dishing the Whigs. Dilke, his closest political associate, was distinguished from other Radicals by his realism in foreign affairs, on which he was an expert; he was a precursor of the Liberal imperialists. Dilke shared Chamberlain's objective of a Radical takeover of the Liberal party, but could not approve of Gladstone's stand on the Eastern Question. Harcourt was all for attacking the government, but did not want the return of Gladstone, who disliked him with unusual intensity. Joseph Cowen, the Newcastle Radical, hated Russia passionately and came to hate Gladstone. Bright was rather aloof, opposed to any sort of active policy and in favour of total non-intervention. The majority of Radical Nonconformists, men like Mundella, Samuel Morley, Stansfeld, Leader, Henry Richard and so on, were, of course, entirely with Gladstone and for them the Eastern Question was the cause which made them forget any past grievances they had had against him. Gladstone's fundamental simplicity and innocence did not exclude a great deal of political cunning. He was aware of many cross-currents; to him the moral issue of the Balkan problem was paramount and he did not want to be anybody's tool or stalking-horse.

If Gladstone was still hoping for a change of government policy, his intervention had put Disraeli on his mettle and made him more obdurate. The personal dual between the two great leaders now came to a climax and added a further twist to the tangled political web. It is difficult to believe that Gladstone was not also affected by it. He wrote to his wife of Disraeli's Judaic feeling 'the deepest and truest, now that his wife has gone, in his whole mind'. Beaconsfield wrote to Lord Derby of Gladstone's pamphlet: 'Vindictive and ill-written – that of course. Indeed in that respect of all the Bulgarian horrors perhaps the greatest.'[6] The Prime Minister replied to Gladstone's Blackheath speech at Aylesbury eleven days later; he spoke of 'designing politicians' who exploited the noble sentiments of the British people 'for the furtherance of sinister ends'.

The battle was now truly joined. Rarely had the country been so divided on a question of foreign policy. In general 'the upper ten thousand', as Gladstone now frequently called them bitterly, were pro-Disraeli; 'when did the Upper Ten Thousand ever lead the attack in the cause of humanity? Their heads are always full of class interests and the main chance,' his niece, Lady Frederick Cavendish, reports him as saying;[7] the provinces were more Gladstonian than London and so was the intelligentsia. The Church of England, except the High Church party, was pro-Disraeli and so were Roman Catholics and Jews, and Nonconformity was Gladstonian. To all these generalizations there were many exceptions; for example among intellectuals Matthew Arnold, Jowett and Fitzjames Stephen cared nothing for the atrocity agitation.[8] The Queen's strong animus against Gladstone dates from this period and she now often referred to him as a madman. For Gladstone faith in the 'virtuous passion' of the masses took the place of the democratic or egalitarian beliefs which he otherwise totally lacked. 'The superiority of the popular judgement in politics, so far as it is superior, is, according to my view, due mainly to moral causes, to a greater mental integrity, which, again, is greatly owing to the comparative absence of the more subtle agencies of temptation,' he wrote in the *Nineteenth Century* in 1878.

In October 1876 Gladstone went on a series of country-house visits in the North and became the focus of great demonstrations of popular enthusiasm. His restraint was sometimes wearing thin and he found it increasingly difficult to keep in line with Granville's caution. On the other hand it was clear to him that it would be very difficult to maintain the momentum of the popular agitation and that it was a blunt weapon for influencing the policy of a government. Gladstone became further discouraged when Forster, who like his rival Hartington had gone to the Near East to collect first-hand information, returned critical of the agitation. However much he disliked the Turks, Forster saw no immediate future in working for independence for the Balkan nationalities. He expressed this view in a speech to his Bradford constituents early in October. Gladstone took fresh heart when it was announced that there would be a Conference of the Powers in Constantinople, starting in mid-December. This seemed a victory for the movement that Gladstone led and an attempt to bring into play again the Concert of Europe. Beaconsfield's speech at the Lord Mayor's Banquet in November convinced Gladstone that he must continue the atrocity campaign as hard as possible, for the Prime Minister again stressed both his commitment to Turkish integrity and Britain's readiness for war if necessary. Those who wished to restrain the government were now bending their efforts to the organization of a great National Conference on the Eastern Question which was to be held at St James's Hall early in December. Gladstone gave these efforts his blessing and spoke at the meeting. It was held just as Salisbury was about to attend as British representative the Conference of the Powers at Constantinople. Gladstone made a moderate speech at St James's Hall. He saw the function of the National Conference as a means of strengthening the hand of Salisbury at Constantinople in his efforts to press reforms and concessions on the Turks; also as a means of backing up the moderate elements in the Cabinet. The other speakers included Shaftesbury, Liddon, Freeman, Fawcett and a good many others, but it was a predominantly Liberal demonstration and there was only a sprinkling of Conservatives. Gladstone was trying to exert a moderating and constructive influence on the policy of the government, but the more excitable and extreme elements on both sides of the divide saw his activities in a much more lurid light. Even Hartington felt that Freeman, Fawcett and others had spoken extravagantly at St James's Hall and that Gladstone should have repudiated them.

The Constantinople Conference was a failure and in the spring of 1877 the situation drifted towards the Russo-Turkish War. The fact that events were thus moving in the direction opposite to what he thought right heightened Gladstone's emotional commitment to his own views. His desire to get back to theology and Homer was genuine, but his moral indignation on the Eastern Question was an overwhelming preoccupation and often he could talk of little else. At a more superficial level he was feeling somewhat guilty at the difficulties he was creating for Granville and Hartington, but in the complex recesses of his mind his explicit posture as the 'non-leader' of the Liberal party must have been an alibi not without its curious satisfaction. Granville and Hartington had to represent to him that much of Liberal opinion, let alone public opinion at large, was not so exclusively concerned with the sins of the Sultan. They were afraid of Russian imperialism, did not care too much for the Balkan nationalities or were perhaps not too interested in the Eastern Question as a whole. As Gladstone perceived that the parliamentary Liberals would not act firmly and unitedly with him he gave encouragement to those forces in the country that seemed to him to represent the genuine voice of the people and to herald a real Liberal revival.

In the House of Commons Gladstone's effort culminated in the five resolutions which he put forward in April 1877 and which amounted to a severe reproof of the Turks and approval of the terms of the Constantinople Conference. This line would have split the Liberals down the middle, and with Granville exerting all his influence as Gladstone's friend, tactics were worked out to avoid this extremity. On 7 May Gladstone made one of his great parliamentary speeches in this debate even though, as he told his niece, he had forgotten his spectacles and could not read some of the quotations he had prepared; he made the House, fundamentally in a hostile mood, listen to him and a week later the Liberals were reasonably united in the lobby, but the government's majority of 121 was still much larger than normal. In fact the parliamentary manoeuvres could achieve little, especially as the cracks in Liberal unity were only so thinly papered over. On the other hand Liberal divisions were paralleled by similar disunity inside the Conservative Cabinet.

Gladstone was therefore driven to pursue his mission outside the House. He published a second pamphlet on the Eastern Question, but it evoked far less response. More significant was his decision to address the inaugural meeting of the National Liberal Federation in Birmingham at the end of May. Chamberlain and Dilke had decided to use the structure of the National Education League and the experience of electoral organization in the Birmingham caucus as the basis for a new, country-wide, permanent party organization. Their intention was to institutionalize the Radical forces within liberalism. They were confident that soon they and the modern radicalism which they represented would take over the party.

To Gladstone their outlook was alien, but the invitation to go to Birmingham reached him in April while his five resolutions on Turkey were being discussed among the party leaders and he accepted it as the parliamentary debate in May was ending. Granville, the Whigs and the respectability of the party were naturally suspicious of Chamberlain and his organization; to Granville Gladstone justified his going to Birmingham by saying that it would do good by 'minimizing the differences which preceded the late debate'. He assured Granville that at Birmingham he would not be associated with any recasting of policy and that Chamberlain's organizational ideas would benefit the party. At Birmingham Gladstone had a triumphal reception and 30,000 people listened to him in Bingley Hall. After briefly blessing the new National Federation he proceeded to fling his thunderbolts against the Turks. He stayed with Chamberlain afterwards, but underneath his Olympian courtesy there was coolness.[9] It was an occasion full of irony. Chamberlain and his friends had sought to enlist the Gladstonian magic in their drive to capture the Liberal party, confident in the belief that Gladstone himself would soon be out of politics. Gladstone had gone to Birmingham because he wished to leave no stone unturned to harness Liberalism to his moral crusade against Disraeli; he had nothing in common with the new radicalism and was careful to keep his distance. In fact he was to dominate the Liberal party for another seventeen years, harness it to his causes, stultify Chamberlainite radicalism and Chamberlain would be forced out of the party.

After Parliament rose for the recess Gladstone retired to Hawarden, but continued his crusade. Deputations and excursions from Northern and Midland towns made the pilgrimage to Hawarden, saw the great man felling trees and were sometimes rewarded with a speech castigating the immorality of the Turk and his allies in Downing Street. To Granville he excused himself: 'You must within these last three weeks have required a large fund of Christian Charity not to give me up for a born fool. I will not explain any more now about the repeated excursions, but only say I could not help myself. . .' In October he paid a visit to Ireland, his only one. Although he did not stray much beyond the Protestant ascendancy, he must have realized that his great measures of 1869 and 1870 had not solved anything. It was a matter of great regret to him that Irish Roman Catholics did not in general support his Bulgarian crusade, but the analogy between the Turkish position in the Balkans and the British position in Ireland must have been in his mind.

The early months of 1878, war hysteria followed by the triumph of Beaconsfieldism, were a difficult time for Gladstone. In London society, where he had occasionally to make an appearance, his name was execrated. In February he had his windows smashed in Harley Street and on several occasions he and his family required police protection. The plaudits of the multitude had often reinforced Gladstone's confidence in the righteousness of his cause; but when his moral fervour was aroused he could swim courageously against the tide and derive satisfaction from it. After the Congress of Berlin he welcomed those features of the settlement for which he had pleaded: the considerable reduction in the Turkish realm in the Balkans, and the extension of independence in the peninsula. He condemned the British acquisition of Cyprus; in his view the conduct of British policy and the work of Disraeli and Salisbury in Berlin had diminished the moral stature of England.

In the earlier phases of the Eastern Question Gladstone had frequently wished for the day when the crisis should be resolved and he could return to his retirement. Now that it was in a fashion resolved he had the feeling that he still had an account to settle with the government; it was a feeling soon reinforced by the unfortunate imbroglios in Zululand and Afghanistan, into which the government allowed itself to drift. At the same time the growing economic depression and the crisis in agriculture cast a cloud over Beaconsfield's fortunes; Gladstone could not but see this as a just retribution for the profligate spending policy of the government and seek the causes in the general disturbance of trade brought about by the government's bellicose policy. Just as Disraeli had been confirmed in his pro-Turkish course by Gladstone's publication of the 'Bulgarian Horrors' pamphlet, so Gladstone was now determined to persevere in his campaign by the apparent triumph of 'Beaconsfieldism'. The personal and public altercations between the two leaders after Beaconsfield's return from Berlin in July must have further stiffened Gladstone's determination to fight; it was then that the Prime Minister spoke of his adversary as 'inebriated with the exuberance of his own verbosity'.

By the autumn of 1878 the tide was beginning to turn and Gladstone was increasingly convinced that the government was heading for a 'smash'. It was to be some time yet before the evidence supplied to him by the whips and electoral pundits would fully bear out this conviction; but nevertheless he was now in a mood for electoral battle. The position of the Liberal party, how it could be reunited and used to put an end to the iniquities of the government was much in his mind and he published an article on this theme entitled

'Electoral Facts' in the November issue of the *Nineteenth Century*. He felt that it had been his role to put forward a cause around which the party could rally and revive. He was still convinced that organization, as in the shape of the National Liberal Federation, had a useful part to play in the revival; but he objected to any attempt by organization to curtail the freedom of members and backed Forster in his brush with the caucus at Bradford. It was at this time, too, that negotiations were in progress to draw him to the central Scottish constituency of Midlothian. He had determined after the last election not to stand for Greenwich again; but many easier constituencies than Midlothian, Leeds for example, were clamouring for his presence. The move to the North was therefore part of a general mood to fight and defy the government, though the call of his Scottish ancestry no doubt also played its part. To Granville, who must have heard the news with mixed feelings, he wrote that his decision to fight Midlothian meant 'a coming forward' and 'if it goes on, it will gather into itself a great deal of force and heat, and will be very prominent'.

The decision to fight Midlothian was definitely taken in January 1879, but the famous campaign when Gladstone introduced himself to his new constituents did not take place till November. By Gladstonian standards the intervening year was a relatively quiet period when he was less in the public eye than he had been. In September and October he spent six weeks on the Continent with his family, during which time he saw Döllinger and Acton. He was, however, anxious that the Liberal attack on the government should not lose momentum and in August, before he went abroad, he wrote to Granville:

It seems to me good policy to join on the proceedings of 1876–9 by a continuous process to the Dissolution. Should this happen, which I think, likely enough, about March, there will have been no opportunity immediately before it of stirring the country. I will not say our defeat in 1874 was owing to the want of such an opportunity but it was certainly I think much aggravated by that want.[10]

The excursion to Midlothian in late November was therefore the creation of such an opportunity and it certainly stirred the country.

The extraordinary enthusiasm aroused by the Midlothian campaign has never been forgotten. Gladstone's daughter Mary described the experience in a letter to her cousin Lavinia Talbot:

. . . the triumphant entry into Edinburgh on a dark, bitter winter's night, with thousands and thousands of people behind barricades, street after street with its crowds of shouting multitudes, our four horses galloping on with five or six policemen outriders, hundreds having escaped from the barricades and running breathlesssly alongside of the carriage . . . Don't you know the look of London with every window stuffed with people waving anything they can lay hold of, but here it is so much more stirring than England, because the faces are so intelligent. There it is a common mob of idlers very likely, here they are strong, thinking, busy men in hundreds and thousands. You can hardly imagine the wild beauty and excitement of one of these galloping drives, the lurid light of the torches and bonfires, the brilliant glare of the electric lights and fireworks, the eager faces and waving hands and shouting voices. He has certainly stood it all wonderfully.[11]

It was no wonder that another of Mary's cousins, Lady Frederick Cavendish, thought that her Uncle William, on his return to Hawarden, was for the first time in her experience 'a little *personally* elated'.

The major themes running through the speeches which Gladstone made in Scotland between 24 November and 6 December 1879 could have been anticipated. There was the attack on Disraeli's foreign policy, the details as well as the spirit of it:

. . . the great duty of a Government, especially in foreign affairs, is to soothe and tranquillize the minds of the people, not to set up false phantoms of glory which are to delude them into calamity, not to flatter their infirmities by leading them to believe that they are better than the rest of the world, and so to encourage the baleful spirit of domination; but to proceed upon a principle that recognises the sisterhood and equality of nations, the absolute equality of public right among them.[12]

He laid down six leading principles of foreign policy:

(1) just legislation and economy at home (2) to preserve to the nations of the world the blessings of peace (3) to strive to cultivate and maintain . . . the Concert of Europe (4) avoid needless and entangling engagements (5) acknowledge the equal rights of all nations and (6) the foreign policy of England should always be inspired by the love of freedom.

He applied these general principles with withering scorn to the government's policies in South Africa and Afghanistan. Another major theme was the attack on the government's extravagant spending: 'I do not hold, gentlemen, that good finance is the beginning and the ending of good government, but I hold this, that it is an essential of good government – it is a condition of good government. Without it you cannot have good government – and with it you almost always get good government.' Other problems to which Gladstone turned his attention were the agricultural depression and the dangers of protection as a remedy for it; disestablishment, the temperance question and the devolution of local government in Scotland and elsewhere. He recognized these problems but gave no specific pledges. Gladstone reckoned that some 87,000 people heard him in Scotland and *The Times* printed 85,000 words of his during those days. He spoke with a freedom and fervour that owed something to the fact that he did not feel the formal responsibilities of party leadership pressing upon him.

The attention aroused by the Midlothian campaign was so great that its effects were perhaps at the time and ever thereafter overestimated. This 'drenching rhetoric', as Beaconsfield called it, was not the main reason for the Liberal victory four months later. Midlothian did, however, bring Gladstone to a position where only an overriding act of renunciation could have prevented his return as Prime Minister in the event of a Liberal victory. Hartington felt this strongly and wished to resign his position as Leader in the Commons. He was dissuaded by Granville, who was closer to Gladstone and knew that ahead of a new Parliament the G.O.M. would not be forced out of his retirement. While still in Scotland Gladstone had spelt out to Bright the reasons why he could not return to the leadership. Perhaps the most compelling of these reasons was that 'a liberal government under me would be the object from the first of an amount and kind of hostility, such as materially to prejudice its acts and weaken or, in given circumstances, neutralize its power for good'. W. P. Adam, the Liberal Chief Whip, shared this opinion and thought that Hartington as leader would be more advantageous in the forthcoming election than Gladstone, though if the latter remained in Parliament he must be the head of a Liberal government. Gladstone himself did not make the ultimate renunciation; to Lord Wolverton, who as George Glyn had been Chief Whip, he wrote that 'the leadership in the next Parliament must, like everything else, be considered in connection with what may appear at the dissolution to be the sense of the country'. Yet by no means all leading Liberals considered Gladstone's return inevitable. Harcourt, for example, Whig in background but with moderately radical leanings, was telling Chamberlain of the great prospects for radicalism under a Hartington premiership uniting both wings of the party.

In January 1880 Gladstone's sister Helen died in Germany. He went to Cologne and brought back her body. He was much exercised by the question whether she could be given an Anglican burial at Fasque; on circumstantial evidence he persuaded himself that she would have preferred this. Politics were again far from his mind and he hoped that it would not be necessary for him to come up for the beginning of the session. But his interest was soon aroused again by two by-elections, Liverpool and Southwark, which, as it happened, were a decisive factor in making Beaconsfield opt for an early dissolution. At Liverpool the Tories held a seat which the Liberals expected to win; but Gladstone, with an expertise worthy of a modern psephologist, pointed out to Granville that the Liberal proportion of the vote had increased. Southwark was worse: the Liberal vote was split between a moderate and a Radical, but the Tory got in by an absolute majority. Gladstone thought that it showed up the weaknesses of the 'Birmingham organization' which up to then he had considered beneficial for the party; he planned to have an interview with Chamberlain on these problems. This kind of concern in a man like Gladstone, whose interest in details of electoral management had until recently been slight, hardly pointed to retreat and retirement.

The by-elections helped to make up Beaconsfield's mind in favour of an early dissolution. The bill to take over and amalgamate the London water companies was another factor in pushing the Cabinet towards a quick dissolution. Accusations of corruption filled the air and a dissolution was an obvious way out. The advice reaching Beaconsfield from his election managers was as inaccurate as the advice given to Gladstone six years earlier.

The dissolution was announced on 8 March and the elections began on 31 March. In the interval the budget brought in by Sir Stafford Northcote, the Tory Chancellor, lent further substance to Gladstone's accusations of extravagance and the high cost of Beaconsfield's foreign policy. The Prime Minister made Ireland the chief theme of his election manifesto; it was prophetic but it evoked little response. Beaconsfield took no further part in the election. He clung to the tradition that peers did not engage in electioneering; in any case he would have been no match for Gladstone in platform oratory and he was a semi-invalid. Gladstone embarked upon a second whirlwind Midlothian campaign. He hammered away at the theme of the classes against the masses; 'we cannot reckon upon the wealth of the country, nor upon the rank of the country . . . nor upon the influence which rank and wealth usually bring . . . Above all these, and behind all these, there is something greater than these – there is the nation itself.' The energy of his electioneering was astonishing in a man of seventy: 'Travelled forty miles and delivered three speeches of forty-five or fifty minutes each . . . Enthusiasm unabated . . . Corrected and dispatched proofs of *Religion, Achaian and Semitic,*' he notes in his diary.

Again it may be doubted if Gladstone's oratory or that of other leading Liberals was a very major factor in the great Liberal victory. If the global number of votes cast for Liberals and Conservatives in 1874 and 1880 is added up, the Liberals were well ahead in both years, though substantially more so in 1880. They were in fact the majority party. The bare figure of votes cast was, of course, not decisive under an electoral system with very uneven constituencies. In 1874 weaknesses of organization, internal divisions and loss of enthusiasm had deprived the Liberals of victory. In 1880 the Conservative organization had declined, the sectionalism of the Liberals was masked largely owing to Gladstone's efforts since 1876 and above all bad trade was working inexorably against the Tories in urban and rural constituencies. The Liberals in 1880 obtained about the same number of seats as the Tories had done in 1874; the Tories had fewer seats than the Liberals in 1874; there was a larger number of Home Rulers, and, even more important, the core of the Irish Nationalist party now led by Parnell had a much more extreme policy as well as a firm popular base in Ireland. Perhaps the most remarkable aspect of the election was that the Tories lost more than twenty-five English county seats, a reflection of the great agricultural depression, and sufficient in itself to blot out the Tory majority in the previous Parliament. The independent Liberal majority was over fifty; with Parnell's party it was about 115.

The moment had arrived when the future of the Liberal leadership would have to be decided and the first move had to be made by the Queen. She was abroad and so confident had Beaconsfield been of victory that he had made no effort to bring her back. When she did return he advised her to send for Hartington. It was not advice she need have accepted, but she was only too glad to clutch at any straw to avoid the dreaded Mr Gladstone. Beaconsfield knew that Granville, whom Gladstone regarded as the overall leader of the Liberals, would never undertake the commission and would merely advise the Queen to send for Gladstone. He had perhaps a slight hope that Hartington might persevere and that, who knows, the Liberal party might split in the process. The Queen certainly tried hard with Hartington, who was, as his biographer put it, 'not devoid of a wish to become Prime Minister'. But Hartington knew that Gladstone would not take any subordinate place in a Liberal government and in these circumstances he could not accept the Queen's commission. All he undertook to do was to ascertain officially that Gladstone would not serve in any but the first position. Honourable as Hartington was, he kept from Gladstone the extent of the Queen's reluctance to readmit him to her service. After a further joint interview of Granville and Hartington with the Queen, Gladstone was at last sent for. These were tense days for all the leading Liberals, even for Gladstone. His sense of mission was fully aroused and it would have been hard for him to relinquish supreme power when it was virtually thrust upon him. On the evening before the day he was called to Windsor Morley met him at a dinner-party: 'He was pale, preoccupied, forced – not at all like himself.' Curiously enough, had Hartington formed a Liberal government at this juncture it would in all likelihood have had to be more radical than the administration which Gladstone now formed. When Gladstone went to Windsor to kiss hands, the Queen's bearing struck him as 'natural under effort'. She reminded him 'with good-natured archness' that he would have to bear the consequences of what he had said in the country.

He was in a position of extraordinary strength. He had not been the *de jure* leader of the party; but even as the *de facto* leader he operated from a position of deliberate detachment. Since 1876 and more latterly in the two Midlothian campaigns his posture had appeared increasingly radical, to none more so than to his opponents. But it was a radicalism of mood, language and moral indignation and it had little in common with the radical programme propounded by men like Chamberlain and Dilke. The Chamberlainites were in any case not the only Radicals in the Liberal party. There were still those who concentrated on single causes, for instance Henry Richard, who had been linked with Edward Miall in the fight for disestablishment, or Sir Wilfrid Lawson the parliamentary leader of the temperance interest; there were others like Mundella or Samuel Morley who were prepared to take Gladstone completely on trust. The Liberals were in fact so heterogeneous that perhaps the only way to lead them was Gladstone's way: by detachment and the choice of great causes emotionally presented.

It was therefore not as surprising as it has often seemed that Gladstone did not allot to the representatives of the 'Birmingham organization', Chamberlain and Dilke, the weight in his government which they thought was due to them. They made large claims about their contribution to the Liberal victory; in the end they used the threat of separate Radical candidatures when they found Gladstone not disposed to give Cabinet office to anyone who had not previously held junior office. With some difficulty they had made a compact that they would both refuse to join the government unless one of them was admitted to the Cabinet. After an intervention by Bright,

Gladstone relented and offered the Board of Trade and a seat in the Cabinet to Chamberlain; Dilke became Under-Secretary for Foreign Affairs. With men like Fawcett, Trevelyan and Mundella also in the government, not to mention radicals of another generation like Bright and Forster in the Cabinet, Gladstone could hardly have gone further. His personal affinities and obligations were to his former colleagues and most clearly to Granville and Hartington.

Gladstone at the beginning of his second ministry was thus in a position of strength, but also of danger. Perhaps not the least of the dangers sprang from his own state of mind. On the day he first went to meet the new Parliament, 20 May 1880, he wrote in his diary:

. . . I do believe that the Almighty has employed me for His purposes in a manner larger or more special than before, and has strengthened me and led me on accordingly, though I must not forget the admirable saying of Hooker, that even ministers of good things are like torches, a light to others, waste and destruction to themselves.

10

THE
AGEING
TITAN
1880–85

Gladstone's second government has often been regarded as inferior in achievement to his first, because at the end of the day it had not passed a long list of specific measures of reform. It is easy to ascribe this alleged lack of achievement to a decline of power and grip in the Prime Minister and to argue that he distorted the course of British politics by not retiring earlier. Lack of achievement in reform can in any case hardly be held against a government that carried through the biggest and most democratic change in the electoral system of the whole of the nineteenth century. The role which Gladstone played in this period was highly complex and is open to many interpretations. One thing is not open to dispute: his continued dominance of the political scene. Harcourt, who more than any other leading Liberal had put his stake on Gladstone's retirement in 1880, wrote to him in June 1885 after the resignation of the government: 'You are the Party and your acts are its acts.' Stansfeld, who in the past had revered Gladstone, wrote in March 1885: 'What we want is that Gladstone should vanish and people reassert themselves.' Gladstone could hardly have towered like a colossus had he really been so much out of line with the mood and requirements of the time. He was getting older and the 'egoism of genius' was sometimes more in evidence than it had been. He was still a liberal conservative and he was out of sympathy with some tendencies of the age, what he himself called 'constructionism'. These tendencies were, however, not yet strong enough to claim predominance in the early 1880s and within the Liberal combination Gladstone's position was still fairly central. The government of 1880 had no programme, but neither had Disraeli's of 1874. Certain issues were coming over the horizon, for example household suffrage in the counties, and these could in due course be taken up. What was exceptional in the 1880 government was the extent of unforeseen problems and events that beset its course: Ireland, Egypt, South Africa, Bradlaugh and others. Gladstone dealt with these matters with his great mastery of detail and powers of work, marred by his lack of proportion and impulsiveness; he did it with a team of able but very disparate men and within a system hardly geared to the dispatch of a large volume of business. Only a young man of exceptional powers could have done as well. When he took office in April 1880 there was a general feeling, shared even by members of his family, that it would be for a couple of years only. It was soon realized, however, on all sides that without him the Liberal government and party could not hold together and so he went on.

In the first short session of the new Parliament, only about half the normal length, the scope for major legislation was limited. Gladstone took the important strategic decision to postpone parliamentary reform until later in the Parliament. In this only Chamberlain disagreed – he would have preferred an early change in the franchise followed swiftly by another election. It was his hope that a greatly enlarged radical Liberal party would be the consequence. In the event preoccupation with Ireland perforce postponed franchise reform till 1884. It was the one major measure that was a *sine qua non* for radicals like Chamberlain; it was mainly due to Gladstone that they eventually got it in such complete form and without a split in the party. This fact alone largely contradicts the picture of Radical frustration during Gladstone's second government.

Two of the main proposals for the 1880 session were in fact directed towards the grievances of the farming community. The farmers were traditionally Tory, but the severity of the agricultural depression had undoubtedly made many of them vote Liberal and the result was the substantial decline of the Tory hold on country seats. The prospect of an extension of the county franchise gave the rural vote the highest importance. The more important of the two government proposals in 1880 was the repeal of the malt tax and its replacement by a beer tax. For this Gladstone was personally responsible, for he was Chancellor of the Exchequer as well as Prime Minister. His criticism of Conservative finance had been a major element in his onslaught on the Beaconsfield government and he assumed responsibility for the Exchequer as an earnest of his intention to institute a sounder financial policy. The farming interest had campaigned against the malt tax for a generation, the Tories had failed to repeal it in their six years of power and it was therefore a not inconsiderable achievement that Gladstone now managed to do so, even though he had to put up the income tax by one penny to make up for it. The second measure of significance to farmers was the Ground Game Bill, also known as the Hares and Rabbits Bill; it made it obligatory to include in all land leases a clause leaving it to the tenant to deal with ground game. It divided landlords and tenants and caused considerable dissension on the Tory benches, thus adding to the demoralized state of the opposition.[1] It also aroused resistance among some Whig members of the Liberal party, but this showed that the government, in spite of its composition, was not necessarily Whiggish in policy. All this was good party stuff and even Beaconsfield thought it 'the most devilish of the A.V.'s schemes'.[2] Arch Villain was now his habitual name for Gladstone in his intimate correspondence. Chamberlain was responsible for a departmental bill, the Employers' Liability Bill, dealing with compensation for industrial accidents. Although this was a problem of great importance for labour, the bill was very limited in scope, in deference to *laissez-faire* principles, yet the attack on it came mainly from employers sitting on the Liberal benches. This again showed how limited the scope for radical reform really was, given the composition of the Liberal party. In the 1880 session Gladstone also proposed a further measure to deal with Irish grievances, although the real flare-up of Ireland was still to come later in the year. The Compensation for Disturbance Bill was yet another attempt to deal with eviction; it was defeated in the Lords and caused the resignation from the government of Lord Lansdowne, a junior minister, and nearly drove out the Duke of Argyll. This again illustrated how divergent a team Gladstone had to drive.

Even in the session of 1880 the planned schemes of the government were from the start upset by the Bradlaugh case, one of the many unforeseen circumstances that affected the course of Gladstone's second government.[3] Charles Bradlaugh, atheist, republican and advocate of birth-control, had been elected Radical member for Northampton, together with Henry Labouchere. He had done much to secure the passage of the Evidence Amendment Acts of 1869 and 1870 under which it was possible to affirm in courts of law instead of taking the oath. It was Bradlaugh's view that these acts together with the Parliamentary Oaths Act of 1866 gave him the right to affirm instead of taking the oath as a new member of the House. He therefore gave notice to the Speaker, Brand, of his intention to affirm. The Speaker sought the opinion of one of the Clerks of the House who reported that Bradlaugh's claim to affirm was not valid. Thus the Speaker proposed to submit the matter to the judgement of the House and suggested to Gladstone that a Select Committee be appointed. Although the Law Officers of the Crown took the view that Bradlaugh's claim was valid, the Prime Minister agreed to the appointment of a Select Committee and so did Sir Stafford Northcote, the Leader of the Opposition. The Select Committee decided by the casting vote of its chairman to reject Bradlaugh's claim to affirm. Bradlaugh thereupon decided to take the oath, but made it clear in a letter to *The Times* that the words of it 'are to me sounds conveying no clear and definite meaning'. It was on 21 May 1880 that Bradlaugh advanced toward the Table of the House and started taking the oath and was immediately interrupted by an objection from Sir Henry Drummond Wolff, the Conservative member for Portsmouth. Thus the Bradlaugh case was born and along with it the Fourth Party, the Tory ginger-group consisting of Wolff, Lord Randolph Churchill, Arthur Balfour and John Gorst. What gave them their opportunity was the weakness of Sir Stafford Northcote who could never quite shake off the devotion he had acquired in many years of being Gladstone's private secretary and agent in successive Oxford elections. Sir Stafford's back-benchers wanted to be 'shown blood', but this he proved quite unable to do. But the Fourth Party also profited from Gladstone's inability to keep silent, his habit of bearing down his opponents by sheer weight of argument and of inflating, through lack of proportion, minor debating points into affairs of state.

On the Bradlaugh case Gladstone was at his best, not perhaps always on the tactics of the matter, but in his refusal to move for the sake of popularity or party advantage from a position that was sound and just. He had no sympathy whatsoever for Bradlaugh's atheism, but he rightly considered that the legal and constitutional question was paramount and not the opinions of Bradlaugh. Beyond the legal niceties Gladstone's view was that the time had long passed when matters of conscience could be used as a justification for a civil disability. It was the logical consummation of the belief in religious liberty that had matured in him over so many years. Unfortunately great sections of public and parliamentary opinion were not interested in legality or even freedom of conscience: they took account only of Bradlaugh's opinions, blasphemous and disloyal. Many were sincere in their abhorrence of these opinions and did not wish to see the Mother of Parliaments tainted with them. Others could not restrain their glee at this spectacle of Gladstone having to take the side of an atheist; both in terms of public opinion and parliamentary skirmishing much party advantage could be derived from the case. Northcote, who often showed signs of wishing to settle the matter decently, could not afford, for the sake of his survival as a leader, to allow his young bloods to make the running. Gladstone's Nonconformist followers were uncertain and divided. They should have nailed freedom of conscience to their mast; but many of them were offended by Bradlaugh's willingness to take the oath, which seemed to them, as well as being blasphemous, to compromise the question of principle. As his parliamentary majority was not reliable on the Bradlaugh case, Gladstone could not always move decisively. So the case dragged on, through a second select committee, Bradlaugh's committal to the Clock Tower, the loss of his case in the courts, his re-election at Northampton and so on. In July 1881 Eddy Hamilton, one of Gladstone's private secretaries, wrote in his diary, 'The sore will be kept open, and the Opposition will continue to have a good and nasty "stick" wherewith "to beat" that "dog" of a Government.'[4]

Gladstone hoped to rid the government of the Bradlaugh incubus and to rescue the House of Commons from the false position into which it had got itself by bringing a bill to allow affirmation in place of the parliamentary oath. It was not until the session of 1883 that time was found to introduce such a bill and even then it was not made an issue of confidence. By this time Gladstone was taking a close personal interest in the question and briefing himself fully on the complex legal and historical problems involved. It was now in his eyes an elementary matter of justice and liberty. How much he was swimming against the tide can perhaps be seen from the fact that there were in 1883 over 700,000 petitions against the bill and only 175,000 in favour. Some of the Nonconformist bodies, though pained by Bradlaugh's views, came out in favour; but otherwise organized religion was strongly opposed. Manning was, in spite of the recent acceptance of Catholics to full civil and religious liberty, a strong opponent. On 26 April 1883 Gladstone made a speech on the Affirmation Bill which he himself signified in his diary with the German word *begeistert* – enthused. Many thought it perhaps his greatest. 'It was the voice and manner, above all the voice, with its marvellous modulations, that made the speech majestic.' One of the most significant passages in this speech illustrates Gladstone's view of the changing religious attitudes in contemporary society:

I do not hesitate to say that the specific evil, the specific form of irreligion, with which in the educated society of this country you have to contend . . . is not blank atheism . . . but what is frequently met with is that form of opinion which would teach us that, whatever may be beyond the visible things of this world . . . you can know nothing of it. . . That is the mischief of the age . . .

The Affirmation Bill was defeated by three votes, a result which caused great jubilation in the Tory ranks and for which much credit was given to Lord Randolph Churchill. In spite of the pressure of public opinion, only nine Liberals had voted against the bill, though more had abstained. But among Irish Nationalists forty-five had voted against the bill and only three in favour. At one time Parnell had been pro-Bradlaugh, but pressure from the Catholic Church had caused many Irish Home Rulers to shift their ground. They were not yet the monolithic party they became under Parnell after 1885; in spasms they were at this stage often anti-Gladstonian. The defeat on the Affirmation Bill shook the government, but for the rest of the Parliament the Bradlaugh case receded from the headlines and the member for Northampton was unable to take his seat.

As soon as the government had been formed at the end of April 1880 questions of foreign and imperial policy began to crowd in upon it, and this continued to be so for the next five years, to a much greater degree than had been the case in Gladstone's first government. The day-to-day conduct of foreign policy rested with the partnership of Gladstone and Granville, still much the closest political relationship in the Cabinet. In this partnership Gladstone was the source of ideas and impulse, Granville the tactful executant. Gladstone had very clear-cut ideas on the aims and methods of foreign and imperial policy and these had supplied the main thrust to his public activities since he abandoned his retirement in 1876. Sometimes these ideas had a great deal of applicability to the problems he now had to deal with as Prime Minister; for example they were applied in the case of the Boers and the Transvaal. In other ways they became more and more difficult to apply; for instance Gladstone's wish to operate through the Concert of Europe, as on the Montenegro question and on Egypt, was not a practical possibility in the age of Bismarck. Gladstone was, however, by no means doctrinaire and in spite of the language of Midlothian recognized that continuity was inevitable in many areas of policy. After five months in office he said to Granville that they 'were certainly not returned to Parliament to carry forward the Foreign Policy of the last Government . . . Nevertheless, sensible of the expediency of maintaining as far as might be a continuity in Foreign Policy, we sought for a ground of action which might be common to both political parties.'⁵ In this instance Gladstone and Granville were, however, applying the principle of continuity somewhat legalistically to pursue a policy the last government would never have adopted: they were trying to force Turkey to carry out the unfulfilled clauses of the Treaty of Berlin relating to Montenegro and Greece. But certainly those who expected a total reversal of policy by the Liberal government were disappointed. As time went on Gladstone was often so preoccupied by Irish and domestic affairs that he could give very little direction to Granville, who in his turn, with advancing age, was less able to pursue a consistent line of policy. Some major blunders were committed and created a general impression of failure in foreign policy, particularly in the minds of those who were hostile to Gladstone's whole approach to international relations.

Two imperial commitments, Afghanistan and South Africa, were inherited from the Conservative government and bulked large in Gladstone's attacks on his rival. In the case of Afghanistan there was a clear decision to reverse the forward policy of Lytton and Beaconsfield, which had been designed to partition the country into spheres of influence. It was fortunate that in this instance retreat took place in the afterglow of a notable feat of arms, Roberts's march on Kandahar. Even so there was much criticism, from the

Queen, and from Beaconsfield who made his last speech on this subject in March 1881. In the South African case the decision was for continuity. Gladstone's notes for one of his early Cabinet meetings, on 12 May 1880, read, 'South Africa – to promote Confederation. Transvaal – retain sovereignty.'[6] These had been the policies of the previous government and the advice of the Colonial Office was to continue them. The most obvious signal of continuity was the decision not to recall Sir Bartle Frere, symbol of the forward policy; perhaps Dilke came near to uncovering the real reason for this decision when he noted that 'as we were retiring from Kandahar we had better not also retire from Pretoria'. The failure to recall Frere was largely responsible for the tension between the government and its back-benchers which developed almost as soon as Parliament assembled. On 31 May Eddy Hamilton wrote in his diary: 'Bradlaugh and Frere have been the main centre of interest during the last week.' At this stage Gladstone was convinced that federation was the solution to the South African problem, a solution that fitted in well with his general concept of self-governing colonies living in harmony and association with the mother country. Concern for the native population was another major argument for not rescinding the annexation of the Transvaal. He parried the attacks from his own side on Frere and on the continued annexation of the Transvaal by holding out the grand prospect of confederation. He was not sufficiently familiar with the situation in South Africa to realize that this vision was a mirage. By July 1880 events in the Cape Assembly had made it clear that there was no hope of a federation and Frere was replaced. The Queen wrote to Gladstone that she 'CANNOT approve of this step, but will not oppose it'.

It was unfortunate that in the case of the Transvaal Gladstone did not have the courage of his conviction to end the annexation when he came to office. It was certainly a deep disappointment for Kruger and the Boers, who fully expected it from the man who had spoken in Midlothian. By the end of the year 1880 much harsher choices were facing the British government in South Africa: war or a retreat from the position that had been taken up. In the interval Gladstone had left the problem mainly in the hands of Kimberley, his Colonial Secretary, and the permanent officials of the Colonial Office. When it reverted to the Prime Minister and the Cabinet in December 1880 they were all deep in the throes of the Irish problem. Ireland and the Boers had much in common: it was a question of finding the right balance between conciliation and coercion and avoiding the worst of both possible worlds. It was a parallel not lost on many, but in terms of sheer pressure of time and business Ireland tended to make it more difficult to deal with South Africa. When the extent of the Boer rebellion became clear to Gladstone he quickly decided that a way out must be sought by negotiation leading to an acknowledgement of Boer independence. Chamberlain and other radical members of the government had advocated this all along. On 21 January 1881 Gladstone made a statement on the Transvaal in the House of Commons which essentially was a smoke-screen to cover the reversal of the government's policy, should the response of the Boers be reasonable enough to make this possible. In the division Chamberlain, Dilke, Bright and Leonard Courtney, who had just joined the government as Under-Secretary at the Home Office, abstained from voting. The government was, as in all such colonial affairs, very much in the hands of its local agent; it was a piece of monstrous bad luck that before the position with the Boers was fully clarified, Sir George Colley, the Governor of Natal, made his ill-fated foray at Majuba Hill which ended in his defeat and death. The news reached London on 25 February 1881, when Gladstone was in bed after slipping on a heap of snow and cutting his head open. The situation was now doubly difficult: on the one side there were those who felt the Boers needed to be taught a lesson first, before any solution could be arrived at, and on the other side were those who wanted the claims of the Boers to be immediately recognized. Among the hawks were the Queen and most of the Whigs in the Cabinet; among the doves were Chamberlain, Bright and above all Gladstone himself. Hamilton wrote in his diary: 'We have . . . just had enough fighting to wound all the susceptibilities of the Peace Party; and just stopped short momentarily, to kindle up all the jingo feelings afresh.'[7] Gladstone now manoeuvred with great skill, containing the impatience of the peace party, who, headed by Bright, threatened to break up the government, while pushing ahead with the policy of coming to terms with the Boers. It was the only possible policy short of mounting a major military effort to defeat the Boers and risking an uprising of the Cape Dutch into the bargain. It did, however, look like weakness to concede after three defeats culminating in Majuba what had been refused before. The result was the Pretoria Convention of August 1881, recognizing the *de facto* independence of the Transvaal under British suzerainty; this was modified in 1884 by the London convention which no longer mentioned suzerainty. All this provided only a temporary respite, but Gladstone could hardly at this stage have provided against all the eventualities arising from the discovery of gold, the great influx of *uitlanders* and the pressures of great-power rivalry in Africa. His handling of the South African crisis illustrates many of the problems he faced in his second administration: the super-imposition of several crises simultaneously, his own 'leadership by detachment' coupled with the principle of leaving cabinet ministers reasonably independent, the divisions in the Cabinet largely along the Whig–Radical fault line, the constant pressure from the Queen, the dilemma between coercion and conciliation, the great tactical and parliamentary skill when under pressure.

Except for a few flashpoints like Majuba, South Africa was overshadowed by the Irish crisis. This crisis caught Gladstone, as he admitted, unaware. Sensitive as he was to Irish grievances and to the claims of Irish nationality, he did not expect an immediate crisis of such severity in 1880. He had been too preoccupied with the Eastern Question; when he had become Chancellor of the Exchequer as well as Prime Minister in April 1880 he had assumed that finance would have first priority as a field for constructive legislation. Nevertheless the agricultural depression had bitten so hard in Ireland in the summer of 1880 that the government had been prodded into an attempt to stop the loopholes in Gladstone's own Irish Land Act of 1870 by the Compensation for Disturbance Bill. The failure of this bill illustrates the great block of prejudice and property interests which all Irish remedial legislation had to encounter. Even had it passed it would have been too late to undo the merger of agrarian revolt and parliamentary action achieved through Parnell's Irish Nationalist party. Henceforth Gladstone was caught in a vicious circle of Irish violence and the repression of it and much of the constructive impact of his legislation for Ireland was, at least in the short run, frustrated.

In the autumn of 1880 Gladstone put forward a scheme of grand committees in Parliament, to deal with Irish, Scottish and English affairs respectively, to lead in due course to a reconstruction of the Irish system of government. The Cabinet did not proceed on these proposals; instead the question arose whether and in what form coercion should be applied in Ireland and whether and in what form remedial legislation should accompany it. These problems caused acute dissension in the Cabinet. Forster, who had initially advocated a conciliatory policy and was the author of the Compensation for Disturbance Bill, was now so convinced of the need for coercion that he threatened to resign if it was not quickly granted. He was backed by most of the Whig members of the Cabinet and Hartington eventually also threatened resignation. On the other wing stood

Bright and Chamberlain. Bright had long been the advocate of a land purchase scheme; Chamberlain hated coercion and also had constructive plans for Ireland. Gladstone, in his Olympian way, steered through these shoals with considerable skill. Eddy Hamilton's comment as early as 18 November 1880 was: 'Here we are in the midst of a ministerial crisis; early days for this certainly. It surely never was the fate of a ministry before to be troubled so much in their early career; – first Ireland (last session), then the Montenegrin business, and now Ireland again.' As far as Bright and Chamberlain were concerned their qualms about coercion were soon overcome by the behaviour of the Parnellites in the House of Commons. Bright became completely disillusioned with Ireland; Chamberlain was restrained by the knowledge that anti-Irish feeling had been fanned among his working-class supporters by the murders and outrages on the other side of St George's Channel.

In the event the government's policies were a compromise, of the kind liable to obtain the worst of both possible worlds. Coercion came, but also Gladstone's great Irish Land Act of 1881 establishing the three Fs: fair rent, free sale and fixity of tenure. He had been slow in seeing his way clear to these principles: at first he had hoped to proceed by a much less drastic amendment of his Land Act of 1870 and he was reluctant to adopt principles which in practice established a form of dual ownership in land. Initially this seemed to him too profound an interference with the ideas of individualism, property and freedom in which he believed. It is a tribute to his remarkable powers of absorbing an immensely complex array of facts that he changed his mind, and it shows that at the age of seventy-one he could discard established ideas if he was convinced that it was intellectually sound to do so. He can be criticized for not having sought advice more widely on the Land Bill, particularly from Parnell and other Irish nationalist quarters. The business of piloting the Irish Land Bill through the House of Commons in the session of 1881 was one of his greatest parliamentary achievements. Few, other than the Irish, understood the intricacies of the bill, and they were only waiting to pounce upon every error or slip. Even fewer of the English and Scottish members of the House cared. At the end of the committee stage, in July, the longest since the great Reform Bill, Hamilton confided to his diary:

The marvellousness of the man who conducted such a measure through such a Committee is now the subject of universal comment. He has achieved many legislative feats, but none so immense and so difficult as this Land Bill. It is impossible to overrate the mastery of detail which he has shown, the tact, judgment, and good temper which he has displayed, the outburst of eloquence which he has occasionally made, and last (and not least) the extraordinary physical power he has exhibited. As the *Daily Telegraph* said the other day, whatever may be our political opinions we all 'must be proud' of such a man.

But there was also coercion and on this the Irish members led by Parnell used to the full their powers of obstruction. There can be little doubt that coercion was painful to Gladstone. Morley, in a letter to Chamberlain, described how Gladstone told him after a dinner-party on New Year's Eve 1880 about coercion 'much as a man might say (in confidence) that he found himself under the painful necessity of slaying his mother. It was downright piteous – his wrung features, his strained gesture, all the other signs of mental perturbation in an intense nature.'[8] In fighting Irish obstruction and defeating it at the end of the famous forty-one-hour sitting in February 1881, Gladstone was again at his best 'with his powerful reasoning, his perfect temper, his high-bred bearing towards those miscreants'. The changes in parliamentary procedure which came about now and in the subsequent session were in the long run to have far more persistent constitutional and political consequences than Irish coercion, and if Gladstone could have foreseen them he would hardly have approved. As for Ireland, Gladstone had not yet fully grasped the reality of Irish national consciousness nor the fact that Parnell was essentially a conservative representative of this consciousness.

Within a few days of the introduction of the Irish Land Bill in the House of Commons Lord Beaconsfield died. Gladstone uttered all the appropriate words required by the occasion, though it cost him a good deal of effort. He declined to attend the private funeral at Hughenden. To the Queen, he wrote:

Mr Gladstone would not seek, nor could he earn, Your Majesty's regard by dissembling the amount or character of the separation between Lord Beaconsfield and himself. But it does not in any degree blind him to the extraordinary powers of the deceased statesman, or to many remarkable qualities, in regard to whom Mr Gladstone, well aware of his own marked inferiority, can only desire to profit by a great example.

The Queen thanked Gladstone warmly for his condolences, but with reference to this passage she wrote: 'The Queen therefore hardly likes to touch on what Mr Gladstone alludes to, viz: the difference between him and Ld Beaconsfield – for she felt much that relates to that keenly and painfully.'[9]

   The Land Act did not bring the hoped-for relief in Ireland, and the agitation of the Land League continued. Even Gladstone felt that Parnell was out to wreck the act. As with many other English statesmen who have dealt with Ireland before or since, he felt the extremists were making the running and the moderates were not coming forward. In October 1881 Gladstone went to Leeds, where he had a triumphant reception. In one of his speeches he gave a clear warning to the extremists of whom he considered Parnell the foremost: 'If it shall appear that there is still to be fought a final conflict in Ireland between law on one side and sheer lawlessness on the other . . . then I say, gentlemen, without hesitation, the resources of civilisation are not yet exhausted.' Parnell referred to him in his reply as 'this masquerading knight errant, the pretending champion of the rights of every other nation except those of the Irish nation'. Within a week Parnell was imprisoned under the Coercion Act.

   When the 1882 session of Parliament began the government was under attack from all sides for its Irish policy. On the one hand the country was not pacified; on the other the imprisonment of Parnell was an extreme use of executive power. There were, however, signs that the Land League was weakened and that more tenants were making use of the Land Act. In one of his speeches on Ireland at this time Gladstone spoke of Home Rule; he saw many difficulties, particularly in the separation of Irish and imperial affairs, but it was clear that he thought the question deserved serious consideration. The affairs of Ireland were still so pressing that it soon became obvious that local government reform, a close concern of Chamberlain and his followers, would not be taken up that session although it had been announced in the Queen's Speech. By April 1882 the seemingly deadlocked Irish situation was in flux. Parnell had public and private reasons for wishing to end his confinement in Kilmainham Gaol. He needed to be back in action in order to maintain his influence in Ireland; he wanted to be with his mistress, Mrs O'Shea, after the death of their first child. Negotiations were carried on between Parnell and the government through Chamberlain and Captain O'Shea. Gladstone was very anxious to grasp any chance of normalization and thus the Kilmainham treaty was concluded. It was not, as Gladstone was always at pains to point out, a 'treaty'. It was merely that the government had enough information to make them aware that the release of Parnell would no longer be detrimental to public order, and that therefore there was no case for detaining a person against whom no charges had been brought. To Lord Richard Grosvenor, his Chief Whip, Gladstone wrote:

'Of a new departure we know nothing; but of new hopes we know much. If wrong in our behalf, we are very wrong and must soon go to the right about.' This was a piece of Gladstonian casuistry, for there had definitely been a bargain. The government undertook to release Parnell and his associates, drop coercion and deal with the problem of rent arrears and leaseholders; Parnell undertook to withdraw the No Rent manifesto and calm the situation in Ireland. It was, however, not a bargain to be ashamed of and there was no justification for the fierce party passion which subsequently represented it as a deal with traitors and a sordid piece of political horse-trading.

The Kilmainham treaty provided Forster with an opportunity to resign. He had been fully aware of the negotiations with Parnell and had not objected to them; on the other hand the 'treaty' could be interpreted as a change of course from the policy of firmness which Forster had pursued and perhaps his main motive was to relinquish his dangerous and thankless task. In later years, after Forster's death, Gladstone always maintained the view that there was no real justification for Forster's resignation.

Gladstone has been criticized for not appointing Chamberlain in his place, the only one among his colleagues with a wider and more conciliatory approach to Irish affairs. But there were difficulties; Chamberlain was highly suspect among Whigs; under new arrangements by which Spencer would replace Lord Cowper as Viceroy the Chief Secretary would no longer have a seat in the Cabinet; the *Pall Mall Gazette* under the editorship of Morley had pushed for Chamberlain's appointment and Gladstone disliked this kind of pressure. An expectation that Chamberlain would succeed Forster had been established and Chamberlain was prepared to make the sacrifice; in these circumstances Gladstone should have conveyed to Chamberlain the reasons why he could not be appointed instead of leaving him to find out from the newspapers. In these minor arts of handling his colleagues Gladstone was often incompetent and unlucky.

Instead Gladstone appointed Lord Frederick Cavendish, the husband of his wife's niece. He was one of several young Whig noblemen who were devoted to him and whom he found attractive. Lord Frederick was particularly close to Gladstone, who clearly hoped through him to keep a personal grip on Irish affairs. The appointment could be helpful in relations with Hartington, Lord Frederick's brother; Hartington had never found it easy to understand Gladstone and was often the focus of opposition to the

Prime Minister's policies in the Cabinet. Within a day of his arrival in Dublin Lord Frederick Cavendish was assassinated while walking in Phoenix Park with Burke, the Permanent Under-Secretary at Dublin Castle. The assassination was as much as anything an indication of the inefficiency of Dublin Castle and its security arrangements. It was one of the worst blows Gladstone had ever suffered and he was never quite the same man afterwards. When the news was broken to him on his return to Downing Street after a dinner at the Austrian Embassy he and Mrs Gladstone fell on their knees and prayed. A few days later in the House of Commons Gladstone with difficulty mastered his misery and 'forced out what was needful'. Party controversy was only briefly interrupted and a week later in the Kilmainham debate raged more fiercely than ever. Two incidents were particularly vicious. Forster, with wounded pride, forced the revelation of a sentence in a letter from Parnell to O'Shea, which had been forwarded to himself, Chamberlain and Gladstone: 'The accomplishment of the programme I have sketched out to you would in my judgment be regarded by the country as a practical settlement of the Land Question, and would enable us to cooperate cordially for the future with the Liberal Party in forwarding Liberal principles and measures of general reform.' Gladstone had explicitly not accepted any deal of this nature, but it now could be made to look like it. On the same theme, Arthur Balfour, in private life a close friend of the Gladstone family, said in the debate: 'I do not believe that any such transaction can be quoted from the annals of our political or parliamentary history. It stands alone – I do not wish to use strong language – it stands alone in its infamy.'[10] Gladstone was deeply wounded by these words. It has to be remembered that some Conservatives had moved for the release of Parnell and his associates and that some kind of *rapprochement* between Tories and Parnellites had been on the cards. The situation looked menacing for the Liberal government and Edward Hamilton confided to his diary:

> I confess that, notwithstanding the acquaintance with all the facts which one has, it requires a very resolute exercise of faith in Mr G and his colleagues not to have qualms, which I confess I cannot wholly banish. I have no apprehensions as to the actual policy taken, but I have the greatest apprehension of anything which implies a belief in the integrity and straight forwardness of any one of the Parnellites including O'Shea, though he does seem like a gentleman.

The effect of the Phoenix Park murders was in fact not as damaging as it appeared at the time. The passions aroused by the event in the country, in Parliament and in the Cabinet forced Gladstone to bring in a Coercion Bill, ahead of the Arrears Bill which had been part of the Kilmainham bargain. This made it appear that the bargain was dead, but Parnell was in fact more anxious than ever to reassert his control in Ireland and divert the agrarian discontent into more constitutional channels. Parnell was somewhat demoralized by Phoenix Park, went in fear of his life and suggested to Gladstone that he might retire from public life. He could now attack the government on coercion and this strengthened his position in Ireland. Gladstone well recognized the fundamentally moderating influence of Parnell; moreover, he instinctively disliked coercion and did what he could to soften the bill, in the face of the Cabinet hawks, for example Harcourt, and against an adverse public opinion. On the Arrears Bill Gladstone got his way much more; he forced the House of Lords under threat of dissolution to accept it in its original form. By this time, August 1882, Egypt was already overshadowing Ireland in the public mind and the Lords gave way. Salisbury, who wanted to fight to the last ditch, was isolated. Throughout these months from May to August 1882 Gladstone was at the centre of manifold pressures on Irish policy: from Chamberlain and other radicals who disliked coercion, from men like Harcourt on his own side and Salisbury on the other who felt that conciliation under threat would get nowhere, from Spencer, the new Viceroy, who was somewhere between these extremes. Gladstone was prepared to use any avenue that might help conciliation – thus his correspondence and interviews with Mrs O'Shea started. He was aware that she was rumoured to be Parnell's mistress, but his highmindedness disinclined him to pay any attention. His view of what the Irish situation required was, as in the case of South Africa, far more realistic than the views of those who advocated repression. He committed tactical blunders and at times he exhibited his 'squeezable nature'. Perhaps in the long run his rational liberal–conservative approach to the Irish problem was bound to be defeated by the extremes inherent in this situation. But his Land and Arrears Acts worked in the short run and agrarian outrages began to decline after 1882; Parnell behaved constitutionally and the Irish party at Westminster were lying relatively low.

In the summer of 1882 Egypt was added to the heavy preoccupations which Irish legislation and the dissensions about it in the Cabinet had placed upon Gladstone. His immediate influence on foreign affairs had markedly declined since his attempts in 1880 to coerce the Porte through the Concert of Europe. On Egyptian affairs

he had only been able to produce some general guidelines. At bottom
he felt that any involvement in Egypt was unnecessary and impossible to justify on grounds of imperial security; already in 1877
he had expressed this view in an article in the *Nineteenth Century*.
The system of dual Anglo-French control over Egyptian finances
had been inherited from the previous government; Gladstone wished
to continue it, use Turkish troops to intervene and avoid isolated
British action. On 13 September 1881 he wrote to Granville:

I sum up thus. 1. Steady concert with France. 2. Turkish General to
go if need be. 3. Turkish troops, in preference to any others. 4. No
British or French force, unless ships be needful for bona fide protection
of subjects. 5. Apart from all this, I long for information on the merits
of the quarrel; as on them I suppose may depend the ulterior question
of reducing, or disbanding, the Army.

The rise of Arabi and Egyptian nationalism took Gladstone by
surprise:

I am not by any means pained, but I am much surprised at this rapid
development of a national sentiment and party in Egypt. The very
ideas of such a sentiment and the Egyptian people seemed quite
incompatible. How it has come up I do not know: most of all is the case
strange if the standing army be the nest that has reared it,

he wrote to Granville on 4 January 1882. His ideas for dealing with
the fast-evolving situation were still rather general and not easily
applied in practice: he wanted to encourage the Egyptian Chamber of
Notables and bring in the Concert of Europe, and he still wanted to
act through the Sultan. 'Think of Bismarck and the Turk fighting
the battle of representative and popular principles against us!'
He did not see in Arabi a genuine manifestation of Egyptian nationalism. 'He seems to me to represent at this time military violence
and nothing else.' The bombardment of Alexandria took place on
11 July 1882 and almost right up to the day Gladstone was reluctant
to agree to such unilateral British action. All this added another
set of dissensions in the Cabinet to those already existing on Irish
affairs at that moment. On Egypt, however, Chamberlain made
common cause with Hartington and they were the chief advocates
of intervention. Bright was the only minister who backed Gladstone's
stand against intervention; when the bombardment was agreed on
he resigned and all the Prime Minister's persuasive powers could not
change his mind. Only a few days later the decision was taken to
send a military expedition under Sir Garnet Wolseley to Egypt.
Again Gladstone was intensely reluctant to act alone, but he was
now convinced of the need for action and had argued on this point

at length with Bright. Once the action was under way Gladstone was, however, pleased with the evidence it gave of British military efficiency, for which his own previous government could take not a little of the credit. Like the Crimean War in its earlier stages he considered this a just war. England had not wished to act alone but in the end the extent of Egyptian disorder and the reluctance of others to co-operate forced her hand. On the day of Tel-el-Kebir he wrote to his wife: 'The war has been undertaken in singleness of purpose, on behalf of justice, peace and liberty, and its progress has thus far been conformable to its origins and its aims.'[11]

On Egypt Gladstone was not at his best: the discrepancy between his own ideology on foreign policy and the realities of the situation was too great. He could not give the matter enough attention; Granville at his best was never an originator of clear policies and he was past his prime; the Cabinet was divided and Gladstone was not a dictator within it. The ramifications of the Egyptian imbroglio on the European power structure were not clearly assessed by Gladstone and Granville and they laid up trouble for themselves for the future. On the morrow of Tel-el-Kebir, however, Gladstone was in high spirits as he left for Hawarden and almost seemed to have caught a touch of jingoism: 'He was quite disappointed at leaving before the guns in honour of the Egyptian victories had been fired, which was his own suggestion, and about which he was quite childishly keen.'

In December 1882 Gladstone celebrated his fiftieth anniversary in politics. More than two and a half years had elapsed since he had taken office again, essentially as he felt on a short lease. On many occasions he spoke to his intimates about retirement; in the autumn of 1881, when he was depressed by Irish affairs, particularly by the arrest of Parnell, he was continually harping on it. He wanted to resign as Chancellor of the Exchequer, for he felt the double burden was too much and that in his ideas on economy he had become 'an old mouldy landmark on a deserted shore'. But he thought his total withdrawal from politics could not be long delayed and therefore it was hardly worth while to do it in two stages. Around his seventy-second birthday in December 1881 he told Acton that 'when the great specialities are disposed of, he (Mr G.) is "outwardly and inwardly bound" to ask for his dismissal'. Yet there were always 'specialities' to detain him, notably the affairs of Ireland. Whenever his resignation appeared to become an imminent reality, irresistible pressures appeared to make him stay. Very often they came from those who frequently opposed him, Hartington and Chamberlain, for only Gladstone could keep the heterogeneous Liberal coalition together and neither of them was yet ready to succeed him. To many it seemed that Gladstone's retirement must mean a major realignment of parties. He was sometimes ill; for example the big Cabinet reconstruction of December 1882, which coincided with his Fiftieth Jubilee, took a lot out of him, as personalities always did, and he retired to Cannes for six weeks. Granville and Hartington laboured hard to prevent his resignation, Chamberlain told Harcourt that he was glad 'to be rid of the nightmare of Mr G.'s resignation'; Harcourt wrote to Ponsonby, the Queen's secretary: 'There are some people I think who have not realized how much more uncomfortable things will be for *everybody* when he is gone. After all, he is the linch-pin of the coach . . .' His illnesses were sometimes due to political vexations rather than physical causes and not infrequently they served a political purpose. He was really very sound in body and limb and his doctor thought that of all his patients he was most likely to live to a hundred. The talk of retirement aided, if anything, his posture of 'leadership by detachment' and he did not need to feel beholden to anybody. Occasionally his political dilemmas made him feel low, but on the whole the fierce controversy of which he was the centre and the malicious slander of London Society made little impact on him. Pessimism and cynicism were not in his nature; his flashes of passion went along with an inner calm that enabled him to switch his mind to scholarship or theology even in the worst moments of political crisis.

Among Gladstone's heaviest burdens was the Queen. Sometimes he felt that his relations with her were intolerable and that she was trying to hound him out of office. On the big political decisions he could stand his ground, although the constant pressure of the Queen's criticism may sometimes have had an effect. More friction was caused by matters like her reluctance to grant Wolseley a peerage in 1881 and to have Dilke in the Cabinet in 1882; ecclesiastical appointments were a constant irritation. All these things came together in December 1882, when Dilke came into the Cabinet as President of the Local Government Board to restore the balance between Whigs and Radicals and Benson, Gladstone's nominee, succeeded Tait as Archbishop of Canterbury, while the Queen was in favour of Browne, the Bishop of Winchester. Edward Hamilton told his chief that

he overrated the gravity of hitches with the Queen; but he would not admit this, attaching as he does so great importance to anything amounting to strained relations with the Sovereign. Not only to my

H

mind does he worry himself too much on the subject, but he imagines the relations are more strained and the estrangement greater than is really the case.

When Gladstone saw the Queen in person matters generally went much better; his courtesy and her good manners overcame political and personal incompatibilities. He described it as 'extreme civility, but keep your distance'. On paper both of them were too 'valiant for truth' to soften any blows.

The session of 1883 was not equal in excitement to the two that had preceded it and for once Gladstone was not himself piloting a major bill through Parliament. Ireland still loomed large in his mind and he was convinced that no solution of the Irish problem would be possible without a measure of self-government for that island. He would have liked to have brought an Irish Local Government Bill that session but circumstances were against him. Most of his colleagues, except Chamberlain and Granville, wanted to let the Irish question rest and it weighed particularly with Gladstone that Spencer, the Irish Viceroy in whom he had complete trust, was strongly of the same opinion. The Phoenix Park murderers were on trial; there were explosions in London outside government offices which could be heard in the House of Commons and explosive substances were sent to prominent men through the post. All this was laid at the door of Irish terrorism and English public opinion was hardly in a mood to see more Irish legislation. Gladstone was persuaded not to legislate on Ireland in 1883, but he did not like it when during his absence in Cannes Hartington said in public that 'it would be madness . . . to give Ireland more extended self-government unless we can receive from the Irish people some assurance that this boon would not be used for the purposes of agitation'. Gladstone called this a 'formidable difference' which 'cuts deep down into my elementary and fixed ideas'. This rebuke to Hartington was neatly counterbalanced by his reaction some months later to a speech Chamberlain made at a dinner to celebrate Bright's jubilee as member for Birmingham. The speech advocated manhood suffrage, equal electoral districts, one man–one vote, payment of members. Within a year at least part of this programme was to be carried, but what particularly irked Gladstone was Chamberlain's disregard of Cabinet policy and above all an ill-chosen phrase which seemed to attack royalty. It was only one among a series of radical speeches by Chamberlain at that period, of which his attack on Salisbury as the representative of a class 'who toil not neither do they spin' is best remembered. The displeasure of the Queen came down upon Gladstone who had to remonstrate with Chamberlain at first indirectly and after a further speech directly.

Thus Gladstone remained the arbiter of his Cabinet, the man whose support all factions were seeking and to whose eventual inheritance they were all looking. What made Gladstone such a villain in Tory eyes was that only he seemed to be holding the Liberal alliance together. As long as he held it together it looked permanently superior to the Conservatives, particularly as they were as seriously divided by the behaviour of Lord Randolph Churchill and the new middle-class activists in the party. And the Liberals still held the trump card of household suffrage in the counties up their sleeve, which the Tories dare not oppose too openly. At the end of the 1883 session Edward Hamilton thought that his master had got through it better than for years past: '. . . his powers as Leader and orator show no sign whatever of failing; indeed they never appeared more resplendent.' His departure to Hawarden was only marred by the receipt of another of the Queen's carping letters: 'The thought that this letter should be the parting words of the Sovereign with forty-five years of experience of constitutional rule to her Prime Minister much concerned Mr G. and filled him with regret . . .' A few weeks later Gladstone went on a highly successful sea trip to Copenhagen where he met many royal personages, including the Tsar of Russia. The Queen was again annoyed and blamed him for going abroad without her permission. His comment was:

She feels aggrieved at the undue reverence shown to an old man of whom the public are being constantly reminded, and who goes on working further beyond the allotted time, while H.M. is, owing to the life she leads, withdrawn from view. Hence comes a dislocation of the natural and just balance of popular interest.

Soon after Gladstone's return from Copenhagen the business for the 1884 session had to be decided. It was almost entirely due to the Prime Minister that it was decided to give first priority to the franchise and to include Ireland in the Franchise Bill; and the tactics for this major change in the electoral system, namely to put forward a Franchise Bill without a Redistribution Bill in the first instance, were also Gladstone's. It is true that in so far as the government had a mandate it was for household suffrage in the counties and that it had been Gladstone's decision to postpone it until later in the life of this Parliament. It was also true that Chamberlain and the National Liberal Federation were giving first priority to the franchise question. At their Leeds conference in October 1883 it was decided to put a Franchise Bill before the reform of local government and to proceed without redistribution in the first instance. None of this was decisive, for even leading Radicals like Dilke would have preferred reform of local government and London government first. Dilke was, after all, at the Local Government Board. Chamberlain was basing his private calculations on the likelihood that the House of Lords would reject a Franchise Bill without redistribution and that it would then be possible to appeal to the country. Such an election would return a Radical majority. None of this influenced Gladstone unduly. On 10 November 1883 he discussed his plans with Edward Hamilton and Lord Richard Grosvenor, the Chief Whip. Franchise reform could not be postponed till 1885: 'with an immediate dissolution confronting you, you will be fighting with your hands behind your back and in a corner (and he ran into the corner of the room to illustrate his meaning).' Ireland would have to be included otherwise the Parnellites and all other Irish factions would combine with the Tories to strangle the bill.

Among his colleagues Gladstone's chief difficulty lay with Hartington. He baulked at the extension of the bill to Ireland – it would mean the return of a solid phalanx of Parnellites, as indeed it did. He wanted to see the outlines of a Liberal redistribution scheme alongside the Franchise Bill – again mainly to safeguard the Protestant minority in Ireland. What really worried Hartington was the prospect of having himself to deal with redistribution after Gladstone's departure, leading a Liberal party in which Chamberlain and Co. held the main influence. Around Christmas 1883 the government, as so often before, was again faced with a split through Hartington's resignation. Gladstone manoeuvred with consummate skill. He put forward his age as a reason for not dealing with franchise and redistribution simultaneously; when he realized Hartington's real fears, he indicated that he would stay on to deal with redistribution, thus further postponing his retirement. Finally he warned Hartington of the consequences of resignation – it might leave the field on the left in politics to Chamberlain, unrestrained by moderates. Hartington stayed and the bill went forward. It was a remarkable triumph for Gladstone, aged seventy-four. Earlier he had been frustrated in his desire to proceed with the solution of the Irish problem by the grant of local self-government. The inclusion of Ireland in the Franchise Bill made it as certain as anything could be in politics that this issue would soon have to be resolved.

Gladstone's handling of the reform legislation of 1884 in Parliament was masterly, almost a counterpiece to his relative failure in

1867. His intentions were fundamentally conservative: he wished for a final settlement of the electoral problem which had never yet reached a resting-point in the course of a century. It was not part of his purpose in the autumn to add the future of the House of Lords to the many problems he was already facing; he merely used the agitation against the Lords by men like Chamberlain as a means to a settlement. Gladstone's task was facilitated by the divisions in the Conservative ranks and the manoeuvres about the Tory leadership between Salisbury, Northcote and Lord Randolph Churchill. It was, moreover, difficult for the Tories to oppose openly the extension of the franchise in itself. On the other hand Egypt loomed large throughout the 1884 session and on this the govern-ment was highly vulnerable. It was part of Gladstone's parlia-mentary skill to use the dangers which threatened the Liberal party on Egypt to bring his followers unitedly through the reform question.

It had always seemed likely that the main battle on the third Reform Bill would revolve round the House of Lords. In the House of Commons Gladstone concentrated on securing the largest possible majorities and the third reading passed in fact without opposition in June. In July the Lords effectively stopped the bill by declining to proceed with it unless it was accompanied by redistribution. Parliament was soon prorogued and an autumn session arranged in which the Franchise Bill was to be passed a second time. The agitation for the bill now started in earnest in the country, but as far as Gladstone was concerned it was a carefully controlled agitation. He made this abundantly clear when he addressed a party meeting at the Foreign Office on 10 July, immediately after the decisive vote in the Lords. It was one of the rare party meetings in Gladstone's career as Liberal leader. The transfer of the franchise question from Parliament to the country enabled Gladstone once more to show his dominance. It was noticeable that in a great and orderly reform demonstration in London on 21 July he and Bright were the heroes of the hour, not Chamberlain or any of the younger men.[12] At the end of August Gladstone went to Midlothian again and made several big speeches, moderate in tone, but not without glancing blows at the Upper House. The Queen complained of these speeches 'under Her own nose' – she was at Balmoral – but she was now impressed with the Prime Minister's moderation. She liked the memorandum on the constitutional position which he presented to her and she was preparing to play the mediatory role towards the eventual achieve-ment of compromise. Her wrath was concentrated on Chamberlain and other Radicals and Gladstone carefully filtered her complaints to his left-wing colleagues.

After the reassembly of Parliament and the second introduction of the Franchise Bill in the Commons the big question was whether the forces of compromise would this time prevail. Nobody could tell with any confidence what the result of a dissolution of Parliament at that time would be. Many radicals believed that a bigger and more radical Liberal majority would be the result; many Tories believed the opposite. Gladstone in any case did not wish to admit the power of the House of Lords to force a dissolution. What predisposed the leading men on both sides to an agreed scheme of redistribution was the realization that either party would be faced with enormous parliamentary difficulties in carrying redistribution as a party question. Anti-reform though many Tories were, it would not have been possible for them to drop the franchise question had they come to power. Gladstone's own principal contribution to the comings and goings between the parties was a secret meeting with Sir Stafford Northcote at the house of his former private secretary, Sir Algernon West. A few days later, on 19 November, Northcote and Salisbury took tea with the Prime Minister at No. 10 Downing Street. Gladstone was 'much struck with the quickness of Lord Salisbury and evidently found it a pleasure to do business with so acute a man'. At subsequent meetings all complications about grouping and separation of rural and urban voters were soon relegated by the decision to go for single-member constituencies, the only exception being those boroughs which by virtue of their size were entitled to two members and already had them. Gladstone was struck by the fact that 'Lord Salisbury, who seems to monopolize all the say on his side, has no respect for tradition. As compared with him, Mr G. declares he is himself quite a Conservative.'[13] The scheme finally agreed represented the most drastic recasting of constituencies in the nineteenth century. Together with the Corrupt Practices Act which Gladstone's government had carried the year before, the third Reform Bill moved the country almost all the way towards political democracy. Gladstone was in the best of humours during his meetings with the opposition leaders: 'Papa apparently extremely cheerful,' wrote his daughter Mary. His still unrivalled parliamentary skill, great political cunning, detachment from all factions combined with his undiminished hold on the party in the country, had enabled him to bring to fruition a matter that was ripe for treatment.

11

HOME RULE

1885–6

If the Franchise Bill was Gladstone's zenith during his second administration, his handling of Egypt, the Sudan and Gordon was his low point and contributed to the collapse of his government. On this problem he was out of humour with the spirit of the age, with the 'evils of jingoism' as he often put it. He could scarcely bring himself to give the affairs of Egypt and the Sudan the attention they deserved and the capriciousness and self-deception of old age got the better of him at times. In politics the intermittent application of determined ideas often obtains the worst of all possible worlds and this was Gladstone's predicament.

There can be no doubt that if he could have had his way he would have wanted the speediest possible evacuation of Egypt after Tel-el-Kebir, and as for the contingent question of the Sudan he wished to have none of it. On Egypt he told Granville within days of Tel-el-Kebir to arrange with the Khedive military and police organization 'as matters of immediate need, with a view to the evacuation'. When evacuation receded as a matter of practical politics, he groaned over the weight of Egyptian business, tried to solve it within a European framework but had little grasp of the place of Egypt in the finely spun web of great-power relations. Repeatedly he deceived himself that matters were near a solution when in fact they were not and he and Granville came up against Bismarck on this question as well as on the beginnings of German colonization in Africa. Between Bismarck's and Gladstone's concept of international relations there was hardly the possibility of a dialogue: for Bismarck Egypt was an element in his policy of controlled tensions between the powers and a useful block to Anglo-French *rapprochement*, while Gladstone still chased the mirage of the 'Concert of Europe'. Bismarck had other reasons for disliking Gladstone, still the foremost figure in European liberalism. He saw the British Prime Minister as an encouragement to his domestic Liberal opponents in his conservative phase; he regarded him as in cahoots with the Crown Princess Frederick, ever a mote in his eye, and the influences emanating from her. He talked about squashing 'Gladstone against the wall, so that he can yap no more' while in Gladstone's entourage there was always talk of Bismarck's jealousy of their own chief's worldwide reputation. The Egyptian question dragged on, leaving the government vulnerable in Parliament; annexation and evacuation, the extreme options, were ruled out, but even within a narrower range of choices the government could not take any decisive action and Gladstone complained about getting deeper and deeper into the Nile mud.

On the Sudan the government's decision early in 1884 was un-equivocally in favour of evacuation. They were frustrated by the course of events and by General Gordon. Gladstone approved of 'Chinese' Gordon's appointment by telegram, but he was not directly party to the considerations, compounded of a press campaign and War Office embarrassment, that led his colleagues to make this curious choice for a mission of inquiry and evacuation. He was quickly aware of the dangers his government was running and was often heard to say that Gordon would be the death of it. In June 1884 he wrote to Granville: 'How tantalising is the rumour about Gordon's "escape". Too good, I fear to be true. God grant it might.' On Egypt and particularly the Sudan Gladstone dealt with affairs with a detachment born of repugnance. He told Hamilton that he would be 'satisfied to be given his congé on the question of sending troops to the Sudan, barring for purely relief purposes, if absolutely necessary', and he declared rather fatalistically that he must 'stand to win or lose by Gordon'. On domestic questions Gladstone's detachment and growing aloofness could be useful; on reform, where the whole nature of the dialogue was so much more under control, he could play off one faction against another, with the help of his considerable powers of casuistry; he could circumvent the Cabinet by not consulting it and use his hold on public opinion. Such devices were worse than useless in matters which were largely outside the control of the government and were dictated by the relentless march of events. There were not really any factions in the Cabinet on Egypt and the Sudan by means of which Gladstone could have imposed his will; only Harcourt was generally with him, while Chamberlain had turned 'jingo'. There was, however, a good deal of support among parliamentary Liberals for a pacific policy. Bright, Morley, Labouchere and many others had attacked the government's Egyptian involvement and were ready to support any policy of withdrawal and limitation in Egypt or the Sudan; Lord Randolph Churchill for a considerable time played the same card from the Conservative side. Gladstone may well have felt justified in the long rearguard action he fought against precipitate moves in the Sudan in the summer of 1884 by the reflection that support for Gordon and a forward policy was much stronger in London drawing-rooms and in the national press than it was among the Liberal rank and file. Gladstone was not much impressed by what he called 'Forsterism', the hawkish policy advocated by W. E. Forster and a few others on the government side; he felt no guilt about Gordon. In August 1884 a relief expedition under Wolseley was at last organized; on 5 February 1885 the news reached London that Khartoum had fallen and that Gordon was probably dead. A flood of obloquy now came down upon the Prime Minister's head the theme of which was 'too late'; it included the famous telegraphic rebuke from the Queen transmitted *en clair*: 'These news from Khartoum are frightful, and to think that all this might have been prevented and many precious lives saved by earlier action is too fearful.' It was 'an act which Mr G. resented not a little' and on this occasion he did not turn the other cheek. He still felt no remorse and he was perhaps a little insensitive in not making some concession to the prevailing emotion. A visit he paid to the theatre a few days later was much held against him. G.O.M. was now short for 'Gordon's Old Murderer'; there was talk of Nero fiddling. In his statement on the fall of Khartoum he could not bring himself to pay tribute to Gordon or to the troops in the Sudan. In the vote of censure on the government moved at the end of February, the Liberal majority fell to fourteen.

It was now a question of judgement whether it was best to carry on or resign. The Redistribution Bill was not yet passed, but as soon as it would be, and it was now an agreed measure, a dissolution of Parliament and an election on the new franchise would follow. It was generally expected that the Liberals stood in a strong position to win, in spite of all the wear and tear of five years in office. Would it not be better therefore to resign, allow a caretaker Tory government to complete the Redistribution Bill and give the electorate a chance to forget Liberal shortcomings in office? Such arguments and a general feeling in favour of escaping the burdens of office made it exceptionally difficult in the ensuing weeks for Gladstone to hold his team together. The imminence of an election under new and unpredictable conditions also explains the frantic manoeuvrings on the Tory side, particularly on the part of Lord Randolph Churchill. The core of these manoeuvres was the attempt to draw Parnell over to the Tory side, thus garnering not merely the eighty votes he was likely to command in the next Parliament, but also the Irish vote in the rest of Great Britain, which, it was thought, would follow his bidding.

Gladstone had no intention of making his 'final bow' on Gordon; it was assumed by all that the end of the 1885 government would be the end of Gladstone's career. He was corresponding with Lord Acton about his personal future at this time. Acton tried to persuade him that it was his duty to see the country across the great political change that was now in prospect and to reassure the world about the stability of England. Gladstone naturally refused to accept that it was his duty to carry on; but he now saw the enemy as 'Tory democracy':

It is demagogism, only a demagogism not ennobled by love and appreciation of liberty, but applied in the worst way, to put down the pacific, law-respecting, economic elements which ennobled the old conservatism, living upon the fomentation of angry passions, and still in secret as obstinately attached as ever to the evil principles of class interest.

If this was the threat, could Gladstone really withhold himself from the task of rescuing the country from it? T.P.O'Connor, the only Irish Nationalist who sat for an English constituency, observed him in the House of Commons in the days following the Gordon disaster :

> He entered rather pale, and he carried a stick on which he leaned –
> even when he rose to speak. It was the first time I ever saw anything
> about him that brought home to the mind the undeniable, but usually
> forgotten fact that he is a very old man. The effect was excellent.
> When he entered, the cheer was not very keen, but when, towards the
> close of question time, he did rise – still with the ominous stick support-
> ing him – there was a really strong and sympathetic cheer. The old man
> could not conceal his delight; he paused for several minutes, gave a
> profound bow after the manner of a prima donna, and paused again
> until the applause had died away with the same – shall I say – simper on
> his face, as if he were a member of a great operatic or theatrical corps.[1]

The fall of Khartoum had in fact reinvigorated Gladstone and restored his will to govern. In January 1885 he had been in low health and spirits, driven almost to despair by the problems of Egyptian finance; his colleagues, sensing his imminent departure, were up to their necks in plots for the succession. A Hartington government seemed the most likely outcome and even Chamberlain and Dilke were adjusting to that possibility. Hartington realized, however, that the old man could not be pushed; when at the end of January the Gladstones came to stay with him at Holker Hall relations between the two men were friendly and intimate.[2] By the end of February Gladstone's determination to carry on was decisive in preventing his government's resignation; but in the next few weeks there were two developments in foreign policy which, from his personal point of view, once more cleared the decks for a possible resignation. One was the London Convention on Egypt which after years of wrangling settled the problem of the Egyptian Finance Commission. About Egypt and Tel-el-Kebir Gladstone had in retro-spect some guilt feelings and he felt a great sense of relief that this incubus was now removed. He did not realize how shallow the co-operation of the Powers on Egypt was and what a considerable mortgage had been put by these arrangements on the conduct of British diplomacy for many years to come. The account he gave to Granville of an after-dinner conversation with Bismarck's son just before the signing of the London Convention could be regarded as jejune, though no doubt it was not meant to be a deep-going foreign policy analysis. Gladstone looked upon German colonization in Africa with restrained benevolence and refused to regard it from the perspective of rivalry. Had this been the general attitude of the age it would have been far wiser.

The second foreign policy development of the spring of 1885 was renewed tension with Russia over Afghanistan culminating in the Penjdeh incident. Here Gladstone and Granville emerged with considerable credit, using the right mixture of firmness and flexibility. They were on strong ground, having in 1880 abandoned the forward policy in Afghanistan; they could hardly allow Russia now to take advantage of the Afghans. Politically this was easier ground: even among the 'non-jingo' radicals Russia was regarded with some ideological disfavour. Labouchere warned in *Truth* against light-heartedly going to war with Russia over a few central Asian villages, but on 27 April the House of Commons unanimously passed a Vote of Credit for which Gladstone had to ask. On such a 'national' occasion he could speak with incomparable dignity, so that even Tories could not avoid a certain sense of pride in having such a man to speak for England. It was a great relief to Gladstone that war with Russia was avoided; the most satisfactory aspect of these developments to him was the fact that they provided an unanswerable argument for withdrawal from the Sudan, a commitment that had been 'torture' to him. It was still a highly controversial matter, but Gladstone managed to avoid a split in his Cabinet. The government had emerged after Penjdeh with more credit in foreign affairs than could have been anticipated a few weeks earlier, but the far from 'splendid' isolation of Britain after five years of Gladstonianism was dangerously evident. Salisbury commented, 'They have at least achieved their long desired "Concert of Europe". They have succeeded in uniting the Continent of Europe – against England.'

The morrow of Penjdeh, early May 1885, was a moment when Gladstone was very much in the mood to 'bolt' and even Mrs Gladstone was packing. It would certainly have been a good moment for him to make his bow, but the consequences to the Liberal party, so all his friends and advisers told him, would be fatal and the split between Whigs and Radicals would become inevitable. Unless he had chosen a moment such as this to leave, his continued leadership over the next election was becoming inevitable. The threat to retire, sincere enough, was itself a means of keeping control over his colleagues. In the meantime Ireland was again becoming the chief problem facing Gladstone's Cabinet. The Coercion Act of 1882 was running out and Spencer, the Irish Viceroy, was adamant that at least some coercive powers must be retained by the Irish administration. Chamberlain and Dilke were completely opposed to coercion; Chamberlain had been negotiating with Parnell through O'Shea and with Manning about Irish local government and a central board scheme with powers over education and similar matters. Chamberlain and Dilke held the view that any even partial renewal of coercion had to be accompanied by a positive measure on Irish government. Gladstone agreed with Chamberlain and Dilke; indeed his own soundings had convinced him that something more far-reaching was required, for he had many correspondents on the Irish problem, including Manning. Gladstone was, however, not prepared to oppose Spencer and in a Cabinet on 9 May a majority of his colleagues, all the peers except Granville, opposed the Irish government scheme; all the commoners bar Hartington were in favour. Gladstone remarked to Chamberlain: 'These men have rejected this scheme, but if God spares their lives for five years more they will be glad to accept something infinitely stronger.' At this moment Gladstone really considered himself free to go, but before evening things were patched up, Harcourt toing and froing as ambassador between the various factions. For another month the government held together, although Chamberlain and Dilke were constantly on the point of resigning. For them political considerations were finely balanced. They considered themselves the future leaders of the Liberal party and they had already in preparation an 'unauthorized programme' of Radical demands for the elections. They could confidently expect the Whigs to become a minor force after the election and thus they would come into their inheritance once Gladstone had retired. It might pay them to be free of Cabinet ties. On the other hand it was preferable for them not to be seen breaking with Gladstone before the election and to make sure that the party would go united into the election, which it could do only under Gladstone. The Prime Minister did not underestimate them. To Hamilton, who said a few days later, 'Why not take them at their word?' he replied, 'If they were ministerial nonentities; but they are great factors; and a quarrel with them is too big a job for me to face lightly.' He did not like their 'constructionism', but eventually, for the 1892 election, he accepted a programme not too unlike what they were proposing. It was in any case a programme behind which the hounds of Henry George, Karl Marx and Keir Hardie were already baying. Gladstone probably did not take Chamberlain and Dilke's position in the Liberal party quite at their own valuation; there were after all Radicals of many persuasions in the party. He would have been prepared to go on without them. There is little doubt that he was beginning to dislike Chamberlain personally, he thought him a careerist, devoid of the instincts of a gentleman; but throughout the time of this government he had agreed with him more often than not. Gladstone would not have been human if he had not somewhat resented the greedy snatching of an inheritance which he had not quite surrendered; also the attempt to mount a campaign in the country along lines that he had first developed.

On 8 June 1885 the government was unexpectedly defeated on the budget by twelve votes. The Parnellites had voted with the Tories and a fair number of Liberals had abstained. Ever since the beginning of the session there had been meetings and negotiations between Parnell and the Tories and most of the time the Parnellites appeared to be hostile to the Liberals. There were now definite indications, from Lord Randolph Churchill and others, that the Tories would not renew coercion. As for the Liberal abstentions, these had probably been caused by the well-advertised dissensions in the Cabinet. Gladstone was not overjoyed by the occasion of the defeat, but he and all his colleagues were agreed that the occasion was too good to be missed for an escape from office and Gladstone resigned. A ministerial crisis unusual in length ensued; the Queen's refusal for some days to return south from Balmoral made its resolution particularly protracted. There was party advantage for the Liberals in leaving office; by the same token there were perils for the Tories in assuming it. An immediate dissolution was not possible and reliance on Irish votes was highly unpopular in the Tory ranks. Lord Salisbury could have refused to take office as Disraeli did in 1873, particularly if Gladstone should decline to give assurances about the conduct of parliamentary business before the dissolution. The issue hung in the balance for nearly a fortnight and the assurances which Gladstone gave were vague and general; nevertheless Salisbury decided to form a government. The Queen offered Gladstone a peerage; he declined with gratitude and told her that her letter would remain 'a precious possession to him and to his children after him'.

During the last six months of his second government Gladstone had pushed his 'leadership by detachment' to dangerous lengths. He was poised between his desire, sincere enough, for retirement; his reluctance to retire at a moment which might seem to be unbefitting to his great career; his reluctance to surrender his power or freedom of movement prematurely and in favour of one particular faction rather than another; his largely subconscious reluctance to surrender for good the exhilaration and excitement of political life. Around him his colleagues were manoeuvring for position; it was hardly surprising that he made a virtue of necessity and that aloofness and an air of mystery were becoming a habit with him. He was still a giant among pygmies, but had he really made up his mind to go there would no doubt have been a sense of relief among many. Gladstone used the Whig–Radical cleavage to emphasize his own indispensability; yet at times this cleavage seemed less important than the gulf between his own Cobdenite economism and the imperialist concerns of so many of his colleagues. In the earlier months of 1885 even Chamberlain and Dilke might have preferred to serve under Hartington, at least for a short spell, and perhaps the experience of managing without Gladstone might have been salutary for the Liberal party. Gladstone's pre-eminence owed much to the fact that he more than anybody else could rally the great public out-of-doors; but now others, notably Chamberlain and Lord Randolph Churchill, were doing the same.

On the resignation of his government Gladstone circulated a memorandum to his colleagues that he would continue as Leader of the Opposition till the end of the session, but reserved his position thereafter. As the election campaign got going and summer gave way to autumn the position remained what it had been throughout that turbulent year; only under his leadership could the Liberal party hold together. It was, however, not until September 1885, after his return from a Norwegian cruise, that it looked certain that he would lead the party through the general election. His main effort as Leader was now bent towards holding the balance between the Radical and the moderate and Whig wing of the party. While he was composing his own address to his constituents in Midlothian he described his problem to Granville, still his closest confidant:

The problem for me is to make if possible a statement which will hold through the Election, and not to go into conflict with either the right wing of the party, for whom Hartington has spoken, or the left wing, or extreme left wing for whom Chamberlain I suppose spoke last night, I do not say they are to be treated as on a footing: but I must do no act disparaging to Chamberlain's wing. Dilke for the moment is under his mantle.

Between Hartington and Chamberlain the gulf was now very wide and there was much talk of a realignment of parties. Gladstone was in constant correspondence with the former and the latter paid a visit to Hawarden in early October. It required all Gladstone's skill and casuistry to prevent a break between those who were campaigning for the unauthorized programme and those who were opposed to most of it. Even Lord Carlingford, a colleague whose feelings for Gladstone were, not surprisingly after the treatment he had received, little short of hatred, wrote in the privacy of his diary about Gladstone's manifesto: 'It is very skilful, and must have a great effect in

keeping the party together – What power he has! What influence
over public opinion and action! – generally well used.'³

The tension between the right and the left in his party was Gladstone's problem as well as his *raison d'être* as leader, but he was no
longer vitally interested in the substance of these differences. On
personal grounds he stood closer to Hartington and still felt slightly
that he was 'taking the bread out of his mouth' by remaining
available to head another government; he disliked the 'constructionism', the tone of 'socialism' in Chamberlain and the Radicals, but
insisted only that in the short term the party should not be committed to principles such as free schools and compulsory purchase
by local authorities, for further he could hardly look. He and Chamberlain were virtually in agreement on moving towards graduated
taxation. But his mind was on Ireland. The Tory flirtation with
Parnell was going ahead: coercion was dropped, in the debate on
the Maamtrasna murders Spencer and the Liberal policy of coercion
was attacked by Tories and behind the scenes Carnarvon, the Irish
Viceroy of the Tories, was talking to Parnell. Gladstone was convinced by all this that the Central Board scheme, which his Cabinet
had refused to accept in May, was no longer enough and that Parnell
would demand a higher price, now that both British parties were
bidding for his favour. The conviction grew in him that Home Rule,
namely a separate Irish Parliament, was now the only way in which
the tragic Anglo-Irish tangle could be resolved. This conclusion
was of course entirely in line with his general philosophy on Ireland,
nationality, morality between nations and elementary justice. It
was precisely the kind of moral cause that nearly ten years earlier
had brought him out of retirement and that seemed to him now to
offer the only justification for postponing his retirement once more.
He was, however, well-nigh certain that Ireland was the great
impending crisis of British politics and that therefore his mission
would have to continue.

As early as July 1885 Gladstone had written to Lord Derby: 'It
is now said that a central board will not suffice, and that there must
be a parliament. This I suppose may mean the repeal of the Act
of Union, or may mean an Austro-Hungarian scheme, or may mean
that Ireland is to be like a great colony such as Canada.' In August
during his Norwegian cruise he had an opportunity to reflect on the
independence of small nations. After his return he told all those
colleagues who were in contact with him that even though he would
lead through the election, only an Irish crisis would bring him
back as Prime Minister. He refused, however, to say clearly what

exactly he had in mind for Ireland for several reasons: he could not anticipate exactly how strong the upsurge of Irish nationalism would be and he did not know precisely what Parnell wanted; he feared that he could not carry the Liberal party with him and he hoped that the Tories would in fact carry on their current policy of themselves providing a positive solution to the problem of Ireland; he did not wish to enter into an auction for the favour of Parnell and feared that any concrete plan that he himself might propose would automatically attract a great deal of hostility. Thus, in spite of the entreaties of his son Herbert, who was already an ardent Home Ruler, he refused to proclaim his future policy for Ireland publicly. Curiously enough Hartington and Chamberlain, whose differences he was always trying to bridge, were united now on one point: no further concessions to Ireland. This had always been Hartington's view; it was now Chamberlain's as well, for he felt bitterly rebuffed by Parnell. In his dealings with both Hartington and Chamberlain in this momentous autumn Gladstone did his best to persuade them to leave themselves 'elbow-room' on Ireland; he did not succeed to any extent and the task was made more difficult by the tone of Parnell's speeches. Gladstone was also in touch again with Parnell through Mrs O'Shea. The information he received about Parnell's ideas for the government of Ireland were useful to him, but he refused to enter into any definite commitment about his own future course of action.

Gladstone campaigned once more in Midlothian in the general election of 1885. At first, when he was at the height of his uncertainty about his future intentions, there was doubt whether he would stand again and Rosebery had gone to the length of fixing up an alternative candidate. While Gladstone was in Midlothian he made a major speech on Ireland at Edinburgh on 9 November: he emphasized the need for the maximum amount of self-government for Ireland compatible with the unity of the Empire. Parnell in a public reply at Liverpool tried to extract a more definite commitment, but Gladstone in his subsequent speech in Scotland refused to go any further. The result was the Parnell Manifesto of 21 November which told Irish voters in Britain to vote Tory. Parnell was expecting a Liberal majority; from his point of view it seemed sound strategy to make it as small as possible so that he could hold the balance.

The result of the general election of 1885 was that 335 Liberals exactly balanced 249 Conservatives and 86 Irish Nationalists. The Liberals suffered big losses in the boroughs but made up for them to some extent by gains in the counties. One can now see that some long-term trends were at work here. The Tories had been improving their position in the largest cities for some time and they were clearly gaining rapidly in the suburbs; on the other hand the absence of household suffrage in the counties had previously prevented the Liberals from showing their true strength in the rural areas. The new system of single-member constituencies allowed these trends to come much more into the open. It can never be accurately known how many borough seats were lost to the Liberals as a result of the Parnell manifesto; contemporary estimates put the number as high as thirty. In Ireland the Nationalists made a remarkably clean sweep everywhere except in eastern Ulster and there could no longer be any doubt about the intensity of the Irish demand for Home Rule.

The situation was now as obscure and complicated as ever. To Gladstone one thing seemed certain: his instinct that Ireland was the critical issue had been borne out. This, however, was not the view taken in many sections of the Liberal party, not by Harting-ton and above all not in the Chamberlain camp. Here the conclusion drawn was that Ireland must on no account be allowed to crowd out the radical programme and a Liberal party still sailing under moderate Gladstonian colours in domestic affairs must not take office dependent on Parnell. It would be better therefore to keep the Tories in office for a time. In practice this meant shelving Mr Gladstone. At Hawarden, however, the G.O.M. had no intention of being shelved by the Birmingham men, but the cause, justice for Ireland, was still more important than any personal considerations. His preference now was for the Tories to meet the aspirations of Ireland; they were the government and with their control of the House of Lords they were in a better position to act. Two months earlier Lord Salisbury had spoken at Newport in a way that had allowed the inference that he would be prepared to see the creation of an autonomous Irish central authority. Gladstone fervently hoped that this was still Tory policy; he was prepared to give it every support and encouragement. The most important support he could give it for the moment was his own silence; but he also conveyed more active encouragement to Salisbury through Arthur Balfour. In the light of our knowledge today we may think Gladstone's belief in the Tories on this matter was naïve. There was in fact no chance that Salisbury would act on behalf of Ireland. Gladstone's hope was understandable in view of the great responsibility that he would be taking upon himself in espousing the cause of Ireland once more with a divided party at his advanced age. Before taking such a course he had to be sure that all other options were closed.

Although Gladstone would have preferred to lie low and let the Tories act, he was not prepared to see his own party turn their backs on Ireland and in the process shelve him. Least of all was he prepared to allow Chamberlain to dictate party strategy in this way; to all the personal and political reservations he had about the Birmingham man there was now added the feeling that he had inflated his electoral prowess. Lord Richard Grosvenor, admittedly biased as a Whig, told Gladstone that only about 100 of the 335 Liberals were Radicals and likely to follow Chamberlain; in fact the poor showing of the Liberals in certain areas was at Hawarden attributed to the Birmingham men. This feeling was particularly strong among the Gladstone family. Mrs Gladstone had some jealousy of Chamberlain's popular appeal; she and Herbert Gladstone were again intensely anxious to see the old man back in harness crowning his great career with an Irish settlement. Matters were precipitated by a speech which Dilke made on 12 December in Chelsea, spelling out the strategy of keeping the Tories in. Hawarden now smelt a plot. On 15 December Hamilton noted in his diary: 'Mr G. . . . will not stand being dictated to by the Birmingham lot. He is disposed to hold aloof from them for the present after the way they have lately behaved. He will take his own line irrespectively of what they may say and do.'[4] This was the background to the Hawarden 'kite'. Herbert Gladstone went up to London and talked amongst others to Wemyss Reid, the editor of the *Leeds Mercury* and an enemy of Chamberlain, and to Labouchere, the man who 'talks to everybody, writes to everybody, and betrays everybody'. On 15 December Hamilton noted after a talk with Herbert Gladstone: 'Herbert's implicit faith in his father is most touching, and his own belief in the efficiency of a Home Rule solution not less strong.' By 17 December the 'kite' was up and blazoned from every headline: 'Mr Gladstone had definitely adopted the policy of Home Rule for Ireland. . .' It achieved its purpose in stopping any possibility of the Liberal party shelving Ireland and Gladstone; it made doubly certain that the Tories would not tackle Ireland; it said nothing that could not have been intelligently guessed, but it was a clumsy move all the same. Gladstone himself had not known anything of what was afoot. One of the immediate and ominous consequences of the publication of the 'kite' was that Hartington, whom Gladstone had been trying to keep as flexible as possible on Ireland, now declared publicly that he was not prepared for any new policy on

Ireland. Many people, from the Queen, through most Tories across to Joseph Chamberlain, thought the 'kite' had been deliberately flown by a 'wild, fanatical old man of seventy-six' who could not resist the lure of office. Hamilton noted that the reaction to the kite at Brooks's was 'We dare not face our constituents with such a programme.'

Until the meeting of Parliament in January 1886 Gladstone continued to lie low. His hopes of a Conservative initiative on Ireland died away. He still refused to commit himself to Parnell, though the correspondence with Mrs O'Shea continued. He refused to call what would now be termed a shadow Cabinet. 'A cabinet does not exist out of office, and no one in his senses could covenant to call *the late cabinet* together, I think, even if there were something on which it was ready to take counsel, which at this moment there is not,' he wrote to Granville on 28 December, the day before his seventy-sixth birthday. Chamberlain swallowed his dislike of Whigs sufficiently to meet with Hartington, in the company of Dilke and Harcourt, on New Year's Day 1886, in an effort to find an agreement to stop Gladstone, but it was entirely in vain. Even to a renewed request for consultation Gladstone returned a peremptory refusal. He knew now that Parnell would turn out the Tories and he was prepared to come in and grasp the Irish nettle. His dominance over the Liberal party appeared to be sufficient to justify the attempt. He saw many leading Liberals individually and thus thwarted any possible combination against him that might have arisen in a shadow Cabinet meeting; it was important that he finally won over Harcourt to Home Rule, for this most flexible of the leaders had links with all factions.

As Parliament assembled there was danger that Hartington would make a declaration in favour of the legislative union between Ireland and Great Britain. Gladstone quickly scotched this move. On 21 January most of the Liberal leaders met at last under Gladstone's chairmanship; as a way out of all their difficulties and perplexities it was decided to vote in favour of a 'three acres and a cow' amendment to be moved in the name of Jesse Collings, one of Chamberlain's lieutenants. This commitment had been drafted by Chamberlain, with Harcourt or possibly Dilke, and it offered a way of defeating the government without raising the Irish issue. Gladstone had never before expressed his agreement with this part of the unauthorized programme. It was now certain that the government would be abandoned by the Irish and they therefore decided to come out in their true colours and propose coercion. Gladstone worked hard to the last, with 'extreme anxiety', to prevent his party from being committed on Ireland; this would have shown up prematurely, and when it was not necessary, the divisions in the party on this issue. In retrospect Gladstone felt that only 200 Liberals might then have voted for Home Rule whereas 300 eventually did six months later. The government was thus defeated on the 'three acres and a cow' amendment. The voting was 331 to 252, but it was ominous that no fewer than 76 Liberals including Bright abstained while 18 including Hartington voted for the government. All knew that Ireland was the real issue. Thus far Gladstone's instinct had been right: the election of 1885 had created a situation that made it imperative to deal with Ireland, one way or the other. He would have preferred a bipartisan approach to Home Rule; it would have been against his entire philosophy to have accepted bipartisan coercion and coercion would have split the Liberals as surely as Home Rule.

In forming his third government Gladstone read to all those whom he hoped to include a short statement that it was his purpose to inquire whether a separate Irish legislative body to deal with Irish affairs was feasible. Hartington declined to join; his overt reason was that he was too much committed against an independent Irish legislature, but he probably hoped that at some juncture it would fall to him to lead a reunited Liberal party after Gladstone's failure. Along with Hartington a number of Gladstone's former Whig colleagues refused to join, among them Northbrook, Selborne and Derby, a recent recruit from the Tories. Gladstone felt most severely the loss of Bright. On the other hand some Whigs remained: notably Spencer, who was now convinced that a return to coercion in Ireland was no longer possible, Granville, Rosebery and Kimberley. Much the most important adherent from among the doubters that Gladstone secured was Chamberlain. Unfortunately the slighting treatment which Chamberlain now received at the hands of the Liberal leader was also the greatest single reason for the failure of the enterprise that now started. Gladstone offered Chamberlain the Admiralty; when Chamberlain indicated his unsuitability he was asked what he would prefer and mentioned the Colonial Office. Gladstone exclaimed: 'Oh, a Secretary of State', and with this tactless remark dismissed what was a serious aspiration. The Colonial Office was already reserved for Granville, whose return to the Foreign Office the Queen, on account of his growing senility, had barred. Instead Chamberlain received the Local Government Board and even here was tactlessly treated over the salary of his junior minister, Jesse Collings, who was one of his closest political collaborators. Hamilton noted in his diary: 'He (G) was very outspoken about Chamberlain. Ch. was wanting in straightforwardness. He was not to be trusted. He badly lacked public spirit.' In view of all that had happened it was perhaps not surprising that Gladstone behaved in this way to Chamberlain; he wanted him as a subordinate or not at all. But in this case the mismanagement of personal relations amounted to a major political misjudgement; it was one indication among many that old age was increasing Gladstone's egotism and loss of touch.

Nevertheless, it was a remarkable achievement, demanding consummate skill and tactical dexterity, that Gladstone managed to form a government, outmanoeuvring his recalcitrant and self-seeking colleagues, yet keeping his hands free to take whatever course he wished. He was convinced that the only way now was to produce boldly a scheme for Ireland and to avoid any piecemeal approach. The state of Ireland was dangerous and large expectations had been raised; now was the moment to meet the situation with a fully fledged scheme. The appointment of a royal commission or the introduction of a few general resolutions of principle on Irish government would not really have appeased the opposition to Home Rule, while it would have been fatal in Ireland and to relations with Parnell. To this extent his statement that the government was based on an 'inquiry' was merely a blind designed to put off as long as possible the defections that were bound to come once the Irish scheme was fully declared. Gladstone did not, however, finally make up his mind on the exact nature of his Irish proposals until at least mid-March 1886.

The proposals which Gladstone eventually presented consisted of two bills, one for the government of Ireland, the other for the buying out of Irish landlords. The main provisions of the Government of Ireland Bill were the creation of a bicameral Irish legislature which could deal with all except a few enumerated matters, of which the principal were defence, foreign affairs and international trade. The Irish members were to be excluded from Westminster. Ireland was to contribute from its own revenues one-fifteenth of total imperial expenditure. In the original draft it would have been possible for the Irish Parliament and executive to levy protective duties against British goods, but this provision was cut out, for it would have made the bill politically too vulnerable. The Land Purchase scheme was coupled with the Home Rule Bill because Gladstone and Morley, his Irish Secretary, felt that the new Irish

Parliament could hardly be saddled with the full weight of the agrarian problem at the outset of its existence. The Anglo-Irish landlords were also, in Gladstone's eyes, the major vested interest liable to be injured by Home Rule. Landlords were given an option to be bought out at twenty years' purchase of their net rental. The scheme involved a credit operation by the British Treasury which was massive by the standards of the time. The details of the two Gladstonian bills owed much to the advice given by Sir Robert Hamilton, the permanent head of the Irish administration; a memorandum envisaging the need for a Home Rule solution, which Hamilton had prepared for Carnarvon the previous October, had greatly impressed Gladstone. It had also contributed to the conversion of Spencer to Home Rule, and this conversion was a factor of major political importance. Gladstone attached great significance to the fact that Spencer was now a Home Ruler; he was much influenced by Spencer's view that a land purchase scheme was needed to accompany Home Rule.

Gladstone's Home Rule scheme was, in the light of subsequent developments, a highly conservative solution. The fact that Parnell, who was hardly consulted, accepted it showed that he was thinking in entirely constitutional terms; it was one of the strongest elements in Gladstone's case that this was perhaps the last opportunity to settle the Irish problem in a non-revolutionary manner. Neither Parnell nor Gladstone could guarantee that this settlement would not in the longer term produce a separation of Ireland from the rest of the United Kingdom, but it stood at any rate a good chance of producing a permanent 'union of hearts'. Perhaps the greatest weakness of the scheme was that it made no provision for Ulster. Gladstone was very much alive to the legitimate claims of the Anglo-Irish landlord class and various arrangements, for example the powers of the second chamber in the proposed Irish Parliament, were designed to take account of these claims. Gladstone was hardly aware yet that there was a separate Ulster problem and he certainly was not prepared to accept any Ulster veto on a separate Irish Parliament. The Ulster problem was in fact relatively new; up to 1885 the representation of Ulster had been divided between Liberals and Tories. In the 1885 election all Liberals were eliminated and Parnell had instructed his followers to vote for the Tory candidates, even though they were Orangemen. Thereafter the differences between Liberals and Conservatives were rapidly pushed into the background and Ulster began to organize itself along sectarian lines, with considerable ramifications within the Tory party in England.

In February 1886 Lord Randolph Churchill went to Belfast and 'played the Orange card': 'Ulster will fight and Ulster will be right.' Neither the Conservatives nor Gladstone, however, took Ulster too seriously. There is little sign that the Prime Minister paid much attention to the contradictory advice he received from two sources available to him; James Bryce, Under-Secretary for Foreign Affairs, Ulsterman by birth and well acquainted with the views of Protestant Liberals in Ulster; and Sir Charles Russell, the Attorney-General, a Catholic Irishman. Bryce warned Gladstone of the opposition in Ulster to an all-Irish Parliament and of the danger that Ulster Liberals would fuse with the Tories to resist it. Russell advised that separate treatment for Ulster was not justified, not even for its most Protestant areas, and backed up his case by population statistics.[5]

Gladstone had a discussion on the Irish problem with Chamberlain on 13 February. It was not a meeting of minds: Chamberlain mentioned the possibility of an Irish Land Purchase scheme, but he was clearly not prepared for an Irish Parliament. A month later Gladstone unveiled to the Cabinet his own far-reaching land purchase scheme and Chamberlain forced him to reveal also the broad outlines of Home Rule. Within two days Chamberlain's letter of resignation was finally in the Prime Minister's hands. Gladstone pleaded for further delay, but on 26 March Chamberlain attended his last Cabinet. After receiving further elucidation from Gladstone about the nature of the Home Rule Bill he left the Cabinet room, accompanied by G. O. Trevelyan, the Scottish Secretary. Gladstone made no effort to detain him and was obviously relieved. His mind was made up and he had no intention of fighting an exhausting rearguard action against a tenacious opponent inside the Cabinet. Harcourt, as always busy mediating, wrote to Gladstone at this time that Chamberlain was not really hostile 'but you have never really discussed the question with him. A great deal in the future depends on how he is personally handled . . . I refer rather to his *post-resignation* attitude.'

Gladstone introduced the Home Rule Bill on 8 April and from that time the whole plan was open to the winds of public opinion. There were a great many cross-currents. On the left there were many who wanted to see justice done to Ireland; but there were many others who cared little for Ireland and saw the chief advantage of the plan in the fact that it removed Ireland as a blockage from the path of reform. In this connection the removal of the Irish members from Westminster seemed particularly attractive. It was, however, in particular this feature of the plan that Chamberlain made his sticking-point, on the ground that it paved the way towards complete separation; in later years he all but admitted that this attitude was only a device to kill the bill. Chamberlain was probably right in sensing that on the left, particularly among working men, there was not only a great deal of apathy about Ireland but downright hostility. The Irish were still the most important source of low-grade labour competing with the British working man. The behaviour of the Irish in recent years, from Parnell's obstruction in the House of Commons through the Phoenix Park murders to the dynamite outrages in London, had increased the antipathy of all classes of Englishman. Thus there were many cross-currents on the left and the divisions would have been much greater still had not the powerful influence of Gladstone propelled the Home Rule cause.

On the right the leading sentiments against Home Rule were national pride and an offended sense of property. Why should the rights of a weak, despised, endemically hostile nation of four million be put before the requirements of a strong nation of thirty million and a powerful Empire? When Ireland was compared with Canada, *The Times* made the point that the Canadians were 3000 miles away and were friendly. The existence of the powerful Anglo-Irish connection, including Ulster, made it doubtful in many eyes whether Ireland was properly a separate nation. It was the danger implied to Anglo-Ireland by Gladstone's plan that constituted the chief affront to property. It was certainly true that Home Rule accelerated the drift of the propertied classes into the Conservative camp; for many like the Hartingtonian Whigs it was the occasion perhaps more than the cause of their apostasy. Gladstone felt more than ever that the moral sense of the masses was being pitted against the corruption of the 'upper ten thousand'. 'The adverse host, then, consists of class and dependants of class,' he said. The Land Purchase Bill attracted hostility from both right and left. It could be represented as an attack on property, an unsound use of the credit of the British treasury on a vast scale. Humble minds could be frightened by the spectre of a vast outpouring of British treasure on behalf of people who little deserved it. Even if the Home Rule Bill had passed it seems doubtful if the Land Bill could have done.

A majority of intellectuals lined up against Home Rule in 1886. The moralism on which the case for Home Rule was ultimately based was out of fashion; too many, moreover, believed that it was not a true moralism but a desire for office and power on Gladstone's part. There was the same distaste of the educated mind for the luxury of moral enthusiasm as there had been on a lesser scale ten years earlier during the Bulgarian agitation; the same hard-headed feeling that force and violence could not be so easily gainsaid. Many who in other circumstances might have come down on the Liberal side were now hostile: Kinglake, Froude, Matthew Arnold, Jowett, Herbert Spencer and many more. Imperialism, seen now by many intellectuals as a progressive force, was coming into fashion and Home Rule was flying in the face of it.

May 1886 was the period when the fate of the Home Rule Bill hung in the balance. Chamberlain held the key to the situation, for it became clear that some fifty Radical anti-Home Rulers would follow him; if they abstained the bill might just pass, but if they voted against the second reading it would fail. If Gladstone were seen to be responsible for a Liberal split he risked being replaced by Hartington, who might have been able to hold office for a long time at the head of a new Palmerstonian majority. In early May negotiations went on with Chamberlain through Labouchere. Chamberlain at this stage was mainly insisting on the retention of Irish members at Westminster, on a separate assembly for Ulster, and the power for the Irish assemblies to deal only with certain enumerated subjects rather than with all residual subjects. What Chamberlain had in mind for the United Kingdom was a form of federalism. Gladstone could not really meet these demands without losing the support of Parnell and thus putting an end to his government. It was now in fact too late to conciliate Chamberlain who was determined to kill the bills either on second reading or in committee. It might still have been possible to isolate Chamberlain or make his position very difficult. On 27 May Gladstone addressed a party meeting at the Foreign Office; only those in favour of an Irish assembly in Dublin were invited, so that the Hartingtonians were definitely excluded. Chamberlain refused to attend, but many of his followers did. The main concession which Gladstone appeared to make was that he agreed that after the passage of the second reading the detailed consideration of the bill would be postponed until the autumn and an amendment on the retention of Irish members at Westminster for imperial purposes might be accepted. Some Liberal waverers appeared to be swayed; but these gains were quickly lost again the following day when Gladstone, taunted by the opposition that he had agreed to a far-reaching restructuring of the bill, shouted, 'Never, never.' Had he been a lesser man he might never have embarked upon the Irish crusade; but a lesser man, using the skills of the party manager, might well have got the bill through its second reading. Gladstone was no doubt influenced by the reports which were reaching him that Liberal organizations almost everywhere except in Birmingham were swinging over to his side; that the enthusiasm evoked by his personality and the Home Rule cause was great and that he would win if he dissolved Parliament. To some extent these were genuine miscalculations; Schnadhorst, the great Liberal organizer who had now switched his allegiance from Chamberlain to Gladstone, backed them with his authority. But there was also in Gladstone now, in his old age, an ever stronger tendency to self-delusion. He heard only what he wanted to hear.

Four days after Gladstone had held his meeting at the Foreign Office Chamberlain called fifty-five Radical anti-Home Rulers together in Committee Room 15, the same room that witnessed more than four years later the agony of Parnell. The crucial moment in Chamberlain's meeting was the reading of a letter from John Bright. The veteran Radical had refused to come to the meeting nor was he prepared to advise anybody on how they should vote. But he did make it plain in the letter that he himself would vote against the second reading of the Home Rule Bill. This was decisive and the meeting decided by an overwhelming majority to vote against the bill. On 8 June, after another great oratorical effort by Gladstone, the second reading was rejected by thirty votes, a larger number than the Prime Minister and his whips had feared. Ninety-three Liberals, nearly a third of all Liberal members, had defied their party. Gladstone had no difficulty in persuading his colleagues that dissolution was now the right course. Resignation would have been tantamount to withdrawing from the Home Rule cause and would have ushered in a period of uncertainty, particularly dangerous in Ireland. Gladstone knew that he would have to fight with his party divided; but whereas at one time he had seen Ireland as the cause which would unify a Liberal party split along Whig–Radical lines, he now persuaded himself that the loss of those who would not rally behind Home Rule was a healthy purge.

Writing to the Queen about the impending election Gladstone confessed that he had little skill in electoral matters 'and dare not lay an opinion before your Majesty on the probable general result'. Schnadhorst, who was present at the Cabinet that decided on dissolution, did not do much better. Great importance was attached to the fact that the Irish vote in Great Britain would now be on the Liberal side; in the event this mattered little. What was of great importance was the efficiency with which the Tory party managers,

Akers-Douglas, the Chief Whip, and Captain Middleton, the chief agent, moved to prevent clashes between Tories and Liberal Unionists. The size of the Liberal defection on the second reading vote owed a good deal to the fact that the dissentient Liberals knew they would not be opposed by Tories in case of a Home Rule election. Thus the Liberal vote was effectively split; on top of this the Gladstonian Liberals, facing a second election in little over six months, left many seats uncontested. Gladstone never took much interest in the details of election management and he was not well served on this occasion. He still thought the vigour of his own election campaign and the magic of his name were all-important. For a man of seventy-six he certainly performed marvels. He plunged into several days of monster meetings and great street demonstrations both in Scotland and Lancashire, all in the heat of summer. He wound up his campaign in Liverpool and T. P. O'Connor, the Irish Nationalist, described the scene.

Gladstone was at his best in his speech – playful, argumentative, solemn; all these moods were conveyed in a voice that, in spite of the terrible strain upon it, seemed as fresh as ever. But there were very palpable evidences of the strain which the exertions of previous days and the stifling heat of the room on the hot June day were making upon him. He began the address wearing one of those very spacious and very erect collars which the genius of the caricaturists has made familiar to the world. By the time the speech was ended the collar had entirely changed its appearance, and from being stiff and upright became moist and flat. There was even more palpable evidence of the strain upon him if you looked at the back of his black coat: it was just as if he had stood out in the open under a heavy shower of rain.

Then he went into the streets and received the same rapturous reception. It was not the first occasion on which I saw proof that the appearance of Gladstone – with his magnificent face, his splendid eyes, the expression at once so benignant as well as so resolute, his broad shoulders, and the sense of vigour and resolution, not weakened by 76 years of life – had almost the effect of the trailing of a miraculous saint among masses of idolators.[6]

While the results were coming in Gladstone stayed at Hawarden and fired off a volley of letters and telegrams to candidates all over the country. Some of them were rather wild in tone and those who wished to regard him as a madman were confirmed in their opinion. Hamilton wrote in his diary:

Our immediate concern is Mr G. He is not fighting with his weapon of yore. He is firing off too many letters and telegrams which are undignified and which give an appearance of impatience and even petulance. He had hitherto always been so scrupulous about descending into the arena of electioneering. Can it be – I dare not admit it to myself – that old age is conducing to tenacity of office ?'[7]

In parliamentary terms the Liberal defeat was massive: 196 Gladstonian Liberals were returned as against 316 Tories, 74 Liberal Unionists and 83 Parnellites. In crude figures Unionists polled some 52–3 per cent of the vote, compared with the 47 per cent polled by the Tories in 1885. But had the Liberals retained a reasonable degree of unity their underlying electoral strength would still have been much greater than that of the Tories. This is a measure of the extent of Gladstone's failure, the most disastrous of his career, a failure that blighted the prospects of the Liberal party for the next twenty years. It cast a shadow over the remarkable *tour de force* he had accomplished in the previous six months. In retrospect he listed his espousal of Home Rule in 1886 as one of the occasions on which his sense of timing had proved correct. In anticipating that Ireland would become the central issue in the autumn of 1885 he was much nearer the truth than others like Hartington or Chamberlain who believed the problem could be side-stepped. He had seized the issue with superb *élan* when the time came in January 1886; in the process he had established his own dominance over the Liberal party and Cabinet to a higher degree than ever before, while the initial defections he suffered were tolerable. Even his estimate of Chamberlain was not so far out: behind the rhetoric of class warfare occasionally brought in for electoral purposes there was a rather 'thin' programme of reform; the element in it that would have troubled Gladstone most, disestablishment, was not considered even by Chamberlain to be immediate practical politics. But Gladstone underestimated the parliamentary damage that Chamberlain could do in a party still smarting from the recent fierce attacks of Parnell whom they were now to treat as an ally. Gladstone's achievement in drafting the complex Home Rule and Land bills was a remarkable intellectual feat; but there was more than a grain of truth in the taunt contained in Lord Randolph Churchill's election manifesto that he was 'an old man in a hurry'. The devoted Hamilton put it not so very differently: 'Herein lies the root of the position which he has taken up. It is for him to settle the Irish difficulty or to put it in train for being settled, he has no time at all to lose. This is how the question comes to have been so rushed.' Perhaps it was not so much a question of speed, for Gladstone's instinct that the nettle must be seized was surely right, but of more flexible management. Sooner or later Gladstone would have come up against the House of Lords, but if he could have preserved the substantial unity of his party in the Commons he would have been in a strong position. His own verdict eleven years later was:

Upon the whole, when I look back upon 1886, and consider the inveterate sentiment of hostility flavoured with contempt towards Ireland which has from time immemorial formed the basis of English tradition, I am much more disposed to be thankful for what we then and afterwards accomplished than to murmur or to wonder at what we did not.

12

ALMOST

A NULLITY

1886–98

When the election results were complete in
early July 1886 Gladstone soon reached the conclusion that the
government must resign without waiting to meet Parliament. The
only justification for hanging on would have been the hope that
among those elected as Liberal Unionists there might be a sufficient
number who could be brought back into the Liberal fold behind some
new version of Irish Home Rule. Nothing was to be hoped for from
Hartington and those who followed him, for he had been wholly
against any Irish concession. Gladstone wrote bitterly to Granville:
'Hartington has displayed much more activity against us than he
ever showed on our behalf as friend and colleague,' but only three

days later he declared: 'There is this difference however between Hartington and C[hamberlain], that the first behaves like and is a thorough gentleman. Of the other it is better not to speak.' To hold on to office by the grace of either Hartington or Chamberlain was clearly not to be contemplated; in any case an anti-Home Rule motion was bound to be moved immediately on the assembly of parliament and this would force Gladstone to resign. It was better therefore to depart immediately and avoid a dangerous interregnum; the government would have to declare their policy and this might help to reunify the opposition.

Gladstone's personal position was that he would continue as leader pending a settlement of the Irish question. To his son Herbert he wrote on 16 July:

> The general outlook is of an uncertain, uneasy, changeful time, until a settlement of the Irish question is reached; and settlement can only be real by Home Rule. . . What I think is possible is that, if such arrangement be cordially accepted by my friends and colleagues, I should obtain a dispensation from ordinary and habitual attendance in Parliament; but should not lay down the leadership so as to force them to choose another leader, and should take an active part when occasion seemed to require it, especially on the Irish Question. The proper policy for the Liberals, put out of Government, will be to promote freely and actively Liberal legislation generally in cooperation with the Dissentients so as to allow the party to reform itself.[1]

Curiously enough there was now less talk of retirement than there had been for a decade or more. Gladstone could not end his great career on a semi-tone, he had to complete the task to which he had put his hand. Moreover, the possibility of Liberal reunion seemed real enough at least for the next year or two. He might soon be back in power to resume the struggle for Ireland.

By dissolving Parliament on his Home Rule policy Gladstone had in a sense restored the two-party system. Parnell's role as arbiter of British politics was a thing of the past and the Irish nationalists were henceforth wedded to the Gladstonian Liberals. The Dissentients, as Gladstone called them, would have to make their choice between the two available alternatives; most of them in due course chose the Tories, but a few drifted back to their former friends. Gladstone's party was now the Irish Home Rule party; the Liberal divisions of the past, the many special interests from temperance to disestablishment, were now swallowed up by the Home Rule cause. Since the end of 1885 Gladstone had taken the view that Ireland was the great blockage in British politics which had to be removed before anything else could be done. This now continued to be the official view of the Liberal party he led. In this way a great simplification of Liberal politics had taken place and it is not surprising that Gladstone often felt the purge had been healthy. Another consequence of the new situation was that the fortunes of the Gladstonian Liberal party were now very closely tied to Parnell and Ireland. The Liberal stock rose when Ireland suffered the rod of coercion; it fell when Irish agrarian outrages caused disgust. When Parnell was vindicated after the exposure of Pigott the Liberals were on the crest of a wave; when he was discredited by the O'Shea divorce case the Liberals faced disaster.

As the years went on without a resolution of the Irish problem there was, however, a growing fatigue with Ireland among Liberals and among the wider public. The demand rose in the Liberal ranks for new and meaningful policies and there was less and less willingness to let Ireland crowd out all other initiatives. Gladstone found himself unable to end his career with the crowning mercy of an Irish settlement and although, with advancing age, his posture remained heroic it became also not a little pathetic. The mastery of extra-parliamentary opinion which had marked him out from all other politicians since the 1860s was fading and in the election of 1886 it had not proved decisive. The masses were no longer responding so fully to his moral appeal and their material class interests became more important. Gladstone was haunted by forebodings that the masses would prove to have no more moral stamina than the upper classes. Others, Chamberlain, Lord Randolph Churchill and many lesser men, were now competitors in mass oratory and were dealing out, as Gladstone saw it, a debased coinage. In order to keep Home Rule in the forefront of Liberal politics Gladstone had to pay a progressively higher price; he had to accept more and more of the 'constructionism' for which he cared so little. Although he accepted more 'constructionism' he took no interest in it and regarded himself as tied to politics by Home Rule only. The result was that he grew more and more detached and the development of the Liberal party and its policies was held in a state of suspended animation; or if it progressed it did so in spite of and not with the assistance of the nominal Leader of the party.

On Gladstone's resignation, Salisbury had offered to serve under Hartington or at least to form a coalition with the Liberal Unionists. This offer was largely window-dressing; the Tory rank and file was not prepared to have Hartington as Prime Minister and most Liberal Unionists were lukewarm about a coalition. Salisbury had made it clear that he could not at this stage join with Chamberlain and this

I

gave Hartington a good reason for declining to enter a coalition in order to maintain the unity of the Liberal dissentients. Thus Salisbury had to form a government based on the Tory party only. The followers of Hartington and Chamberlain took their seats on the Liberal side of the House, but they supported the Tory government, not always actively, but to the extent of keeping it in office. In this situation Gladstone's main hope of an early collapse of Salisbury's government had to be Liberal reunion. There is little doubt that this was what he sincerely hoped for in the autumn of 1886 and in the early months of 1887; not least because his conscience troubled him over the role he had played, albeit under dire necessity, in splitting the Liberal party. Soon after his departure from office he published a pamphlet on the Irish question reiterating his case for Home Rule. He ascribed the defeat of Home Rule in the main to the fact that it was coupled with a Land Bill and indicated that in future these two issues would be separated. He thus removed one possible obstacle to Liberal reunion. There were also hints out of Hawarden that the Irish members might be retained in some form at Westminster and this again might make it easier for some, notably Chamberlain, to return to the Liberal fold. But the obstacles to Liberal reunion were formidable. Gladstone could not, from conviction, retreat from the principle of Home Rule and it would not even have been politically useful, for it would have lost him the support of Parnell. Over sixty of the Liberal Unionists were Whigs or moderate Liberals who followed Hartington; only about a dozen were Radical Unionists following Chamberlain. Only the return of Hartington and his followers would have transformed the political situation; Hartington was also the man whom Gladstone wanted back, on personal grounds and because it would have strengthened the moderate wing of the party. Hartington, however, was totally opposed to Home Rule and felt, moreover, increasingly comfortable in support of the Conservative government. Chamberlain on the other hand had always been prepared to go a long way towards self-government in Ireland; if one wanted to be optimistic about the chances of a reconciliation with him one could believe that some meeting-point might be found between the local Irish self-government he was prepared to grant and the principle of a separate Parliament in Dublin. But Chamberlain had only a handful of followers in the Commons and it was hardly worth while to go to any great length to bring him back to the Liberals. Moreover, Gladstone's opinion of him as a person was no higher than it had been and he was not interested in seeing the Radical wing of the party strengthened.

The moves towards Liberal reunion were given impetus by the resignation of Lord Randolph Churchill as Chancellor of the Exchequer in December 1886. Chamberlain's hopes of forcing the Tory government into progressive policies had rested chiefly on Lord Randolph and both before and after the latter's resignation there was talk of party realignment around a Chamberlain–Churchill axis. As soon as Lord Randolph's departure from the government became public Chamberlain made a speech in which he suggested that, as Liberals were agreed on ninety-nine points of their pro-gramme 'three men sitting round a table' might be able to work out a compromise. Such a Round Table conference of Liberal Unionists and Gladstonian Liberals did in fact take place in January and February 1887. Gladstone gave the enterprise his blessing, but he placed no great hopes in it, nor did he allow it to bulk large in his calculations. The Round Table meetings came to an end when in February 1887 Chamberlain published a letter in the *Baptist* in which he blamed the delay in reforms like Welsh disestablishment on the preoccupation with Home Rule: 'Thirty-two millions of people must go without much-needed legislation because three million are disloyal . . .'[2] It was a reply to a public letter of Glad-stone's blaming the Liberal Unionists for the postponement of Liberal legislation such as Welsh disestablishment. The end of the Round Table conference was not the end of all hope that Chamber-lain at any rate might return to the fold. In April 1887 Gladstone and Chamberlain had a meeting, but neither gave anything away. By this time Chamberlain was in a difficult position, for the Con-servatives had switched to coercion and as a result some prominent Radical Unionists returned to their Gladstonian allegiance. The Liberal Unionist following in the country was visibly diminishing and even Chamberlain's Birmingham base was no longer safe. Gladstone had no reason now to make any concessions to Chamber-lain, and Hartington was not attainable. In August Chamberlain had to vote with Gladstone and against the government when the National League in Ireland, the new Nationalist organization, was being proclaimed as illegal. By this time Chamberlain's gesture was no longer a signal for Liberal reunion, but a warning to Salisbury that he could not be taken for granted; his future now lay clearly with the Tories. Thus Gladstone and Chamberlain finally parted company. Both were men who could put a political cause above party; only the early retirement of Gladstone would have made a return of Chamberlain to the Liberals possible.

In the meantime Salisbury's government had overcome the

threat to its existence caused by Lord Randolph's resignation. He had been replaced by Goschen who had drifted so much to the right in the Liberal party that he could never join Gladstone's second government and was now a Liberal Unionist. Thus the Tories managed to stay in office; Hartington, although compelled by circumstances to refuse the premiership for the third time in his career, was determined to keep Salisbury in power. But as Gladstone had predicted, the Tories could not escape the Irish problem; the adoption of Home Rule as the centrepiece of Liberal policy had, however, somewhat changed the emphasis of the Irish question. Parnell was now just as much wedded to Gladstone as the Liberals to Parnell. Gladstone had to be the hero of Irish nationalism, 'a white old man with a face like a benediction and a voice like an Archangel's', as William O'Brien put it.[3] The consequence was that Parnell, who was never a revolutionary, had to turn his face more resolutely than ever against Irish political extremism. He must do nothing to embarrass 'the illustrious Englishman who towers head and shoulders over all living men . . .' in his ability to deliver the priceless gift of Irish autonomy. Parnell was successful in containing Irish political extremism, but he could not halt a fresh wave of agrarian unrest. He warned that it was coming when he introduced a Tenants' Relief Bill in September 1886, to deal with the problem of eviction and rent arrears, which Gladstone's 1881 Land Act had by no means completely resolved. Gladstone was consulted and approved of Parnell's bill, but the government rejected it out of hand, not without causing a good deal of heart-searching among Chamberlain's Radical Unionists. Then the 'Plan of Campaign' started: the tenants on Irish estates banded together, asked the landlord for rent abatement; if he refused they paid the reduced rent into a campaign fund. It was the application of trade union and collective-bargaining principles to the Irish agrarian situation. Parnell for political and personal reasons took no part in the launching or the organization of the Plan of Campaign. He knew that it could embarrass his Liberal allies, but he could not and did not disavow it. Gladstone in his turn refused the demands of Hartington and the Tories to condemn the Plan of Campaign. His considered verdict on it, given in a speech in July 1887, was that it 'was one of those devices that cannot be reconciled with the principles of law and order in a civilized country. Yet we all know that such devices are the certain result of misgovernment.'

The Plan of Campaign finally forced the Conservative government back to coercion. Hicks Beach, the Chief Secretary for Ireland, was replaced by Balfour; this outwardly languid nephew of the Prime Minister, whose nickname was 'Clara', became the strong man of Ireland, one of the few politicians who have enhanced their reputation as a result of dealing with the affairs of that country. At the end of March 1887 a Crimes Act was introduced, the chief novelty of which was that it was not limited in time as previous coercion acts had been. Dublin Castle was thus granted special powers in perpetuity, to be used when required. There was also a more conciliatory side to the Tory strategy on Ireland. It arose out of the recommendations of the Cowper Commission whose appointment had been the opening move on Ireland of the Salisbury government. Leaseholders were now to be included in the provisions of the 1881 Land Act and judicial rents fixed under the act could be revised according to the movement of agricultural prices. The adoption of such policies represented a considerable reversal of previous Tory attitudes about the sanctity of property and contracts in Ireland. On the other hand they had already during their brief period in office passed a Land Purchase Act, the Ashbourne Act, and in the next few years Tory propaganda made much of its beneficent working. An even tighter grip on parliamentary procedure, to prevent Irish obstruction at Westminster, was the third element in Tory policy; in June 1887 the guillotine was introduced with no more than verbal opposition from the Liberals.

Thus the Tory alternative to Gladstone's Irish policy stood unveiled by the summer of 1887. To Gladstone it afforded ample justification that his championship of Home Rule was right and that it was necessary to put it into the forefront of Liberal policies. Tory coercion became a potent Liberal propaganda weapon. Many English sympathizers went over to Ireland to see for themselves the rigours of oppression and the sufferings of prisoners. Certain incidents became symbolic: the evictions on the Clanricarde estates, the owner of which was the most notorious and eccentric landlord in Ireland; the deliberate martyrdom of Wilfrid Scawen Blunt who had himself arrested at a prohibited meeting on one of the Clanricarde estates;[4] and above all the Mitchelstown affair in September 1887 when after provocative behaviour by the police three men were shot dead. Gladstone himself coined the phrase 'Remember Mitchelstown'. The situation was made for another Gladstonian crusade and he himself felt passionately and ardently for the Irish cause. He was trying, as it were, to 'bulgarianize' the Irish question. Oratory gave him release for his feelings. In June 1887 he made a triumphal tour of South Wales and at the end of July he made a big speech in

London. He conceded one important point: in future he would not necessarily exclude the Irish members from Westminster, a policy which had driven many into the Unionist camp. The government was losing by-elections and all the indications were that the Home Rule cause was gaining.

The reverses of the government in 1887 and the impression that the Liberal tide was flowing was probably as much due to the economic depression that reached its nadir that year as it was to Home Rule. Nevertheless the repression of a popular movement in Ireland by Tories undoubtedly evoked much sympathy in the British working class. The famous Trafalgar Square riots of November 1887 arose from a protest demonstration againt the imprisonment of William O'Brien. Among the Irish nationalist leaders Michael Davitt had the closest links with the British labour movement.[5] It was mostly radical back-benchers in the Liberal party who went over to Ireland to view the horrors of coercion. All this presented something of a dilemma for Gladstone. He felt that the withdrawal of Whigs and moderate Liberals and the line taken by Hartington since the split had strengthened the Radical tendencies in the party. In November 1887 he wrote to Rosebery:

> To me as a politician it is probably nothing, but to me as an individual this advance of radicalism is a matter of great regret. Even Hartington in his venom against Home Rule, is giving it countenance. When Home Rule is settled, Chamberlain will atone for his defection on this question by greater intensity on others. In 1866 John Mill said the Liberal party were 'a broad church' and it was true. But it will be difficult to keep them so.[6]

For Gladstone this kind of argument was an alibi: it was not he who had by taking up Home Rule caused the Liberal schism. In public he had to face both ways: he had to tell moderates that delay over Home Rule would strengthen radicalism; and he told Radicals that the swift realization of Home Rule was also the quickest path to the achievement of their aims. It would be overstating the case to say that Gladstone's single-minded obsession with Ireland was solely responsible for blocking the Radical advance. The Liberal party as a whole, even without Hartington and the moderates, was not ready to advance with rapid strides towards 'Radicalism, Socialism and Bradlaughism' as Gladstone put it to Hamilton. It was still a middle-class party, but middle-class radicalism, with its emphasis on religious and civil equality, had largely shot its bolt – it had won its objectives. The party was, however, not ready to allow the politically conscious working class to occupy positions of real influence in its organization, either locally or nationally. Socialism, the 'New Unionism', strikes, unemployment – these were bogies rather than real problems to most Liberals. Radicalism within the Liberal party was a ragbag of ideas and causes, disestablishment, local option, electoral reform, the status of the House of Lords, employers' liability, shorter hours; the leading Radicals were anti-authoritarian gadflies like Labouchere. Had Gladstone been radical rather than conservative in his views he might have given the Liberal party a new radical impetus. As it was he remained a Peelite Conservative who gradually reconciled himself to a few items from the Radical ragbag; from a left-wing point of view his sin was one of omission rather than commission.

The Tory policy of coercion in Ireland, as it unfolded in the spring of 1887, was accompanied by a series of articles in *The Times* entitled *Parnellism and Crime*. The editor, G.E.Buckle, was a strong anti-Gladstonian and this bias is not absent from those parts of Disraeli's biography which he later wrote. The most sensational feature of the articles was the publication on 18 April 1887, to coincide with the second reading of the Coercion Bill, of the facsimile of a letter from Parnell. In this letter, dated 15 May 1882, Parnell appeared to apologize for having had to condemn the Phoenix Park murders. The Irish leader immediately denounced this letter as a forgery in the House of Commons; it was, however, difficult for him to bring a libel action in England, for in a case politically so contentious he could not rely on the verdict of an English jury. This conclusion seemed to be borne out by the fact that Salisbury made a speech within days of Parnell's denunciation of the forgery, in which he took the Irish leader's guilt for granted. Six months later, however, F.H. O'Donnell, a former associate of Parnell, brought a libel action of his own against *The Times*. It was one of the curious features of this case that Sir Richard Webster, the Attorney-General, appeared on behalf of the newspaper. He used the opportunity to broadcast further evidence incriminating Parnell as an accomplice of assassins. Although Morley advised him to continue to lie low the Irish leader was not prepared to do so any longer. He asked for the appointment of a select committee; this the government refused, but offered instead to appoint a special commission of inquiry. It was again an extraordinary mode of proceeding, for thereby the inquiry was widened into an investigation into the connection between the Irish nationalist movement and violence. A revolutionary movement was put on trial and the judges were appointed by their political opponents. Parnell was, however, so eager to have an opportunity to clear himself that he did not refuse even this form of investigation where the dice were loaded against him. It was Gladstone's instinct also that it was better to have an inquiry, however unsatisfactory its form, than to bury the matter. There was much uneasiness about the Special Commission even on the Unionist side. Hartington tried to dissuade the government from taking this course; Lord Randolph Churchill was strongly and consistently against the commission; Sir Richard Webster was with difficulty persuaded by his colleagues to appear again.

The proceedings dragged on for four months before the question of the incriminating letters was reached in February 1889. The results were melodramatic. Sir Charles Russell, Parnell's counsel, exposed Pigott in the witness-box as a forger; Pigott deposited a signed confession with Labouchere, fled the country and shot himself in a Madrid hotel. Parnell was on a pedestal of public esteem and the Home Rule cause seemed assured of victory. There was corresponding demoralization on the other side. Salisbury's verdict was: 'As to internal affairs – they do not look promising. The life of the Ministry and the life of the G.O.M. are both ebbing – the question is which will ebb the fastest. On the answer to that question the fate of Ireland – and possibly of England – depends.'[7] The episode was highly discreditable to the government and particularly its relations with *The Times* form a murky chapter of history. The adoption of such low and as it turned out risky tactics was a measure of the fear Home Rule inspired in the Unionist camp as a force disintegrating the Empire. On the other hand there was also danger to the Liberals in the sharp swing of opinion in favour of Parnell. Gladstone's daughter Mary wrote after watching him in the witness-box before the Special Commission in May 1889: 'He really exhibited all the fruits of the Spirit, love, peace, patience, gentleness, forbearance, long-suffering meekness. His personality takes hold of one, the refined, delicate face, illuminating smile, fire-daring eyes, slight tall figure.'[8] Parnell received the accolade of respectability when he visited Hawarden in December 1889. He and Gladstone had a long discussion on the form of a future Irish settlement, particularly on the vexed question of Irish representation at Westminster after the setting up of a Parliament in Dublin. No definite conclusions were reached, but Gladstone's view of his visitor was that he 'is certainly one of the very best people to deal with that I have ever known'. On another occasion, when Parnell met Gladstone at a dinner-party, the G.O.M. launched into a long historical disquisition on the iniquities of the Act of Union. Parnell's comment was, 'The old gentleman is very talkative.' The report of the Special Commission did not appear until February 1890. The Conservatives tried to make the most of the blame the three judges attached to Irish nationalist M.P.s for failing to give support to law and order in Ireland. For the general public the salient fact, however, remained the acquittal of Parnell and therefore the tide was still flowing in favour of the cause for which Gladstone remained in politics.

The tide was flowing, the government's majority was being whittled down through by-election losses, but time was passing. The hope that the government might actually be brought down by Liberal Unionist defections had faded after 1887. One fact had emerged clearly from all the Liberal Unionist perplexities and divisions: they would never as a body return to the Liberal fold as long as Gladstone remained in the lead and with him Home Rule as the foremost Liberal cause. Even the vindication of Parnell could not assuage the feeling in many sections of the Liberal party that policies other than, and additional to, Home Rule must be developed. In 1889 about seventy Radical M.P.s formed their own parliamentary organization, with their own Whips. A spate of resolutions was adopted each year at the meeting of the National Liberal Federation, ranging from disestablishment to local option. In 1889 Gladstone himself voted for the first time for a private member's bill to disestablish the Scottish Church. It had been a hotly debated issue in Scotland for a long time and as a candidate for a Scottish constituency Gladstone had had to step very warily. In 1885 he had not considered the issue 'mature' and a declaration from him in favour of Scottish disestablishment would have had serious repercussions on Liberal prospects in England in that election. By 1889 Gladstone had become convinced that Scottish Liberals were clearly in favour of disestablishment and that therefore he could no longer withhold his vote from that cause. He refused, however, to commit himself about timing or whether Scottish or Welsh disestablishment should have priority after Home Rule was achieved. The feeling of Welsh members was well known to Gladstone through his close friendship with Stuart Rendel, long known as 'the member for Wales'. The Liberal party could not, however, devote itself solely to the causes of the Celtic fringe; but Gladstone refused to give any lead towards the evolution of other policies. When the Home Rule cause appeared to be riding high, as it was in 1889 and 1890, he was merely confirmed in this attitude. Even on Home Rule Gladstone refused to lay down a clear policy on such contentious matters as the retention of Irish members at Westminster; the Liberal imperialists, particularly Rosebery, were very anxious to present Home Rule as a positive scheme of federation within the Empire. Gladstone realized that to stir up such matters in public would merely raise fresh obstacles. On the other hand he was reluctant to engage even in private consultations with his colleagues. Meetings of Liberal leaders were rare and generally inconclusive. Gladstone still felt that he and what he stood for was seen by the public as the beginning and end of the Liberal party. As Hamilton put it, 'He feels "you must take me as you find me, or else get rid of me".'

In 1889 Gladstone celebrated two anniversaries: his Golden Wedding in July and his eightieth birthday in December. For a man of his age the range of his activities was still remarkable. He wrote a great deal and was a fairly regular contributor to the *Nineteenth Century*. In the pages of this review he had, at the height of the political crisis of 1885 and 1886, engaged in a controversy with T. H. Huxley about the relationship between modern science and the account of the Creation given in the Book of Genesis. Somewhat naïvely Gladstone had urged that science bore out the broad order of events given in the Bible and that this confirmed the basis of Holy Scripture in divine revelation. Huxley had no great difficulty in demolishing this argument, though Gladstone could legitimately cling to his view that the conflict between science and religion was unreal and unnecessary. Between October 1887 and September 1891 Gladstone contributed three articles to the *Nineteenth Century* on 'Electoral Facts' which show him as a keen student of the political scene, though some of his arguments would scarcely survive in the hard light of modern psephology. His refusal to play the role of an ordinary party leader was not due to any loss of interest in politics.

Gladstone was, however, now a very old man and particularly after his eightieth birthday even his close and loyal followers, men like Lord Acton or Sir Edward Hamilton, had to admit that he was showing signs of ageing. His sight and hearing were deteriorating and this added physical to the psychological obstacles to communication. He was a living myth and his family and friends rallied round to maintain its purity. Catherine, Herbert, after his father politically the most prominent Gladstone, and the other members of the family were not only devoted to him personally but believed totally in the myth and in the cause. Gladstone knew he was 'a survival', but he also believed that he had been spared for a divine purpose; undoubtedly he found it in his nature very difficult to 'stand aside'. Thus he was a willing collaborator in the maintenance of his own myth. For him and his entourage the popular acclaim he could still evoke on his public appearances seemed to confirm the righteousness of his mission. When he visited Birmingham, the Chamberlain bastion, in November 1888, his daughter Mary noted in her diary:

Special train only stopping at Willington when flowers and addresses and crowds and magnificent luncheon handed in. This we greedily ate on way to B'ham . . . we drove in procession slowly thro' the packed streets, great enthusiasm . . . He spoke nearly 2 hours and never seemed tired. Tremendous reception.

Others helped to maintain the Olympian existence of the G.O.M. Stuart Rendel, former chief of Armstrong & Whitworth, the armament firm, and George Armitstead, a financier and member for Dundee, were wealthy friends able to put their houses in London and abroad at the disposal of the Gladstone family. That such friendships could be misinterpreted never occurred to Gladstone. John Morley was politically closest to the Liberal leader; he shared to the full the preoccupation with Ireland. But Morley was an intellectual recently arrived in politics; his personal advancement was bound up with the Home Rule cause, but he hardly carried the guns for long-term survival in high politics. Many of the men to whom Gladstone was linked by a life-time of endeavour and correspondence were leaving the scene: Döllinger, Newman, Manning; Acton survived him. Gladstone was now frequently in a reminiscing mood; he talked much and ranged freely over his eventful life. Morley, Rendel, Lionel Tollemache and others recorded his table talk. As with all old men, he dwelt lovingly on the past, while some manifestations of the present alarmed him. It was a particularly nostalgic moment when he visited Oxford soon after his eightieth birthday. During his stay at All Souls he had much to say about the unreformed Oxford and the greatness of English institutions in the past. About the present he was less sanguine; 'For me Socialism has no attractions: nothing but disappointment awaits the working classes if they yield to exaggerated anticipations which are held out to them by the Labour party'; but he was never one to surrender to general gloom about the future.

Gladstone, ageing, remote and obsessed with Ireland, continued to dominate the Liberal party and there was as yet no one in the whole of British politics who could equal him. His colleagues might get irritated with his failure to consult them or discuss new policies; but whenever they contemplated his disappearance from active politics they recoiled: they had nothing to put in his place. Morley said in 1892: '. . . Mr Gladstone is very old . . . There is an old Indian idea that when a great chief dies, his friends and horses and dogs should be buried with him. So it must be with us!'[9] At the end of the year 1890, however, an event occurred which put the continued leadership of Gladstone and the Home Rule cause seriously in doubt. A divorce suit had been filed by Captain O'Shea, citing Parnell as co-respondent, within days of the latter's visit to Hawarden in December 1889. The suit was not heard until 15 November 1890. Gladstone had known at least since the days of the Kilmainham Treaty in 1882 that Mrs O'Shea was rumoured to be Parnell's mistress. He shut his ears to such rumours; it was the normal reaction of Victorian public men as long as there was no public scandal. Hartington had, after all, an equally famous liaison with the Duchess of Manchester. A few days before the divorce suit was heard, Gladstone had premonitions of disaster and wrote to Arnold Morley, the Liberal Chief Whip, that 'a thundercloud is about to burst over Parnell's head'. Parnell, however, had always reassured his followers that he would emerge without discredit from the divorce suit and he gave the same reassurance to John Morley a few days before the trial. He hoped until the last moment that O'Shea would be bought off and withdraw. When this failed to happen he preferred the divorce to take its course, for he wanted passionately to make Mrs O'Shea his wife and to have done with secrecy and deceit. The proud, defiant attitude of Parnell was the central element in the tragedy that now unfolded; he defied convention, hypocritical public opinion in England, his own dumbfounded followers, the Catholic Church, his Liberal allies and even Gladstone; he paid for defiance with life itself.

The court proceedings appeared to reveal a story of

domestic treachery, systematic and long-continued deception, the whole squalid apparatus of letters written with the intent of misleading, houses taken under false names, disguises and aliases, secret visits and sudden flights . . . comparable only to the dreary monotony of French middle-class vice, over which the scalpel of M. Zola so lovingly lingers.

In these words *The Times* lingered lovingly over the discomfiture of its enemy. We now know that the facts were far more discreditable to Captain O'Shea than to Parnell. Almost certainly O'Shea had been a *mari complaisant* since 1882 and had shamelessly tried to use the situation to extract political and pecuniary advantages. But contemporaries could not know this. The reaction of Gladstone's daughter Mary was typical and inevitable: 'He and she undefended, and he has lived this life of lies all these years. A heart-breaking revelation. "Blot out his name."' Gladstone himself, as soon as he heard the news, so staggeringly different from the reassurance that

had just reached him through John Morley, kept repeating to himself 'in the interior and silent forum' the words 'it'll na dae' and
said so to his family. The National Liberal Federation was meeting
at Sheffield and the reports which Harcourt and Morley gave him
of opinion there confirmed his instinctive reaction.

On 24 November 1890 Gladstone came up to London to stay with
Stuart Rendel at Carlton Gardens. He immediately saw Harcourt,
Granville, John and Arnold Morley. Convinced as he was that
Parnell was now impossible, he refused to be stampeded by Harcourt
into writing directly to the Irish leader to tell him so. Gladstone
thought it would be 'intolerable' if he as a party leader had to set
himself up as a judge and censor of morals. He hoped that Parnell
would of his own accord withdraw and knew that a direct letter
from him would have exactly the opposite effect. He chose, however,
two methods of conveying to Parnell indirectly that his continuation
as Irish leader would make it impossible for him to go on as Liberal
leader. One method was an interview with Justin McCarthy, the
Vice-Chairman of the Irish party, who described it as 'a momentous
interview – well-nigh tragic milestone. It touched me deeply.'[10] It is,
however, not quite clear whether Gladstone, with his deeply en-
grained habit of circumlocution, really succeeded in conveying to
McCarthy that he would retire if Parnell stayed on. The second
method was a letter which Gladstone wrote Morley to be shown to
Parnell. It was not easy for Gladstone to bring himself to write this
letter and the crucial passage in it was inserted after further consultation with Morley. It read:

. . . the continuance I speak of [Parnell's as Irish leader] would not
only place many hearty and effective friends of the Irish cause in a
position of great embarrassment, but would render my retention of the
leadership of the liberal party, based as it has been mainly upon the
prosecution of the Irish cause, almost a nullity.

Gladstone had used similar words to Harcourt earlier. The final
version of Gladstone's letter was completed while the Liberal
leaders were dining together on the evening of 24 November. 'We
were all gay enough, and as unlike as possible to a marooned crew'[11]
was Morley's description of the atmosphere. Only Spencer 'doubted
whether we were right in putting any screw at all upon Parnell, and
he pressed earnestly that P. was the only man who could drive the
Irish team'.

Unfortunately neither of these warnings reached Parnell before
he attended a meeting of Irish members on the following day, at
which he was due to be re-elected, in accordance with normal practice,

as Leader of the party. Parnell avoided an appointment with Morley before the Irish party meeting; at the meeting McCarthy, perhaps out of timidity or because he had not fully grasped the situation, did not speak out. Gladstone learnt of Parnell's re-election shortly after the event from Morley when he entered his room at the House of Commons:

'Well?' he asked eagerly the moment the door was closed, and without taking off cape or hat. 'Have you seen him?' 'He is obdurate,' said I. I told him shortly what had passed. He stood at the table, dumb for some instants, looking at me as if he could not believe what I had said. Then he burst out that we must at once publish his letter to me; at once, that very afternoon.

Up to then Gladstone had acted with great forbearance and circumspection, but this was a blunder. The letter to Morley, when published, sounded like an ultimatum to the Irish members to depose their leader. Parnell now fought back fiercely; he issued a manifesto in which he accused Gladstone of nothing less than treachery to Ireland and the cause of Home Rule. He claimed that during his conversations with Gladstone at Hawarden a year earlier it had become clear that in many important respects the Liberal leader had abandoned the promises made to Ireland. After the publication of Gladstone's letter to Morley it had thus become Parnell's strategy to save his own position by evoking the deep Irish suspicion of English perfidy and treachery. By this strategy Parnell failed to save himself, but he created a myth in Ireland that even Gladstone, a man deserving of Irish gratitude if ever there was one, was in fact not to be trusted. Parnell's dramatic fight for survival in Committee Room 15 now started. In the course of it an attempt was made to extract fresh assurances from Gladstone about Home Rule in return for Parnell's withdrawal from the leadership of the Irish party. Gladstone categorically refused to give any promises about the shape of a future Home Rule Bill. The Irish Nationalist party now split into a majority of anti-Parnellites and a minority of Parnellites. For some years therefore the Irish nationalist movement became involved in internecine warfare; the fight was particularly bitter during the ten months that remained of Parnell's life.

The shock of all this to the cause of Home Rule, to the Liberal party and to Gladstone was profound. Even if Parnell could have been induced quietly to withdraw from active politics the damage would have been great. On the Liberal side the Nonconformists, still the backbone of the party, were outraged; the Nonconformist moral conscience was one of the mainstays of the Home Rule cause and it was now seriously alienated. On the Unionist side the divorce case reinforced the contempt, mingled with fear, in which Irish nationalism had always been held. The attacks on Gladstone by Parnell and his followers in Ireland and the struggle between the two Irish factions worsened the situation even more. The way in which the Catholic Church threw its influence against Parnell and helped to destroy him seemed to confirm the fear that 'Home Rule meant Rome rule'. It was almost a miracle that in these circumstances Gladstone was able and willing to remain the Liberal leader and that his party continued to be willing to support Home Rule. In December 1890 a by-election took place in Bassetlaw and Gladstone spoke on behalf of the Liberal candidate. After a long series of by-election reverses the Unionists found their vote increasing. Morley, visiting Hawarden at this time, found Gladstone more depressed than he had ever seen him. Even the G.O.M. felt for a moment that Home Rule might have to be temporarily shelved. To Acton he wrote: 'I consider the Parnell chapter of politics finally closed for us, the British liberals, at least during my time.' He wrote round to his colleagues suggesting that new policies should be devised to repair the damage to the party and even proposed a consultative meeting.

It soon became apparent that it was by no means easy to devise new policies and that shelving Home Rule, not that Gladstone ever seriously proposed it, was not practical politics after so many years' commitment to it. Apart from the broad questions of morality and consistency even tactical considerations virtually blocked the abandonment of Home Rule. It would drive the Irish party into the arms of Parnell; it would lose the Irish vote in England and above all there was no real substitute for it in Liberal politics. As the Liberal leaders now, after four and a half years in opposition, turned their minds to alternative policies, they found the cupboard still very bare. Local option, Welsh or Scottish disestablishment was of interest to limited sections only of the Liberal constituencies. Free schools and allotments were of more general interest, but the Tory government, which had established county councils in 1888, was about to legislate on both questions. Education was, because of its denominational implications, always at least as difficult for the Liberals to tackle as it was for the Tories; allotments for agricultural labourers proved in an increasingly urbanized society a damp squib. This left the possibility of further changes in the political system; improvements in the electoral machinery in the direction of 'one man, one vote', and reform of the House of Lords. It was clear that the problem of the House of Lords would be most likely to be brought to a decision by Home Rule; as for electoral reform Ripon pointed out to Gladstone that the 'working classes will, no doubt, be glad enough of a reform which will increase their power. But they will ask what is it going to lead to? What will be the result of it?'[12] The eight-hour day was a result which many in the labour movement were now actively working for. But this was just the kind of commitment which most Liberals were unwilling to enter into. Gladstone refused to adopt the eight-hour day as Liberal policy ahead of the 1892 election and regarded the pressure for it as a sign of 'the labouring class beginning to be corrupted by the semblance of power as the other classes have been tainted and warped by its reality . . .'. To Gladstone it was a moral question; most of his colleagues were on other grounds fearful to allow the politics of class to occupy a central position in the Liberal programme. Harcourt was probably the Liberal leader most lukewarm about Home Rule and most insistent that it should be supplemented by other policies. To Morley he wrote in January 1891: 'Like the Kingdom of Heaven the Liberal Party is a house of many mansions. It is a party of progress and if its advance is checked by insuperable obstacles in one direction it will not dash itself to pieces like a foolish bird, but will go on and prosper in another.' But even Harcourt had to admit now to Gladstone that Home Rule would have to remain in first place.

Thus Gladstone and Home Rule survived the crisis of the Parnell divorce case, but both were weakened by it. A general election was approaching and the Liberal prospects in 1891 were not what they had been a year earlier. To the victor of the Bassetlaw by-election Salisbury quoted Shakespeare: 'Now is the winter of our discontent made glorious summer by the sun of York.' Liberal confidence recovered somewhat through later by-elections and through the clear signs of Parnell's failure in Ireland, but the rank and file were more restless than ever.

This was the background to the Newcastle conference of the National Liberal Federation in October 1891. There was no novelty in these annual meetings passing resolutions on the many topics of concern to Liberals; nor was there anything new in Gladstone addressing the gathering, for he had done so in most years since 1886. The approach of a general election and the weakness of Home Rule as an election slogan meant greater importance was being attached to what might emerge from this conference. There was a feeling that the growing concern of the electorate about social and economic reforms must be harnessed to the Liberal party, for the indications were that the Tories were also trying to catch this wind. 'Socialism', in the guise of independent labour candidates, the Social Democratic Federation, the Fabians, the labour movement in general, was on the scene; there was beginning to be a feeling in Liberal quarters that they must look to their left flank. Gladstone was receiving advice from many quarters before he went to Newcastle that he must give encouragement to a wide-ranging programme of reforms; he was also warned, for example by Schnadhorst, that he must not commit himself too far on questions like the limitation of hours, on which the party was deeply divided. Thus Gladstone in a speech at Newcastle on 2 October 1891 gave his endorsement to what came to be known as the Newcastle Programme and this was something he had not done at previous meetings of the National Liberal Federation. Even now the commitment was sufficiently vague: Home Rule still topped the list and no attempt was made to establish any kind of priority among the other items, which included disestablishment, 'one man, one vote', local option on the licensing laws, district and parish councils and employers' liability; on divisive questions like limitation of hours and the House of Lords the programme was very vague. Gladstone, having been subjected to much pressure to relent from his obsession with Home Rule, was in later years blamed for putting the Newcastle Programme like an albatross around the neck of the Liberal party. Immediately he was attacked for insincerity in proposing a programme in which he did not believe. When he spoke at Newcastle he no doubt did so because he saw it as a way of propelling the one cause that really concerned him, Ireland, while the rest of the programme would really touch him little during the short time left to him in politics. He was not an anti-reformer; but he felt that the ultimate purpose of all social and political action was to raise the moral stature of the individual and this could not be done by redressing his material grievances. Gladstone waxed really eloquent at Newcastle when he spoke of the evacuation of Egypt and even more so when he attacked the House of Lords: he raised his arms higher and higher while his knees bent lower and lower as he uttered his words of condemnation.

For Gladstone the year 1891 had been difficult. Apart from his political tribulations, he had lost both his eldest son after a long illness and his close associate of former years, Lord Granville. At the end of the year he and Mrs Gladstone spent two and a half months in Biarritz and in the South of France as guests of George Armitstead. When they returned at the end of February 1892 a dissolution of Parliament was in the offing. In his last article on 'Electoral Facts' in the *Nineteenth Century*, published in September 1891, Gladstone had through various calculations predicted a Liberal majority of somewhere between forty-six and ninety-seven. These expectations were lower than they would have been in 1890, but the hope was still for an independent Liberal majority. Liberal spirits were raised by their victory in the Rossendale by-election, caused by the elevation of Hartington to the Dukedom of Devonshire. The election campaign finally took place in July 1892 and Gladstone was again a candidate for Midlothian. He spent most of the election period, as so often in the past, as the guest of Rosebery at Dalmeny. The impact he could now make on the public mind was on a much lesser scale than it had been in the great days of the Midlothian campaign of 1879, but even now there was no one on either side of politics who could equal the attention he could command. Almost all commentators on the 1892 election were agreed that Irish Home Rule had become boring to the British electorate. 'The Irish are a bad lot, if Home Rule will keep them quiet, let them have Home Rule' – this is how a perceptive Tory observer, Edward Dicey, had summed up the attitude of the man in the street to the Irish problem.[13] In so far as Home Rule was still the major single issue in the election, Gladstone laid himself open to attack on two points in particular: his refusal to reveal the details of his Home Rule scheme and his failure to recognize the Ulster problem. The Unionists tried to exploit Nonconformist sympathies for their co-religionists in Ulster. On domestic affairs the government fought on their record, which was respectable; the wide scope of the Newcastle Programme made the Liberals vulnerable. A number of independent labour candidates were in the field; Gladstone's refusal to accept the eight-hour day, while Chamberlain had supported the miners' 'Eight Hours' Bill, damaged the Liberals in the eyes of labour. On foreign affairs it was a favourite gambit of Tory speakers to contrast Salisbury's success and firmness with the failure and vacillation of Gladstone's second government. The result of the election was that 273 Liberals and 82 Home Rulers, of whom a few were Parnellites, confronted 269 Tories and 46 Liberal Unionists. The Liberals would be dependent on the Irish if they formed a government. Gladstone was severely disappointed and cried, 'Too small, too small.' It was particularly galling for him that his own majority in Midlothian dropped from over 4500 in 1885 to under 700. The elections indicated more clearly than before that the country was moving away from the politics of communities, localities and religious affiliations towards greater national homogeneity based mainly on socio-economic class. The Liberal party had for a generation been a product of the old politics and had not yet, quite apart from Gladstone, found a way of adjusting to the new politics.

Salisbury waited to meet the new Parliament in August 1892 and resigned on his defeat. There was never any doubt in Gladstone's mind that he would have to form a fourth government, though he had hoped to do it under much more auspicious circumstances. He was still 'fast bound to Ireland as Ulysses was to his mast', 'chained to the oar' of Home Rule. The Queen was appalled that a wild, incomprehensible old man of eighty-two should rule her country and had hoped to summon Rosebery or Harcourt instead. She bowed to the inevitable and Gladstone tried to reassure her that 'Home Rule was a very Conservative measure as it would bring peace and contentment to Ireland'. In forming his last government he had less of a free hand than he had had in 1886 and he was 'beset right and left' with a number of personal difficulties. The most important of these was Rosebery, a man with whom Gladstone's relations had always been ambivalent. On the one hand there was close friendship and a complicated nexus of personal and political obligation. Gladstone had always admired Rosebery's brilliance and had entertained the highest expectations of his political future. But Gladstone was too self-centred a man to be able to meet with sympathy the hypersensitivity and inner weaknesses of Rosebery. The younger man had resigned from his first ministerial post in 1883, and before doing so had joined the Queen in the gallery of Gladstone's most severe personal irritants. But Rosebery had taken office again in 1885 to show his solidarity with Gladstone after the death of Gordon. His tenure of the Foreign Office in 1886 had given him a presumptive claim to return to the same post in 1892. In the meantime the death of his wife had caused Rosebery to lose much of his savour for political life. During the last Midlothian campaign, an occasion made particularly cheerless by the memory of past splendours, the Gladstones had again been Rosebery's guests at Dalmeny. Rosebery suffered from 'the lack of nous', as Morley put it, with which Gladstone treated him, and Mrs Gladstone was no better. The result was that formidable pressure had to be put on Rosebery before he would finally consent to return to the Foreign Office. Gladstone had no sooner secured Rosebery than he regretted it. The Foreign Secretary was in fact a Liberal Imperialist and on the two major problems of foreign policy that now faced the new government, Egypt and Uganda, he and his Prime Minister were fundamentally out of sympathy. Rosebery's political position was strong and he knew that Gladstone's outlook on foreign affairs was out of joint with an age of clashing imperialisms. The result was that he went ahead with his own policies and practised something approaching deceit on Gladstone and those members of the Cabinet, like Harcourt and Morley, who tended to agree with the Prime Minister on foreign affairs. Writing in 1896 Gladstone blamed Rosebery for 'his total gross misconception of the relative position of the two offices we respectively held' and described him as 'rather seriously imbued with that territorial greed, which constitutes for us one of the grave dangers of the time'. Rosebery was not the only personal difficulty for Gladstone in the formation of his last government. The Queen barred Labouchere from Cabinet office; Gladstone wanted Spencer, in whom he had the utmost confidence, back on Irish affairs, but the 'Red Earl' preferred the Admiralty; Harcourt was holding meetings at his house in Brook Street to discuss the shape of the Cabinet and the press talked of the 'Brook Street Conspiracy'. Gladstone managed nevertheless to give office to a number of men like Asquith and Acland in the Cabinet and Sir Edward Grey as Under-Secretary at the Foreign Office, who were to carry the Liberal banner for many years to come.

To be Prime Minister in the circumstances in which Gladstone found himself now was inevitably not without pathos. His return to office to deliver justice to Ireland had been too long delayed; the vicissitudes on the way and his own failing faculties now deprived him of his former dominance. His wife and family more than ever formed a wall of devotion around him and Sir Algernon West, who returned to him from the Inland Revenue to head his private secretariat, found the situation often very trying. Gladstone could be fully effective only fitfully and was more than ever a law unto himself. Cabinet meetings were infrequent; to begin with Gladstone adopted the curious practice of seating himself at a small table apart from his colleagues with Rosebery beside him; later Harcourt and Rosebery, disgusted by the prevalence of Irish business, would retire to what they called the 'English bench'. In the House of Commons, Gladstone could still be marvellously effective, even though he sometimes had difficulty, because of his failing eyesight, in reading vital papers or notes. His style was now less monumental and more mellow and occasionally laced with gentle humour. He was a popular speaker; the House could not fail to take pride in such a veteran and occasionally the edge was taken off the fiercest controversy.

Gladstone's one remaining purpose in politics was to bring in another Home Rule Bill. He knew that it would be rejected by the House of Lords. He felt therefore that there should be a reasonable programme of English reforms to accompany the Irish Bill; some of the English legislation would also fall foul of the Lords and thus sufficient pressure would be built up to confront the peers and submit the question of their powers to the electorate. But how could an old man of eighty-three, holding on to office from day to day and having behind him only a precarious majority, follow out such a complicated strategy, which would necessarily take years to develop? Morley and Spencer pressed Gladstone to get on with the preparation of a Home Rule Bill, for they knew that it would be a lost cause once he had gone. Harcourt was making hectoring demands for a large Radical programme and many other ministers backed him. At his first Cabinet on 19 August 1892 Gladstone said 'he thought it of great importance that English measures should be pressed on concurrently with Home Rule'. In fact a number of departmental measures were brought forward. Fowler's Parish Councils Bill was eventually passed just before Gladstone retired, after a prolonged wrangle with the Lords; the Employers' Liability Bill brought in by Asquith was killed by the Lords through amendment. Gladstone was not able to concern himself much with either bill and in the event they could not contribute to the strategy of confronting the Peers.

Yet Gladstone was slow to get to work on the Home Rule Bill. Although there was a respite from parliamentary work in the autumn of 1892, much of his energy was absorbed by the angry disputes with Rosebery over Uganda. Visions of the Gordon case rose up before him 'on which we adopted a ruinous decision under the most seductive appearances . . .'[14] On the margin of a telegram stressing the dangers to the Christian missions in Uganda in case of a British evacuation he wrote, 'I wonder how much the transmission of this very unimportant *jingo* paper cost.'[15] Gladstone had to give way on Uganda and after his retirement Rosebery declared it a British protectorate. Early in 1893 the request for more British troops in Egypt made Gladstone almost as angry: 'I would as soon set a torch to Westminster Abbey . . .' he told Harcourt, but again, if the government was to survive for Home Rule, he had to give way. When Morley saw him at Hawarden in December 1892 he was angry about Uganda and depressed by his failing sight and hearing.

Work on the second Home Rule Bill started in November 1892 and was undertaken by a small Cabinet committee including

Gladstone, Spencer, Morley, Herschell, Campbell-Bannerman and Bryce. Discussion of it in the Cabinet itself was often sidetracked by Uganda and Egypt and there were wrangles over the financial clauses. Morley sometimes complained to Sir Algernon West how old and difficult to work with Gladstone was; but the G.O.M.'s parliamentary performances on this bill showed his grip on the intricate details to be still very remarkable. The chief difference between the first and the second Home Rule Bill lay in the treatment of Irish representation at Westminster. Eighty Irish members were to remain at Westminster, but they were not to vote on English or Scottish bills. On its passage through the House the bill was amended so that the eighty Irish members would have unlimited voting rights at Westminster. Total exclusion of the Irish from the Imperial Paliament meant taxation without representation and might prove the way to complete separation. Total inclusion meant that Ireland would get not only self-government but would retain the ability to disturb the rest of the United Kingdom as heretofore. Partial inclusion still left the Irish the power to topple British governments. The financial clauses in the Home Rule Bill caused a good deal of controversy in the Cabinet. Morley clashed with Harcourt; these two had previously been linked in the 'Malwood Compact' and their disagreement now was not without influence on the accession of Rosebery rather than Harcourt to the premiership in 1894.

The Home Rule Bill was introduced in February 1893, had its second reading in April, finally passed the Commons early in September with a vote of 347 to 304 and was within less than a week rejected by the Lords with a vote of 419 to 41. Within this bare framework there was encompassed a parliamentary drama seldom excelled. The eighty-three-year-old premier, virtually living in the House during the committee stage, was the centre of it; perhaps his most worthy antagonist was Joseph Chamberlain, himself nearing sixty, but looking about half Gladstone's age. It was a battle not without its moments of chivalry: when Chamberlain's son Austen made a maiden speech the G.O.M. complimented him with the august courtesy of which he was a master. The Liberal Unionist leader was deeply moved and bowed low to his great opponent. But mostly the battle was fierce and on one occasion there were fisticuffs, exaggerated no doubt by the press, but still unheard of in those days. The government had to introduce a new guillotine procedure, greeted by the Unionists with shouts of 'The gag, the gag.' What did Gladstone achieve by this labour of Sisyphus? He made an eventual attempt to take up Home Rule again that

much more certain, and he helped to keep Irish nationalism in constitutional channels for a time; he posed with more insistence than
before the question of the House of Lords. In a longer perspective
the verdict of history has gone to him. He saw the Irish situation
more clearly than those who feared Home Rule as revolution and
disruption of Empire. Only on Ulster was his vision defective.

Gladstone did not, even now, feel that it was for him the end of
the Home Rule story. He proposed to proceed with his strategy of
attacking the House of Lords and suggested a dissolution to his
colleagues. They refused. There was now a good deal of resentment
against their ageing, unpredictable, autocratic leader among the
members of his Cabinet, but it was still counterbalanced by fears of
the consequences of his departure. Everybody was manoeuvring
against the day but nobody was quite ready yet. Among the radical
elements in the party feeling was more bitter. Labouchere, disappointed of office, wrote to Dilke, another disappointed man, in
October 1893: 'We are in the hands of an aged fetish of nothing
but HR, senilely anxious to retain power, and fancying he can do so
by tricking and dodging everyone.' Sidney Webb, who had once
'half killed Mr G., with his long yarns' and Bernard Shaw chose
this moment to announce the end of their co-operation with the
Liberals in an article 'To Your Tents, O Israel!' In December 1893
the matter of increasing the naval estimates came to the centre of
the stage. The Franco-Russian *rapprochement* made it seem more
important than ever that the British navy should remain superior
to any possible hostile combination; there was alarm about the loss
of a battleship in the Mediterranean as the result of a collision and
a more professional Board of Admiralty felt in a strong position to
ask for greater resources. The naval question spilt over into the
press and in the House of Commons Lord George Hamilton, the
opposition spokesman on naval affairs, moved for an increase in
the strength of the navy. It was a matter which touched Gladstone
on the raw: all his deeply held beliefs about militarism and economy
were under attack; the ghosts of Peel, Cobden, Bright, Aberdeen,
rose within him. Repeatedly he called the naval proposals 'drunk
and mad' and he despised his colleagues for not standing up to the
admirals. It was particularly painful to him that the trusted
Spencer backed these naval estimates as First Lord of the Admiralty.
Harcourt, who was usually with him on such an issue, at first
opposed Spencer, but afterwards became converted. Later Gladstone
suspected that Harcourt made a common cause with Spencer
because he wanted to go ahead with his ambitious budget. This

budget of 1894 introduced graduated estate duties and Gladstone after his retirement commented how much such an arrangement went against his own financial principles. On 9 January 1894 Gladstone confronted the Cabinet with his absolute opposition to the naval estimates and with the possibility of his resignation. He spoke for fifty minutes. His notes on his personal position read:

a Silent – and disgraced
b A survival.
   ¾ of my life, a continuous effort for economy
   Who could thus break himself in pieces?
c Eyes and ears.
   Warrant ample for going.
   Scanty for staying.[16]

Four days later Gladstone went to Biarritz. West, his secretary, went backwards and forwards between Biarritz and London to get him to relent on the estimates, as he had given way on Egypt and Uganda, but this time he would not give way. He wrote to Mundella, one of his most faithful supporters:

Liberalism cannot put on the garb of Jingoism without suffering for it . . . I am told that the govt cannot go on without me . . . If this be so some essential part of that confidence is confidence in me. If it is confidence in me, it is founded on my life and my actions. Now in them had been embedded for sixty years a constant effort to do all I could for economy and for peace . . . If the thing is to be done at all let it be done by those who think it *right* . . .[17]

Morley tried by letter to dissuade Gladstone from resigning and told him that the naval estimates would not be accepted by many as sufficient ground for so great a step. But in London Morley was shifting his ground and taking the resignation for granted. Gladstone had one more shot left in his locker. He once more proposed a dissolution of Parliament on the issue of the House of Lords. Looking back on his resignation later he listed this as one of the occasions in his life when his gift for right timing had been at work. But in the meantime his colleagues in London were coming to terms with his resignation and when West, largely for form's sake, consulted them on the dissolution proposal they were unanimously hostile. Harcourt telegraphed from his house in the New Forest: 'I consider proposal from abroad simply insane. Tell colleagues.' Gladstone's colleagues were in fact gradually overcoming the danger to a continuation of the Liberal government arising from the absence of an acknowledged heir. Gladstone had refused to raise up a Crown Prince. The choice lay between Harcourt and Rosebery and the scales were tilting towards the latter.

Gladstone returned to London on 10 February 1894. He still had not entirely given up the plan of a dissolution but events and his colleagues were steadily foreclosing the possibility. On 17 February there was a Cabinet dinner and ministers hoped that the Prime Minister would announce his resignation. 'After the servants had left the room ministers made constant pauses in the general conversation to allow Gladstone to commence any statement he had to make, but he never did so,' noted Harcourt's son in his Journal.[18] By now Gladstone must have felt considerable contempt for his colleagues and he hit back by letting them dangle a little longer. It was not until 27 February that Gladstone's resignation became definite. He had been turning over in his mind and seeking medical advice on whether his eyesight could be given as a sufficient reason for his retirement. This was the reason now given to the Queen for it was not desirable that she should learn of the deep divisions in the Cabinet on the naval estimates. Gladstone had an interview with the Queen, who was cheerful and clearly much relieved. On 1 March Gladstone held his last Cabinet. Kimberley tried to say a few appropriate words, but broke down. Then Harcourt took over; ' . . . he pulled from his pocket a handkerchief and a manuscript and at once commenced weeping loudly.' Gladstone remained impassive and it is difficult to tell whether he was moved or disgusted. Later he called it the 'blubbering Cabinet'. In the afternoon Gladstone made his last speech in the House of Commons in which he pointed to the position of the House of Lords as a major problem for the future. The following day he and Mrs Gladstone went to Windsor. His treatment there wounded the old man deeply and he kept reverting to it in the few remaining years of his life. He considered that the circumstances of his farewell 'were altogether without parallel'. He sometimes dreamt that the Queen had asked him to breakfast alone with her at 10 o'clock, but 'the hour never came'. He thought those dreams were an indication that 'the subject of my personal relations to the Queen, and all the unsatisfactory ending of my over half a century of service, had more hold upon me, down at root, than I was aware'. He was surprised that she did not ask his advice about his successor; had he been asked he would have named Spencer. He was the only one among those who were *papabile* with a real interest in Home Rule. Failing Spencer, Gladstone would have preferred Harcourt; his political differences with Rosebery had cut very deep. It was a consolation to Gladstone that the Queen felt more sympathetic towards his wife; retirement was probably a greater blow to her than to him. 'Mama has borne it very bravely, tho' nobody knows the blow it is to her. You know how she loves being inside the mainspring of history, and all the stir and stress and throb of the machine is life and breath to her,' wrote her daughter.

Gladstone was not the first overpowering public figure to find that his retirement was greeted with relief rather than regret in many quarters. He had retired for the first time nearly twenty years earlier; with the end of his second government in 1885 his political life was generally assumed to be over or nearly over. Then he had with a passion born of his religious faith taken up the cause of Irish Home Rule. Imperiously and sometimes with scant regard for realities or personalities, he had foisted this cause on his reluctant party and had in the process given a violent twist to the political kaleidoscope. For another eight years he had upheld the Home Rule banner, kept his own party and indeed the whole political dialogue upon his chosen track. Only the crushing disappointment of Parnell's fall had begun to weaken his hold on his followers. Would it have been better if he had stood aside earlier? Perhaps there might have been a better chance for the Liberal party to adapt itself to new social forces and to acquire new leaders. As the final crisis over naval estimates showed, the centre of Gladstone's career lay in the 1860s, in the age of economy, free trade, removal of religious inequalities. In the age of rival imperialisms, armaments races, Protectionism and class warfare he was 'a survival'. His point of reference was still an aristocratic society, based on land, but with a strong sense of moral obligation; to him the aim of social policy was to remove all the obstacles to the full expression of the individual moral personality. On the wider world stage the aim was to produce a community based on the freedom and self-expression of national groups. Some of these values seemed out of date in the 1890s or others, like the material welfare of the masses or the pursuit of national power and self-interest, seemed more important. Gladstone's values were, however, of perennial validity and he was determined never to allow his capacity for righteous indignation to wither or his sense of sin to be blunted.

Gladstone survived what he called his political death by four years. After an operation for cataract in 1894 he was still able to read and write, though more slowly and with greater difficulty. He wrote further articles on theology for the *Nineteenth Century*; brought out his edition of the works of Bishop Butler, who was to him throughout his life a guide of the greatest authority; and he put together a further volume of *Gleanings*. In spite of what he had said about Harcourt's death duties, he believed that men had an obligation to dispose much of their wealth before they died on charitable work. One of his major preoccupations was the foundation and endowment of St Deniol's Library at Hawarden as a centre of 'divine learning' and to combat unbelief. He contributed £30,000 to this foundation, as well as a large library, which he personally helped to arrange.

Even politically he was not quite dead yet. The Armenian mass-acres were the issue which forced him back into public pronounce-ments, for the first time at the end of 1894 and for the last time at Liverpool on 24 September 1896. Even had he been a younger man he would now have found it difficult to arouse the public conscience to the extent he had done twenty years before, although the atrocities were on a greater scale and occurred more repeatedly. Glad-stone's authority was, however, still so great that any move on his part caused more than a ripple in the muddied waters of Liberal politics. Nobody could be quite certain that he might not sweep back into the arena as he had done before. Rosebery in particular felt himself under the Gladstonian shadow and he took Gladstone's last public speech at Liverpool as the occasion for laying down the Liberal leadership.

Gladstone met the Queen for the last time in Cannes in March 1897. He took elaborate steps not to be seen to be forcing his presence on her, but he was much relieved when she held out her hand to him, a gesture she had never made even in the dim and distant past when he was in favour. He found her much altered and her facility for polite conversation almost gone. He thought she must soon abdicate. His own final illness, a painful cancer behind the cheekbone, showed its first symptoms in the autumn of 1897. He had often been unwell, but he had never been really ill and he found the pain hard to bear. 'In his worst bouts you may hear him in a voice of extraordinary fervour, "Praise to the Holiest in the height",' wrote his daughter, ' . . . but I never saw anybody mind it as he does.' He died on 19 May 1898 and was given a state funeral in Westminster Abbey. Rosebery, one of his pallbearers, described the scene:

A noble sight and ceremony. Mrs Gladstone a figure of indescribable pathos. Supported by her two sons she knelt at the head of the coffin, and when it was lowered seemed to wish to kiss the ground, saying 'once more, only once more' (I was close) with a dim idea, I think, that she was to kiss him, but the two sons gently raised her.[19]

CONCLUSION

Throughout his long life Gladstone was surrounded by controversy which increased in intensity as he came to the forefront of the public stage. Even now it is not easy to make a dispassionate assessment of him. His was an ardent, zealous personality and no one could remain indifferent to it. Was he the 'arch villain' of Disraeli's letters? Whatever Disraeli himself thought this is what many of Gladstone's opponents believed. Or was he 'a white old man with a face like a benediction and a voice like an Archangel's', as many of his adherents sincerely felt? Was the note of moral righteousness genuine or was it merely the result of an unusual capacity for self-deception? Was the sense of mission real or did it merely disguise a craving for power and self-importance? Such were the questions about him that contemporaries asked themselves and they were deeply divided in their answers.

To see Gladstone's career in perspective it is useful to divide it into phases. The first twenty years of his public life, from 1833 to 1853, were the formative phase, when his ideas and beliefs ripened in the light of experience. During the second phase, from 1853 to 1868, he was a major public figure, whose contribution to the national life, even had his career ended there, would have been regarded as of high historical importance. During the last phase, from 1868 until his retirement, he was a dominant figure, with paramount influence to shape the framework and the substance of British politics for his time and for many years to come.

During the formative period Gladstone's liberal–conservative outlook became established. His identification with ultra-Toryism was temporary and went deep only on religious and ecclesiastical questions. Within less than two years of entering Parliament he had become a 'ministerial man'; a personal follower of Peel and of the enlightened, pragmatic Conservatism characteristic of Peel. Gladstone's assimilation to Peelite Conservatism was completed during his membership of Peel's government from 1841 through the practical experience of dealing with trade and industry. Along with his chief he advanced towards acceptance of most of the prevailing tenets of *laissez-faire* economics on internal as well as external trade. His views on the Church and her position within the civil community were slower to change; in his personal religious beliefs he remained the High Anglican which he had become after moving away from the evangelicalism of his family background. Gladstone's great moral sensitivity and acute feeling for justice made him aware, however, that his view of the Church as the sole legitimate expression of the spiritual aspect of the nation could no longer be maintained without serious injustice to the large non-Anglican part of the population. Thus he came to embrace the idea of religious liberty in its fullest sense. His support for the Maynooth grant in 1845 was an indication that he had advanced to this position. The same sense of justice and morality helped him in the evolution of his ideas on the international community. The Peelite tradition of foreign policy was one of cautious stewardship of the national interest combined with a commitment to peace and economy in defence expenditure. Gladstone had in addition a lively sense of the unity of European civilization which came to him through his study of the classics and of the Christian religion and churches. It only needed the contact with flagrant injustice and oppression, such as he experienced in the Neapolitan prisons, to bring his dedication to international justice to full flower.

By the time he became Chancellor of the Exchequer in 1853 Gladstone's ideological position was fully formed and only the emphasis changed here and there in the light of subsequent circumstances and experience. He had also found his personal style. In a sense his political vocation remained always a second best to the call to enter the Church which he had felt so strongly towards the end of his Oxford days. He was always searching – for God, for truth, for justice. Only when he found a cause to which he could fully commit himself were his highest powers released. He was also a preacher – oratory gave him his hold over men and from it he drew exhilaration. He could persuade and overpower with words and he could even persuade himself. Once in later life he exclaimed: 'I wish you knew the state of total impotence to which I should be reduced if there were no echo to the accents of my own voice.' In many ways his motive and temperament were not those most suitable to a politician, but here his great and efficient intellect helped him. He had the stature to act without the slightest regard to expediency and he could be utterly innocent; but he also developed great powers of casuistry and manoeuvre, at once feared and derided by his opponents.

The budget of 1853 made Gladstone into a national figure of the first rank. At the Board of Trade a decade earlier he had already given proof of his vast capacity for work and high administrative ability. Now he demonstrated his gifts on an even wider stage; over the next ten to fifteen years he was given much credit for the growth of national prosperity. He became the hero of the middle classes and increasingly of those below them who shared in the general prosperity. For some years yet, however, his own future between the parties remained uncertain and for a time after the Crimean War his career seemed to be becalmed; but his standing in Parliament was so high that in spite of his own doubts and indecisions there was never much likelihood that he would be left out in the cold. In 1859 he at last threw in his lot with the Whig–Radical amalgam that was to become the Liberal party. His views, the actions of his remaining Peelite friends, personalities, particularly Disraeli's, and calculations of personal advantage contributed to this decisive step. As a member of Palmerston's government he further enhanced his reputation as a public financier and gradually moved into a position where the succession to the party leadership was likely to fall upon him after the departure of the 'two terrible old men', Palmerston and Russell.

The most important factor in Gladstone's advancement was the growing *rapport* between him and the masses who were still outside the *pays politique*. Without departing from his essential liberal conservatism, he felt an increasing confidence in their moral sense, respectability and responsibility; while they saw in him the one major parliamentary and governmental figure who sympathized with their aspirations. Gladstone now found that his oratorical gift was as effective on the platform as it had been in the House of Commons; this helped him to forge his link with the masses while giving him extra weight on the parliamentary scene. After Palmerston's death he reached the first place on the Liberal side in the House of Commons; even his indifferent performance over reform in 1866 and 1867, which showed up his weakness as a manager of men, could not prevent his eventual succession to the leadership.

Gladstone's personality and leadership were two of the key factors in the formation of the Liberal party and in the history of the party for the next quarter of a century. 'When I do not know what to say, I say "Gladstone" and then they are sure to cheer, and I have time to think,' said a candidate in the election of 1868. In many ways Gladstone and the Liberal 'broad church' made strange bedfellows. He was not completely identified with any of the sections that made up the party. Perhaps the Whigs were closest to him on personal grounds; through the Glynnes he was related to many of them. Granville was his most intimate political friend; he felt a strong sense of obligation to men like Hartington and regarded it as natural that they should occupy the leading positions in his Cabinets. He continued to believe that the aristocracy had an essential role to play in government and in society at large. Yet Gladstone was by no stretch of the imagination a Whig; most Whigs were very conscious that he was not one of them and 'Liverpool underneath'. Politically they were intensely suspicious of him and finally they parted company from him in 1886.

The relationship between Gladstone and the Nonconformists was complex. He and they believed firmly that public action had to come from a basis of morality, and this was a very strong bond between them. It gave Gladstonian liberalism its particular flavour. Much of what he wanted to do to free individuals and society from unjust restraints was precisely what the Nonconformists also wanted. Yet he was not one of them; as a High Churchman he was far removed from them in doctrine and undoubtedly it came hard to him to deliver some of the things they wanted. The relationship had its ups and downs: formed in the 1860s, it was seriously disturbed after 1870 by the education controversy, only to be repaired in the days of the Bulgarian atrocities campaign.

Gladstone had sprung from that middle class engaged in commerce and industry which still formed the backbone of the Liberal party. But he had long grown away from his roots and the Flintshire landowner with many aristocratic connections and a lifetime in high politics had little in common with the middle classes of the later nineteenth century. As for the working classes, the masses, Gladstone's ability to appeal to them had helped his rise to the top. Increasingly he persuaded himself that their moral instincts were sound while that of the classes had been corrupted; only right at the end of his public life did he in turn begin to doubt the moral soundness of the masses. That a patrician sounding a note of conscience could appeal so strongly to a large number of people in the Victorian age is a remarkable fact; it owed little to Gladstone's understanding of the masses and not much to their understanding of him.

He was therefore a leader detached from those he led and that is how he saw his position. He was in politics for a cause and if men would follow whither he thought it right to go he eagerly seized the opportunity. But when his ammunition was spent he would rather withdraw than drift into a humdrum administration of affairs. Thus for all but the first three or four of his twenty-five years as Liberal leader he was always contemplating, more or less realistically, the possibility of retirement. When he was in charge he did not see his function in the same light as many modern prime ministers and party leaders would. In Cabinet he would have thought himself as usurping the prerogatives of others if he had not left his colleagues their full autonomy within their departmental responsibilities; but once measures had been agreed he supported them with the full weight of his great authority in the House of Commons. He made little attempt to control his parliamentary followers through the normal devices of party management; with them he again relied on the power of his oratory and the respect and veneration inspired by his personality. As time went on and the moment of retirement was forever postponed his position of detachment became perhaps less convincing than he himself cared to admit. His family and entourage found it even more difficult than he did to give up their position at the centre of affairs and thus there was an element of inertia in Gladstone's prolonged retention of the Liberal leadership in the 1880s.

K

During his first government, however, Gladstone was at the height of his powers and entirely in tune with the spirit of the age. The political lethargy of Palmerston's final years had been dispelled and work was waiting to be done. Gladstone could lend his powerful support to virtually all of it with conviction, even if some of it was on the periphery of his own interests. The common denominator of the policies and legislation of this period was the removal of unjust barriers and privileges that inhibited individuals and groups from finding full self-expression. Gladstone's own particular crusade on Ireland was based on the concept of justice and fair dealing between nations; if this was the basis of Gladstonian foreign policy, how much more important that it should be fully implemented in respect of a country like Ireland, over which Britain had full control. It was with such altruistic arguments above all that he tried to convince his countrymen that they should support him in his long Irish campaign.

When Gladstone emerged from his retirement in 1876 it was to put the same arguments in an even greater and more general cause. In the campaign over the Bulgarian atrocities and the Eastern Question he reached his peak as a popular statesman; one of the two camps into which the nation was split at this time, a camp that included all manner of men, from Dissenters to High Anglicans, from the working man to the intellectual, hung upon his every word. As long as he was in opposition he could, in spite of his eloquence and large following, do little to change policy. When the election of 1880 brought him back into office he felt it to be his main task before his final retirement to reverse the policies of 'Beaconsfieldism', for which the nation had given him a mandate. But now his retirement receded forever over the horizon: the opportunity to depart somehow never came. Ireland again kept him chained to the mast; but, above all, his overpowering presence seemed the only barrier to factional chaos in the Liberal party. At least one more major reform, a further extension of the franchise, was waiting to be accomplished; he engaged his still incomparable powers as a parliamentarian in this cause and without him this question could perhaps not have been so completely settled. But in foreign policy these years were frequently agonizing; the gulf between Gladstonian principles and the realities of a world dominated by imperial rivalries became too great. Even in home affairs Gladstone was increasingly out of sympathy with what he called the 'constructionism' that was being demanded by the radical wing of his party. Had he retired in 1885, however, no marked decline in his powers could have been recorded, nor could there have been, given his achievements over the third Reform Bill, a feeling that he had seriously outrun his lease.

Instead he took the fateful decision not only to continue to lead the Liberals through the next election, but after the election to attempt the Home Rule solution for Ireland, which must seriously divide his followers. In many ways it was a heroic effort, justified in the light of history because it was one of the few real opportunities to cut through the unhappy tangle of Anglo-Irish relations. But it was largely due to Gladstone's personality and his handling of the Home Rule crisis that so deep, damaging and lasting a split occurred in the Liberal ranks. In this lay the obverse of his greatness and his genius. The question arises how great a blight not only the split but the further continuation of Gladstone's leadership for another eight years cast upon Liberal prospects. In many ways the party was not ready to produce the new progressive policies which the conditions of the age and the electors increasingly demanded and even if Gladstone had retired in 1885 it would have required time to find new leaders and new ideas and adapt the structure of the party to changing needs. The fate and development of parties has, however, often depended on small events which tilt the balance hither or thither. The split of 1886 was a major blow that stacked the cards against the Liberals for many years to come, though it can also be seen as a reassertion of the two-party system by the two major party leaders, Gladstone and Salisbury. The continuing presence of Gladstone's towering figure until 1894 made the emergence of new leaders and new ideas much more difficult. Gladstone was now neither able nor willing to initiate new policies. Most of the new proposals that were in the air were uncongenial to him and he was only reluctantly prepared to accept them. In his conversation in these final years of his public life he was often in a backward-looking and reminiscing mood. When he was a guest at All Souls in February 1890 he said that all the real reforms of the period between 1830 and 1880 would have been carried by the unreformed House of Commons. A wide franchise was not an advantage to the cause of reform, he felt, though he accepted democracy. Such talk, to be expected from an old man, perhaps exaggerates his alienation from the times in which he was now living. For his age he still had an astonishing sense of purpose and his ideals were by no means blunted. Even in 1896 Balfour could still say of him: 'He is, and always was, in everything except essentials a tremendous Tory,' but Gladstone's grasp of essentials had not slipped. Nevertheless, it is difficult to avoid the conclusion that his final years added little to his reputation and did harm to the Liberal party which was so much of his own creation.

Peel was the first major political figure alongside whom Gladstone worked and in some ways he remained all his life a Peelite liberal-conservative. Great as his admiration for Peel was, the two men were temperamentally very different. Although there was warmth beneath Peel's cold exterior, he had none of Gladstone's ardour or quest for causes; the volcanic eruptions which from time to time resolved Gladstone's doubts and propelled him with great force along a new path were quite alien to Peel. Gladstone and Palmerston had virtually nothing in common; reason occasionally told Gladstone to respect Palmerston's professional ability, but most of the time he found it hard to approve so pagan a figure. Palmerston's hatred for Gladstone, so strenuous, so unrelenting, was only thinly disguised. It is astonishing that in the eight years during which they were leading men in the same Cabinets they did not clash even more frequently and violently. The man to whom Gladstone is most often held up for comparison is his great antagonist Disraeli. It is hardly necessary to enlarge on the depth of the gulf that divided them politically, morally and temperamentally. In constructive achievement and sheer energy over a wide range of human activity Gladstone was much the greater man. Disraeli excelled him clearly in one vital respect: imagination, sometimes quaint and quixotic, but occasionally visionary and percipient. It is for this reason that Disraeli's name continues to be invoked by Tories as having a message relevant right into our own day; while Gladstone, so powerful an inspiration in his lifetime, was soon felt to belong entirely to the past. Such a judgement does not do him full justice. When he was at his best, Gladstone's vision went deep and was very radical. From his immensely strong and firmly rooted Christian frame of reference he could assess a problem *sub specie aeternitatis* and find the right solution. When he had done so nothing could stop him from throwing the whole weight of his dynamic personality into the task of achieving the solution. Such a man can sometimes deceive himself and he may commit gross tactical errors. But he can also move mountains, and this is the lesson to be learnt from Gladstone's life.

NOTES

Chapter 1: Liverpool Underneath 1809–32

1. S.G.Checkland, *The Gladstones, A Family Biography 1764–1851*, Cambridge University Press, 1971, pp. 414–16
2. John Brooke and Mary Sorensen, eds., *The Prime Ministers' Papers: W.E.Gladstone I: Autobiographica*, H.M.S.O., 1971, p. 13
3. W.R.Ward, *Victorian Oxford*, F.Cass, 1965, particularly pp. 50 ff.; also David Newsome, *The Parting of Friends. A Study of the Wilberforces and Henry Manning*, Murray, 1966, pp. 62 ff.
4. Brooke and Sorensen, op. cit., p. 35
5. ibid., pp. 220–29
6. M.R.D.Foot, ed., *The Gladstone Diaries*, Oxford University Press, 1968, vol. I, pp. 495, 473. See also W.E. Gladstone, 'The Evangelical Movement; its parentage, progress and issue', *Gleanings of Past Years*, John Murray, 1879, vol. VII, pp. 201–41

Chapter 2: The Rising Hope 1832–41

1. A.F. Robbins, *The Early Public Life of William Ewart Gladstone*, Methuen, 1894, pp. 116–18
2. S.G.Checkland, *The Gladstones. A Family Biography 1764-1851*, Cambridge University Press, 1971, p. 259
3. John Brooke and Mary Sorensen, eds., *The Prime Ministers' Papers: W.E.Gladstone II : Autobiographical Memoranda*, H.M.S.O., 1972, p. 5
4. Robbins, op. cit., pp. 134–5
5. B.Disraeli, *Coningsby* (Bradenham Edn), p. 97
6. O.Macdonagh, *A Pattern of Government Growth, 1800–60: The Passenger Acts and their Enforcement*, MacGibbon & Kee, 1961, pp. 85–9
7. N.Gash, *Sir Robert Peel: The Life of Sir Robert Peel after 1830*, Longman, 1972, pp. 121 ff.
8. P.Magnus, *Gladstone: A Biography*, Murray, 1954, pp. 23 ff.
9. M.R.D.Foot, ed., *The Gladstone Diaries*, Oxford University Press, 1968, vol. II, pp. 189, 252, 23 August 1835 and 4 August 1836
10. Robbins, op. cit., p. 289
11. Select Committee on the Working of the Apprenticeship System in the Colonies, 1836 (560) xv. 1 and 1837 (510) vii. 745
12. A.R.Vidler, *The Orb and the Cross*, S.P.C.K., 1954, p. 44
13. Georgina Battiscombe, *Mrs Gladstone: The Portrait of a Marriage*, Constable, 1954, pp. 23 ff.

Chapter 3: Governing Packages 1841–6

1. F.E.Hyde, *Mr Gladstone at the Board of Trade*, Cobden, Sanderson, 1934, p. 43
2. John Brooke and Mary Sorensen, eds., *The Prime Ministers' Papers: W.E.Gladstone II : Autobiographical Memoranda*, H.M.S.O., 1972, p. 170
3. Lucy Brown, *The Board of Trade and the Free Trade Movement 1830–1842*, Oxford University Press, 1958, pp. 225 ff.
4. John Brooke and Mary Sorensen, eds., *The Prime Ministers' Papers: W.E.Gladstone I : Autobiographica*, H.M.S.O., 1971, p. 46
5. Hyde, op. cit., p. 73
6. H.Parris, *Government and the Railways in Nineteenth Century Britain*, Routledge & Kegan Paul, 1965, pp. 55 ff.
7. W.P.Morrell, *British Colonial Policy in the Age of Peel and Russell*, Oxford University Press, 1930, pp. 393–4

Chapter 4: A Party of Observation 1846–53

1. W.R.Ward, *Victorian Oxford*, F.Cass, 1965, p. 44
2. J.B.Conacher, *The Peelites and the Party System, 1846–52*, David & Charles, Newton Abbot, 1972, pp. 23–4
3. D.C.Lathbury, ed., *Correspondence on Church and Religion of W.E.Gladstone*, John Murray, 1910, vol. II, p. 5
4. Conacher, op. cit., Appendix A

5. P.Magnus, *Gladstone: A Biography*, Murray, 1954, pp. 92–4
6. D.W.R.Bahlman, ed., *The Diary of Sir Edward Hamilton*, Oxford University Press, 1972, vol. I, pp. 269–70
7. J.Prest, *Lord John Russell*, Macmillan, 1972, pp. 275–9
8. E.S.Purcell, *Life of Cardinal Manning*, Macmillan, 1896, vol. I, pp. 569–75
9. R.Blake, *Disraeli*, Eyre & Spottiswoode, 1966, p. 297
10. Conacher, op. cit., p. 70
11. J.T.Ward, *Sir James Graham*, Macmillan, 1967, p. 257
12. R.Stewart, *The Politics of Protection: Lord Derby and the Protectionist Party, 1841–1852*, Cambridge University Press, 1971, p. 199

Chapter 5: A Most Rigid Economist 1853–8

1. J.Ridley, *Palmerston*, Constable, 1970, p. 105
2. A.C.Benson, Esher, Viscount and Buckle,G.E., eds., *Letters of Queen Victoria 1837-61*, John Murray, 1907–32, vol. II, p. 491
3. W.R.Ward, *Victorian Oxford*, F.Cass, 1965, p. 177
4. J.B.Conacher, *The Aberdeen Coalition 1852–1855: A Study in Mid-Nineteenth-Century Party Politics*, Cambridge University Press, 1968, p. 227
5. K.Martin, *The Triumph of Lord Palmerston: A Study of Public Opinion in England before the Crimean War*, Hutchinson, 1963, p. 153
6. O.Anderson, *A Liberal State at War. English Politics and Economics during the Crimean War*, Macmillan, 1967, pp. 194 ff.
7. E.Hughes, 'Sir Charles Trevelyan and Civil Service Reform, 1853–5', *English Historical Review* LXIV (1949), and 'Civil Service Reform, 1853–5', *History* XXVII (1942)
8. Conacher, op. cit., p. 340–41
9. ibid., p. 408
10. ibid., p. 532
11. W.D.James, *Lord Derby and Victorian Conservatism*, Oxford University Press, 1956, p. 218
12. W.E.Gladstone, *Gleanings of Past Years*, John Murray, 1879, vol. VI, p. 49

Chapter 6: Getting Unmuzzled 1858–65

1. Lord Stanmore, *Sidney Herbert, Lord Herbert of Lea: A Memoir*, John Murray, 1906, vol. II, pp. 167–8
2. ibid., vol. II, pp. 196–7
3. D.Read, *Cobden and Bright: A Victorian Political Partnership*, Arnold, 1967, pp. 111 ff.
4. A.A.Iliasu, 'The Cobden–Chevalier Commercial Treaty of 1860', *Historical Journal* XIV (1971)
5. P.Guedalla, ed., *Gladstone and Palmerston*, Gollancz, 1928, p. 212
6. ibid., p. 169
7. J.Ridley, *Lord Palmerston*, Constable, 1970, p. 497
8. J.R.Vincent, *The Formation of the Liberal Party, 1857–1868*, Constable, 1966; Penguin Books, Harmondsworth, 1972, p. 219

9. R. Harrison, *Before the Socialists: Studies in Labour and Politics 1861-1881*, Routledge & Kegan Paul, 1965, pp. 40–77
10. G.M.Trevelyan, *The Life of John Bright*, Constable, 1913, p. 320
11. Georgina Battiscombe, *Mrs Gladstone: The Portrait of a Marriage*, Constable, 1954, p. 126
12. Ridley, op. cit., p. 563
13. W.R.Ward, *Victorian Oxford*, F.Cass, 1965, p. 232

Chapter 7: The Pale of the Constitution 1865–8

1. M.Cowling, *1867: Disraeli, Gladstone and Revolution: The Passing of the Second Reform Bill*, Cambridge University Press, 1967, pp. 101–2
2. Paul Smith, ed., *Lord Salisbury on Politics. A Selection from his Articles in the Quarterly Review, 1860–1883*, Cambridge University Press, 1972, p. 229
3. Cowling, op. cit., p. 105
4. D.C.Lathbury, ed., *Correspondence on Church and Religion of W.E.Gladstone*, John Murray, 1910, vol. I, p. 57
5. F.B.Smith, *The Making of the Second Reform Bill*, Cambridge University Press, 1966, p. 159
6. R.Blake, *Disraeli*, Eyre & Spottiswoode, 1966, p. 465
7. F.B.Smith, op. cit., p. 184
8. H.J.Hanham, *Elections and Party Management: Politics in the Time of Disraeli and Gladstone*, Longman, 1959, p. 294
9. W.E.Gladstone, *Gleanings of Past Years*, John Murray, 1879, vol. VII, pp. 97–151
10. F.M.Leventhal, *Respectable Radical: George Howell and Victorian Working Class Politics*, Weidenfeld & Nicolson, 1971, pp. 93 ff.
11. J.D.Clayton, 'Mr Gladstone's Leadership of the Parliamentary Liberal Party 1868–1874', D.Phil. thesis, Oxford University, 1960, pp. 27 ff.

Chapter 8: Zenith 1868–73

1. J.L.Hammond, *Gladstone and the Irish Nation*, F.Cass, 1964, p. 98; E.D.Steele, *Irish Land and British Politics. Tenant-Right and Nationality 1865–1870*, Cambridge University Press, 1974, passim
2. A.Ramm, ed., *The Political Correspondence of Mr Gladstone and Lord Granville 1868–1876*, Oxford University Press, 1952, vol. I, pp. 170–72
3. Asa Briggs, Introduction to Francis Adams, *History of the Elementary School Contest* (1873), reprinted, Harvester Press, Brighton, 1972, p. xxix
4. 'Mr Forster and Ireland', *Nineteenth Century* XXIV (1888), p. 453
5. W.E.Gladstone, 'Germany, France and England 1870', *Gleanings of Past Years*, John Murray, 1879, vol. IV, pp. 197–257
6. E.Drus, ed., *John, First Earl of Kimberley, A Journal of Events during the Gladstone Ministry 1868–1874*, Royal Historical Society, London, 1958, p. 23

7. W.H.G.Armytage, *A.J.Mundella, 1825–1897: The Liberal Background to the Labour Movement*, Benn, 1951, p. 96
8. Sir R.Biddulph, *Lord Cardwell at the War Office*, John Murray, 1904, p. 103
9. B.Harrison, *Drink and the Victorians: The Temperance Question in England, 1815–1872*, Faber & Faber, 1971, p. 269
10. A.Ponsonby, *Henry Ponsonby*, Macmillan, 1943, p. 252
11. E.R.Norman, *The Catholic Church and Ireland in the Age of Rebellion*, Longman, 1965, p. 443
12. Drus, op. cit., p. 37
13. J.D.Clayton, 'Mr Gladstone's Leadership of the Parliamentary Liberal Party, 1868–1874', D.Phil. thesis, Oxford University, 1960, p. 118

Chapter 9: Bag and Baggage 1873–80

1. R.R.James, 'Gladstone and the Greenwich Seat', *History Today* IX (1959); W.H.Maehl, 'Gladstone, the Liberals and the Election of 1874', *Bulletin of the Institute of Historical Research* XXXVI (1963)
2. D.Bowen, *The Idea of the Victorian Church: A Study of the Church of England 1833–1889*, McGill-Queen's University Press, London, 1968, p. 167
3. R.T.Shannon, *Gladstone and the Bulgarian Agitation 1876*, Nelson, 1963, pp. 99 ff.
4. Lucy Masterman, ed., *Mary Gladstone (Mrs Drew): Her Diaries and Letters*, Methuen, 1930, p. 109
5. J.Bailey, ed., *The Diary of Lady Frederick Cavendish*, John Murray, 1927, vol. II, p. 204
6. R.Blake, *Disraeli*, Eyre & Spottiswoode, 1966, p. 602
7. Bailey, op. cit., vol. II, p. 199
8. Shannon, op. cit., pp. 202–11
9. J.L.Garvin, *Life of Joseph Chamberlain*, Macmillan, 1932, vol. I, pp. 260–61
10. A.Ramm, *The Political Correspondence of Mr Gladstone and Lord Granville 1876–1886*, Oxford University Press, 1962, vol. I, p. 99
11. Masterman, op. cit., p. 183
12. M.R.D.Foot, ed., *Midlothian Speeches 1879*, Leicester University Press, 1971, p. 37

Chapter 10: The Ageing Titan 1880–85

1. E.J.Feuchtwanger, *Disraeli, Democracy and the Tory Party*, Oxford University Press, 1968, pp. 63–4
2. *Letters of Disraeli to Lady Bradford and Lady Chesterfield 1873–81*, 2 vols., Benn, 1929, vol. II, p. 278
3. W.L.Arnstein, *The Bradlaugh Case: A Study in Late Victorian Opinion and Politics*, Oxford University Press, 1965, pp. 59 ff.
4. D.W.R.Bahlman, ed., *The Diary of Sir E.W.Hamilton*, Oxford University Press, 1972, vol. I, p. 151

L

5. A. Ramm, ed., *The Political Correspondence of Mr Gladstone and Lord Granville 1876–1886*, Oxford University Press, 1962, vol. I, p. 181

6. D. M. Schreuder, *Gladstone and Kruger: Liberal Government and Colonial 'Home Rule' 1880–85*, Routledge & Kegan Paul, 1969, p. 60

7. Bahlman, op. cit., vol. I, p. 114

8. J. L. Garvin, *Life of Joseph Chamberlain*, Macmillan, 1932, vol. I, p. 332

9. P. Guedalla, ed., *The Queen and Mr Gladstone*, Hodder & Stoughton, 1933, vol. II, p. 153

10. J. L. Hammond, *Gladstone and the Irish Nation*, F. Cass, 1964, p. 290

11. A. T. Bassett, ed., *Gladstone to his Wife*, Methuen, 1936, p. 239

12. A. Jones, *The Politics of Reform 1884*, Cambridge University Press, 1972, p. 15

13. Bahlman, op. cit., vol. II, p. 741

Chapter 11: Home Rule 1885–6

1. Quoted in A. Jones, *The Politics of Reform 1884*, Cambridge University Press, 1972, p. 51, n. 4

2. A. B. Cooke and John Vincent, *The Governing Passion. Cabinet Government and Party Politics in Britain 1885–86*, Harvester Press, Brighton, 1974, pp. 25–30 and 173–89

3. A. B. Cooke and J. R. Vincent, eds., *Lord Carlingford's Journals: Reflections of a Cabinet Minister, 1885*, Oxford University Press, 1971, p. 134

4. Diary of Sir E. W. Hamilton, Add. MS 48642

5. Macmillan's Morley Box, Add. MS 56447, Bryce to Gladstone, 12 March 1886, Russell to Gladstone, 17 March 1886; see also Cooke and Vincent, *The Governing Passion*, pp. 156–7

6. T. P. O'Connor, *Memoirs of an Old Parliamentarian*, Benn, 1929, vol. II, pp. 43–4

7. Diary of Sir E. W. Hamilton, Add. MS 48644

Chapter 12: Almost a Nullity 1886–98

1. Macmillan's Morley Box, Add. MS 56445, typed copy

2. M. Hurst, *Joseph Chamberlain and Liberal Reunion: The Round Table Conference of 1887*, David & Charles, Newton Abbot, 1967, p. 286

3. C. C. O'Brien, *Parnell and His Party, 1880–90*, Oxford University Press, 1957, p. 193

4. L. P. Curtis, Jr, *Coercion and Conciliation in Ireland, 1880–92: A Study in Conservative Unionism*, Princeton University Press, Princeton, N.J., 1963, p. 205

5. T. W. Moody, 'Michael Davitt and the British Labour Movement', *Transactions of the Royal Historical Society*, 5th series, vol. III (1953)

6. D. A. Hamer, *Liberal Politics in the Age of Gladstone and Rosebery*, Oxford University Press, 1972, p. 147
7. Curtis, op. cit., p. 290
8. Lucy Masterman, ed., *Mary Gladstone (Mrs Drew): Her Diaries and Letters*, Methuen, 1930, p. 408
9. H. G. Hutchinson, ed., *The Private Diaries of Sir Algernon West*, John Murray, 1922, p. 96
10. F. S. L. Lyons, *The Fall of Parnell, 1890–91*, Routledge & Kegan Paul, 1960, pp. 85–9
11. J. Morley, *Recollections*, Macmillan, 1921, vol. I, p. 236
12. Hamer, op. cit., p. 170
13. E. Dicey, 'The Rival Coalitions', *Nineteenth Century*, January 1891
14. P. Stansky, *Ambitions and Strategies: The Struggle for the Leadership of the Liberal Party in the 1890s*, Oxford University Press, 1964, p. 8
15. R. R. James, *Rosebery: A Biography of Archibald Philip, Fifth Earl of Rosebery*, Weidenfeld & Nicolson, 1963, p. 266
16. ibid., p. 294
17. Stansky, op. cit., p. 35
18. A. G. Gardiner, *The Life of Sir William Harcourt*, Constable, 1923, vol. II, p. 262
19. James, op. cit., p. 401

BIBLIOGRAPHY

The Gladstone Papers, mostly in the British Museum (Add. MSS 44086–835), is the largest nineteenth-century collection of private papers. A recent addition to them are papers which Morley abstracted from the archives at Hawarden while writing his Life of Gladstone and deposited with his publisher, Macmillans (Add. MSS 56444–53). Significant material remains at Hawarden. Many of the most important documents on Gladstone's life can be consulted in print in the following works:

Bassett, A.T., ed., *Gladstone to his Wife*, Methuen, 1936
Brooke, John and Sorensen, Mary, eds., *The Prime Ministers' Papers: W.E.Gladstone I: Autobiographica. II: Autobiographical Memoranda*, H.M.S.O., 1971–2

Foot, M.R.D. and Matthew, H.C.G., eds., *The Gladstone Diaries* (*1825–54*), 4 vols., Oxford University Press, 1968–75

Guedalla, P., ed., *Gladstone and Palmerston*, Gollancz, 1928

Guedalla, P., ed., *The Queen and Mr Gladstone*, 2 vols., Hodder & Stoughton, 1933

Lathbury, D.C., ed., *Correspondence on Church and Religion of W.E. Gladstone*, 2 vols., John Murray, 1910

Morley, John, *Life of William Ewart Gladstone*, 3 vols., Macmillan, 1903

Ramm, Agatha, ed., *The Political Correspondence of Mr Gladstone and Lord Granville 1868–1876*, 2 vols., Oxford University Press, 1952

Ramm, Agatha, ed., *The Political Correspondence of Mr Gladstone and Lord Granville 1876–1886*, 2 vols., Oxford University Press, 1962

The Diary of Sir Edward Hamilton, one of Gladstone's private secretaries during his second period as Prime Minister, is available in print for the years 1880–85 (2 vols., edited by Dudley W.R.Bahlman, Oxford University Press, 1972). Subsequent volumes of the diary are in the British Museum (Add. MSS 48641–83).

Other biographies, diaries, memoirs, etc., concerning Gladstone and the Gladstone family:

Archer, T., *William Ewart Gladstone and his Contemporaries*, Blackie, Edinburgh, 1883

Bagehot, Walter, *Biographical Studies*, 1881

Bailey, J., ed., *The Diary of Lady Frederick Cavendish*, 2 vols., John Murray, 1927

Battiscombe, G., *Mrs Gladstone: The Portrait of a Marriage*, Constable, 1954

Birrell, Francis, *Gladstone*, Duckworth, 1933

Burdett, O.H., *W.E.Gladstone*, Constable, 1927

Checkland, S.G., *The Gladstones. A Family Biography 1764–1851*, Cambridge University Press, 1971

Eyck, Erich, *Gladstone*, trans. Bernard Miall, F. Cass, 1938

Fletcher, C.R.L., 'William Ewart Gladstone at Oxford, 1890', Cornhill Magazine, 1908

Gladstone, Viscount, *After Thirty Years*, Macmillan, 1928

Hamilton, Sir E.W., *Mr Gladstone*, John Murray, 1898

McCarthy, Justin, *The Story of Gladstone's Life*, A. & C. Black, 1898

Magnus, Philip, *Gladstone: A Biography*, Murray, 1954

Masterman, Lucy, ed., *Mary Gladstone (Mrs Drew): Her Diaries and Letters*, Methuen, 1930

Paul, H.W., *Life of W.E.Gladstone*, Smith, Elder, 1901

Reid, Sir Thomas Wemyss, ed., *The Life of William Ewart Gladstone*, Cassell, 1899

Robbins, Sir Alfred Farthing, *The Early Public Life of William Ewart Gladstone*, Methuen, 1894

Russell, G.W.E., *The Right Honourable W.E.Gladstone*, 5th edn, Dent, 1906

Tollemache, Lionel Arthur, *Talks with Mr Gladstone*, Arnold, 1898

Works by W.E.Gladstone:

The State in its Relations with the Church, John Murray, 1838
Church Principles Considered in their Results, John Murray, 1840
Gleanings of Past Years, 7 vols., John Murray, 1879
Midlothian Speeches 1879, intro. M.R.D.Foot, Leicester University Press, 1971
The Irish Question, John Murray, 1886
'The History of 1852–1860 and Greville's Latest Journals', *English Historical Review* II (1887)
Later Gleanings, John Murray, 1897
Bassett, A.T., *Gladstone's Speeches: descriptive index and bibliography*, Methuen, 1916

Biographies, diaries, memoirs, etc.:

Akers-Douglas, E.A. (3rd Viscount Chilston), *Chief Whip: the political life and times of Aretas Akers-Douglas, 1st Viscount Chilston*, Routledge & Kegan Paul, 1961
Ashwell, A.R., and Wilberforce, R.G., *Life of Samuel Wilberforce*, 3 vols., John Murray, 1880–82
Argyll, Dowager Duchess of, ed., *George Douglas, eighth Duke of Argyll, Autobiography and Memoirs*, 2 vols., John Murray, 1906
Armytage, W.H.G., *A.J.Mundella 1825–1897: the Liberal Background to the Labour Movement*, Benn, 1951
Bell, H.C.F., *Lord Palmerston*, 2 vols., F.Cass, 1936
Benson, A.C., Esher, Viscount, and Buckle, G.E., eds., *Letters of Queen Victoria*, 3rd series, 9 vols., John Murray, 1907–32
Best, G.F.A., *Shaftesbury*, Batsford, 1964
Blake, R., *Disraeli*, Eyre & Spottiswoode, 1966
Cecil, Lady Gwendolen, *The Life of Robert, Marquis of Salisbury*, 4 vols., Hodder & Stoughton, 1921–31
Cooke, A.B., and Vincent, J.R., eds., *Lord Carlingford's Journals: Reflections of a Cabinet Minister, 1885*, Oxford University Press, 1971
Drus, E., ed., John, First Earl of Kimberley, *A Journal of Events during the Gladstone Ministry 1868–1874*, Royal Historical Society, London, 1958
Figgis, J.N., and Lawrence, R.V., eds., *Selections from the Correspondence of the First Lord Acton*, Longman, vol. I, 1917
Fitzmaurice, Lord Edmond, *The Life of Granville George Leveson-Gower, second Earl Granville*, 2 vols., Longman, 1905
Fraser, P., *Joseph Chamberlain, Radicalism and Empire, 1868–1914*, Cassell, 1966
Fulford, Roger, ed., *The Greville Memoirs, 1814-1860*, 8 vols., Macmillan, 1938
Gardiner, A.G., *The Life of Sir William Harcourt*, 2 vols., Constable, 1923
Garvin, J.L., *Life of Joseph Chamberlain*, vols. I and II, Macmillan, 1932
Gash, Norman, *Mr Secretary Peel: The Life of Sir Robert Peel to 1830*, Longman, 1961

Gash, Norman, *Sir Robert Peel: The Life of Sir Robert Peel after 1830*, Longman, 1972

Gooch, G.P., ed., *The Later Correspondence of Lord John Russell*, 2 vols., Longman, 1925

Hamer, D.A., *John Morley. Liberal Intellectual in Politics*, Oxford University Press, 1968

Hamer, F.E., ed., *The Personal Papers of Lord Rendel*, Benn, 1931

Hammond, J.L. and B., *Lord Shaftesbury*, F.Cass, 1923

Holland, Bernard, *The Life of Spencer Compton, Eighth Duke of Devonshire*, 2 vols., Longman, 1911

Howard, C.H.D., ed., Joseph Chamberlain, *A Political Memoir 1880–92*, Batchworth Press, 1953

Hutchinson, H.G., ed., *The Private Diaries of Sir Algernon West*, John Murray, 1922

James, R.R., *Rosebery. A Biography of Archibald Philip, Fifth Earl of Rosebery*, Weidenfeld & Nicolson, 1963

James, R.R., *Lord Randolph Churchill*, Weidenfeld & Nicolson, 1959

Jenkins, R., *Sir Charles Dilke. A Victorian Tragedy*, Collins, 1958

Kilbracken, Lord, *Reminiscences*, Macmillan, 1931

Leventhal, F.M., *Respectable Radical: George Howell and Victorian Working Class Politics*, Weidenfeld & Nicolson, 1971

Maxwell, Sir Herbert, *The Life and Letters of George William Frederick Fourth Earl of Clarendon, K.G., G.C.B.*, 2 vols., Arnold, 1913

Monypenny, W.F., and Buckle, G.E., *Life of Benjamin Disraeli*, 6 vols., John Murray, 1910–20

Morley, John, *Recollections*, 2 vols., Macmillan, 1921

Morley, John, *The Life of Richard Cobden*, 2 vols., Chapman & Hall, 1881

O'Connor, T.P., *Memoirs of an Old Parliamentarian*, Benn, 1929

Ornsby, R., *Memoirs of J.R.Hope-Scott*, 2 vols., John Murray, 1884

Ponsonby, Arthur, *Henry Ponsonby*, Macmillan, 1943

Prest, J., *Lord John Russell*, Macmillan, 1972

Purcell, E.S., *Life of Cardinal Manning*, 2 vols., Macmillan, 1896

Read, Donald, *Cobden and Bright: A Victorian Political Partnership*, Arnold, 1967

Reid, T. Wemyss, *Life of the Right Honourable William Edward Forster*, 2 vols., Chapman & Hall, 1888

Reid, Sir T.W., *Politicians of Today* (1880), reprinted Richmond Publishing Co., 1972

Ridley, Jasper, *Lord Palmerston*, Constable, 1970

Russell, Lord John, *Recollections and Suggestions, 1813–1873*, Longman, 1875

Stanmore, Lord, *The Earl of Aberdeen*, Sampson Low, 1893

Stanmore, Lord, *Sidney Herbert, Lord Herbert of Lea: A Memoir*, 2 vols., John Murray, 1906

Selborne, Earl of (Roundell Palmer), *Memorials*, 4 vols., Macmillan, 1896–8

Trevelyan, G.M., *The Life of John Bright*, Constable, 1913

Walling, R.A.J., ed., *The Diaries of John Bright*, Cassell, 1930

Ward, J.T., *Sir James Graham*, Macmillan, 1967

West, Sir Algernon, *Recollections, 1832 to 1886*, 2 vols., Smith, Elder, 1899

Zetland, Marquis of, ed., *Letters of Disraeli to Lady Bradford and Lady Chesterfield 1873–81*, 2 vols., Benn, 1929

Secondary works:

Adams, Francis, *History of the Elementary School Contest* (1873), intro. Asa Briggs, reprinted, Harvester Press, Brighton, 1972

Adamson, J.W., *English Education, 1789–1902*, Cambridge University Press, 1930

Anderson, Olive, *A Liberal State at War. English Politics and Economics during the Crimean War*, Macmillan, 1967

Arnstein, W.L., *The Bradlaugh Case. A Study in Late Victorian Opinion and Politics*, Oxford University Press, 1965

Bell, P.M.H., *Disestablishment in Ireland and Wales*, S.P.C.K., 1969

Best, G.F.A., *Temporal Pillars: Queen Anne's Bounty, the Ecclesiastical Commissioners, and the Church of England*, Cambridge University Press, 1964

Biddulph, Sir R., *Lord Cardwell at the War Office*, John Murray, 1904

Blake, R., *The Conservative Party from Peel to Churchill*, Eyre & Spottiswoode, 1970

Bowen, D., *The Idea of the Victorian Church: a Study of the Church of England 1833–1889*, McGill-Queen's University Press, London, 1968

Brown, Ford Keeler, *Fathers of the Victorians: the Age of Wilberforce*, Cambridge University Press, 1961

Brown, Lucy, *The Board of Trade and the Free Trade Movement, 1830–42*, Oxford University Press, 1958

Chadwick, Owen, *The Victorian Church*, 2 vols., A.C.Black, 1966–70

Chadwick, Owen, ed., *The Mind of the Oxford Movement*, A.C.Black, 1960

Clark, G.Kitson, *Churchmen and the Condition of England 1832–1885*, Methuen, 1973

Clark, G. Kitson, *Peel and the Conservative Party*, F.Cass, 1929

Clarke, P.F., *Lancashire and the New Liberalism*, Cambridge University Press, 1971

Clayden, P.W., *England under Lord Beaconsfield* (1880), reprinted, Richmond Publishing Co., 1972

Clayden, P.W., *England under the Coalition. The Political History of Great Britain and Ireland from the General Election of 1885 to May 1892*, T.Fisher Unwin, 1892

Conacher, J.B., *The Aberdeen Coalition 1852–1855. A Study in Mid-Nineteenth Century Party Politics*, Cambridge University Press, 1968

Conacher, J.B., *The Peelites and the Party System, 1846–52*, David & Charles, Newton Abbot, 1972

Cooke, A.B., and John Vincent, *The Governing Passion. Cabinet, Government and Party Politics in Britain 1885–86*, Harvester Press, Brighton, 1974

Coupland, Sir Reginald, *The British Anti-Slavery Movement*, F.Cass, 1933

Cowling, M., *1867: Disraeli, Gladstone and Revolution. The Passing of the Second Reform Bill*, Cambridge University Press, 1967

Curtis, L.P., Jr, *Coercion and Conciliation in Ireland 1880–1892: A Study in Conservative Unionism*, Princeton University Press, Princeton, N.J., 1963

Eldridge, C.C., *England's Mission. The Imperial Idea in the Age of Gladstone and Disraeli 1868–1880*, Macmillan, 1974

Feuchtwanger, E.J., *Disraeli, Democracy and the Tory Party*, Oxford University Press, 1968

Gash, Norman, *Politics in the Age of Peel. A Study in the Technique of Parliamentary Representation 1830–1850*, Longman, 1953

Gash, Norman, *Reaction and Reconstruction in English Politics, 1832–1852*, Oxford University Press, 1965

Hamer, D.A., *Liberal Politics in the Age of Gladstone and Rosebery*, Oxford University Press, 1972

Hamer, D.A., ed., *Joseph Chamberlain and Others, The Radical Programme* (1885), reprinted, Harvester Press, Brighton, 1971

Hammond, J.L., *Gladstone and the Irish Nation*, intro. M.R.D.Foot, F.Cass, 1964

Hammond, J.L., and Foot, M.R.D., *Gladstone and Liberalism*, English Universities Press, 1952

Hanham, H.J., *Elections and Party Management: Politics in the Time of Disraeli and Gladstone*, Longman, 1959

Harrison, Brian, *Drink and the Victorians: The Temperance Question in England, 1815–1872*, Faber & Faber, 1971

Harrison, Royden, *Before the Socialists. Studies in Labour and Politics 1861–1881*, Routledge & Kegan Paul, 1965

Himmelfarb, Gertrud, *Victorian Minds*, Weidenfeld & Nicolson, 1968

Hirst, F.W., *Gladstone as Financier and Economist*, Benn, 1931

Hurst, Michael, *Joseph Chamberlain and Liberal Reunion. The Round Table Conference of 1887*, David & Charles, Newton Abbot, 1967

Hyde, Francis Edwin, *Mr Gladstone at the Board of Trade*, Cobden, Sanderson, 1934

James, W.D., *Lord Derby and Victorian Conservatism*, Oxford University Press, 1956

Jones, Andrew, *The Politics of Reform 1884*, Cambridge University Press, 1972

Kebbel, T.E., *A History of Toryism* (1886), reprinted, Richmond Publishing Co., 1972

Kelly, R., *The Transatlantic Persuasion. The Liberal-Democratic Mind in the Age of Gladstone*, Knopf, New York, 1969

Knaplund, P.A., *Gladstone and Britain's Imperial Policy*, F.Cass, 1927

Knaplund, P.A., *Gladstone's Foreign Policy*, F.Cass, 1935

Lloyd, Trevor, *The General Election of 1880*, Oxford University Press, 1968

Lucy, H.W., *A Diary of Two Parliaments. The Disraeli Parliament, 1874–1880. The Gladstone Parliament, 1880–1885*, 2 vols., Cassell, 1885

Lynd, H.M., *England in the Eighteen-Eighties. Towards a Social Basis for Freedom*, F.Cass, 1945

Lyons, F.S.L., *The Fall of Parnell 1890–91*, Routledge & Kegan Paul, 1960

Macdonagh, Oliver, *A Pattern of Government Growth, 1800–60: The Passenger Acts and their Enforcement*, MacGibbon & Kee, 1961

Martin, Kingsley, *The Triumph of Lord Palmerston: A Study of Public Opinion in England before the Crimean War*, rev. edn, Hutchinson, 1963

Millman, R., *British Foreign Policy and the Coming of the Franco-Prussian War*, Oxford University Press, 1972

Morrell, William Parker, *British Colonial Policy in the Age of Peel and Russell*, Oxford University Press, 1930

Newsome, David, *The Parting of Friends. A Study of the Wilberforces and Henry Manning*, Murray, 1966

Norman, E.R., *The Catholic Church and Ireland in the Age of Rebellion, 1859–73*, Longman, 1965

Northcote, Sir Stafford, *Twenty Years of Financial Policy* (1862), reprinted, Kelley, New York, 1973

O'Brien, C.C., *Parnell and His Party, 1880–90*, Oxford University Press, 1957

Parris, Henry, *Government and the Railways in Nineteenth Century Britain*, Routledge & Kegan Paul, 1965

Pelling, H., *Social Geography of British Elections, 1885–1910*, Macmillan, 1967

Pelling, H., *Popular Politics and Society in Late Victorian Britain*, Macmillan, 1968

Richter, M., *The Politics of Conscience. T.H.Green and his Age*, Weidenfeld & Nicolson, 1964

Schreuder, D.M., *Gladstone and Kruger: Liberal Government and Colonial 'Home Rule' 1880–85*, Routledge & Kegan Paul, 1969

Seton-Watson, R.W., *Disraeli, Gladstone and the Eastern Question*, F.Cass, 1935

Seymour, Charles, *Electoral Reform in England and Wales: the development and operation of the parliamentary franchise, 1832–1885*, Oxford University Press, 1915

Shannon, R.T., *Gladstone and the Bulgarian Agitation 1876*, Nelson, 1963

Smith, F.B., *The Making of the Second Reform Bill*, Cambridge University Press, 1966

Smith, Paul, *Disraelian Conservatism and Social Reform*, Routledge & Kegan Paul, 1967

Smith, Paul, ed., *Lord Salisbury on Politics. A Selection from his Articles in the Quarterly Review, 1860–1883*, Cambridge University Press, 1972

Southgate, Donald, *The Passing of the Whigs*, Macmillan, 1962

Stansky, P., *Ambitions and Strategies: The Struggle for the Leadership of the Liberal Party in the 1890s*, Oxford University Press, 1964

Steele, E.D., *Irish Land and British Politics: Tenant-Right and Nationality 1865–1870*, Cambridge University Press, 1974

Stewart, Robert, *The Politics of Protection: Lord Derby and the Protectionist Party, 1841–1852*, Cambridge University Press, 1971

Taylor, A.J.P., *Englishmen and Others*, Hamish Hamilton, 1956

Vidler, A.R., *The Orb and the Cross*, S.P.C.K., 1945

Vincent, J.R., *The Formation of the Liberal Party, 1857–1868*, Constable, 1966; Penguin Books, Harmondsworth, 1972

Ward, W.R., *Victorian Oxford*, F. Cass, 1965

White, W., *The Inner Life of the House of Commons*, 2 vols., 1897; reprinted, Richmond Publishing Co., 1973

Williams, W.E., *The Rise of Gladstone to the Leadership of the Liberal Party, 1859–1868*, Cambridge University Press, 1934

Theses and articles:

Clayton, J.D., 'Mr Gladstone's Leadership of the Parliamentary Liberal Party, 1868–1874', D.Phil. thesis, Oxford University, 1960

Close, D., 'The Formation of Two-party Alignment in the House of Commons between 1832 and 1841', *English Historical Review* XXXIV, 1969

Dicey, E., 'The Rival Coalitions', *Nineteenth Century* XXIX, January 1891

Foot, M.R.D., 'Morley's Gladstone: A Reappraisal', *Bulletin of the John Rylands Library* LI (1968–9)

Iliasu, A.A., 'The Cobden–Chevalier Commercial Treaty of 1860', *Historical Journal* XIV (1971)

James, R.R., 'Gladstone and the Greenwich Seat: the Dissolution of 26th January 1874', *History Today* IX (1959)

Koss, Stephen E., 'Morley in the Middle', *English Historical Review* LXXXII (1967)

Machin, G.I.T., 'The Maynooth Grant, the Dissenters and Disestablishment 1845–1847', *English Historical Review* LXXXII (1967)

Maehl, W.H., 'Gladstone, the Liberals and the Election of 1874', *Bulletin of the Institute of Historical Research* XXXVI (1963)

Moody, T.W., 'Michael Davitt and the British Labour Movement', *Transactions of Royal Historical Society*, 5th series, vol. III (1953)

Savage, D.C., 'The General Election of 1886 in Great Britain and Ireland', Ph.D. thesis, London University, 1958

Stephen, M.D., 'Gladstone and the Composition of the Final Court in Ecclesiastical Causes, 1850–73', *Historical Journal* IX (1966)

Stuart, C.H., 'The Formation of the Coalition Cabinet of 1852', *Transactions of Royal Historical Society*, 5th series, vol. IV (1954)

Thompson, A.F., 'Gladstone's Whips and the General Election of 1868', *English Historical Review* LXIII (1948)

INDEX

Hours (1891), 264; Employers' Liability (1880), 199, (1893), 267; Ground Game (1880), 199

Ireland: Arrears (1882), 212; Church Disestablishment (1869), 122, 142, 143, 144–5, 150, 151–2, 153; Church Reform (1833), 23, (1834), 24; Coercion (1881), 208–9, (1882), 212, 226; Compensation for Disturbance (1880), 199–200, 206; Crimes (1887), 251; Home Rule (1886), 236–41, (1893), 267–9; Land (1870), 150, 153–4, 206, (1881), 153, 207–9, 212, 251; Land Purchase (1885), 251, (1886), 236, 239; Local Government (1883), 216; Tenant Relief (1886), 250; University (1873), 150, 169–70, 173, 176

Jewish Disabilities (1848), 65, 77; Licensing (1871–2), 166, 176, 177; Navigation (1848–9), 66; Oxford University Reform (1854), 92–3; Parish Councils (1894), 267; Public Worship Regulation (1874), 178, 182; Reform (1832), 4, 11, 13, 56, 129, (1854), 87, (1859), 104, (1860), 110, 128, (1866), 127–31, (1867), 39, 135–41, (1884), 197, 217–20, 221, 224, 280; Ten-Hour (1833), 21, (1844), 47, (1847), 63; Trade Unions (1871), 164–5; University Tests (1871), 164

Bismarck, Prince Otto von (1815–98), 117, 159, 160, 180, 203, 213, 222, 225

Blomfield, C.J. (1786–1857), Bishop of London, 70

Blunt, Wilfrid Scawen (1840–1922), poet and politician, 251

Bonham, F.R. (1785–1863), 55

Boord, Sir William (1838–1912), 1st Bt, M.P. for Greenwich, 177

Bradlaugh, Charles (1833–91), 198, 200, 201, 202, 204, 252

Brand, H.B.W. (1814–92), 1st Viscount Hampden, Liberal Chief Whip, Speaker, 125, 131, 133, 134, 139, 141, 200

Bright, John (1811–89), 83, 88, 98,

108, 119, 120, 121, 126, 131, 135, 136, 146, 147, 192, 195, 205, 207, 214, 216, 219, 223, 269; first meets Gladstone, 45; on Oxford University Reform, 93; urges new start on Gladstone, 97, 100; formation of Liberal party, 105; excluded from Palmerston government, 106; shares Gladstone's views on international order, 107; disagrees with him on American Civil War, 107, 114, 115; talks with him on Ireland and Liberal party, 118; attitude on franchise reform, 127–8, 134, 138; joins Gladstone's first government, 146; on Irish Land Bill (1870), 154; returns to Cabinet (1873), 174; fails to support Gladstone on Eastern Question, 184; joins Cabinet (1880), 196; resigns on Egypt (1882), 213; refuses to join Gladstone's third Government, 235; opposes Home Rule, 241

Brook Street Conspiracy (1892), 266

Brougham, 1st Lord (1778–1868), 4

Brown, James Baldwin (1820–84), Nonconformist leader, 124

Browne, E.H. (1811–91), Bishop of Winchester, 215

Bruce, H.A. (1815–95), 1st Lord Aberdare, Home Secretary 1868–73, 147, 164, 166, 174

Bryce, James (1838–1922), 1st Viscount, later Ambassador to Washington, 238, 268

Buccleuch, 5th Duke of (1806–84), 54

Buckingham, 2nd Duke of (1797–1861), 43, 107

Buckingham, 3rd Duke of (1823–89), 107

Buckle, G.E. (1854–1935), 253

Bulgarian atrocities, 181–3, 185, 186, 188, 189, 240, 251, 279, 280

'Bulgarian Horrors and the Question of the East, The' (1876), 183, 185, 189

Bunsen, Baron Christian (1791–1860), Prussian Ambassador in London, 50

and death, 222–4; on Tory democracy, 224; Egyptian Finance Commission, 225; possible resignation, 225, 226; Penjdeh incident, 226; renewal of Irish Coercion Act (1885), 226; attitude to 'constructionism', 227, 247, 280; third Midlothian campaign (1885), 231; Hawarden 'kite', 233; formation of third government, 235–6; first Home Rule Bill, 236–41; Irish Land Purchase Bill (1886), 236–7; Ulster problem, 237–8; resignation of Chamberlain, 238; dissolution of Parliament (1886), 241; 1886 general election, 241–3; resignation (1886), 245; Liberal reunion, 248–9; Round Table conference (1887), 249; Parnell inquiry (1888–90), 253–5; Scottish and Welsh disestablishment, 255; effects of old age, 256–7; O'Shea divorce case, 258; fall of Parnell, 260–61; Liberal programme, 261–2; Newcastle programme (1891), 262–3; fourth Midlothian campaign (1892), 264; 1892 general election, 264–5; formation of fourth government, 265; second Home Rule Bill, 267–9; policy on Uganda, 267; naval estimates (1894), 269; final resignation, 271; Armenian massacres, 273; death, 273;

Relations with:

Bright, 45, 97, 100, 107, 115, 118, 120, 131, 135, 136, 146, 184, 213–14, 235; Chamberlain, 158, 188, 227, 232, 233, 235, 238, 240, 241, 246, 247, 248, 249; Cobden, 43, 46, 97, 107; Disraeli, 31, 72, 78, 84, 93, 95, 97, 101, 139, 181, 182, 185, 189, 191, 199, 208, 277, 282; Granville, 151, 159, 161, 183, 184, 185, 187, 188, 192, 194, 196, 203, 229, 278; Hartington, 174, 182, 184, 186–7, 194, 196, 210, 216, 218, 225, 230, 246, 252; Palmerston, 72, 74, 80, 88, 96, 97, 99, 101, 105–6, 109, 111, 115, 116, 119, 282; Parnell, 209–10, 230, 231, 234, 236, 240, 248, 254,

259–60; Peel, 21, 22, 25–6, 34, 36–7, 41–2, 43, 46, 47, 49, 52, 53, 57, 63, 64, 66, 67, 72, 276, 282; Queen Victoria, 69, 97, 117, 143, 167, 185, 194–5, 208, 215–16, 223, 234, 265, 271, 273; Russell, 69, 70, 75, 77, 78, 87–8, 94, 96, 110, 126, 127, 128, 130, 142

Gleanings (1897), 272

Glenelg, Lord (1778–1866), Colonial Secretary, 31

Glyn, George, *see* Wolverton, Lord

Glynne, Sir Stephen (1807–74), 9th Bt, 35, 60

Gordon, Arthur, *see* Stanmore, Lord

Gordon, General Charles (1833–85), 221, 222–4, 225, 267

Gorham, Rev. G.C. (1787–1857), 70, 71

Gorst, Sir John (1835–1916), Conservative politician, 200

Gortchakoff, Prince A.M. (1798–1883), 161

Goschen, G.J. (1831–1907), 1st Viscount, President of Poor Law Board 1868–71, 147, 175, 250

Goulburn, Henry (1784–1856), Chancellor of the Exchequer 1841–6, 47, 57, 66, 67, 68

Graham, Sir James (1792–1861), Home Secretary 1841–6, 24, 26, 47, 54, 55, 66, 67, 75, 77, 83, 95, 100, 101; refuses Russell's offer of Admiralty (1849), 68, 71; returns to Whigs, 76; opposes competitive entry into Civil Service, 91; resigns from Palmerston government, 96; moves closer to Liberals, 104, 106; death of, 117

Granville (1815–91), 2nd Earl, 130, 146, 150, 155, 171, 174, 175, 177, 182, 183, 190, 193, 196, 213, 215, 216, 225, 229, 234, 245, 259; close relations with Queen, 151; on Irish Church Disestablishment Bill, 152; on Franco-Prussian War, 159–61; on American arbitration, 162; Liberal leader, 180; on Eastern Question, 184–5, 187; embarrassed by Gladstone's presence at inau-

Newcastle, 5th Duke of (1811–64), Lord Lincoln until 1851, 9, 10, 13, 14, 26, 63, 66, 68, 75, 76, 88, 94, 96, 117

Newman, Cardinal J.H. (1801–90), 49, 50, 51, 54, 257

Nicholas I (1796–1855), Tsar of Russia, 87, 97

Nineteenth Century Review, 185, 190, 213, 256, 264, 272

Northbrook, 1st Earl of (1826–1904), First Lord of Admiralty 1880–85, 235

Northcote, Sir Stafford (1818–87), 1st Earl of Iddesleigh, 83, 91, 92, 170, 193, 200, 201, 219, 220

Oak Farm, 60, 68

O'Brien, William (1852–1928), Irish nationalist leader, 250, 252

O'Connell, Daniel (1775–1847), 24, 29, 30, 50

O'Connor, Feargus (1794–1855), 45

O'Connor, T.P. (1848–1929), 224, 242

O'Donnell, F.H. (1848–1916), 253

O'Shea, Mrs Catherine (1845–1921), 209, 212, 231, 234, 247, 258

O'Shea, Capt. W.H. (1840–1905), 211, 226, 258

Otto, King of Greece (1815–67), 71

Overend and Gurney, 130

Oxford, 7, 10, 11, 14, 15, 61, 91, 98, 101, 107, 118, 124, 129, 164, 257, 281; reform of university (1854), 92–3; Gladstone ceases to be member for university, 122–3

Oxford Movement, 10, 32, 33, 46, 49, 51, 61, 65, 69, 75, 83, 97, 116, 122

Pacifico, Don David (1784–1854), 71, 72, 73

Palmer, Roundell, *see* Selborne, 1st Earl of

Palmerston, Henry John Temple (1784–1865), 3rd Viscount, 53, 86, 94, 97, 101, 105, 107, 108, 113, 114, 115, 123, 126, 128, 143, 146, 147, 150, 159, 162, 166, 277, 278, 280, 282; accused by Gladstone on Chinese Opium War, 35; frustrates formation of Russell government, 54; on Don Pacifico case, 71–2; on *Letters to Lord Aberdeen*, 73–4; estrangement from Russell, 75–6; collaborates on free-trade resolution with Gladstone, 80; Home Secretary (1853), 82; resignation and return (December 1853), 87–8; forms government, 95–6; wins 1857 election, 98; clashes with Gladstone on Divorce Bill, 99; defeated on Orsini case, 100; Gladstone joins his government, 106; clash with Gladstone on foreign policy, 109; fails to support Gladstone over paper duties, 111; relations with Gladstone, 116–17; his low-church appointments, 116, 122; on Schleswig-Holstein, 117–18; rebukes Gladstone over franchise speech, 119; demonstration against him at Bradford, 120–21; death of, 125

Papacy, Papal States, 14, 133, 153

paper duties (1860–61), 110–11

Paris, Treaty of (1856), 159, 161

Parnell, Charles Stewart (1846–91), 194, 206, 214, 226, 236, 240, 248, 262; is anti-Bradlaugh, 202; Gladstone fails to consult him on Land Bill, 207; obstructs coercion, 208; Kilmainham treaty, 209–11; offers to retire after Phoenix Park murders, 212; courted by Tories, 224; votes with Tories (June 1885), 228; negotiates with Carnarvon, 230; throws Irish vote to Tories, 231; Gladstone negotiates with him through Mrs O'Shea, 234; accepts Gladstone's Home Rule proposals, 237; no longer arbiter of British politics, 246; Gladstonian party tied to him, 247; restrains Irish extremism, 250; *Parnellism and Crime*, 253; special commission vindicates him, 254; divorce case, 258; fall, 259–61, 272

Peel, General Jonathan (1799–1879), younger brother of Sir Robert, 135, 136

Peel, Sir Robert (1788–1850), 10, 13,

Hampden appointment, 69–70; Ecclesiastical Titles Bill, 75; Gladstone objects to his pandering to 'No Popery' hysteria, 75, 78, 79; fall of government, 76; difficulty in placing him in Aberdeen Coalition, 82; differences with Gladstone over Reform Bill (1854), 87–8; objects to competitive entry into Civil Service, 91; clash with Gladstone over Kennedy affair, 94; fails to form government (1855), 96; resigns from Palmerston government, 97; rapprochement with remaining Peelites, 101; formation of Liberal party, 105; Gladstone wants him to withdraw Reform Bill (1860), 110; supports mediation between North and South in American Civil War, 114; succeeds Palmerston, 125–6; asks for dissolution (1866), 130, 131; tells Gladstone of wish to retire, 142; opposes conciliatory attitude on *Alabama* claims, 163; presses Gladstone to condemn Bulgarian atrocities, 182

Russell, Lady (1815–98), 94

Sadler, Michael Thomas (1780–1835), 18

St Asaph (Bishopric), 1843, 46

Salisbury, 3rd Marquess of (1830–1903), 189, 219, 226, 248, 249, 254; opposes Palmerston (1857), 98; articles in *Quarterly*, 110, 123, 130–31; opposes Disraeli's Reform Bill (1867), 135, 136, 137, 139; votes for Second Reading of Irish Church Disestablishment Bill, 152; tries to block abolition of university tests, 164; at Constantinople Conference (1877), 186; tries to block Arrears Bill (1882), 212; attacked by Chamberlain, 216; interparty conference on redistribution (1884), 220; forms government (1885), 228; Newport speech, 232; offers to serve under Hartington (July 1886), 247; appoints Goschen to replace Lord Randolph Churchill, 250;

assumes Parnell's guilt, 253; elated by victory in Bassetlaw by-election, 262; resigns (1892), 265; reassertion of two-party system in 1886, 281

Sandon, Viscount (1798–1882), 2nd Earl of Harrowby, 22, 32

Schleswig-Holstein, 117, 118, 120, 159

Schnadhorst, Francis (1840–1900), Secretary of the National Liberal Federation, 241, 263

Schwarzenberg, Prince (1800–1852), Austrian Chancellor, 73

Seaforth House, 5

Selborne, 1st Earl of (1812–95), Roundell Palmer until 1872, 93, 122, 235

Selwyn, George A. (1809–78), Bishop of New Zealand and Lichfield, 9

Shaftesbury, 7th Earl of (1801–85), 21, 32, 47, 60, 116, 186

Shaw, George Bernard (1856–1950), 269

Simeon, Charles (1759–1836), Evangelical divine, 5

Sinope (1853), 87

Smith, Goldwin (1823–1910), Regius Professor of Modern History at Oxford 1858–66, 83, 145

Smith, John (1790–1824), 18

Social Democratic Federation, 263

Somerset, 12th Duke of (1804–85), Whig minister, 147

South Africa, 198, 203, 204, 205

Spencer, 5th Earl (1835–1910), 210, 212, 216, 226, 227, 230, 235, 259, 266, 267, 268, 269, 271

Spencer, Herbert (1820–1903), 240

Stanley, A.P. (1815–81), Dean of Westminster, 61, 116

Stanley, Lord, *see* Derby, 14th *and* 15th Earls of

Stanmore, 1st Lord (1829–1912), Arthur Gordon, 94, 104

Stansfeld, Sir James (1820–98), 145, 184, 198

State in its Relations with the Church, The, 29, 32, 33, 34, 41, 145

Stead, W.T. (1849–1912), 182